KV-045-133

Temple of Antoninus.

Basilica of Constantine.

Temple of Romulus (Augustulus).

Colosseum. Temple of Venus and Roma.

Arch of Titus. Temple of Castor.

Temple of Vespasian.

Arch of Severus.

Temple of Saturn.

Basilica Julia.

THE ROMAN FORUM LOOKING EAST.

Frontispiece.

A SMALLER HISTORY OF ROME FROM THE EARLIEST TIMES TO THE ESTABLISHMENT OF THE EMPIRE

BY SIR WILLIAM SMITH, D.C.L., LL.D.

NEW AND THOROUGHLY REVISED
EDITION BY A. H. J. GREENIDGE, M.A.

LECTURER AND LATE FELLOW OF HERTFORD COLLEGE, LECTURER IN ANCIENT
HISTORY AT BRASENOSE COLLEGE, OXFORD

WITH COLOURED MAP, PLANS
AND ILLUSTRATIONS

LONDON
JOHN MURRAY, ALBEMARLE STREET
1897

LONDON:
PRINTED BY WILLIAM CLOWES AND SONS, LIMITED,
STAMFORD STREET AND CHARING CROSS.

PREFACE.

In this new edition of the "Smaller History of Rome" care has been taken not to alter any of the essential characteristics which have long made this book such a valuable instrument of education. Its original proportions have been, as far as possible, preserved, and no special department of history has been allowed to curtail the space which was due to others. Such alterations as those which deal with the original populations of Italy and the constitutional arrangements of Rome, are merely the inevitable result of the progress of recent historical research in these directions.

Throughout the work the language has been simplified as much as possible, and the quantities of names, where necessary, have been added in the index.

All the maps and a large proportion of the illustrations have been specially prepared for this edition. Some of the latter were suggested by the editor; but whatever merit this feature of the work may possess is due far more to the publishers than to him.

A. H. J. G.

Oxford, *May*, 1897.

LIST OF MAPS.

Julius Caesar.

CONTENTS.

CHAPTER I.

THE PEOPLES OF ITALY.

CHAPTER II.

THE EARLY KINGS AND THE ORIGINAL CONSTITUTION OF ROME, 753-617 B.C.

CHAPTER III.

THE LAST THREE KINGS OF ROME, AND THE ESTABLISHMENT OF THE REPUBLIC, DOWN TO THE BATTLE OF THE LAKE REGILLUS, 616-498 B.C.

CHAPTER IV.

FROM THE BATTLE OF THE LAKE REGILLUS TO THE DECEMVIRATE, 498–451 B.C.

CHAPTER V.

THE DECEMVIRATE, 451–449 B.C.

CHAPTER VI.

FROM THE DECEMVIRATE TO THE CAPTURE OF ROME BY THE GAULS, 448–390 B.C.

CHAPTER VII.

From the Capture of Rome by the Gauls to the Final Union of the Two Orders, 390–367 B.C.

CHAPTER VIII.

From the Licinian Rogations to the End of the Samnite Wars, 367–290 B.C.

CHAPTER IX.

FROM THE CONCLUSION OF THE SAMNITE WAR TO THE SUBJUGATION OF ITALY, 290-265 B.C.

CHAPTER X.

THE FIRST PUNIC WAR, 264–241 B.C.

CHAPTER XI.

THE CONQUEST OF NORTHERN ITALY. THE CARTHAGINIANS IN SPAIN. 240–219 B.C.

CHAPTER XII.

THE SECOND PUNIC WAR: FIRST PERIOD DOWN TO THE BATTLE OF CANNAE, 218–216 B.C.

CHAPTER XIII.

SECOND PUNIC WAR: SECOND PERIOD, FROM THE REVOLT OF CAPUA TO THE BATTLE OF THE METAURUS, 215–207 B.C.

CHAPTER XIV.

SECOND PUNIC WAR: THIRD PERIOD, FROM THE BATTLE OF THE METAURUS TO THE CONCLUSION OF THE WAR, 206–201 B.C.

CHAPTER XV.

WARS IN THE EAST: THE MACEDONIAN, SYRIAN, AND GALATIAN WARS, 214–188 B.C.

CHAPTER XVI.

WARS IN THE WEST: THE GALLIC, LIGURIAN, AND SPANISH WARS, 200–175 B.C.

CHAPTER XVII.

THE ROMAN CONSTITUTION AND ARMY.

CHAPTER XVIII.

INTERNAL HISTORY OF ROME DURING THE MACEDONIAN AND SYRIAN WARS. CATO AND SCIPIO.

CHAPTER XIX.

THE THIRD MACEDONIAN, ACHAEAN, AND THIRD PUNIC WARS, 179–146 B.C.

CHAPTER XX.

SPANISH WARS, 153-133 B.C FIRST SERVILE WAR, 134-132 B.C.

CHAPTER XXI.

THE GRACCHI AND THE ATTACK ON THE GOVERNMENT, 133-121 B.C.

40

CHAPTER XXII.

The Jugurthine War and the Defeat of the Government, 118–104.

CHAPTER XXIII.

THE CIMBRI AND TEUTONES, 113–101 B.C. SECOND SERVILE WAR IN SICILY, 103–101 B.C.

CHAPTER XXIV.

THE DOWNFALL OF THE OPPOSITION, AND THE ATTEMPT OF DRUSUS AT REFORM, 100-91 B.C.

CHAPTER XXV.

THE SOCIAL OR MARSIC WAR, AND THE INCORPORATION OF ITALY, 90–89 B.C.

CHAPTER XXVI.

First Civil War, 88-86 B.C.

CHAPTER XXVII.

First Mithridatic War, 88-84 B.C.

CHAPTER XXVIII.

Second Civil War. Sulla's Dictatorship, Legislation, and Death, 83-78 B.C.

CHAPTER XXIX.

FROM THE DEATH OF SULLA TO THE CONSULSHIP OF POMPEY AND CRASSUS, 78–70 B.C.

CHAPTER XXX.

THIRD OR GREAT MITHRIDATIC WAR, 74-61 B.C.

CHAPTER XXXI.

INTERNAL HISTORY, FROM THE CONSULSHIP OF POMPEY AND CRASSUS TO THE RETURN OF POMPEY FROM THE EAST: THE CONSPIRACY OF CATILINE. 69-61 B.C.

CHAPTER XXXII.

From Pompey's Return from the East to Cicero's Banishment and Recall, 62–57 B.C.

CHAPTER XXXIII.

Caesar's Campaigns in Gaul, 58–51 B.C.

CHAPTER XXXIV.

Internal History from the Return of Cicero from Banishment to the Commencement of the Civil War: Expedition and Death of Crassus. 57–50 B.C.

CHAPTER XXXV.

The Beginning of the Civil War to Caesar's Death, 49–44 B.C.

CHAPTER XXXVI.

FROM THE DEATH OF CAESAR TO THE BATTLE OF PHILIPPI, 44-42 B.C.

CHAPTER XXXVII.

FROM THE BATTLE OF PHILIPPI TO THE BATTLE OF ACTIUM, 41-30 B.C.

CHAPTER XXXVIII.

SKETCH OF THE HISTORY OF ROMAN LITERATURE FROM THE EARLIEST TIMES TO THE DEATH OF AUGUSTUS.

Vergil.

LIST OF ILLUSTRATIONS.

ABBREVIATED FORMS OF ROMAN PERSONAL NAMES (*praenomina*).

A.	represents	Aulus.
Ap.	,,	Appius.
C.	,,	Caius, or Gaius.
Cn.	,,	Cnaeus, or Gnaeus.
D.	,,	Decimus.
L.	,,	Lucius.
M.	,,	Marcus.
M'.	,,	Manius.
P.	,,	Publius.
Q.	,,	Quintus.
Ser.	,,	Servius.
Sp.	,,	Spurius.
T.	,,	Titus.
Ti.	,,	Tiberius.

London. John Murray, Albemarle Street.

John Bartholomew & Co., Edinr.

Urn showing forms of cottages of the ancient Latins.

HISTORY OF ROME.

CHAPTER I.

THE PEOPLES OF ITALY.

The peninsula of Italy.

Italy is the central one of the three great peninsulas which project from the south of Europe into the Mediterranean Sea. It is bounded on the north by the chain of the Alps, which form a natural barrier against invasion; on the west its shores are washed by the Tyrrhenian Sea, called by the Romans the Lower Sea (Mare Infĕrum), on the east by the Adriatic or Upper Sea (Mare Supĕrum). All its best harbours lie on the west, and consequently it is in this direction that Rome's earliest trade-routes lay, and her earliest imperial acquisitions were made.

The peninsula itself may be divided into two parts, the northern consisting of the great plain drained by the river Padus or *Po* and its numerous tributaries, and the southern being a long tongue of land, with the Apennines as a back-bone running down its whole extent from north to south. The extreme length of the peninsula from the Alps to the Straits of Messina is 700 miles. The breadth of Northern Italy is 350 miles, while that of the southern portion is on an average not more than 100 miles. But till the time of the Empire the Romans never included the plain of the Po in Italy. To this country they gave the name of GALLIA CISALPINA, or Gaul on this (the Roman) side of the Alps, in consequence of its being inhabited by Gauls. The westernmost portion of the plain was peopled by Ligurian tribes, and was therefore called LIGURIA, while its eastern extremity was inhabited by the VENETI.

The name Italia.

The name ITALIA was originally applied to a very small tract of country. It was confined to the extreme south of the peninsula, which at a still earlier period had been called Oenotria; by the fifth century B.C. it had come to include the territory, subsequently known as Lucania and Bruttium, stretching along the shores of the Tarentine gulf south of a line drawn from Metapontum to Paestum, and by the time of the Punic wars, in the third century B.C., it had spread over the whole peninsula south of the rivers Rubicon and Macra, which parted Umbria and Etruria from the northern districts of the valley of the Po. Italy, properly so called, is a very mountainous country, being filled up more or less by the broad mass of the Apennines, the off-shoots or lateral branches of which, in some parts, descend quite to the sea, but in others leave a considerable space of level or low country. There are fewer land-locked valleys than in Greece, and the open plains are eminently suitable for the growth of leagues or federations between towns.

Peoples of Italy.

The population of the peninsula south of the Alps was of a very varied character. It may be divided into no less than six great branches.

The Gauls.

1. The GAULS represent at once the most northerly and the youngest of the races of Italy. They belong to the great family of the Celts, whose presence in the peninsula was due to two separate migrations, both of which took place long after the other races of Italy had been settled in their separate localities. Tradition says that the first swarm of Celts passed the Alps in the reign of the elder Tarquin

(616–578 B.C.); a second migration, which planted the Senones, the most southerly of these tribes, on the shores of the Adriatic east of Umbria, is connected with the great Gallic invasion which ended in the capture of Rome (390 B.C.). Previously to these movements the northern regions of Cisalpine Gaul had been in the hands of the Ligurians, the southern in those of the Umbrians, while the Etruscans possessed scattered settlements north of the Apennines. The result of the migrations was to spread the Gallic name from the Alps to the Apennines and the Adriatic. The most important of the Gallic tribes were the Insubres and Cenomani to the north of the Po, and the Boii and Lingones to the south of that river.

The Ligurians.

2. West and south of Gaul lay LIGURIA, the country of the Ligures (or Ligues, as they were called by the Greeks). The origin of this race is quite unknown; it had once occupied much of the territory subsequently overrun by the Gauls, and in historical times it extended at least from the upper reaches of the Po, but possibly even from the Poenine Alps (the Great St. Bernard) to the river Macra on the south. The chief northern tribe was that of the Taurini, but the tribes with which we find Rome most frequently brought into hostile contact were those of the south, the Intemilii, Ingauni, and Apuani, lying between the Apennines and the sea, and the Friniates to the east of this range.

The north-eastern portion of Italy, from the river Athesis (*Adige*) to the Julian Alps was occupied by the VENETI. They were doubtless of the same race as the Istrians and Liburnians on the other side of the Adriatic, and are said to have belonged to the great Ligurian stock.

The Etruscans.

3. The ETRUSCANS were known as Etrusci or Tusci to the Romans, as Tyrrheni to the Greeks; but their own native name for themselves was Rasena. They formed a striking contrast to the nations of Central and Southern Italy; for their language is wholly different from that of the other Italian tribes, and shows no resemblance to the languages of the Indo-European group, while their manners and customs clearly prove them to be a people originally quite distinct from the Greek and Italian races, although they showed themselves very susceptible to Greek culture. Their influence on the early customs of Rome was

necessarily great, for the Etruscans possessed a fully developed civilization when Rome was but an infant state; but it was an influence that, so far as we can see, affected little beyond the ceremonies and religious institutions of Rome. It was from them that she derived the science of augury, and perhaps the very idea of priestly colleges or guilds; while tradition adds that the symbols of Roman royalty, the purple robe, the ivory sceptre, and the curule chair, came from Etruria. The origin of this strange race is wholly uncertain. Most ancient writers relate that the Etruscans were Lydians who had migrated by sea from Asia to Italy; it is now more generally believed that they descended into Italy from the Rhaetian Alps. Yet Etruscan civilization shows the deepest traces of Oriental influence, and, if the hypothesis that connects the Etruscans with the Rhaeti is correct, it is probable that they were an Alpine people, whose art and customs were profoundly modified by intermixture with immigrants from the East. In early times they had maintained settlements in the great plain of the Po, until they were expelled or subdued by the invading Gauls. The country known as ETRURIA in historic times extended along the coast of the Lower Sea from the river Macra on the north to the Tiber on the south. Inland, the Tiber also formed its eastern boundary, dividing it first from Umbria, afterwards from the Sabines, and, lastly, from Latium.

The Italian races.

4. We next come to the Italian races proper, which inhabited the centre and most of the south of the peninsula. The evidence of language proves that the common stock from which these races sprang falls into two great branches: (1) the Umbrian and Sabellian; (2) the Latin. The differences between these groups of languages are little more than the differences between dialects of the same tongue, and show the clearest traces of a common origin. They are closely related to the Greek, but still more closely to the Celtic; and this connection, combined with the great resemblance between the fundamental social and political institutions of the Greeks and Romans, make it probable that the Italian, Celtic, and Greek races dwelt together for a long period during their journey from the East, and that when the Greeks parted from their kinsmen at the head of the Adriatic, Italians and Celts still continued for a time in close contact with one another. The Gauls, in fact, were not only near neighbours, but near kinsmen of the Romans.

The Umbrians.

The UMBRIANS dwelt, in historic times, in Eastern Italy between Etruria and the Adriatic. The district of UMBRIA had once been far more extensive, but its possessions west of the Apennines had fallen to Etruria, and the Gallic tribe of Senones finally annexed the territory on the Adriatic coast. The language of the Umbrians is the most ancient tongue of the family to which it belongs, and verifies the tradition that the Umbrians were one of the oldest nations of Italy.

The Volscians.

The VOLSCIANS, a race afterwards merged in Latium, show the nearest resemblance in language to the Umbrians. They were at first a nation distinct from the Latins, and, though they lost their independence as a separate state, inscriptions show that they long preserved their language unimpaired. Other tribes bordering on Latium are the AEQUIANS and HERNICANS. We know little of them beyond their close international relations with the Volscians.

The Sabines.

It is doubtful to which division of the family of the Umbrians and Sabellians the SABINES belonged; for their language early fell into disuse, and only a few words have been preserved. But they probably belonged to the Sabellian branch. They are said to have been originally a mountain race dwelling near the sources of the Arnus on the ridge of the Apennines which lies between Umbria and Etruria. Thence they descended into the valleys between Umbria and Latium, which they occupied in historic times. They preserved their simple mountaineering habits, and are described as brave, hardy, and frugal. Tradition has much to tell of their early influence on Rome, and this is natural, for the Sabine city of Cures was but twenty-four miles from Rome. Amongst Sabine tribes we may, perhaps, reckon the PICENTINES, occupying a fertile strip of territory on the coast of the Adriatic; and the PAELIGNI, MARSI, MARRUCINI, and VESTINI, lying south of this district.

The Sabellian races.

The SABELLIAN races are those which are known to have spoken a common tongue, sometimes called Oscan. They spread over the greater part of Central and Southern Italy, and are represented by the Samnites, with their offshoots the Campanians and Lucanians.

The SAMNITES, the most powerful of these races, occupied an inland district in the region of the central Apennines. On the west they commanded the valley of the Vulturnus bordering on Campania. On the east they early extended beyond the limits of Samnium proper to the sea; for the Frentani on the north-east were a Samnite people, and it is probable that at least the northern part of Apulia was conquered and occupied by Samnite tribes. But their greatest conquests were on the west and south. In the fifth century B.C. they conquered the whole of the rich province of Campania, the garden of Italy. This district, stretching from the Liris to the Silarus, forms, for the most part, an unbroken plain, celebrated in ancient as well as in modern times for its extraordinary beauty and fertility. The Greek cities of this coast alone retained their independence and their territories. Shortly afterwards the Samnites spread through the whole of Lucania. But, although the LUCANIANS appear in history as a Samnite people, they have broken away from the control of the main body of their countrymen. They have formed a state of their own, and they rule not only over Lucania, but over the native peoples to the south as far as the strait which separates Italy from Sicily.

These native peoples at last threw off the Lucanian yoke, and appear in history as the BRUTII.

The Latins.

The LATINS, like the Samnites, are represented as having been originally a mountaineering race dwelling in the central Apennines, from which they descended into the regions between the mountains and the sea. Even here the Latins were for a time but an insignificant people overshadowed by the great Etruscan power in the north and surrounded on all other sides by hostile tribes. The original Latium was a narrow territory extending from the Tiber to the Volscian mountains, and from the Apennines about Praeneste to the sea. But Latin conquest subsequently absorbed the Volscians and Aurunci, and the name Latium was spread to the Liris on the borders of Campania. The original abode of the Latins is of volcanic origin. The Alban mountains are a great volcanic mass, and several of the craters have been filled with water, forming lakes, of which the Alban lake is one of the most remarkable. The plain in which Rome stands, now called the *Campagna*, is not an unbroken level, but a broad undulating tract, intersected by numerous streams, which have cut themselves deep channels through the soft volcanic tufa of which the soil is composed. The climate of Latium was not healthy even in ancient times. The malaria of the Campagna renders Rome itself unhealthy in the summer and autumn; and the Pontine marshes, which extend along the coast in the south of Latium for a distance of thirty miles, are still more pestilential.

The Iapygians.

5. A primitive people, whose language, as known from inscriptions, differs widely from those of the Umbrians and Sabellians, were represented by the Iapygians and Messapians of Calabria. Yet the language shows resemblances to both Greek and Latin, and bears out the tradition that the Iapygians were Pelasgi, or pre-historic inhabitants of Italy. They were probably the earliest Aryan settlers who were driven towards the extremity of the peninsula as the Latins and Sabellians pressed further to the south.

The Greeks.

6. The *Greeks* planted so many colonies upon the coasts of Southern Italy that they gave to that district the name of Magna Graecia. The most ancient, and at the same time the most northerly, Greek city in Italy was Cumae in Campania. Most of the other Greek colonies were situated farther to the south, where many of them attained to great power and wealth. Of these some of the most distinguished were Tarentum, Croton, Metapontum, and Sybaris, which was destroyed in 510 B.C., and was replaced in 443 B.C. by the town of Thurii.

Prehistoric gate at Arpinum.

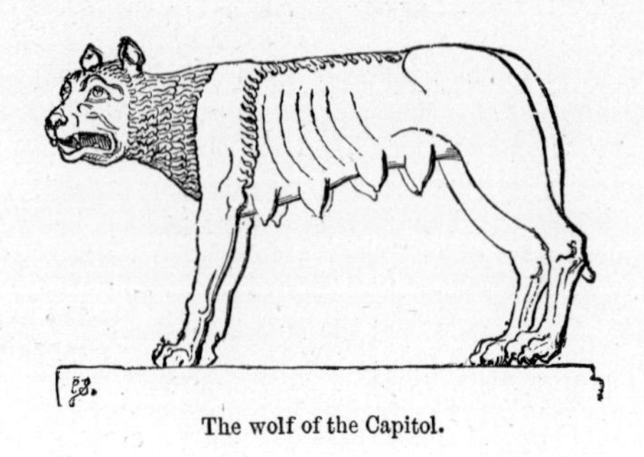

The wolf of the Capitol.

CHAPTER II.

THE EARLY KINGS AND THE ORIGINAL CONSTITUTION OF ROME.

THE history of Rome is that of a city which originally had only a few miles of territory, and gradually extended its dominion at first over Italy and then over the civilized world. The city lay in the central part of the peninsula, on the left bank of the Tiber, and about fifteen miles from its mouth. It appears from the first as the most important town of Latium, and this importance must have been due to its site. Its commercial greatness was due to its situation on a navigable river, which provided a safe refuge for ships at a time when the Lower Sea was swept by Etruscan fleets; its military strength was due to its position upon the borders of two of the most powerful races in Italy, the Sabines and the Etruscans.

The city of Rome.

Though originally a Latin town, it received at an early period a considerable Sabine population, while it appears nearly certain that a part of its population was of Etruscan origin, and that the two Tarquins represent the establishment of an Etruscan dynasty at Rome.* But Roman civilization is in all essential points different from the Etruscan, and that the Latin element predominated over the Sabine is evident from the fact that the

* See ch. iii. p. 20.

language of the Romans was a Latin and not a Sabellian dialect.

The early traditions.

The early history of Rome as given by the Roman writers is a mass of popular tradition worked up by poets, annalists, and antiquarians into a professed record of fact. Not only is it full of marvellous tales and poetical embellishments, of contradictions and impossibilities, but it wants the very foundation upon which all history must be based. Many of the legends are simply attempts to explain the origin of certain political and religious customs existing in the Republic; and, although the political civilization of early Rome can be discovered with some degree of certainty, it is not until we come to the war with Pyrrhus that we can place full reliance upon the narrative as a trustworthy statement of events. With this caution we now proceed to relate the celebrated legends of the foundation and early history of Rome.

The story of Aeneas.

Rome is thought to have arisen with the fall of Troy, for, on the capture of that town, Aeneas, son of Anchises and Venus, fled to seek a new home in a foreign land. He carried with him his son Ascanius, the Penates or household gods, and the Palladium of Troy.* Upon reaching the coast of Latium he was kindly received by Latinus, the king of the country, who gave him his daughter Lavinia in marriage. Aeneas now built a city, which he named Lavinium, in honour of his wife. But Lavinia had been previously promised to Turnus, the leader of the Rutulians. This youthful chief, enraged at the insult, attacked the strangers. He was slain, however, by the hands of Aeneas; but in a new war which broke out three years afterwards, the Trojan hero disappeared amid the waters of the river Numicius, and was henceforward worshipped under the name of Jupiter Indiges, or "god of the country."

The kings of Alba Longa.

Ascanius, who was also called Iulus, removed from Lavinium, thirty years after its foundation, and built Alba Longa, or the "Long White City," on a ridge of the Alban Mount about fifteen miles south-east of Rome. It became the most powerful city in Latium, and the

* The Palladium was a statue of Pallas, or Minerva, which was said to have fallen from heaven, and was preserved at Rome with the most sacred care.

head of a confederacy of Latin cities. Twelve kings of the family of Aeneas succeeded Ascanius. The last of these, named Procas, left two sons, Numitor and Amulius. Amulius, the younger, seized the kingdom; and Numitor, who was of a peaceful disposition, made no resistance to his brother.

Amulius, fearing lest the children of Numitor might not submit so quietly to his usurpation, caused his only son to be murdered, and made his daughter, Rhea Silvia, one of the vestal virgins, who were compelled to live and die unmarried. But the maiden became, by the god Mars, the mother of twins. She was in consequence put to death, because she had broken her vow, and her babes were doomed to be drowned in the river. The Tiber had overflowed its banks far and wide; and the cradle in which the babes were placed was stranded at the foot of the Palatine, and overturned on the root of a wild fig tree. A she-wolf, which had come to drink of the stream, carried them into her den hard by, and suckled them; and when they wanted other food, the woodpecker, a bird sacred to Mars, brought it to them. At length this marvellous spectacle was seen by Faustulus, the king's shepherd, who took the children home to his wife, Acca Larentia. They were called Romulus and Remus, and grew up along with the sons of their foster-parents on the Palatine hill.

Romulus and Remus.

A quarrel arose between them and the herdsmen of Numitor, who stalled their cattle on the neighbouring hill of the Aventine. Remus was taken by a stratagem, and carried off to Numitor. His age and noble bearing made Numitor think of his grandsons; and his suspicions were confirmed by the tale of the marvellous nurture of the twin brothers. Soon afterwards Romulus hastened with his foster-father to Numitor; suspicion was changed into certainty, and the old man recognized them as his kindred. They now resolved to avenge the wrongs which their family had suffered. With the help of faithful comrades they slew Amulius, and placed Numitor on the throne.

Romulus and Remus loved their old abode, and therefore left Alba to found a city on the banks of the Tiber. But a dispute arose between the brothers where the city should be built, and after whose name it should be called. Romulus wished to build it on the Palatine, Remus on the Aventine. It was agreed that the question should be decided by the gods; and each took his station on the top of his chosen hill, awaiting the pleasure of the gods by some striking sign. The night passed away, and as the day was dawning Remus saw six vultures; but at sunrise, when these tidings were brought to Romulus, twelve vultures flew by him. Each claimed the augury in his own favour; but the shepherds decided for Romulus, and Remus was therefore obliged to yield. Such was the legendary explanation of the later Roman custom of the taking of auspices by a magistrate.

1. REIGN OF ROMULUS, 753–717 B.C.—Romulus, on gaining this divine sanction, proceeded to mark out the boundaries of his city. He yoked a bullock and a heifer to a plough, and drew a deep furrow round the Palatine. This formed the sacred limits of the city, and was called the *Pomerium*. To the original city on the Palatine was given the name of *Roma Quadrata*, or Square Rome, to distinguish it from the one which subsequently extended over the seven hills.

Foundation of Rome.

The traditional date for the founding of Rome was the 21st of April, 753 years before the Christian era.

On the line of the Pomerium Romulus began to raise a wall. One day Remus leapt over it in scorn; whereupon Romulus slew him, exclaiming, "So die whosoever hereafter shall leap over my walls." Romulus now found his people too few in numbers. Accordingly, he set apart on the Capitoline hill an asylum, or a sanctuary, in which homicides and runaway slaves might take refuge. The city thus became filled with men, but they wanted women, and the inhabitants of the neighbouring cities refused to give their daughters to such an outcast race. Romulus accordingly resolved to obtain by force what he could not gain by entreaty. He proclaimed that games were to be celebrated in honour of the god Consus, and invited his neighbours, the Latins and Sabines, to the festival. Suspecting no treachery, they came in numbers with their wives and children; when suddenly the Roman youths rushed upon their guests and carried off the virgins. The bereaved parents hastened home and prepared for vengeance.

Rape of the Sabines.

The inhabitants of three of the Latin towns, Caenina, Antemnae, and Crustumerium, took up arms one after the other, but were defeated by the Romans. Romulus slew with his own hand Acron king of Caenina, and dedicated his arms and armour, as *spolia opima*, to Jupiter. These were offered when the commander of one army slew with his own hand the commander of another, and were only gained twice afterwards in Roman history.

Wars with the Latins and Sabines.

At last Titus Tatius, the king of Cures, the most powerful of the Sabine states, marched against Rome. His forces were so great that Romulus, unable to resist him in the field, was obliged to retire into the city. Besides the city on the Palatine, Romulus had also fortified the top of the Capitoline hill, which he intrusted to the care of Tarpeius. But his daughter Tarpeia, dazzled by the golden bracelets of the Sabines, promised to betray the hill to them "if they would give her what they wore on their left arms." Her offer was accepted. In the night-time she opened a gate and let in the enemy, but when she claimed her reward they threw upon her the shields "which they wore on their left arms," and thus crushed her to death. Thus was explained the later custom of hurling traitors from the Tarpeian rock.

On the next day the Romans endeavoured to recover the hill. A long and desperate battle was fought in the valley between the Palatine and the Capitoline. At one time the Romans were driven before the enemy, when Romulus vowed a temple to Jupiter Stator, the Stayer of Flight, whereupon his men took courage and returned again to the combat. At length the Sabine women, who were the cause of the war, rushed in between them, and prayed their husbands and fathers to be reconciled. Their prayers were heard: the two people not only made peace, but agreed to form only one nation. The Romans dwelt on the Palatine under their king Romulus, the Sabines on the Capitoline under their king Titus Tatius.* The two kings and their senates met for deliberation in the valley between the two hills, which was hence called *Comitium*, or the place of meeting, and which afterwards became the Roman Forum.

Union with the Sabines.

But the double monarchy did not last long. Titus Tatius

* The Sabines were called *Quirites*, and this name was afterwards applied to the Roman people in their civil capacity.

was slain at Lavinium by some Latins to whom he had refused satisfaction for outrages committed by his kinsmen. Henceforward Romulus ruled alone over both Romans and Sabines. He reigned in all thirty-six years.

Translation of Romulus.

One day, as he was reviewing his people in the Campus Martius, near the Goat's Pool, the sun was suddenly eclipsed, and a dreadful storm dispersed the people. When daylight returned Romulus had disappeared, for his father Mars had carried him up to heaven in a fiery chariot. Shortly afterwards he appeared in more than mortal beauty to the senator Proculus Sabinus, and bade him tell the Romans to worship him under the name of the god Quirinus.

2. REIGN OF NUMA POMPILIUS, 715-673 B.C.—The choice of the people next fell upon the wise and pious Numa Pompilius, a

Salii carrying the ancilla.

native of the Sabine Cures who had married the daughter of Tatius. The forty-three years of Numa's reign glided away in quiet happiness without any war or any calamity.

Religious institutions of Numa.

Numa was regarded as the author of the chief religious institutions of the state. Instructed by the nymph Egeria, whom he met in the sacred grove of Aricia, he instituted three priests called Flamens, each of whom attended to the worship of separate deities—Jupiter,* Mars, and Quirinus; four Vestal Virgins, who kept alive the sacred fire of Vesta brought from Alba Longa; and

* The Flamen of Jupiter was called Flamen Dialis.

twelve Salii, or priests of Mars, who had the care of the sacred shields.* Numa reformed the calendar, encouraged agriculture, and marked out the boundaries of property, which he placed under the care of the god Terminus. He also built the temple of Janus, a god represented with two heads looking different ways. The gates of this temple were to be open during war and closed in time of peace.

3. REIGN OF TULLUS HOSTILIUS, 673–642 B.C.—Upon the death of Numa, Tullus Hostilius, a Roman, was elected king. His reign was as warlike as that of Numa had been peaceful. The most memorable event in it is the destruction of Alba Longa. A quarrel having arisen between the two cities, and their armies having been drawn up in array against each other, the princes determined to avert the battle by a combat of champions chosen from each army. There were in the Roman army three brothers, born at the same birth, named Horatii; and in the Alban army, in like manner, three brothers, born at the same birth, and called Curiatii. The two sets of brothers were chosen as champions, and it was agreed that the people to whom the conquerors belonged should rule the other. Two of the Horatii were slain, but the three Curiatii were wounded, and the surviving Horatius, who was unhurt, had recourse to stratagem. He was unable to contend with the Curiatii united, but was more than a match for each of them separately. Taking to flight, he was followed by his three opponents at unequal distances. Suddenly turning round, he slew, first one, then the second, and finally the third. The Romans were declared the conquerors, and the Albans their subjects. But a tragical event followed. As Horatius was entering Rome, bearing his threefold spoils, his sister met him and recognized on his shoulders the cloak of one of the Curiatii, her betrothed lover. She burst into such passionate grief that the anger of her brother was kindled, and stabbing her with his sword he exclaimed, "So perish every Roman woman who bewails a foe." For this murder he was condemned by the two judges of blood to be hanged upon the fatal tree, but he appealed to the people, and they gave him his life.

War with Alba Longa.

* These shields were called *Ancilia*. One of these shields is said to have fallen from heaven; and Numa ordered eleven others to be made exactly like it, that it might not be known and stolen.

Shortly afterwards Tullus Hostilius made war against Fidenae and the Etruscans of Veii. The Albans, under their dictator Mettius Fuffetius, followed him to the war as the subjects of Rome. In the battle against the Etruscans the Alban dictator, faithless and insolent, withdrew to the hills; but when the Etruscans were defeated he descended to the plain, and congratulated the Roman king. Tullus pretended to be deceived. On the following day he summoned the two armies to receive their praises and rewards. The Albans came without arms, and were surrounded by the Roman troops. They then heard their sentence. Their dictator was to be torn in pieces by horses driven opposite ways; their city was to be razed to the ground; and they themselves, with their wives and children, transported to Rome. Tullus assigned to them the Caelian hill for their habitation. Some of the noble families of Alba were enrolled among the Roman patricians, but the great mass of the Alban people were not admitted to the privileges of the ruling class.

Destruction of Alba.

After carrying on several other wars Tullus fell sick, and sought to win the favour of the gods, as Numa had done, by prayers and divination. But Jupiter was angry with him, and smote him and his whole house with fire from heaven. Thus perished Tullus after a reign of thirty-one years.

4. REIGN OF ANCUS MARCIUS, 642–617 B.C.—Ancus Marcius, the successor of Tullus Hostilius, was a Sabine, being the son of Numa's daughter. He sought to tread in the footsteps of his grandfather by reviving the religious ceremonies which had fallen into neglect; but a war with the Latins called him from the pursuits of peace. He conquered several of the Latin cities, and removed many of the inhabitants to Rome, where he assigned them the Aventine for their habitation. Ancus instituted the Fetiales, whose duty it was to demand satisfaction from a foreign state when any dispute arose, to determine the circumstances under which hostilities might be commenced, and to perform the proper religious rites on the declaration of war. He also founded a colony at Ostia at the mouth of the Tiber, built a fortress on the Janiculum as a protection against the Etruscans, and united it with the city by a bridge across the Tiber, called

Conquest of Latin cities.

the Pons Sublicius because it was made of wooden piles, and he erected a prison to restrain offenders. He died after a reign of twenty-five years.

THE ORIGINAL CONSTITUTION OF ROME.

From the earliest times the population of Rome was divided into two distinct classes, the patricians and plebeians. The patricians were the members of a certain limited number of noble clans (*gentes*). These clans may have represented the chief families in the tribes which amalgamated to form Rome, or may have been composed of all the original settlers in the territory, but there is no clear evidence to show how they attained their pre-eminence. The patricians, who may originally have formed quite the larger portion of the population, alone possessed full political and religious privileges. They had the exclusive right of voting in the assembly of the people, of serving in the army, and of filling the priesthoods of the state.

The patricians.

All outside this select circle were known as the *plebs*, or plebeians. They did not, however, form a simple, uniform class; for their condition depended on their origin. Some of the plebeians were sprung from emancipated slaves, and, where this servile taint could be proved to exist, they were clients (*clientes*) * of the patrician who had emancipated them, remained dependent members of his clan, and owed personal duties to him as their patron (*patronus*) and to his descendants after him. A large number had also sprung from the inhabitants of conquered cities who had been deported to Rome. These, too, seem to have been attached as clients to patrician *gentes*. But one class, at least, of the plebeians, which was composed of individuals who had voluntarily migrated to Rome from allied cities, seems to have been personally free. These plebeians formed clans of their own, did not attach themselves to the *gens* of a patrician, were under no obligation to a patron, and bequeathed this freedom from clientship to their descendants. Yet they, too, were, like the other members of this order, devoid of political privileges.

The plebeians.

The earliest constitution of Rome was a limited monarchy.

* The word *clientes* is connected with *cluere* ("to hear"). They were dependants who listened to their masters' bidding.

The king was in theory only a magistrate, to whom the people had given the management of the chief business of the state; but he was a sole magistrate holding office for life, and his powers were so enormous that they required very little straining to make his rule degenerate into a tyranny. The authority of the king was expressed in the word *Imperium*, and included supreme command in war, with the power of life and death over the citizens, supreme civil and criminal jurisdiction, and the sole right of summoning the people and laying measures before them for their approval.

The king.

Although the actual mode of appointment of the king is somewhat uncertain, it seems best to consider that it was both the right and the duty of the reigning monarch to nominate his successor. But this nomination was not final. The new king had no right to reign until he had challenged the allegiance of the people and his appointment had been ratified by them. This ratification was expressed in a law of the *comitia* of the *curiae* (*lex curiata*).* In the case of a king's dying without nominating a successor, this duty fell to the senate. That body appointed a series of interim-kings (*inter-reges*) (never less than two), who held office for five days in turn, and the last of whom nominated a candidate for the throne. This nomination had then to be ratified by the *curiae*. Although tradition represents the Sabine Numa, the foreigner Tarquin, and the slave's son Servius as having been elected kings of Rome, it is almost certain that the king had to be both a Roman citizen and a patrician—qualifications that we know were required for the inter-rex.

As the king was sole magistrate, all the other officials of the state were merely delegates appointed by him. Chief of these was the prefect of the city, an official left behind for the control of the capital when the king was absent in the field.

The whole of the patrician population of Rome is said to have been divided by Romulus into three tribes (*tribus*), each of which was held to represent one of the three nationalities present in the Roman state. The Ramnes were the original Romans of Romulus, the Tities (or Titienses) the Sabines of Titus Tatius, while the Luceres were regarded as Etruscan. Closely connected with this division was the corps of 300 knights (*equites*), each tribe

The patrician tribes.

* See next page.

supplying a "century" of 100 men. The number is said to have been doubled by Tullus Hostilius, and 600 probably remained the maximum for this corps until the time of Servius Tullius.

Each of the tribes was further subdivided into ten parishes called "curiae." Each of these thirty curies had its peculiar worship and chapel; but their importance was chiefly political. In the popular assembly the votes of each curia were first taken, and all questions were decided by a majority of these groups. Hence this assembly, composed at this time exclusively of patricians, was known as the "comitia curiata." This was nominally the sovereign body of Rome, which the king was morally bound to consult on all questions of legislation and all changes in the constitution. It also listened to appeals from the king's criminal jurisdiction, but only on his permission, for there was as yet no law giving every one the right of appealing against his judgments.* The comitia had no power of debate, and could only answer "Yes" or "No" to the question put before it by the king.

The curiae.

The comitia curiata.

The assembly, fettered as it was by its dependence on the king, could be no real check on his authority. The greatest limitation on his power was supplied by the ever-present council of elders, the senate, composed, we are told, originally of 100, afterwards of 200 members. This council was chosen by the king from the heads of the patrician families (hence its members were called *patres*), and, though in theory only an advising body, the age and experience of its members led it to gain certain definite prerogatives. One of the fundamental principles of the Roman commonwealth, that a magistrate should never undertake an important matter without consulting a body of advisers, was the reason both of the existence and of the power of the senate.

The senate.

Most of the foregoing institutions were naturally attributed to the founder Romulus. Another series of creations, all of a religious character, were attached to the name of the priest-king Numa. Besides the priesthoods and the worships which we have already mentioned, he was held to have instituted the two great religious colleges of Pontiffs and Augurs. The four Pontiffs were the interpreters of

The priestly colleges.

* Compare ch. iii. p. 32.

the sacred law (*jus divinum*), which, besides directing the ritual of the priesthoods, included in these early times most of the criminal and civil law. The four Augurs were the interpreters of omens and portents. The Romans believed that religious guidance could be obtained for almost every act of their daily life. When starting on an enterprise they looked for the will of the gods in the changing expressions of the sky, in the flight of birds or the manner in which they fed, and in the marks on the vitals of slain animals. The meaning of these signs was interpreted by the Augurs, and thus they largely guided the actions of the state. The king himself was Chief Pontiff (*Pontifex Maximus*), and thus the head of the religious as he was of the civil life of the community.

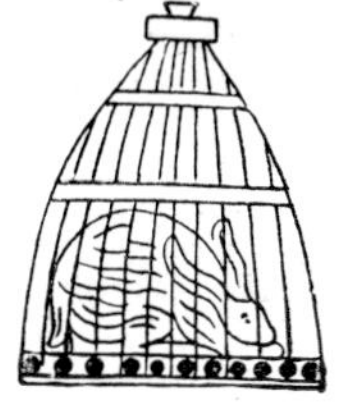

Augur's victims.

Remains of the Servian wall.

CHAPTER III.

THE LAST THREE KINGS OF ROME, AND THE ESTABLISHMENT OF THE REPUBLIC DOWN TO THE BATTLE OF THE LAKE REGILLUS. 616–498 B.C.

5. Reign of Lucius Tarquinius Priscus, or the Elder Tarquin, 616–579 B.C.—The fifth king of Rome was an Etruscan by birth, but a Greek by descent. His father Demaratus was a wealthy citizen of Corinth, who settled in the Etruscan city of Tarquinii, where he married an Etruscan wife. Their son wedded Tanaquil, who belonged to one of the noblest families in Tarquinii, and himself became a *Lucumo*,* or a noble in the state. But he aspired to still higher honours; and, urged on by his wife, who was an ambitious woman, he resolved to try his

The Etruscan dynasty.

* This was an Etruscan word originally meaning an "insane" or "frenzied" person. It was thus applied to any one supposed to be inspired.

fortune at Rome. Accordingly he set out for this city, accompanied by a large train of followers. When he had reached the Janiculum an eagle seized his cap, and, after carrying it away to a great height, placed it again upon his head. Tanaquil, who was skilled in the Etruscan science of augury, bade her husband hope for the highest honours. Her predictions were soon verified. He took the name of Lucius Tarquinius, and gained the favour both of Ancus Marcius and the people. Ancus appointed the stranger guardian of his children; and, when he died, the senate and the people unanimously elected Tarquin to the vacant throne.

Reign of the elder Tarquin.

The reign of Tarquin was distinguished by great exploits in war and by great works in peace. He defeated the Sabines, and took their town Collatia, which he placed under his nephew Egerius, who was thence called Collatinus. He also captured many of the Latin towns, and became the ruler of all Latium; but the important works which he executed in peace have rendered his name still more famous. The great *cloacae*, or sewers, by which he drained the lower parts of the city, still remain, after so many ages, with not a stone displaced. He laid out the Circus Maximus, and instituted the Great or Roman games performed in the circus. He also made some changes in the constitution of the state. He added to the senate 100 new members, taken from the Luceres, the third tribe, and called *patres minorum gentium* to distinguish them from the old senators, who were now termed *patres majorum gentium;* the numbers of this council were thus raised to 300. The number of vestal virgins was also increased from four to six, the two new vestals being probably taken from the Luceres.

Tarquin had a favourite, Servius Tullius, said to have been the son of a female slave taken at the capture of the Latin town Corniculum. His infancy was marked by prodigies which foreshadowed his future greatness. On one occasion a flame played around his head, as he was asleep, without hurting him. Tanaquil foresaw the greatness of the boy, and from this time he was brought up as the king's child. Tarquin afterwards gave him his daughter in marriage, and left the government in his hands. But the sons of Ancus Marcius, fearing lest Tarquin should transmit the crown to his son-in-law, hired two countrymen to assassinate the king. These men, feigning to have a quarrel, came before the king to have their dispute decided; and while he was listening to the complaint of one, the other gave him a deadly wound with his axe. But the sons of Ancus did not reap the fruit of their crime; for Tanaquil, pretending that the king's wound was not mortal, told them that he would soon return, and that he had, meantime, appointed

The Cloaca Maxima.

Servius to act in his stead. Servius forthwith proceeded to discharge the duties of king, greatly to the satisfaction of the people; and when the death of Tarquin could no longer be concealed, he was already in firm possession of the regal power. Tarquin had reigned thirty-seven years.

6. SERVIUS TULLIUS, 578–535 B.C.—Servius thus succeeded to the throne by the strictly recognized method of nomination.

The reign of this king is almost as barren of military exploits as that of Numa. His great deeds were those of peace; and he was regarded by posterity as the author of the later Roman constitution, just as Romulus was of the earlier. Three important acts are assigned to Servius by universal tradition. Of these the greatest was—

Servius Tullius.

(1) The reform of the Roman constitution. In this reform his main object was to distribute the burdens of taxation and military service as evenly as possible amongst all the members of the state. The effect of his scheme was to give to the wealthy classes as a whole the influence which had formerly depended on patrician birth, and thus to grant privileges to the well-to-do plebeians. To carry his purpose into effect he made a twofold division of the Roman people, one according to their residence, the other according to their property.

Reform in the constitution.

(*a*) It must be recollected that the only existing political organization was the division into three tribes, and of these tribes into thirty curiae, composed exclusively of patrician gentes; but Servius now divided the whole Roman territory into Four Tribes, and, as this division was simply local, these tribes contained plebeians as well as patricians. But though the institution of these local tribes made the plebeians members of the state, it conferred upon them no right to take part in the elections, or in the management of public affairs, for the powers of electing the king and of ratifying the laws were possessed exclusively by the purely patrician "comitia curiata."

(*b*) The means by which Servius indirectly gave the plebeians a share in the government was by dividing the whole body of citizens into classes according to their wealth for the purposes of taxation and the military levy. But this new arrangement was soon made the basis of a new Popular Assembly, in which patricians and plebeians alike voted. The result of the arrangement was that the wealthiest persons, whether patricians or plebeians, possessed the chief power. In order to ascertain the property of each citizen, Servius instituted the *Census*, which was a register of Roman citizens and their property. All Roman citizens possessing a certain amount of landed property afterwards valued at 12,500

The Servian census.

asses and upwards * were divided into five great *Classes*. The First Class contained the richest citizens, the Second Class the next in point of wealth, and so on. The whole arrangement was of a military character. Each of the five Classes was divided into a certain number of Centuries or Companies, half of which consisted of Elders (*Seniores*) from the age of 46 to 60, and half of younger members (*Juniores*) from the age of 18 to 46. All the Classes had to provide their own arms and armour, but the expense of the equipment was in proportion to the wealth of each Class. The Five *Classes* formed the infantry (*pedites*). To these five classes were added two centuries of smiths and carpenters, and two of trumpeters and horn-blowers. These four centuries voted with the Classes. Those persons whose property did not amount to 12,500 asses were not included in the Classes, and formed a single century.

At the head of the Classes were the Equites or cavalry. These consisted of eighteen centuries, six being the old patrician Equites, as founded by Romulus and augmented by Tarquinius Priscus, and the other twelve being chosen from the chief plebeian families.†

* The *as* was originally a pound weight of copper of twelve ounces. Although the census is always given in terms of copper money, there is little doubt that originally it was an assessment on hides of land (*jugera*), and perhaps on sheep and cattle.

† The following table will show the census of each class, and the number of centuries which each contained:—

Equites.—Centuriae		18
First Class.—Census, 100,000 asses and upwards.		
Centuriae Seniorum	40	
Centuriae Juniorum	40	82
Centuriae Fabrum (smiths and carpenters)	2	
Second Class.—Census, 75,000 asses and upwards.		
Centuriae Seniorum	10	20
Centuriae Juniorum	10	
Third Class.—Census, 50,000 asses and upwards.		
Centuriae Seniorum	10	20
Centuriae Juniorum	10	
Fourth Class.—Census, 25,000 asses and upwards.		
Centuriae Seniorum	10	20
Centuriae Juniorum	10	
Fifth Class.—Census, 12,500 asses and upwards		
Centuriae Seniorum	15	
Centuriae Juniorum	15	32
Centuriae cornicinum, tubicinum	2	
Centuria capite censorum		1
Sum total of the centuriae		193

The Centuries formed the new National Assembly. They mustered as an army in the Campus Martius, or the Field of Mars, on the banks of the Tiber outside the city. They voted by Centuries, and were hence called the *Comitia Centuriata*. Each Century counted as one vote, but did not consist of the same number of men. On the contrary, in order to give the preponderance to wealth, the first or richest class contained a far greater number of centuries than any of the other classes (as will be seen from the table on p. 24), although they must at the same time have included a much smaller number of men. The Equites and First Class alone amounted to 100 centuries, or more than half of the total number; so that, if they agreed to vote the same way, they possessed at once an absolute majority. An advantage was also given to age; for the Seniores, though possessing an equal number of votes, must of course have been very inferior in number to the Juniores.

The comitia centuriata.

This system, therefore, only admitted to power the classes who possessed a certain amount of wealth, but it was far more a government by the people than the rule of the patrician nobles which it replaced. The Comitia Centuriata became the sovereign assembly of the nation; it finally usurped from the Comitia Curiata the right of ratifying the election of kings and magistrates, of enacting and repealing laws, and of deciding in cases of appeal from the sentence of a judge. Eventually the *Comitia Curiata* came itself to include plebeians. This old assembly was not abolished, and a trace of its ancient ascendency remained in the formality of the *lex curiata*,* which even in the Republic was required to ratify the election of a magistrate with *imperium*.

(2) The second great work of Servius was the extension of the Pomerium, or hallowed boundary of the city, and the completion of the city by incorporating with it the Quirinal, Viminal, and Esquiline hills.† He surrounded the whole with a stone wall, called after him the wall of Servius Tullius; and from the Porta Collina to the Esquiline Gate, where the hills sloped gently to

Extension of the city.

* See p. 17.

† The celebrated seven hills upon which Rome stood were the Palatine, Aventine, Capitoline, Caelian, Quirinal, Viminal, and Esquiline. The Mons Pincius was not included within the Servian Wall.

the plain, he constructed a gigantic mound nearly a mile in length and a moat 100 feet in breadth and thirty in depth, from which the earth of the mound was dug. Rome thus acquired a circumference of five miles, and this continued to be the legal extent of the city till the time of the emperors, although suburbs were added to it.

Alliance with the Latins.

(3) An important alliance with the Latins, by which Rome and the cities of Latium became the members of one great league, was one of the great events which distinguished the reign of Servius.

Servius gave his two daughters in marriage to the two sons of Tarquinius Priscus. Lucius, the elder, was married to a quiet and gentle wife; Aruns, the younger, to an aspiring and ambitious woman. The character of the two brothers was the very opposite of the wives who had fallen to their lot; for Lucius was restless and haughty, but Aruns retiring and unambitious. The wife of Aruns, enraged at the long life of her father, and fearing that at his death her husband would tamely resign the sovereignty to his elder brother, resolved to murder both her father and husband. Her fiendish spirit put into the heart of Lucius thoughts of crime which he had never entertained before. Lucius made away with his wife, and the younger Tullia with her husband; and the survivors, without even the show of mourning, were straightway joined in unhallowed wedlock. Tullia now incessantly urged her husband to murder her father, and thus obtain the kingdom which he so ardently coveted. Tarquin formed a conspiracy with the patricians, who were enraged at the reforms of Servius; and when the plot was ripe he entered the forum arrayed in the kingly robes, seated himself in the royal chair in the senate-house, and ordered the senators to be summoned to him as their king.

Death of Servius.

At the first news of the commotion Servius hastened to the senate-house, and, standing at the doorway, bade Tarquin to come down from the throne; but Tarquin sprang forward, seized the old man, and flung him down the stone steps. Covered with blood, the king staggered home; but, before he reached it, he was overtaken by the servants of Tarquin, and murdered. Tullia drove to the senate-house and greeted her husband as king; but her transports of joy struck even him with horror. He bade her go home; and, as she was returning, her charioteer pulled up and pointed out the corpse of her father lying in his blood across the road. She commanded him to drive on: the blood of her father spurted over the carriage and on her dress; and from that day forward the place bore the name of the Wicked Street. The body lay unburied; for Tarquin said scoffingly, "Romulus too went without burial;" and this impious mockery is said to have given rise to his surname of Superbus, or the Proud. Servius had reigned forty-three years.

7. Reign of LUCIUS TARQUINIUS SUPERBUS, or THE PROUD, 535–510 B.C.—Tarquin commenced his reign without any of the forms of election. One of his first acts was to abolish all the privileges which had been conferred upon the plebeians by Servius. He also compelled the poor to work at miserable wages upon his magnificent buildings, and the hardships which they suffered were so great that many put an end to their lives. But he did not confine his oppressions to the poor. All the senators and patricians whom he mistrusted, or whose wealth he coveted, were put to death or driven into exile. He surrounded himself with a body-guard, by whose means he was enabled to carry out his designs.

Tarquinius Superbus.

But, although a tyrant at home, he raised the state to great influence and power among the surrounding nations, partly by his alliances and partly by his conquests. He gave his daughter in marriage to Octavius Mamilius of Tusculum, the most powerful of the Latins, by whose means he acquired great influence in Latium. Any Latin chiefs like Turnus Herdonius, who attempted to resist him, were treated as traitors, and punished with death. At the solemn meeting of the Latins at the Alban Mount, Tarquin sacrificed the bull on behalf of all the allies, and distributed the flesh to the people of the league.

Supremacy of Rome in Latium.

Strengthened by this Latin alliance, Tarquin turned his arms against the Volscians. He took the wealthy town of Suessa Pometia, with the spoils of which he commenced the erection of a magnificent temple on the Capitoline hill, which his father had vowed. This temple was dedicated to the three gods of the Latin and Etruscan religions, Jupiter, Juno, and Minerva. A human head (*caput*), fresh bleeding and undecayed, is said to have been found by the workmen as they were digging the foundations, and being accepted as a sign that the place was destined to become the head of the world, the name of CAPITOLIUM was given to the temple, and thence to the hill. In a stone vault beneath were deposited the Sibylline books, containing obscure and prophetic sayings. One day a sibyl, a prophetess from Cumæ, appeared before the king and offered to sell him nine books. Upon his refusing to buy them she went away and burned three, and then demanded the same sum for the remaining six as she had asked for the nine. But the king laughed, whereupon she again burnt three, and then demanded the same sum as before for the remaining three. Wondering at this strange conduct, the king purchased the books. They were placed under the care of two patricians, and were consulted when the state was in danger.

Tarquin next attacked Gabii, one of the Latin cities which refused to enter into the league. Unable to take the city by force, he had recourse to stratagem. His son, Sextus, pretending to be illtreated by his father, and covered with the bloody marks of stripes, fled to Gabii. The infatuated inhabitants intrusted him with the command of their troops; and when he had obtained the unlimited confidence of the citizens, he sent a messenger to his father to inquire how he should deliver the city into his hands. The king, who was walking in his garden when the messenger arrived, made no reply, but kept striking off the heads of the tallest poppies with his stick. Sextus took the hint. He put to death or banished, on false charges, all the leading men of the place, and then had no difficulty in compelling it to submit to his father.

In the midst of his prosperity Tarquin was troubled by a strange portent. A serpent crawled out from the altar in the royal palace, and seized on the entrails of the victim. The king, in fear, sent his two sons, Titus and Aruns, to consult the famous oracle of the Greeks at Delphi. They were accompanied by their cousin, L. Junius Brutus. One of the sisters of Tarquin had been married to

Brutus.

M. Brutus, a man of great wealth, who died, leaving two sons under age.* Of these the elder was killed by Tarquin, who coveted their possessions; the younger escaped his brother's fate only by feigning idiotcy. On arriving at Delphi, Brutus propitiated the priestess with the gift of a golden stick enclosed in a hollow staff. After executing the king's commission, Titus and Aruns asked the priestess who was to reign at Rome after their father. The priestess replied, whichsoever should first kiss his mother. The princes agreed to keep the matter secret from Sextus, who was at Rome, and to cast lots between themselves. Brutus, who better understood the meaning of the oracle, fell, as if by chance, when they quitted the temple, and kissed the earth, the mother of them all.

Crime of Sextus Tarquinius.

Soon afterwards Tarquin laid siege to Ardea, a city of the Rutulians. The place could not be taken by force, and the Roman army lay encamped beneath the walls. Here, as the king's sons, and their cousin Tarquinius Collatinus, were feasting together, a dispute arose about the virtue of their wives. As nothing was doing in the field, they mounted their horses to visit their homes by surprise. They first went to Rome, where they surprised the princes' wives at a splendid banquet. They then hastened to Collatia, and there, though it was late in the night, they found Lucretia, the wife of Collatinus, spinning amid her handmaids. The beauty and virtue of Lucretia excited the evil passions of Sextus. A few days after he returned to Collatia, where he was hospitably received by Lucretia as her husband's kinsman. In the dead of night he

* The following genealogical table exhibits the relationship of the family:—

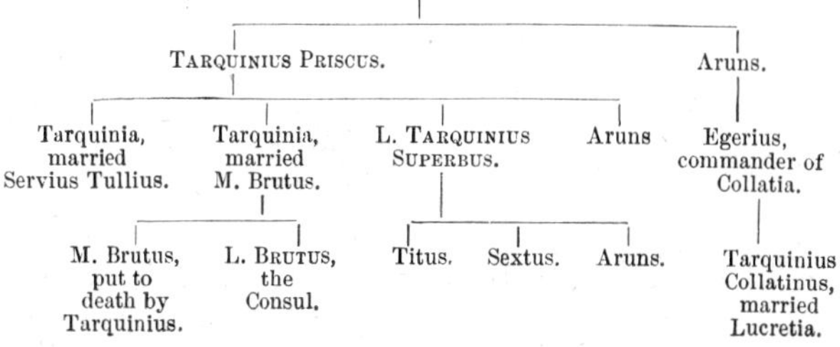

entered her chamber with a drawn sword, threatening that, if she did not yield to his desires he would kill her and lay by her side a slave with his throat cut, and would declare that he had killed them both taken in adultery. Fear of such a shame forced Lucretia to consent; but, as soon as Sextus had departed, she sent for her husband and father. Collatinus came, accompanied by L. Brutus; her father, Lucretius, brought with him P. Valerius. They found her in an agony of sorrow. She told them what had happened, enjoined them to avenge her dishonour, and then stabbed herself to the heart. They all swore to avenge her. Brutus threw off his assumed stupidity, and placed himself at their head. They carried the corpse into the market-place of Collatia. There the people took up arms, and renounced the Tarquins. A number of young men attended the funeral procession to Rome. Brutus summoned the people, and related the deed of shame. All classes were inflamed with the same indignation.

Downfall of the monarchy.

A decree was passed deposing the king, and banishing him and his family from the city. Brutus now set out for the army at Ardea. Tarquinius meantime had hastened to Rome, but found the gates closed against him. Brutus was received with joy at Ardea; and the army renounced their allegiance to the tyrant. Tarquin, with his two sons, Titus and Aruns, took refuge at Caeré, in Etruria. Sextus fled to Gabii, where he was shortly after murdered by the friends of those whom he had put to death.

Tarquin had reigned twenty-five years when he was driven out of Rome. In memory of this event an annual festival was celebrated on the 24th of February, called the *Regifugium* or *Fugalia*.

Creation of consuls.

THE REPUBLIC.—Thus ended monarchy at Rome. Here, however, the revolution stopped. The form of the constitution remained unaltered; but the power of the chief magistrate was limited in three ways. The office was no longer entrusted to a single individual, the time for which it might be held was shortened, and direct election by the people was substituted for the older principle of nomination. Two men of equal authority, who held office only for a year, were entrusted with the regal *imperium*. Each was given the power of commanding, judging, and proposing laws, and each with the power of overriding his colleague's actions. In later times they were called *Consuls*, but at their first institution they were named *Praetors.** They were elected by the Comitia Centuriata, and possessed the honours and most of the emblems of authority (*insignia*) of the king. The first consuls were L. Brutus and Tarquinius Collatinus (509 B.C.). But the people so hated the very name and race of Tarquin, that Collatinus was obliged to resign his office and retire from Rome. P. Valerius was elected consul in his place.

Meantime ambassadors came to Rome from Tarquin, asking that his private property should be given up to him. The demand seemed just to the senate and the people; but while the ambassadors were making preparation for carrying away the property, they formed a conspiracy among the young Roman nobles for the restoration of the royal family. The plot was discovered by means of a slave, and among the conspirators were found the two sons of Brutus himself. But the consul would not pardon his guilty children, and ordered the lictors † to put them to death with the other traitors. The agreement to surrender the property was made void by this attempt at treason, and the royal goods were given up to the people to plunder.

War with the Etruscans.

As the plot had failed, Tarquin now endeavoured to recover the throne by arms. The people of Tarquinii and Veii espoused the cause of their Etruscan kinsmen, and marched against Rome. The two consuls advanced to meet them. When Aruns, the king's son, saw Brutus at the head of the Roman cavalry he spurred his horse to the charge. Brutus did not shrink from the combat; and both fell from their horses mortally wounded by each other's spears. A desperate battle between the two armies now followed. Both parties claimed the victory, till a voice was heard in the dead of night, proclaiming that the Romans had conquered, as the Etruscans had lost one man more. Alarmed at this, the Etruscans fled; and Valerius, the surviving consul, returned to Rome, carrying with him the dead body of Brutus.

* Cf. p. 62.

† The *lictores* were public officers who attended upon the Roman magistrate. Each consul had twelve lictors. They carried upon their shoulders *fasces*, which were rods bound in the form of a bundle, and containing an axe in the middle.

The matrons mourned for Brutus a whole year, because he had revenged the death of Lucretia.

Valerius was now left without a colleague; and as he began to build a house on the top of the hill Velia, which looked down upon the forum, the people feared that he was aiming at kingly power. Thereupon Valerius not only pulled down the house, but, calling an assembly of the people, he ordered the lictors to lower the fasces before them, as an acknowledgment that their power was superior to his. He likewise brought forward a law enacting that every citizen who was condemned by a magistrate to be executed, should have a right of appeal to the people. Valerius became in consequence so popular that he received the surname of *Publicola*, or "The People's Friend."

Valerius then summoned an assembly for the election of a successor to Brutus; and Sp. Lucretius was chosen. Lucretius, however, lived only a few days, and M. Horatius was elected consul in his place. It was Horatius who had the honour of consecrating the temple on the Capitol, which Tarquin had left unfinished when he was driven from the throne.

The second year of the republic (508 B.C.) witnessed the second attempt of Tarquin to recover the crown. He now applied for help to Lars Porsena, the powerful ruler of the Etruscan town of Clusium, who marched against Rome at the head of a vast army. The Romans could not meet him in the field; and Porsena seized without opposition the Janiculum, a hill immediately opposite the city, and separated from it only by the Tiber.

The Etruscans besiege Rome.

Rome was now in the greatest danger, and the Etruscans would have entered the city by the Sublician bridge had not Horatius Cocles, with two comrades, kept the whole Etruscan army at bay while the Romans broke down the bridge behind him. When it was giving way he sent back his two companions, and withstood alone the attacks of the foe till the cracks of the falling timbers and the shouts of his countrymen told him that the bridge had fallen. Then praying, "O Father Tiber, take me into thy charge and bear me up!" he plunged into the stream and swam across in safety amid the arrows of the enemy. The state raised a statue in his honour, and allowed him as much land as he could plough round in one day. Few legends are more celebrated in

Horatius.

Roman story than this gallant deed of Horatius, and Roman writers loved to tell

"How well Horatius kept the bridge
In the brave days of old."

The Etruscans now proceeded to lay siege to the city, which soon began to suffer from famine. Thereupon a young Roman, named C. Mucius, resolved to deliver his country by murdering the invading king. He accordingly went over to the Etruscan camp; but, ignorant of the person of Porsena, killed the royal secretary instead. Seized and threatened with torture, he thrust his right hand into the fire on the altar, and there let it burn, to show how little he heeded pain. Astonished at his courage, the king bade him depart in safety; and Mucius, out of gratitude, advised him to make peace with Rome, since three hundred noble youths, he said, had sworn to take the life of the king, and he was the first upon whom the lot had fallen. Mucius was henceforward called Scaevola, or the *Left-handed*, because his right hand had been burnt off. Porsena, alarmed for his life, which he could not secure against so many desperate men, forthwith offered peace to the Romans on condition of their restoring to the Veientines the land which they had taken from them. These terms were accepted, and Porsena withdrew his troops from the Janiculum, after receiving ten youths and ten maidens as hostages from the Romans. Cloelia, one of the maidens, escaped from the Etruscan camp, and swam across the Tiber to Rome. She was sent back by the Romans to Porsena, who was so amazed at her courage that he not only set her at liberty, but allowed her to take with her those of the hostages whom she pleased.

Thus ended the second attempt to restore the Tarquins by force.*

War with the Latin league.

After Porsena quitted Rome, Tarquin took refuge with his son-in-law, Octavius Mamilius of Tusculum. The thirty Latin cities now espoused the cause of the exiled king, and declared war against Rome.

The Romans in their peril had recourse to a dictatorship.

* There is, however, reason to believe that these brilliant stories conceal one of the earliest and greatest disasters of the city. It is probable that Rome was really conquered by Porsena, and lost all the territory which the kings had gained on the right side of the Tiber.

This was a temporary revival of the monarchy for the purpose of meeting some emergency, whether within or without the city, which seemed beyond the powers of the ordinary magistrates with their divided authority. The dictator was nominated by one of the consuls, and held office only for six months. His absolute power was shown by the fact that the lictors attending him bore the axes in the fasces even within the city, to signify that from him, as from the kings, there was no appeal. From the time of his appointment the independent powers of all other magistrates ceased, and the only other authority was exercised by his lieutenant, the Master of the Horse, who commanded the cavalry. A. Postumius was appointed Dictator, and he named T. Aebutius Master of the Horse; at the head of the Latins were Tarquin and Octavius Mamilius. The armies met near the lake Regillus, and the struggle was fierce and bloody, but the Latins at length fled. Almost all the chiefs on either side fell in the conflict, or were grievously wounded. Titus, the son of Tarquin, was killed; and the aged king was wounded, but escaped with his life. It was related in the old tradition, that the Romans gained this battle by the assistance of the "Great Twin Brethren," Castor and Pollux, who were seen charging the Latins at the head of the Roman cavalry, and who afterwards carried to Rome the tidings of the victory. A temple was built in the forum on the spot where they appeared, and their festival was celebrated yearly.

Appointment of a dictator.

This was the third and last attempt to restore the Tarquins. The Latins were completely humbled by this victory. Tarquinius Superbus had no other state to which he could apply for assistance. He had already survived all his family; and he now fled to Cumae, where he died a wretched and childless old man (496 B.C.).

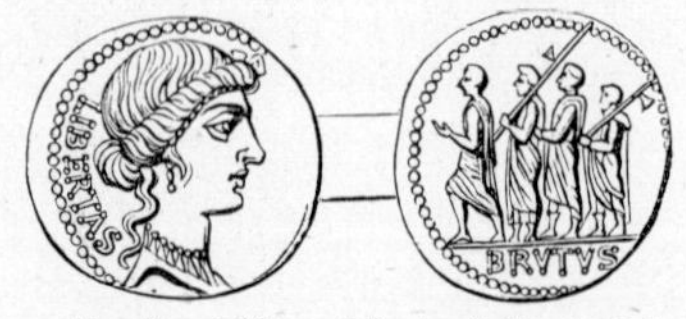

Coin representing the children of Brutus led to death by lictors.

The Campagna.

CHAPTER IV.

FROM THE BATTLE OF THE LAKE REGILLUS TO THE DECEMVIRATE. 498–451 B.C.

THE infant Republic was now saved from its immediate danger, a forcible restoration of the monarchy; but the state was for a long time in the most grievous peril: it needed consolidation from within, and was at the same time mercilessly attacked by enemies from without.

The internal history of Rome during this period is marked by the struggle between the patricians and plebeians, who formed two distinct orders in the state. After the banishment of the kings, the patricians retained exclusive possession of political power. The plebeians, it is true, could vote in the Comitia Centuriata; but, as they were mostly poor, they were outvoted by the patricians and their clients. The consulship and all other magistracies

Grievances of the plebeians.

were legally confined to the patricians, so that the executive power was entirely in their hands, while the pontiffs, who were the authorized interpreters of the law, were drawn entirely from that order. The state was still practically governed by a handful of nobles, and there was no possibility of bridging the gulf between the classes; for intermarriage between the orders was forbidden, and in the sacred rites of the patrician clans the plebeians had no share.

The plebeians had to complain, not only of disadvantages in social and public life, but also of private wrongs. The law of debtor and creditor was very severe at Rome. An agreement called *nexum* was often concluded, by which the debtor pledged his body and his future services for the repayment of the loan, and if the borrower did not refund the money by the time agreed upon, his person was seized by the creditor, and he was obliged to work as a slave.* Slavery was also the penalty for ordinary debts; and if there were more creditors than one, the debtor's body might be cut in pieces and divided among them. The whole weight of this oppressive law fell upon the plebeians; and what rendered the case still harder was that they were frequently compelled, through no fault of their own, to become borrowers. They were small landholders, living by cultivating the soil with their own hands; but as they had to serve in the army without pay, they had no means of engaging labourers in their absence. Hence on their return home they were left without the means of subsistence or of purchasing seed for the next crop, and borrowing was their only resource.

Another circumstance still further aggravated the hardships of the plebeians. The state possessed a large quantity of land called *Ager Publicus*, or the "Public Land." This land originally belonged to the kings, partly for their own use, partly in trust for the people; and it was constantly increased by conquest, as it was the practice, on the subjugation of a people, to deprive them of a certain portion of their land. This public land was either divided amongst the poorer citizens or left by the state to any occupier subject to a rent; but as the patricians possessed the political power, they occupied the public land themselves, and paid for it only a nominal rent. Thus the plebeians, by whose blood and unpaid toil much of this land

* Debtors thus given over to their creditors were called *nexi*.

had been won, were excluded from all share in the fruits of their conquest.

The struggle that ensued was, therefore, partly social, partly political. But protection was what the plebeians desired even more than power; the cruelty of the patrician creditors was the most pressing evil, and led to the first reform. In 494 B.C. the plebeians, after a campaign against the Volscians, instead of returning to Rome, suddenly turned aside to the Sacred Mount, a hill about three miles from the city, near the junction of the Anio and the Tiber. Here they determined to settle and found a new town, leaving Rome to the patricians and their clients. This event is known as the *Secession to the Sacred Mount.* The patricians, alarmed, sent several of their number to persuade the plebeians to return. Among the deputies was the aged Menenius Agrippa, who had great influence with the plebeians. He related to them the celebrated fable of the Belly and the Members—

First secession of the plebeians.

"Once upon a time," he said, "the Members refused to work any longer for the Belly, which led a lazy life and grew fat upon their toils. But receiving no longer any nourishment from the Belly, they soon began to pine away, and found that it was to the Belly they owed their life and strength."

The fable was understood, and the plebeians agreed to treat with the patricians. It was decided that existing debts should be cancelled, and that all debtors in bondage should be restored to freedom. Slavery for debt was not, however, forbidden, and as it was necessary to provide security for the future, the plebeians insisted that two of their own number should be elected annually, to whom the plebeians might appeal for assistance against the decisions of the patrician magistrates. These officers were called *Tribunes of the Plebs.* They were not magistrates, and had no *imperium;* their sole duty was that of protection; they could forbid the fulfillment of any decree aimed against a citizen—a right which gradually became a power of declaring any proposal made by a magistrate to be null and void.* Their persons were declared sacred and inviolable; they were never to quit the city during

Appointment of tribunes.

* This was called the right of *intercessio,* from *intercedo,* "to come between."

their year of office; and their houses were to remain open day and night, that all who were in need of help might apply to them. Their number was soon afterwards increased to four, and at a later time to ten.* At the Sacred Mount the plebeians also obtained the privilege of having two *aediles* of their order appointed. These officers had at a later time the care of the public buildings and roads, and the superintendence of the police of the city.

Agrarian law of Spurius Cassius.

Emboldened by this success, the plebeians now demanded a share in the public land. And in this they found an unexpected supporter among the patricians themselves. Sp. Cassius, one of the most distinguished men in the state, brought forward in his third consulship a law by which a portion of the public land was to be divided among the plebeians (486 B.C.). This was the first *Agrarian Law* mentioned in Roman history. It must be recollected that all Agrarian laws dealt only with the public land, and, though often infringing private rights, never touched what was actually private property. Notwithstanding the violent opposition of the patricians, the law was passed; but it was never carried into execution, and the patricians soon revenged themselves upon its author. In the following year he was accused of aiming at the kingly power, and condemned to death. He was scourged and beheaded, and his house razed to the ground.

Foreign relations of Rome.

We now turn to the external history of Rome. Under the kings Rome had risen to a superiority over her neighbours; she had extended her dominion over the southern part of Etruria, and she had acquired the headship of the Latin league: this headship taking the form of an alliance between Rome on the one hand and all the cities of the league on the other. The early history of the Republic presents a very different spectacle. She is now isolated, and for the next 100 years engaged in a constant defensive war with her neighbours, the Etruscans on the one hand and the Volscians and Aequians on the other.

An attempt to break this isolation was made by Sp. Cassius in the days of his power by the alliance which he effected

* The tribunes were originally elected by the assembly of the Plebs which met by curiae (*concilium plebis curiatim*); but by the Publilian Law, proposed by the tribune Publilius Volero, and passed 471 B.C., the election was transferred to the assembly of the Plebs meeting by tribes (*concilium plebis tributim*).

between Rome and the Latin and Hernican leagues (486 B.C.). It was this union which kept the Volscians and Aequians at bay in the defensive contest now carried on by Rome. It would be unprofitable to relate the details of these petty campaigns; but there are three celebrated legends connected with them which must not be passed over.

Renewal of the Latin league.

1. CORIOLANUS AND THE VOLSCIANS, 488 B.C.—C. Marcius, surnamed Coriolanus, from his valour at the capture of the Latin town of Corioli, was a brave but haughty patrician youth. He was hated by the plebeians, who refused him the consulship. This inflamed him with anger; and accordingly, when the city was suffering from famine, and a present of corn came from Sicily, Coriolanus advised the senate not to distribute it among the plebeians, unless they gave up their tribunes. Such insolence enraged the plebeians, who would have torn him to pieces on the spot, had not the tribunes summoned him before the Assembly of the Plebs. Coriolanus himself breathed nothing but defiance; and his kinsmen and friends interceded for him in vain. He was condemned to exile. He now turned his steps to Antium, the capital of the Volscians, and offered to lead them against Rome. Attius Tullius, king of the Volscians, persuaded his countrymen to appoint Coriolanus their general. Nothing could check his victorious progress: town after town fell before him; and he advanced within five miles of the city, ravaging the lands of the plebeians, but sparing those of the patricians. The city was filled with despair. The ten first men in the senate were sent in hopes of moving his compassion. But they were received with the utmost sternness, and told that the city must submit to his absolute will. Next day the pontiffs, augurs, flamens, and all the priests, came in their robes of office, and in vain prayed him to spare the city. All seemed lost, but Rome was saved by her women. Next morning the noblest matrons, headed by Veturia, the aged mother of Coriolanus, and by his wife Volumnia, holding her little children by the hand, came to his tent. Their lamentations turned him from his purpose. "Mother," he said, bursting into tears, "thou hast saved Rome, but lost thy son!" He then led the Volscians home. Some say that they put him to death because he had spared Rome.

War with the Volscians.

But others tell that he lived among the Volscians to a great age, and was often heard to say that "none but an old man can feel the misery of living in a foreign land."

2. THE FABIA GENS AND THE VEIENTINES, 477 B.C.—The Fabii were one of the most powerful of the patrician houses.

War with Veii.

For seven successive years one of the consuls was always a Fabius. This clan had furnished the leading opponents of the Agrarian Law; and Kaeso Fabius had taken an active part in obtaining the condemnation of Sp. Cassius. But shortly afterwards we find this same Kaeso the advocate of the popular rights, and proposing that the Agrarian Law of Cassius should be carried into effect. He was supported in his new views by his powerful house; though the reasons for their change of opinion we do not know. But the Fabii made no impression upon the great body of the patricians, and only earned for themselves the hearty hatred of their order. Finding that they could no longer live in peace at Rome, they determined to leave the city, and found a separate settlement, where they might still be useful to their native land. One of the most formidable enemies of the Republic was the Etruscan city of Veii, situate about twelve miles from Rome. Accordingly the Fabian house, consisting of 306 males of full age, accompanied by their wives and children, clients and dependents, marched out of Rome by the right-hand arch of the Carmental Gate, and proceeded straight to the Cremera, a river which flows into the Tiber below Veii. On the Cremera they established a fortified camp, and sallying thence, they laid waste the Veientine territory. For two years they sustained the whole weight of the Veientine war; and all attempts to dislodge them proved in vain. But at length they were enticed into an ambuscade, and were all slain. The settlement was destroyed, and no one of the house survived except a boy, who had been left behind at Rome, and who became the ancestor of the Fabii, afterwards so celebrated in Roman history. The Fabii were sacrificed to the hatred of the patricians; for the consul T. Menenius was encamped a short way off at the time, and he did nothing to save them.

3. CINCINNATUS AND THE AEQUIANS, 458 B.C.—The Aequians in their numerous attacks upon the Roman territory generally occupied Mount Algidus, which formed a part of the group of

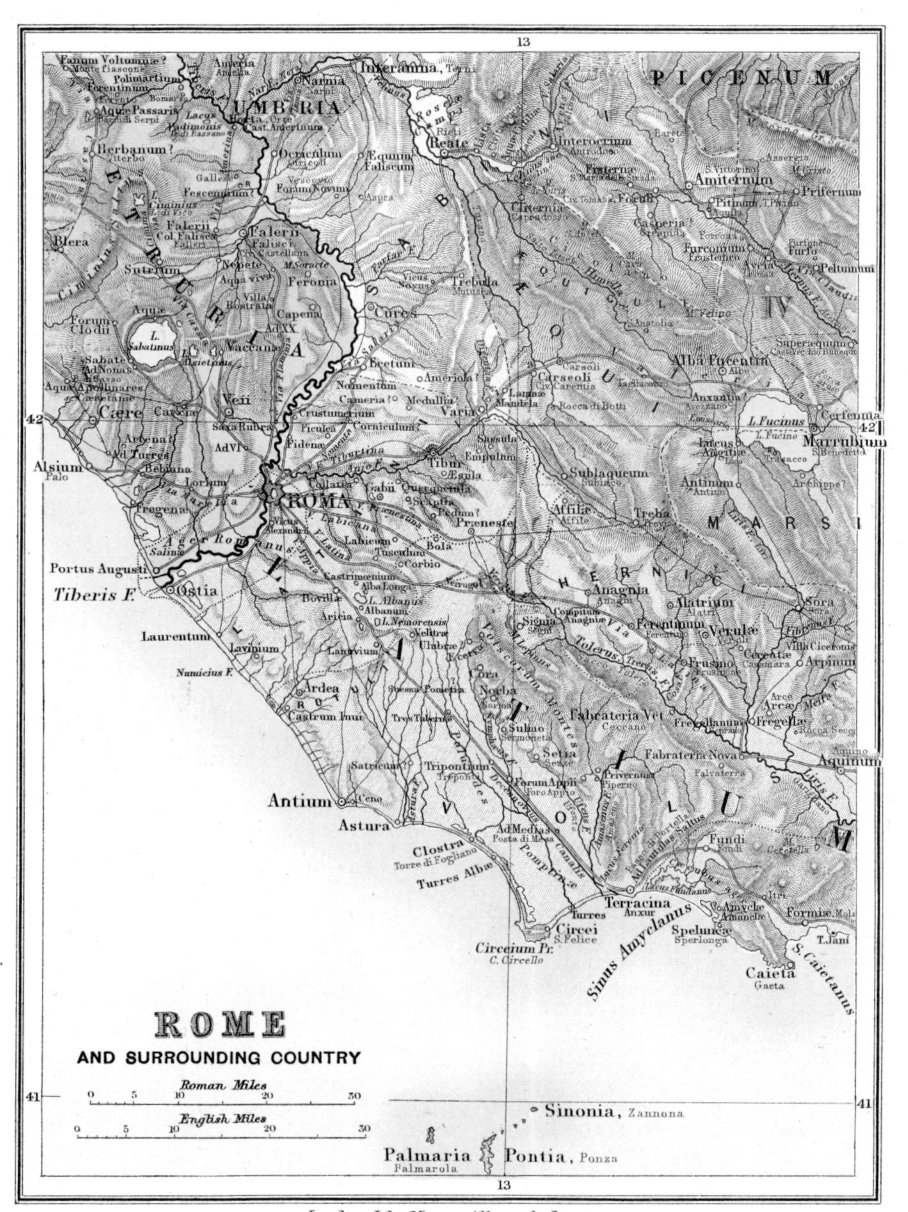

London. John Murray, Albemarle Street.

the Alban hills in Latium. It was accordingly upon this mount that the battles between the Romans and Aequians most frequently took place. In the year 458 B.C. the Roman consul L. Minucius was defeated on the Algidus, and surrounded in his camp. Five horsemen, who made their escape before the Romans were completely encompassed, brought the tidings to Rome. The senate forthwith appointed L. Cincinnatus dictator.

War with the Aequians.

L. Cincinnatus was one of the heroes of old Roman story. When the deputies of the senate came to him to announce his elevation to the dictatorship, they found him driving a plough, and clad only in his tunic or shirt. They bade him clothe himself, that he might hear the commands of the senate. He put on his toga, which his wife Racilia brought him. The deputies then told him of the peril of the Roman army, and that he had been made dictator. The next morning, before daybreak, he appeared in the forum, and ordered all the men of military age to meet him in the evening in the Field of Mars, with food for five days, and each with twelve stakes. His orders were obeyed; and with such speed did he march, that by midnight he reached Mount Algidus. Placing his men around the Aequian camp, he told them to raise the war-cry, and at the same time to begin digging a trench and raising a mound, on the top of which the stakes were to be driven in. The other Roman army, which was shut in, hearing the war-cry, burst forth from their camp, and fought with the Aequians all night. The dictator's troops thus worked without interruption, and completed the entrenchment by the morning. The Aequians found themselves hemmed in between the two armies, and were forced to surrender. The dictator made them pass under the yoke, which was formed by two spears fixed upright in the ground, while a third was fastened across them. Cincinnatus entered Rome in triumph, only twenty-four hours after he had quitted it, having thus saved a whole Roman army from destruction.

It is impossible from the scattered legendary notices to gauge accurately the result of these struggles. We can only say that Rome issued from the contest with unimpaired strength—a result partly due to the renewed consolidation of the Latin league, partly to the weakening of her great rival Etruria. The

Decline of the Etruscan power.

Etruscans had been defeated in a great naval battle off Cumae by Hiero, king of Syracuse, in 474 B.C., and from this event dates the decline of their power. Henceforth Etruria was the object of attack, and not the aggressor, and Rome was left free to cope with the Aequians and Volscians, her warlike neighbours on the east and south.

Tarpeian Rock.

CHAPTER V.

THE DECEMVIRATE. 451–449 B.C.

FROM the Agrarian Law of Sp. Cassius to the appointment of the decemvirs was a period of more than thirty years. At the close of this period the contest between the patricians and the plebeians had reached an acute stage. The latter had constantly demanded, and the former as firmly refused, the execution of the Agrarian Law of Cassius. But though the plebeians

Renewed struggle between the orders.

failed in obtaining this object, they nevertheless made steady progress in gaining for themselves a more important position in the city. In 471 B.C. the Publilian Law, passed by the Tribune Publilius Volero,* had enacted that the election of the tribunes and plebeian aediles should take place in an Assembly of the Plebs which met by tribes.† From this time the Concilium of the Plebs, presided over by the tribunes, may be regarded as one of the political assemblies of the state, ranking with those of the centuries and the curies. But the patricians still retained exclusive possession of the powers of carrying out the laws and of giving judgments, and there were no written rules to limit their authority and to regulate their decisions.

Proposal to codify the law.

Under these circumstances, the Tribune C. Terentilius Arsa proposed, in 462 B.C., that a Commission of Ten Men (Decemviri) should be appointed to draw up a code of laws, by which a check might be put to the arbitrary power of the patrician magistrates. This proposition, as might have been expected, met with the most vehement opposition from the patricians. But the plebeians were firm and for five successive years the same tribunes were re-elected. At length, after a struggle of eight years, a compromise was effected, and it was arranged that Three Commissioners (Triumviri) were to be sent into Greece to collect information respecting the laws of Solon at Athens, as well as of the other Greek states.

Appointment of decemvirs.

After an absence of two years the three commissioners returned to Rome (452 B.C.), and it was now resolved that a Council of Ten, or Decemvirs, should be appointed to draw up a code of laws, and at the same time to carry on the government and administer justice without appeal. All the other magistrates were obliged to abdicate, and no exception was made even in favour of the tribunes. The decemvirs were thus entrusted with supreme power in the state. They entered upon their office at the beginning of 451 B.C. They were all patricians. At their head stood Appius Claudius and T. Genucius, who had been

* This Publilian law must be carefully distinguished from the *leges Publiliae* of the dictator Q. Publilius Philo, passed in 339 B.C. See p. 62.

† See note on p. 38, and cf. p. 63. This assembly was the *concilium plebis tributim* (sometimes loosely called the *comitia tributa*). Strictly the word *concilium* denotes an assembly of part of the people; the word *comitia*, an assembly of the whole people.

already appointed consuls for the year. They discharged the duties of their office with diligence, and dispensed justice with impartiality. Each administered the government day by day in succession, and the fasces were carried only before the one who presided for the day. They drew up a Code of Ten Tables, in which equal justice was dealt out to both orders. The Ten Tables received the sanction of the Comitia of the Centuries, and thus became law.

Their reappointment.

On the expiration of their year of office all parties were so well satisfied with the manner in which the decemvirs had discharged their duties, that it was resolved to continue the same form of government for another year; more especially as some of them said that their work was not finished. A new Council of Ten was accordingly elected, of whom Appius Claudius alone belonged to the former body. He had so carefully concealed his pride and ambition during the previous year that he had been the most popular member of the council, and the patricians, to prevent his appointment for another year, had ordered him to preside at the Comitia for the elections, thinking that he would not receive votes for himself. But Appius set such scruples at defiance, and not only returned himself as elected, but took care that his nine colleagues should be subservient to his views.

Their tyranny.

He now threw off the mask he had hitherto worn, and acted as the tyrant of Rome. Each decemvir was attended by twelve lictors, who carried the fasces with the axes in them, so that 120 lictors were seen in the city instead of twelve. The senate was rarely summoned. No one was now safe, and many of the leading men quitted Rome. Two new Tables were added to the Code, making twelve in all; but these new laws contained clauses which confirmed the patricians in their most odious privileges.

When the year came to a close, the decemvirs neither resigned nor held Comitia for the election of successors, but continued to hold their power in defiance of the senate and of the people. Next year (449 B.C.) the Sabines and Aequians invaded the Roman territory, and two armies were despatched against them, commanded by some of the decemvirs. Appius remained at Rome to administer justice. But the soldiers fought with no spirit under the command of men whom they detested, and two acts of outrageous tyranny caused them to turn their arms against their hated masters.

Murder of Dentatus.

In the army fighting against the Sabines was a centurion named L. Sicinius Dentatus, the bravest of the brave. He had fought in 120 battles; he had slain eight of the enemy in single combat; he had received forty wounds, all in front; he had accompanied the triumphs of nine generals; and had war-crowns and other rewards innumerable. As Tribune of the Plebs four years before, he had taken an active part in opposing the patricians, and was now suspected of plotting against the decemvirs. His death was accordingly resolved on, and he was sent with a company of soldiers as if to reconnoitre the enemy's position. But in a lonely spot they fell upon him and slew him, though not until he had destroyed most of the traitors. His comrades, who were told that he had fallen in an ambush of the enemy, discovered the foul treachery that had been practised when they saw him surrounded by Roman soldiers who had evidently been slain by him. The decemvirs prevented an immediate outbreak only by burying Dentatus with great pomp, but the troops were ready to rise in open mutiny upon the first provocation.

Verginia.

In the other army sent against the Aequians there was a well-known centurion named Verginius. He had a beautiful daughter, betrothed to L. Icilius, an eminent leader of the plebeian order. The maiden had attracted the notice of the Decemvir Appius Claudius. He at first tried bribes and allurements, but when these failed he had recourse to an outrageous act of tyranny. One morning, as Verginia, attended by her nurse, was on the way to her school, which was in one of the booths surrounding the forum, M. Claudius, a client of Appius, laid hold of the damsel and claimed her as his slave. The cry of the nurse for help brought a crowd around them, and all parties went before the decemvir. In his presence Marcus repeated the tale he had learnt, asserting that Verginia was the child of one of his female slaves, and had been imposed upon Verginius by his wife, who was childless. He further stated that he would prove this to her father as soon as he returned to Rome, and he demanded that the girl should meantime be handed over to his custody. Appius, fearing a riot, said that he would let the cause stand over till the next day, but that then, whether her father appeared or not, he should know how to maintain the laws. Straightway two friends of the family made all haste to the camp, which they reached the same evening. Verginius immediately obtained leave of absence, and was already on his way to Rome when the messenger of Appius arrived, instructing his colleagues to detain him. Early next morning Verginius and his daughter came into the forum with their garments rent. The father appealed to the people for aid, and the women in their company sobbed aloud. But, intent upon the gratification of his passions, Appius cared nought for the misery of the father and the girl, and hastened to give sentence, by which he consigned the maiden to his client. Appius, who had brought with him a large body of armed patricians and their clients, ordered his lictors to disperse the mob. The people drew back, leaving Verginius and his daughter alone before the judgment-seat. All help was gone. The unhappy father then prayed the decemvir to be allowed to speak one word to the nurse in his daughter's hearing, in order to ascertain whether she was really his daughter. The request was granted. Verginius drew them both aside, and, snatching up a butcher's knife from one of the stalls, plunged it in his daughter's breast, exclaiming, "There is no way but this to keep thee free." In vain did Appius call out to stop him. The crowd made way for him, and, holding his bloody knife on high, he rushed to the gate of the city and hastened to the army. His comrades espoused his cause, expelled their commanders, and marched towards Rome. They were soon joined by the other army, to whom Numitorius and Icilius had carried the tidings. The plebeians in the city flocked to them, and they all resolved to retire once more to the Sacred Mount.

Second secession of the plebeians.

This second secession extorted from the patricians the second great charter of the plebeian rights. The patricians compelled the decemvirs to resign, and sent L. Valerius and M. Horatius, two of the most eminent men of their order, to negotiate with the plebeians. It was finally agreed that the tribunes should be restored, that the authority of the Concilium Plebis should be recognized, and that the right of appeal to the people against the power of the supreme magistrates should be confirmed. The plebeians now returned to the city, and elected ten tribunes

—a number which remained unchanged down to the latest times. Verginius, Icilius, and Numitorius were among the new tribunes.

Two consuls were elected in place of the decemvirs, and the choice of the Comitia Centuriata naturally fell upon Valerius and Horatius. The new consuls now redeemed their promises to the plebeians by bringing forward the laws which are called after them, the *Valerian and Horatian Laws.* These celebrated laws enacted—

Valerio-Horatian Laws.

1. That every Roman citizen should have a right of appeal against the sentence of the supreme magistrate within the limits of the city. This was, in fact, a solemn confirmation of the old law of Valerius Publicola, passed in the first year of the Republic. The reason for its re-enactment on this occasion was the recent existence of the decemvirate, from the members of which there had been no appeal. But, as great difficulty was found in controlling the executive officials, it was enacted again a third time in 300 B.C., on the proposal of M. Valerius, the consul. The Roman soldier in the field (*militiae*) had no right of appeal, and was still subject to martial law.

2. That the *Plebiscita,* or resolutions passed by the plebeians in the Concilium Plebis, should have the force of laws, and should be binding alike upon patricians and plebeians.

3. That the persons of the tribunes, aediles, and other plebeian magistrates, should be sacred, and whoever injured them should be outlawed.

Verginius now accused Appius Claudius, who was thrown into prison to await his trial. But the proud patrician, seeing that his condemnation was certain, put an end to his own life. Oppius, another of the decemvirs, and the personal friend of Appius, was condemned and executed. The other decemvirs were allowed to go into exile, but they were all declared guilty, and their property confiscated to the state.

The Twelve Tables.

The Twelve Tables were always regarded as the foundation of the Roman law, and long continued to be held in the highest estimation. They probably did little more than fix in a written form a large body of customary law; but this was plebeian law, and in most of the relations of private life the two orders were now on an equality. The patricians still, however, retained their exclusive political privileges; and the eleventh table even gave the sanction of law to the old custom which prohibited all intermarriage (*conubium*) between the two orders, since this prohibition was thought to be connected with the maintenance of the state religion.

View from the neighbourhood of Veii.

CHAPTER VI.

FROM THE DECEMVIRATE TO THE CAPTURE OF ROME BY THE GAULS. 448-390 B.C.

Lex Canuleia.

THE efforts of the leaders of the plebeians were now directed to removing disadvantages, based in the main on religious prejudice, under which their order laboured; they aimed at securing the permission of intermarriage between patricians and plebeians, and at opening the consulship to their own order. The first object was attained four years after the decemvirate by the Lex Canuleia, proposed by Canuleius, one of the tribunes (445 B.C.). But the Plebs did not carry this law without a third secession, in which they occupied the Janiculum. At the same time, a compromise was effected with respect to the consulship.

The patricians agreed that the supreme power in the state should be entrusted to new officers bearing the title of *Military*

Tribunes with Consular Power, who might be chosen equally from patricians and plebeians. Their number varied in different years from three to six. In 444 B.C. three Military Tribunes were nominated for the first time. In the following year (443) two new magistrates, called *Censores*, were appointed. They were always to be chosen from the patricians; and the effect of their institution was to deprive the Military Tribunes of some of the most important functions which had been formerly discharged by the consuls. The original duty of the censors was that of registering the names of Roman citizens in their various tribes and centuries. This was done once every five years, the interval being called a *lustrum*, from the sacrifice of purification which closed the ceremony; but the censors' tenure of office was fixed at eighteen months, as early as ten years after their institution, by a law of the Dictator Mamercus Aemilius, though they continued to be appointed only once in five years. As the taxation of citizens depended on their place in the census, the duty of registration gave the censors important financial functions.

Appointment of Military Tribunes and Censors.

Though the Military Tribunes could from their first institution be chosen from either order, yet such was the influence of the patricians in the Comitia of the Centuries that it was not till 400 B.C., or nearly forty years afterwards, that any plebeians were actually elected. In 421 B.C. the quaestorship was also thrown open to them. The *Quaestores* were the paymasters of the state; and as the custom was now growing up of filling up the senate from ex-magistrates, the plebeians thus became eligible for a seat at the great council of the Republic.

In spite of these concessions, there was soon ground for fear that plebeian discontent might give rise to tyranny. In the year 440 B.C. there was a great famine at Rome. Sp. Maelius, one of the richest of the plebeian knights, expended his fortune in buying up corn, which he sold to the poor at a small price, or distributed among them gratuitously. The patricians thought, or pretended to think, that he was aiming at kingly power; and in the following year (439) the aged Quinctius Cincinnatus, who had saved the Roman army on Mount Algidus, was appointed dictator to save the state from this supposed internal danger.

Spurius Maelius.

He nominated C. Servilius Ahala his Master of the Horse. During the night the Capitol and all the strong posts were garrisoned by the patricians, and in the morning Cincinnatus appeared in the forum with a strong force, and summoned Maelius to appear before his tribunal. But seeing the fate which awaited him, he refused to go, whereupon Ahala rushed into the crowd and struck him dead upon the spot. His property was confiscated, and his house levelled to the ground. The deed of Ahala is frequently mentioned by Cicero and other writers in terms of the highest admiration, but it was regarded by the plebeians at the time as an act of murder. Ahala was brought to trial, and only escaped condemnation by a voluntary exile.

In their foreign wars the Romans continued to be successful, and, aided by their allies the Latins and Hernicans, they made steady progress in driving back their old enemies the Volscians and Aequians. About this time they planted several *coloniae* in the districts which they conquered, to consolidate their dominion. These Roman colonies differed widely from those of ancient Greece and of modern Europe. They were of the nature of garrisons established in conquered towns, and served both to strengthen and extend the power of Rome. The colonists, who remained citizens of Rome, received a portion of the conquered territory, and lived as a ruling class among the old inhabitants, who retained the use of the rest of the land, and probably possessed a partial citizenship.

Foundation of colonies.

The league now turned its attention to Etruria, its great enemy in the north, and a war ensued, in the course of which Rome made her first acquisition in the territory of an alien nationality.

Northern Etruria was at this time hard pressed by the Gauls, and Veii, which was the chief object of the Roman attack, was almost isolated. It was, however, closely allied with Fidenae, a town of Latium, not more than five or six miles from Rome. The two cities frequently united their arms against Rome, and in one of these wars Lars Tolumnius, the king of Veii, was slain in single combat by A. Cornelius Cossus, one of the Military Tribunes, and his arms dedicated to Jupiter—the second of the

Siege and capture of Veii.

three instances in which the *Spolia Opima* were won (437 B.C.). A few years afterwards Fidenae was taken and destroyed (426 B.C.), and at the same time a truce was granted to the Veientines for twenty years. At the expiration of this truce the war was renewed, and the Romans resolved to subdue Veii, as they had done Fidenae. The siege of Veii, like that of Troy, lasted ten years, and the means of its capture was almost as marvellous as the wooden horse by which Troy was taken. The waters of the Alban Lake, close to the ancient town of Alba Longa, rose to such a height as to deluge the neighbouring country. An oracle declared that Veii could not be taken until the waters of the lake found a passage to the sea. This reached the ears of the Romans, who thereupon constructed a tunnel to carry off its superfluous volume.* The formation of this tunnel is said to have suggested to the Romans the means of taking Veii. M. Furius Camillus, who was appointed dictator, commenced digging a mine beneath the city, which was to have its outlet in the citadel, in the temple of Juno, the guardian deity of Veii. When the mine was finished, the attention of the inhabitants was diverted by feigned assaults against the walls. Camillus led the way into the mine at the head of a picked body of troops, and emerged on the Veientine Capitol in time to complete an unfinished sacrifice which the priest was offering to Juno. The soldiers who guarded the walls were now taken in the rear, the gates were thrown open, and the city soon filled with Romans. The booty was immense, and the few citizens who escaped the sword were sold as slaves. The city was abandoned, and its territory divided amongst the plebeians. Falerii was almost the only one of the Etruscan cities which had assisted Veii, and she was now exposed single-handed to the vengeance of the Romans; but she avoided the fate of her sister city by a timely surrender, and the Etruscan war was over (394 B.C.)

Two circumstances, of great importance for later history, originated from the long campaign against Veii. As the soldiers were obliged to pass the whole year under arms, in order to invest the city during the winter as well as the summer, they now for the first time received pay, and to this circumstance

* This remarkable work, which, after the lapse of more than two thousand years, still continues to serve the purpose for which it was originally designed, is cut through the soft volcanic tufa of which the Alban hill is composed. The length of the tunnel is about 6000 feet, and it is 4 feet 6 inches wide.

we may trace the beginnings of a standing army at Rome. At the same time, the cavalry was increased by allowing any one possessed of a certain income to serve on horseback at his own expense (*eques equo privato*), and thus the term *equites*, originally applied to the horsemen of the eighteen centuries, was extended to the wealthy members of the middle-class.

Camillus.

Camillus celebrated a splendid triumph for his conquest of Veii. He entered the city in a chariot drawn by white horses, and he brought with him from the conquered town the statue of Juno, for whom a splendid temple was now erected on the Aventine. But the victories of Camillus did not win him popularity. His extravagant triumph was taken as a sign of more than human pride, and he now incurred the hatred of the plebeians by calling upon every man to refund a tenth of the booty taken at Veii, because he had made a vow to consecrate to Apollo a tithe of the spoil. He was himself accused of having appropriated the great bronze gates at Veii, and was impeached by one of the tribunes. Seeing that his condemnation was certain, he went into exile, with the disloyal prayer that the Republic might soon have cause to regret him (391 B.C.). His prayer was heard, for the Gauls had already crossed the Apennines, and next year Rome was in ashes.

Fragment of sculpture from the pediment of the Temple of Jupiter Capitolinus.

CHAPTER VII.

FROM THE CAPTURE OF ROME BY THE GAULS TO THE FINAL UNION OF THE TWO ORDERS. 390–367 B.C.

Invasion of Italy by the Gauls.

THE Gauls were a branch of the Celtic race which in ancient times spread over the greater part of Western Europe. It inhabited Gaul and the British Isles, and it had, as we saw, in the time of the Tarquins crossed the Alps and taken possession of Northern Italy. These Gallic invaders now spread further south, crossed the Apennines, and laid waste with fire and sword the provinces of Central Italy. Rome fell before them, and was reduced to ashes; but the details of its capture are clearly legendary. The common story runs as follows:—

The Senones, a tribe of the Gauls, under the leadership of "the Brennus," * laid siege to Clusium, the powerful Etruscan city over which Lars Porsena once reigned. Such reputation

* Brennus, given by our authorities as a proper name, is probably a title, the Cymric *brenhin*, or king.

had Rome gained through her conquests in Etruria, that Clusium applied to her for aid (391 B.C.). The senate sent three ambassadors of the Fabian house to warn the barbarians not to touch an ally of Rome. But the Gauls treated their message with scorn; and the ambassadors, forgetting their sacred character, fought in the Clusine ranks. One of the Fabii slew with his own hands a Gallic chieftain, and was recognized while stripping off his armour. "The Brennus" therefore sent to Rome to demand satisfaction. It might have been granted by the senate, but the current of popular feeling was too strong; the Roman people not only refused to give it, but elected the guilty ambassadors Military Tribunes for the following year. On hearing of this insult, the Gauls broke up the siege of Clusium, and hastened southwards towards Rome. All the inhabitants fled before them into the towns. They pursued their course without injuring any one, crying to the guards upon the walls of the towns they passed, "Our way lies for Rome."

Battle of the Allia.

On the news of their approach the Roman army hurried out of the city, and on the 16th of July (390 B.C.), a day ever after marked with black letters on the calendar, they met the Gauls on the Allia, a small river which flows into the Tiber, on its left bank, about eleven miles from Rome. The Roman legions, unfamiliar with the impetuous character of the Celtic attack, broke at the first furious onset of the Gauls. Most of the soldiers were cut down, others turned and fled; even such as escaped by crossing the Tiber found themselves on the wrong side of the river, and the path to Rome lay open to the Gauls.

The loss at the Allia had been so great that enough men were not left to guard the walls of the city. It was therefore resolved that those in the vigour of their age should withdraw to the Capitol, taking with them all the provisions in the city; that the priests and vestal virgins should convey the objects of religious reverence to Caeré; and that the rest of the population should disperse among the neighbouring towns. But the aged patricians who had held high rank, seeing that their lives were no longer of any service to the state, sat in the porches of their houses in full official robes, awaiting death. When the Gauls entered the city they found it desolate and deathlike. They marched on, without seeing a human being, till they came to the forum.

Here they beheld the aged senators sitting immovable, like beings of another world. For some time they gazed in awe at this strange sight, till at length one of the Gauls ventured to go up to M. Papirius and stroke his white beard. The old man struck him on the head with his ivory sceptre; whereupon the barbarian slew him, and all the rest were massacred. The Gauls now began plundering the city; fires broke out in several quarters; and with the exception of a few houses on the Palatine, which the chiefs kept for their own residence, the whole city was burnt to the ground.

Siege of the Capitol.

The Capitol was the next object of attack. There was only one steep way leading up to it, and all the assaults of the besiegers were easily repelled. They thereupon turned the siege into a blockade, and for seven months were encamped amid the ruins of Rome. But their numbers were soon thinned by disease, for they had entered Rome in the most unhealthy time of the year, when fevers have always prevailed. The failure of provisions obliged them to ravage the neighbouring countries, the people of which began to combine for defence against the marauders. Meantime the scattered Romans took courage. They collected at Veii, and here resolved to recall Camillus from banishment, and appoint him dictator. In order to obtain the consent of the senate, a daring youth, named Pontius Cominius, offered to swim across the Tiber and climb the Capitol. He reached the top unperceived by the enemy, obtained the approval of the senate to the appointment of Camillus, and returned safely to Veii. But next day some Gauls observed the traces of his steps, and in the dead of night they climbed up the same way. The foremost of them had already reached the top, unnoticed by the sentinels and the dogs, when the cries of some geese roused M. Manlius from sleep. These geese were sacred to Juno, and had been spared notwithstanding the gnawings of hunger; and the Romans were now rewarded for their piety. M. Manlius thrust down the Gaul who had clambered up, and gave the alarm. The Capitol was thus saved; and down to latest times M. Manlius was honoured as one of the greatest heroes of the early Republic.

Still no help came, and the Gauls remained before the Capitol. The Romans suffered from famine, and at length agreed to pay the barbarians 1000 pounds of gold, on condition of their quitting the city and its territory. "The Brennus" brought false weights, and, when the Romans exclaimed against this injustice, the Gallic chief threw his sword also into the scale, crying, "Woe to the vanquished!" (*Vae victis!*). The Gauls then retired, having bartered victory for gold. Tradition, indeed, tells that at this very moment Camillus marched into the forum, ordered the gold to be taken away, and drove the Gauls out of the city, and that another battle was fought on the road to Gabii, in which the Gauls were completely destroyed, and their leader Brennus taken prisoner. But this is an invention of Roman vanity. We learn from other sources that the Gauls retreated because their settlements in Northern Italy were attacked by the Venetians; nor was their withdrawal final: they frequently repeated their inroads, and for many years to come were the constant dread of Rome.

The Gauls quit Rome.

When the Romans returned to the heap of ruins which was once their city, their hearts sank within them. The people shrank from the expense and toil of rebuilding their houses, and loudly demanded that they should all remove to Veii, where the private dwellings and public buildings were still standing. But Camillus strongly urged them not to abandon the homes of their fathers; and they were at length persuaded to remain. Within a year the city rose from its ashes; but the streets were narrow and crooked; the houses were frequently built over the sewers; and the city continued to show, down to the great fire of Nero, evident traces of the haste and irregularity with which it had been rebuilt.

Rome after the Gallic invasion.

Rome was now deprived of almost all her subjects, and her territory was reduced to nearly its original limits. The Latins and Hernicans dissolved the league with the Romans, and wars broke out on every side. In these difficulties and dangers Camillus was the soul of the Republic. Again and again he led the Roman legions against their enemies, and always with success.

The rapidity with which the Romans recovered their power after so terrible a disaster would seem unaccountable, but for the facts that the other nations had also suffered greatly from the inroads of the Gauls, who still continued to ravage Central Italy, and that these Gallic invasions forced the Italians to

Renewed incursions of the Gauls.

recognize in Rome their bulwark against the barbarians. Two famous family legends grew out of these invasions, which may be related here, though they belong to a later period.

In 361 B.C. the Gauls and Romans were encamped on either bank of the Arno. A gigantic Gaul stepped forth from the ranks and insultingly challenged a Roman knight. T. Manlius, a Roman youth, obtained permission from his general to accept the challenge, slew the giant, and took from the dead body the golden chain (*torques*) which the barbarian wore around his neck. His comrades gave him the surname of Torquatus, which he handed down to his descendants.

In 349 B.C. another distinguished Roman family earned its surname from a single combat with a Gaul. Here again a Gallic warrior of gigantic size challenged any one of the Romans to single combat. His challenge was accepted by M. Valerius, upon whose helmet a raven perched; and as they fought, the bird flew into the face of the Gaul, striking at him with his beak and flapping his wings. Thus Valerius slew the Gaul, and was called in consequence "Corvus," or the "Raven."

Distress of the plebeians.

Meanwhile, Rome, though she had survived the stress of war, was again on the verge of a social revolution. Great suffering and discontent prevailed. Returning to ruined homes and ravaged lands, the poor citizens had been obliged to borrow money to rebuild their houses and cultivate their farms. The law of debtor and creditor at Rome, as we have already seen, was very severe, and many unfortunate debtors were carried away to bondage.

Manlius.

Under these circumstances, M. Manlius, the preserver of the Capitol, came forward as the patron of the poor. This distinguished man had been bitterly disappointed in his claims to honour and gratitude. While Camillus, his personal enemy, who had shared in none of the dangers of the siege, was repeatedly raised to the highest honours of the state, he, who had saved the Capitol, was left to languish in a private station. Neglected by his own order, Manlius turned to the plebeians. One day he recognized in the forum a soldier who had served with him in the field, and whom a creditor was carrying away in fetters. Manlius paid his debt upon the spot, and swore that, as long as he had a single pound, he would not allow any Roman to be imprisoned for debt. He sold a large part of his property, and applied the proceeds to the liberation of his fellow-citizens from bondage. Supported now by the plebeians, he came forward as the accuser of his own order, and charged them with appropriating to their own use the gold which had been raised to ransom the city from the Gauls. The patricians, in return, accused him, as they had accused Sp. Cassius, of aspiring to the tyranny. When he was brought to trial before the Comitia of the Centuries, in the Campus Martius, he proudly showed the spoils of thirty warriors whom he had slain, the forty military distinctions which he had won in battle, and the innumerable scars upon his breast, and then, turning towards the Capitol, he prayed the immortal gods to remember the man who had saved their temples from destruction. After such an appeal his condemnation was impossible; and his enemies therefore contrived to break up the assembly. Shortly afterwards he was arraigned on the same charges before the Comitia, at a place without the walls from which the Capitol could be no longer seen. Here he was at once condemned, and was hurled from the Tarpeian rock. His house, which was on the Capitol, was razed to the ground (384 B.C.).

Licinian Rogations.

The death of Manlius, however, was only a temporary check to the cause of reform. The agitation was now taken up by the rich plebeians, who aspired to public office; but it was necessary to enlist the rank and file of their order in the cause by proposing social reforms. In 376 B.C. C. Licinius Stolo and his kinsman L. Sextius, being Tribunes of the Plebs, brought forward three laws, which are celebrated in history under the name of THE LICINIAN ROGATIONS.* These were—

I. That in future consuls, and not Military Tribunes, should be appointed, and that one of the two consuls *must* be a plebeian.

II. That no citizen should possess more than 500 jugera † of the public land, nor should feed upon the public pastures more than 100 head of large and 500 of small cattle, under penalty of a heavy fine.

* A *Rogatio* differed from a *Lex*, as a *Bill* from an *Act* of Parliament. A rogatio was a law submitted to the assembly of the people, and only became a lex when enacted by them.

† A *jugerum* was rather more than half an acre.

III. That the interest already paid for borrowed money should be deducted from the principal, and that the remainder should be repaid in three yearly instalments.

These great reforms naturally excited the most violent opposition, and the patricians induced some of the tribunes to put their veto upon the measures of their colleagues. But Licinius and Sextius were not to be baffled in this way, and they exercised their veto by preventing the Comitia Centuriata from electing any magistrates for the next year. Hence no consuls, military tribunes, censors, or quaestors, could be appointed; the tribunes and the aediles of the plebs, who were elected by the Concilium Plebis, were the only magistrates in the state, most of the public business was suspended, and all the courts were closed. For five years did this anarchy continue. C. Licinius and L. Sextius were re-elected annually, and prevented the Comitia of the Centuries from appointing any magistrates. At the end of this time they allowed Military Tribunes to be chosen in consequence of a war with the Latins; but so far were they from yielding any of their demands, that to their former Rogations they now added another: That the care of the Sibylline books, instead of being entrusted to two men (*duumviri*), both patricians, should be given to ten men (*decemviri*), half of whom should be plebeians.

Political struggle between the orders.

Five years more did the struggle last, but the firmness of the tribunes at length prevailed. In 367 B.C. the Licinian Rogations were passed, and L. Sextius was elected the first plebeian consul for the next year. But the patricians made one last effort to evade the law. By the Roman constitution the consuls, after being elected by the Comitia Centuriata, required the ratification of their imperium from the Comitia Curiata. The patricians, who exercised great influence in this assembly, persuaded it to nullify the election of L. Sextius; and they had already made Camillus, the great champion of their order, dictator, to support them in their new struggle. But the old hero saw that it was too late, and determined to bring about a reconciliation between the opposing parties. A compromise was effected. The imperium was conferred upon L. Sextius; but the judicial duties were taken away from the consuls, and

Consulship open to the plebeians.

given to a new magistrate, called *praetor*.* Camillus vowed to the goddess Concord a temple for his success.

Further concessions. The long struggle between the patricians and plebeians was thus brought to a virtual close. The patricians still clung obstinately to the exclusive privileges which they still possessed; but when the plebeians had once obtained a share in the consulship, it was evident that their participation in the other offices of the state could not be much longer delayed. We may therefore anticipate the course of events by narrating in this place that the first plebeian dictator was C. Marcius Rutilus, in 356 B.C., that the same man was the first plebeian censor five years afterwards (351 B.C.); that the praetorship was thrown open to the plebeians in 337 B.C.; and that the Lex Ogulnia in 300 B.C., which increased the number of the pontiffs from four to eight, and that of the augurs from four to nine, also enacted that four of the pontiffs and five of the augurs should be taken from the plebeians.

Publilian Laws. About thirty years after the Licinian Rogations, another important reform, which abridged still further the privileges of the patricians, was effected by the PUBLILIAN LAWS, proposed by the Dictator Q. Publilius Philo in 339 B.C. These were—

I. That the resolutions of the plebs (*plebiscita*) passed in the Concilium Plebis should be binding on all the Quirites.†

II. That all laws passed at the Comitia Centuriata must receive the sanction of the patrician members of the senate (*patrum auctoritas*) *before* and not *after* their enactment; this sanction was soon reduced to a mere formality.

III. That one of the censors must be a plebeian.

Close of the struggle between the orders. The first of these laws seems to be little more than a re-enactment of one of the Valeriano-Horatian Laws, passed after the expulsion of the decemvirs;‡ but it is possible that those measures, and even the Publilian Law of 339 B.C., merely provided facilities for bringing *plebiscita* before the Comitia Centuriata, there to be passed into law. It was an enactment of the Dictator Q. Hortensius in 287 B.C. that first gave *plebiscita* the force of *leges*. In this year the last secession of the plebeians took place, and the LEX HORTENSIA is always

* Cf. p. 31. † *Ut plebiscita omnes Quirites tenerent.* ‡ See p. 49.

mentioned as the law which gave to plebiscita passed at the Concilium of the Tribes the full power of laws binding upon the whole nation. During this period we can also trace the growth of a third assembly composed of patricians and plebeians, and meeting by tribes (*Comitia Tributa*), which possessed legislative and judicial power and elected the lower magistrates.*

The close of the long struggle between the orders had left victory with the plebeians. They formed the majority of two of the sovereign assemblies (the *Comitia Centuriata* and *Tributa*), and the whole of the third (the *Concilium Plebis*); one place in the highest magistracies and half the vacancies in the priestly colleges were assured them, the other places and vacancies they might secure. Rome was now nearer a democracy than at any other period of her history, for the great power of the senate had not yet cast its shadow over the state.

* See note on p. 44.

Temple of Jupiter Capitolinus (from a coin).

Samnite warriors (from a mural painting at Paestum).

CHAPTER VIII.

THE LATIN AND SAMNITE WARS. 367–290 B.C.

UNITED at home, the Romans were now prepared to carry on their foreign wars with more vigour. But the years which immediately followed the Licinian Laws were times of great suffering. A pestilence raged in Rome, which carried off many of the most distinguished men, and among others the aged Camillus (362 B.C.). The Tiber overflowed its banks, the city was shaken by earthquakes, and a yawning chasm opened in the forum. Superstitious fears were excited, and the soothsayers declared that the gulf could never be filled up except by throwing into it that which Rome held most valuable. The tale runs that, when every one was doubting what the gods could mean, a noble youth named Mettus Curtius came forward, and, declaring that Rome possessed nothing so valuable as her brave citizens, mounted his steed and leaped into the abyss in full armour, whereupon the earth closed over him (362 B.C.).

During the next few years the Gauls renewed those inroads, in which Manlius Torquatus and Valerius Corvus gained such glory. The Romans steadily extended their dominion over the southern part of Etruria and the country of the Volscians; the alliance with the Latin league stood firm, and the cities of this league were rapidly becoming mere dependencies of Rome, for she remodelled their constitutions and treated defection from the league as revolt from herself. Fifty years had elapsed since the capture of the city by the Gauls, and Rome was now strong enough to enter into a contest with the most formidable enemy which her arms had yet encountered.

Extension of Roman dominion.

The SAMNITES were at the height of their power, and the contest between them and the Romans was virtually for the supremacy of Italy. The Samnites, as we have already seen, were a people of Sabellian origin, and had emigrated to the countries which they inhabited at a comparatively late period. Not contented with their mountain-homes, they had, as we saw, overrun the rich plains which lay at their feet; already they had become the masters of Campania and Lucania, and had spread themselves almost to the southern extremity of Italy. But the Samnites of Campania and Lucania had in course of time broken off all connection with the parent nation, and were sometimes engaged in hostilities with the latter.

Conquests of the Samnites.

It was a contest of this kind that led to the war between the Romans and the Samnites of the Apennines. On the borders of Campania and Samnium dwelt a people called the Sidicini, who had hitherto preserved their independence. Being attacked by the Samnites, this people implored the assistance of the Campanians, which was readily granted. Thereupon the Samnites turned their arms against the Campanians, and, after occupying Mount Tifata, which overlooks the city of Capua, they descended into the plain, and defeated the Campanians in a pitched battle at the very gates of Capua. The Campanians, being shut up within the city, now applied for assistance to Rome, and offered to place Capua in their hands. The Romans had only a few years previously concluded an alliance with the Samnites; but the bait of the richest city and the most fertile soil in Italy was irresistible; and they resolved to comply with the request. Thus

The Campanians join Rome.

began the Samnite Wars, which, with a few intervals of peace, lasted fifty-three years.

First Samnite War.

FIRST SAMNITE WAR, 343–341 B.C.—The Romans commenced the war by sending two consular armies against the Samnites; and the first battle between the rival nations was fought at the foot of Mount Gaurus, which lies about three miles from Cumae. The Samnites were defeated with great loss; and it has been justly remarked that this battle may be regarded as one of the most memorable in history, since it was a kind of omen of the ultimate issue of the great contest which had now begun between the Samnites and Romans for the sovereignty of Italy. The Romans gained two other decisive victories, and both consuls entered the city in triumph. But two causes prevented the Romans from prosecuting their success. In the first place, the Roman army, which had been wintering in Capua, rose in open mutiny; and the poorer plebeians in the city, who were oppressed by debt, left Rome and joined the mutineers. In the second place, the increasing disaffection of the Latins warned the Romans to husband their resources for another and more terrible struggle. The Romans, therefore, abandoning the Sidicini and Campanians, concluded a treaty of peace and alliance with the Samnites in 341 B.C., so that in the great Latin war, which broke out in the following year, the Samnites fought on the side of the Romans.

Demands of the Latins.

THE LATIN WAR, 340–338 B.C.—The increasing power of Rome had excited the alarm of the Latin states; and it became evident to them that, though nominally on a footing of equality, they were in reality becoming her subjects. This feeling was confirmed by the treaty of alliance which the Romans had formed with the Samnites. The Latins, therefore, determined to bring matters to a crisis, and sent two praetors, who were their chief magistrates, to propose to the Romans that the two nations should henceforth form one state, that half of the senate should consist of Latins, and that one of the two consuls should be chosen from Latium. These requests excited the greatest indignation at Rome, and were rejected with the utmost scorn. The senate met in the temple of Jupiter, in the Capitol, to receive the Latin deputation, and, after hearing their proposals, the consul T. Manlius Torquatus, the same who had slain the Gaul in single combat, declared that, if the Republic should be so cowardly as to yield to these demands, he would come into the senate-house sword in hand, and cut down the first Latin he saw there. The tale goes on to say that in the discussion which followed, when both parties were excited by anger, the Latin praetor defied the Roman Jupiter; that thereupon an awful peal of thunder shook the building; and that, as the impious man hurried down the steps from the temple, he fell from top to bottom, and lay there a corpse.

War with the Latin league.

War was now declared, and the most vigorous efforts were made on both sides. The contest was to decide whether Rome should become a simple member of the Latin league, or the Latins be subject to Rome. The Romans had elected to the consulship two of their most distinguished men. The patrician consul was, as already mentioned, T. Manlius Torquatus; his plebeian colleague was P. Decius Mus, who had gained great renown in the recent war against the Samnites. Meantime Capua, freed from fears of the Samnites, had thrown off its half-hearted allegiance to Rome and joined the Latins in their revolt. The two consuls now marched straight on Capua, and the contest was thus withdrawn from the territory of Rome and transferred to Campania, where the Romans could receive assistance from the neighbouring country of their Samnite allies.

Battles of Veseris and Trifanum.

It was at the river Veseris near the foot of Mount Vesuvius that the two armies met, and here the battle was fought which decided the contest. It was like a civil war. The soldiers of the two armies spoke the same language, had fought by each other's sides, and were well known to one another. Under these circumstances, the consuls published a proclamation that no Roman should engage in single combat with a Latin on pain of death. But the son of Torquatus, provoked by the insults of a Tusculan officer, accepted his challenge, slew his adversary, and carried the bloody spoils in triumph to his father. The consul had within him the heart of Brutus; he would not pardon this breach of discipline, and ordered the unhappy youth to be beheaded by the lictor in the presence of the assembled army.

In the night before the battle a vision appeared to each

consul, announcing that the general of one side and the army of the other were doomed to destruction. Both agreed that the one whose wing first began to waver should devote himself and the army of the enemy to the gods of the lower world. Decius commanded the left wing; and when it began to give way, he resolved to fulfil his vow. Calling the Pontifex Maximus, he repeated after him the form of words by which he devoted himself and the army of the enemy to the gods of the dead and the mother earth; then leaping upon his horse, he rushed into the thickest of the fight, and was slain. The Romans gained a signal victory. Scarcely a fourth part of the Latins escaped (340 B.C.).

Yet this victory (decisive as the legend makes it) did not conclude the war. It required another battle fought at Trifanum in the same year to make the Romans masters of Latium and Campania. The war continued two years longer, each city confining itself to the defence of its own walls, and hoping to receive help from others in case of an attack. But in 338 B.C. all the Latins had laid down their arms, and garrisons were placed in their towns. The Romans were now absolute masters of Latium, and their first act was to dissolve the league. For this purpose not only were all assemblies for political purposes forbidden; but separate treaties were made with the separate states, and in order to keep the cities completely isolated, the citizens of one town were forbidden to marry or make a legal contract of bargain or sale with another.* Tibur and Praeneste, the two most powerful cities of the league, which had taken the most active part in the war, were deprived of a portion of their land, but were allowed to retain a nominal independence, preserving their own laws and renewing their treaties (*foedera*) with Rome. The inhabitants of several other towns, such as Aricia, Pedum, and Lanuvium, lost their independence and received the full Roman franchise. In Campania the private rights of citizenship were given to Fundi, Formiae, Cumae, and Capua.

Dissolution of the Latin league.

Twelve years elapsed between the subjugation of Latium and the commencement of the Second Samnite War. During this

* According to the Roman expression, the *Jus Conubii* and *Jus Commercii* were prohibited.

time the Roman arms continued to make steady progress. One of their most important conquests was that of the Volscian town of Privernum in 330 B.C., from which time the Volscians, so long the formidable enemies of Rome, disappear as an independent nation. The extension of the Roman power naturally awakened the jealousy of the Samnites; and the assistance rendered by them to the Greek cities of Palaeopolis and Neapolis was the immediate occasion of the Second Samnite War. These two cities were colonies of the neighbouring Cumae, and were situated only five miles from each other. The position of Palaeopolis, or the "Old City," is uncertain; but Neapolis, or the "New City," stands on the site of a part of the modern Naples. The Romans declared war against the two cities in 327 B.C., and sent the Consul Q. Publilius Philo to reduce them to subjection. The Greek colonists had previously formed an alliance with the Samnites, and now received powerful Samnite garrisons. Publilius encamped between the cities; and as he did not succeed in taking them before his year of office expired, the important step was for the first time taken of continuing the consul in his command with the title of *proconsul*. At the beginning of the following year Palaeopolis surrendered; and with Neapolis was admitted to alliance with Rome on favourable terms. Meanwhile the Romans had declared war against the Samnites.

Conflict with Greek cities.

SECOND OR GREAT SAMNITE WAR, 326–304 B.C.—The Second Samnite War lasted twenty-two years, and was by far the most important of the three wars which this people waged with Rome. During the first five years (326–322 B.C.) the Roman arms were generally successful. The Samnites became so disheartened that they sued for peace, but obtained only a truce for a year. It was during this period that the well-known quarrel took place between L. Papirius Cursor and Q. Fabius Maximus, the two most celebrated Roman generals of the time, who constantly led the armies of the Republic to victory. In 326 B.C. L. Papirius was dictator, and Q. Fabius his Master of the Horse. Recalled to Rome by some defect in the auspices, the dictator left the army in charge of Fabius, but with strict orders not to venture upon an engagement. Compelled or provoked by the growing boldness of the enemy, Fabius attacked and defeated them with

Second Samnite War.

great loss. But this victory was no extenuation for his offence in the eyes of the dictator. Papirius hastened back to the camp, burning with indignation that his commands had been disobeyed, and ordered his lictors to seize Fabius and put him to death. The soldiers, whom Fabius had led to victory, rose in his defence; and in the night he escaped to Rome, to implore the protection of the senate. He was stating the case to the Fathers, when Papirius entered the senate-house followed by his lictors, and demanded that the offender should be delivered up for execution. But the senate, the people, and the aged father of Maximus interceded so strongly for his life, that the dictator was obliged to give way, and to grant an ungracious pardon.

The year's truce had not expired when the Samnites again took up arms, and for the next seven years (321–315 B.C.) the balance of success inclined to their side. This appears to have been mainly owing to the military abilities of their general C. Pontius, who deserves to be ranked among the chief men of antiquity. In the first year of his command he inflicted upon the Romans one of the severest blows they ever sustained in the whole course of their history.

In 321 B.C. the two consuls, T. Veturius and Sp. Postumius marched into Samnium by the road from Capua to Beneventum. Near the town of Caudium they entered the celebrated pass called the CAUDINE FORKS (Furculae Caudinae). It consisted of two narrow defiles or gorges, between which was a tolerably spacious plain, but shut in on each side by mountains. The Romans, thinking the Samnites to be far distant, had marched through the first pass and the plain; but when they came to the second they found it blocked up by works and trunks of trees, so as to be quite impassable. Retracing their steps to the pass by which they had entered, they found that the enemy had meantime taken possession of this also. They were thus blocked up at either end, and, after making vain attempts to force their way through, were obliged to surrender at discretion. Thus both consuls and four legions fell into the hands of the Samnites. C. Pontius made a merciful use of his victory. He agreed to dismiss them in safety upon their promising to restore the ancient alliance on equal terms between the two nations, and

Disaster of the Caudine Forks.

to give up all the places which they had conquered during the war. The consuls and the other superior officers swore to these terms in the name of the Republic, and 600 Roman knights were given as hostages. The whole Roman army was now allowed to depart, and each Roman soldier marched out singly under the yoke.

When the news of this disaster reached Rome, the senate refused to ratify the peace, on the ground that an *imperator* in the field had no power to make a sworn treaty on behalf of the state; for, according to the convenient theory of the senate, this could only be done by a *fetialis* sent from Rome. The two consuls and all the officers who had sworn to the peace were delivered up as scape-goats to the Samnites; but Pontius refused to accept the persons who were thus offered, and told them, if they wished to nullify the treaty, to send back the army to the Caudine Forks. Thus Postumius and his companions returned to Rome, and the 600 knights were alone left in the hands of the Samnites.

Breach of the treaty with the Samnites.

The disaster of Caudium shook the faith of many of the Roman allies, and the fortune of war was for some years in favour of the Samnites. But in 314 B.C. the tide of success again turned, and the decisive victory of the consuls in that year opened the way into the heart of Samnium. From this time the Romans were uniformly successful; and it seemed probable that the war was drawing to a close, when the Etruscans created a powerful diversion by declaring war against Rome in 311 B.C. But the energy and ability of Q. Fabius Maximus averted this new danger. He boldly carried the war into the very heart of Etruria, and gained a decisive victory at Perusia over the forces of the league. The Samnites also were repeatedly defeated; and, after the capture of Bovianum, their chief stronghold, they were compelled to sue for peace. It was granted them in 304 B.C., and they were admitted to terms of alliance with Rome.

Victories over Etruscans and Samnites.

At the conclusion of the Second Samnite War the Hernicans, who had joined the Samnites in 306 B.C., were reduced to subjection after a brief struggle, and their league was dissolved. The Sabellian tribes (the Marsi, Marrucini, Paeligni, and other nations of Central Italy) entered into a league with the Romans on equal terms. Thus, in 300 B.C., the power of Rome seemed firmly established in Central Italy. But this very power awakened the jealousy of the surrounding nations, and the Samnites exerted themselves to form a new and formidable coalition. The Etruscans and Umbrians agreed to make war against Rome, and called in the assistance of the Senonian Gauls.

Dissolution of the Hernican league.

THIRD SAMNITE WAR, 298–290 B.C.—As soon as the Etruscans and Umbrians were engaged with Rome, the Samnites invaded Lucania. The Lucanians invoked the assistance of the Romans, who forthwith declared war against the Samnites. The Republic had now to contend at one and the same time against the Etruscans, Umbrians, Gauls, and Samnites; but she carried on the struggle with the utmost energy, attacking the Etruscans, Umbrians, and Gauls in the north, and the Samnites in the south.

Third Samnite War.

At length, in 295 B.C., the Samnites joined their confederates in Umbria. In this country, near the town of Sentinum, a desperate battle was fought, which decided the fortune of the war. The two Roman consuls were the aged Q. Fabius Maximus and P. Decius Mus, son of the consul who had sacrificed his life at the battle of Veseris (p. 68). The victory was long doubtful. The wing commanded by Decius was giving way before the terrible onset of the Gauls, when he determined to imitate the example of his father, and to devote himself and the enemy to destruction. His death gave fresh courage to his men, and Fabius gained a complete and decisive victory. Gellius Egnatius, the Samnite general, who had taken the most active part in forming the coalition, was slain. But, though the league was thus broken up, the Samnites continued the struggle for five years longer. During this period a C. Pontius, perhaps the very general who had defeated the Romans at the Caudine Forks twenty-seven years before, or possibly his son, appears as the leader of the Samnites, but he was defeated by Q. Fabius Maximus with great loss and taken prisoner. Being carried to Rome, he was put to death as the triumphal car of the victor ascended the Capitol (292 B.C.).* This shameful act has been justly branded as one of the greatest

Final victory of Rome.

* See p. 152.

stains on the Roman annals. Two years afterwards the Samnites were unable to continue any longer the hopeless struggle, and were forced to renew their league with Rome (290 B.C.). The complete incorporation of the conquered nation was not desired. For the issue of the Latin and Samnite wars had given Rome all that she wished. It had enabled her to effect the dissolution of the two leagues, to control the Campanian coast, and to reduce to impotence the only rival who could dispute her sway in the peninsula.

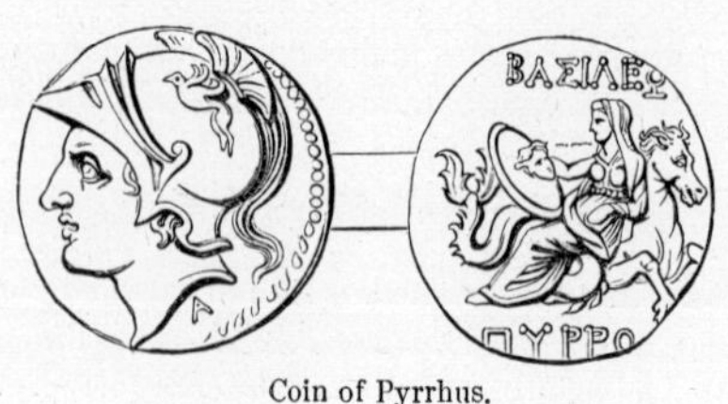

Coin of Pyrrhus.

CHAPTER IX.

FROM THE CONCLUSION OF THE SAMNITE WAR TO THE SUBJUGATION OF ITALY. 290–265 B.C.

TEN years elapsed from the conclusion of the Third Samnite War to the arrival of Pyrrhus in Italy. During this time the Etruscans and Gauls renewed the war in the north, but were defeated with great slaughter near the lake Vadimo (*Vadimonis lacus*), in Etruria. This decisive battle appears to have completely crushed the Etruscan power; and it inflicted so severe a blow upon the Gauls that we hear no more of their ravages for the next sixty years.

Rome and the Greek cities.

The extension of the Roman dominion in the south of the peninsula had brought the state into connection with the Greek cities, which at one period were so numerous and powerful as to give to this part of Italy the name of Magna Graecia.* Many of these cities had now fallen into decay through internal dissensions and the conquests of the Lucanians and other Sabellian tribes; but Tarentum, originally a Lacedaemonian colony, still maintained her former power and splendour, and, jealous of the progress of the Roman arms in the south of Italy, had secretly instigated the Etruscans and Lucanians to form a new coalition against Rome. But it was assistance rendered to the Greek city of Thurii which brought Rome into immediate conflict with the Tarentines. Attacked by the Lucanians, Thurii applied to Rome for aid, and the Consul C. Fabricius not only relieved the city, but defeated the Lucanians and their allies in several engagements (282 B.C.).

* See p. 7.

Upon the departure of Fabricius, a Roman garrison was left in Thurii. The easiest mode now of maintaining communication between Rome and this garrison was by sea; this, however, was virtually forbidden by a treaty which the Romans had made with Tarentum many years before, in which it was stipulated that no Roman ships of war should pass the Lacinian promontory. But circumstances were now changed, and the senate determined that their vessels should no longer be debarred from the gulf of Tarentum. There was a small squadron of ten ships in those seas under the command of L. Valerius; and one day when the Tarentines were assembled in the theatre, which looked over the sea, they saw the Roman squadron sailing towards their harbour. This open violation of the treaty roused the fury of the people, and, urged on by the vehement eloquence of a demagogue, they rushed down to the harbour, quickly manned some ships, and gained an easy victory over the small Roman squadron. Only half made their escape, four were sunk, one taken, and Valerius himself killed. After this the Tarentines marched against Thurii, compelled the inhabitants to dismiss the Roman garrison, and then plundered the town.

War declared with Tarentum.

The senate sent an embassy to Tarentum to complain of these outrages and to demand satisfaction. L. Postumius, who was at the head of the embassy, was introduced with his colleagues into the theatre, to state to the assembled people the demands of the Roman senate. He began to address them in Greek, but his mistakes in the language were received with peals of laughter from the thoughtless mob. Unable to obtain a hearing, much less an answer, Postumius was leaving the theatre when a drunken buffoon rushed up to him and sullied his white robe. The whole theatre rang with shouts of laughter and clapping of hands, which became louder and louder, when Postumius held up his sullied robe and showed it to the people. "Laugh on now," he cried, "but this robe shall be washed in torrents of your blood."

Arrival of Pyrrhus.

War was now inevitable. The luxurious Tarentines sent an embassy to Pyrrhus, king of Epirus, begging him, in the name of all the Italian Greeks, to cross over into Italy in order to conduct the war against the Romans. They told him that they only wanted a general, and that all the nations of Southern Italy would flock to his standard. Pyrrhus, whose ambition soared beyond the limits of his poverty-stricken kingdom of Epirus, readily listened to the offer. The conquest of Italy might lead to the sovereignty of Sicily and perhaps of Africa, and to the founding of a great Hellenic kingdom in the West. But as he would not trust the success of his enterprise to the valour and fidelity of Italian troops, he began to make preparations to carry over a powerful army. Meantime he sent Milo, one of his generals, with a detachment of 3000 men to garrison the citadel of Tarentum. Pyrrhus himself crossed over from Epirus towards the end of 281 B.C., taking with him 20,000 foot, 3000 horse, and twenty elephants.

Upon reaching Tarentum, he began to make preparations to carry on the war with activity. The Tarentines soon found they had obtained a master rather than an ally. He shut up the theatre and all other public places, and compelled their young men to serve in his ranks. Notwithstanding all his activity, the Romans were first in the field. The Consul M. Valerius Laevinus marched into Lucania; but as the army of Pyrrhus was inferior to that of the Romans, he attempted to gain time by negotiation, in order that he might be joined by his Italian allies. He accordingly wrote to the consul, offering to arbitrate between Rome and the Italian states; but Laevinus bluntly told him to mind his own business and retire to Epirus.

Battle near Heraclea.

Fearing to remain inactive any longer, although he was not yet joined by his allies, Pyrrhus marched out against the Romans with his own troops and the Tarentines. He took up his position between the towns of Pandosia and Heraclea, on the river Siris. The Romans, who were encamped on the other side of the river, were the first to begin the battle. They crossed the river, and were immediately attacked by the cavalry of Pyrrhus, who led them to the charge in person, and distinguished himself, as usual, by the most daring acts of valour. The Romans, however, bravely sustained the attack; and Pyrrhus, finding that his cavalry could not decide the day, ordered his infantry to advance. The battle was still contested most furiously: seven times did the legions and the phalanx meet; and it was not till Pyrrhus brought forward his elephants, which bore down everything before them, that the Romans took to flight, leaving their camp to the conqueror (280 B.C.).

This battle taught Pyrrhus the difficulty of the enterprise he had undertaken. Before the engagement, when he saw the Romans forming their line as they crossed the river, he said to his officers, "In war, at any rate, these barbarians are not barbarous;" and afterwards, as he saw the Roman dead lying upon the field with all their wounds in front, he exclaimed, "If these were my soldiers, or if I were their general, we should conquer the world." And, though his loss had been inferior to that of the Romans, still so large a number of his officers and best troops had fallen, that he said, "Another such victory, and I must return to Epirus alone." He therefore resolved to avail himself of this victory to conclude, if possible, an advantageous peace. He sent his minister Cineas to Rome, with the proposal that the Romans should recognize the independence of the Greeks in Italy, restore to the Samnites, Lucanians, Apulians, and Bruttians all the possessions which they had lost in war, and make peace with himself and the Tarentines. He promised, if peace was concluded on these terms, to return all the Roman prisoners without ransom.

Rome refuses peace.

Cineas, whose persuasive eloquence was said to have won more towns for Pyrrhus than his arms, neglected no means to induce the Romans to accept these terms. The prospects of the Republic seemed so dark and threatening, that many members of the senate thought it would be more prudent to comply with the demands of the king; and this party would probably have carried the day had it not been for the patriotic speech of the aged Ap. Claudius Caecus. He denounced the idea of a peace with a victorious foe, and stimulated the senate to make the proud reply (now heard for the first time) that Rome never negotiated with an enemy on Italian soil.

Pyrrhus marches on Rome.

Cineas returned to Pyrrhus, and told him he must hope for nothing from negotiation, that the city was like a temple of the gods, and the senate an assembly of kings. Pyrrhus now advanced by rapid marches towards Rome, ravaging the country as he went along, and without encountering any serious opposition. He at length arrived at Anagnia, in the country of the Hernicans.

Another march would have brought him within sight of the walls of Rome; but at this moment he learnt that peace was concluded with the Etruscans, and that the other consul had returned with his army to Rome. All hope of compelling the Romans to accept the peace was now gone, and he therefore resolved to retreat. He retired slowly into Campania, and from thence withdrew into winter quarters at Tarentum.

As soon as the armies were quartered for the winter, the Romans sent an embassy to Pyrrhus to negotiate the ransom or exchange of prisoners. The ambassadors were received by Pyrrhus in the most distinguished manner; and his interviews with C. Fabricius, who was at the head of the embassy, form one of the most famous stories in Roman history. Fabricius was a fine specimen of the sturdy Roman character. He cultivated his farm with his own hands, and, like his contemporary Curius, was celebrated for his incorruptible integrity. The king attempted in vain to work upon his cupidity and his fears. He steadily refused the large sums of money offered by Pyrrhus; and when an elephant, concealed behind him by a curtain, waved his trunk over his head, Fabricius remained unmoved. Such respect did his conduct inspire, that Pyrrhus attempted to persuade him to enter into his service and accompany him to Greece. The object of the embassy failed. The king refused to exchange the prisoners; but to show them his trust in their honour, he allowed them to go to Rome in order to celebrate the Saturnalia, stipulating that they were to return to Tarentum if the senate would not accept the terms which he had previously offered through Cineas. The senate remained firm in their resolve, and all the prisoners returned to Pyrrhus, the punishment of death having been denounced against those who should remain in the city.

Fabricius.

In the following year (279 B.C.) the war was renewed, and a battle was fought near Asculum. The Romans fled to their camp, which was so near to the field of battle that not more than 6000 fell, while Pyrrhus lost more than half this number. The victory yielded Pyrrhus little or no advantage, and he was obliged to retire to Tarentum for the winter without effecting anything more during the campaign. In the last battle, as well as in the former, the brunt of the action had fallen almost exclusively upon his Greek

Battle near Asculum.

troops; and the state of Greece, which this year was overrun by the Gauls, made it hopeless for him to expect any reinforcements from Epirus. He was therefore unwilling to hazard his surviving Greeks in another campaign with the Romans, and accordingly lent a ready ear to the invitations of the Greeks in Sicily, who begged him to come to their assistance against the Carthaginians. It was necessary, however, first to suspend hostilities with the Romans, and to find a fair pretext for bringing the war to a conclusion. This was afforded at the beginning of the following year (278 B.C.) by one of the servants of Pyrrhus deserting to the Romans, and proposing to the consuls to poison his master. They sent back the deserter to the king, saying that they abhorred a victory gained by treason. Thereupon Pyrrhus, to show his gratitude, sent Cineas to Rome with all the Roman prisoners without ransom and without conditions; he made fresh proposals for peace, but Rome was now in alliance with Carthage, and could not make terms with the king.

Pyrrhus crosses to Sicily.

But the safety of Syracuse was at stake, and, in spite of the protection which he owed to his Italian allies, Pyrrhus left Milo with part of his troops in possession of Tarentum, and crossed over into Sicily. He remained there upwards of two years. At first he met with brilliant success, and deprived the Carthaginians of a great part of the island, although he failed to dislodge them from the impregnable fortress of Lilybaeum. He had built a fleet, communications were kept up between Syracuse and Tarentum, and everything seemed to favour his designs. But Pyrrhus ruled the Sicilians as though they were his own Epirote peasants, and the Greeks, unaccustomed to strong government, now began to form cabals and plots against him.

Pyrrhus returns to Italy.

This led to retaliation on his part, and he soon became as anxious to abandon the island as he had been before to leave Italy. Accordingly, when his Italian allies again begged him to come to their assistance, he readily complied with their request, and arrived in Italy in the autumn of 276 B.C. His troops were now almost the same in number as when he first landed in Italy, but very different in quality. The faithful Epirots had for the most part fallen, and his present soldiers consisted chiefly of mercenaries whom he had levied in Italy. One of his first operations was the recovery of Locri, which had revolted to the Romans; and, as he here found himself in great difficulties for want of money to pay his troops, he was induced to take possession of the treasures of the temple of Persephone in that town; but the ships conveying the money were wrecked. This circumstance deeply affected the mind of Pyrrhus; he ordered the treasures which were saved to be restored to the temple, and from this time became haunted by the idea that the wrath of Persephone was pursuing him and dragging him down to ruin.

The following year (275 B.C.) closed the career of Pyrrhus in Italy. The Consul M'. Curius marched into Samnium, and his colleague into Lucania. Pyrrhus advanced against Curius, who was encamped in the neighbourhood of Beneventum, and resolved to fight with him before he was joined by his colleague. As Curius, not wishing to risk a battle with his own army alone, declined to leave his camp, Pyrrhus planned a night-attack. But he miscalculated the time and the distance; the torches burnt out, the men missed their way, and it was already broad daylight when he reached the heights above the Roman camp. Still, their arrival was quite unexpected; but as a battle was now inevitable, Curius led out his men. The troops of Pyrrhus, exhausted by fatigue, were easily put to the rout; two elephants were killed and eight more taken. Encouraged by this success, Curius no longer hesitated to meet the king in the open plain, and gained a decisive victory. Pyrrhus arrived at Tarentum with only a few horsemen. Shortly afterwards he crossed over to Greece, leaving Milo with a garrison at Tarentum. Two years afterwards he perished in an attack upon Argos, ingloriously slain by a tile hurled by a woman from the roof of a house.

Battle of Beneventum.

The departure of Pyrrhus left the Lucanians and other Italian tribes exposed to the full power of Rome. They nevertheless continued the hopeless struggle a little longer; but in 272 B.C. Tarentum fell, and in a few years afterwards every nation in Italy, to the south of the Macra and the Rubicon, owned the supremacy of Rome. She had now become the first power of the Western, and one of the first powers in the ancient, world. The defeat of Pyrrhus attracted the attention of the nations of

Supremacy of Rome in Italy.

the East; and in 273 B.C. Ptolemy Philadelphus, king of Egypt, sent an embassy to Rome, and concluded a treaty with the Republic.

Organization of Italy.

But Rome did not mean to rule as a mistress over the subject cities of Italy. Empire was still far from her thoughts, and, though she continued the policy adopted on the dissolution of the Latin league, destroyed the existing confederations and isolated the cities from one another, yet she granted them the rights of self-government, and, where possible, incorporated them more or less completely with herself. The population of Italy was divided into three broad classes—*Cives Romani*, inhabitants of *municipia*, and *Socii*.

I. CIVES ROMANI, or ROMAN CITIZENS.—These consisted: (1) Of the citizens of the thirty-three tribes into which the Roman territory was now divided, and which extended north of the Tiber a little beyond Veii, and southwards as far as the Liris; though even in this district there were some towns, such as Tibur and Praenesté, which did not possess the Roman franchise. (2) Of the citizens of Roman colonies planted in different parts of Italy. (3) Of the citizens of municipal towns upon whom the Roman franchise was conferred.

II. The *municipia* were towns to which the Roman citizenship without the right of voting (*civitas sine suffragio*) or of holding office had been given. They possessed, therefore, the rights of trade and intermarriage with Rome (*jus conubii et commercii*).

III. The SOCII were divided into the two classes of (1) the Latins, or cities of the Latin name; and (2) the free and allied communities.

(1) The term *Latini* was applied to the colonies founded by Rome which did not enjoy the rights of Roman citizenship, and which stood almost in the same position with regard to the Roman state as had been formerly occupied by the cities of the Latin league. The name originated at a period when colonies were actually sent out in common by the Romans and Latins, but similar colonies continued to be founded by the Romans alone long after the extinction of the Latin league. These colonists possessed privileges in private and public law. In private law they had the right of trade (*jus commercii*), and could sue and be sued in Roman courts. Their distinctive

public right was capacity for acquiring Roman citizenship. The citizen of any Latin colony might emigrate to Rome, and be enrolled and give his vote in one of the Roman tribes. But after 267 B.C. this right of exile (*jus exsulandi*) was abolished and replaced by the later Latin right which gave full citizenship to any one who had held a magistracy in his native town.

(2) The free and allied cities (*civitates liberae* or *foederatae*) included the rest of Italy. Rome had either formed a treaty (*foedus*) with, or given a charter (*lex data*) to, each of these cities; and this treaty or charter determined its rights and duties. The relation of all the Italian cities to Rome was that of a very close military alliance. Contingents of men were drawn from most of the states, and requisitions for ships of war were made from the Greek cities in the south.

Votes of the freedmen and artisans.

The political changes in Rome itself, from the time of the Latin wars, have been already in great part anticipated. Appius Claudius, afterwards named Caecus, or the Blind, introduced a dangerous innovation in the constitution during the Second Samnite War. Slavery existed at Rome, as among the other nations of antiquity; and as many slaves, from various causes, acquired their liberty, there gradually sprung up at Rome a large and, in many cases, indigent population of servile origin. These freedmen, whose interests became merged in those of the class of landless citizens and artisans, were enrolled only in the four city-tribes, so that, however numerous they might become, they could influence only the votes of four tribes. Appius Claudius, in his censorship (312 B.C.), when making out the lists of citizens, allowed the freedmen and landless citizens to enrol themselves in any tribe they pleased; but this dangerous innovation was abolished by the Censors Q. Fabius Maximus and P. Decius Mus (304 B.C.), who restored these classes to the four city-tribes. The censorship of Appius is, however, memorable for the great public works which he executed. He made the great military road called the Appian Way (Via Appia), leading from Rome to Capua, a distance of 120 miles, which long afterwards was continued across the Apennines to Brundusium. He also executed the first of the great aqueducts (Aqua Appia) which supplied Rome with such an abundance of water.

This period is also remarkable for the growth of a class of lawyers who were no longer members of the sacred guilds. Cn. Flavius, the son of a freedman, and secretary to Appius Claudius, divulged the forms and times to be observed in legal proceedings. These had formerly been the monopoly of the priestly colleges; but Flavius, having become acquainted with these secrets by means of his patron, published in a book a list of the formularies to be observed in the several kinds of actions, and also set up in the forum a whited tablet containing a list of all the days on which the courts could be held. His action was a prelude to the final divorce of Roman law from the trammels of the *jus pontificium*.

Publication of the forms of law.

Coin representing Temple of Vesta.

Roman galley (from Trajan's Column).

CHAPTER X.

THE FIRST PUNIC WAR. 264–241 B.C.

ROME, now the mistress, was also the protectress of Italy, and the defence of her Italian dependencies necessarily entailed on her a long and arduous struggle with Carthage, the undisputed mistress of the western waters of the Mediterranean. This great and powerful city was founded by the Phoenicians * of Tyre in 825 B.C., according to the common chronology. Its inhabitants were consequently a

Carthage.

* The Phoenicians were called by the Latins *Poeni*, whence the adjective *punicus*, like *munire* from *moenia*, and *punire* from *poena*.

branch of the Semitic race, to which the Hebrews also belonged. Carthage rose to greatness by her commerce, and gradually extended her empire over the whole of the north of Africa, from the Straits of Hercules to the borders of Cyrene. Her Libyan subjects she treated with extreme harshness, and hence they were always ready to revolt against her so soon as a foreign enemy appeared upon her soil.

The two chief magistrates at Carthage were elected annually out of a few of the wealthiest families, and were called *Suffetes*.* There was a senate of large numbers; but its power was inferior to that of a smaller council of 104, which was created to control the authority of the generals, and which, by the exercise of its judicial power, held an almost sovereign position. The assembly of the people was sometimes consulted, but the government was practically an oligarchy; and a few old, rich, and powerful families divided among themselves the great offices of state. All power was acquired by commercial wealth, as all policy was subservient to commercial motives.

Relations of Carthage with Sicily.

The mercantile had also crushed the military spirit, and in her foreign wars Carthage depended upon mercenary troops, which her great wealth enabled her to procure in abundance from Spain, Italy, and Greece, as well as from Libya. Sardinia and Corsica were among her earliest conquests, and her most cherished object was the possession of Sicily. The Phoenician colonies in this island came under her dominion as the power of Tyre declined; and having thus obtained a firm footing in Sicily, she carried on a long struggle for supremacy with the Greek cities. It was here that she came into contact with the Roman arms. The relations of Rome and Carthage had hitherto been peaceful, and a treaty, concluded between the two states in the first years of the Roman Republic, had been renewed more than once. But the extension of Roman dominion had excited the jealousy of Carthage; it was evident that a struggle was not far distant, and Pyrrhus could not help exclaiming, as he quitted Sicily, "How fine a battle-field are we leaving to the Romans and Carthaginians!"

The city of Messana, situated on the straits which divide Sicily from Italy, was occupied at this time by the Mamertini.

* Probably the same as the Hebrew *shofetim*, i.e. judges.

They were a body of Campanian mercenaries, chiefly of Sabellian origin, who had served under Agathocles, and after the death of that tyrant (289 B.C.) were marched to Messana, in order to be transported to Italy. Being hospitably received within the city, they suddenly rose against the inhabitants, massacred the male population, and made themselves masters of their wives and property. They now took the name of Mamertini, or "Children of Mars," from Mamers, a Sabellian name for that deity. They rapidly extended their power over a considerable portion of the north of Sicily, and were formidable enemies to Syracuse. Hiero, having become king of Syracuse, determined to destroy this nest of robbers, advanced against them with a large army, defeated them in battle, and shut them up within Messana. The Mamertines were obliged to look out for help; one party wished to appeal to the Carthaginians, and the other to invoke the assistance of Rome. The latter ultimately prevailed, and an embassy was sent to implore immediate aid. The temptation was strong, for the occupation of Messana by a Carthaginian garrison might prove dangerous to the tranquillity of Italy. Still the senate hesitated; for only six years before Hiero had assisted the Romans in punishing the Campanian mercenaries, who had seized Rhegium in the same way as the Mamertines had made themselves masters of Messana. But, though the senate hesitated, the popular assembly, to whom the question was referred, showed no such scruples; it eagerly voted that the Mamertines should be assisted: in other words, that the Carthaginians should not be allowed to obtain possession of Messana; and the decisive step was taken which launched Rome on her career of conquest beyond the limits of Italy.

The Mamertines seek aid from Rome.

The Consul App. Claudius, the son of the blind censor, was to lead an army into Sicily. But during this delay the Carthaginian party in Messana had obtained the scendency, and Hanno, with a Carthaginian garrison, had been admitted into the citadel. Hiero had concluded peace with the Mamertines through the mediation of the Carthaginians, so that there was no longer even a pretext for the interference of the Romans. But a legate of the Consul App. Claudius, having crossed to Sicily, persuaded the Mamertines to expel the Carthaginian garrison. Hiero and

Occupation of Messana War with Carthage.

the Carthaginians now proceeded to lay siege to Messana by sea and land, and the Romans no longer hesitated to declare war against Carthage. Such was the commencement of the First Punic War (264 B.C.).

The Carthaginians commanded the sea with a powerful fleet, while the Romans had no ships of war worthy of the name. But the Consul App. Claudius, having contrived to elude the Carthaginian squadron, landed near the town of Messana, and defeated in succession the forces of Syracuse and Carthage. In the following year (263) the Romans followed up their success against Hiero. The two consuls advanced to the walls of Syracuse, ravaging the territory of the city and capturing many of its dependent towns. The king became alarmed at the success of the Romans; and thinking that they would prove more powerful than the Carthaginians, he concluded a peace with Rome. From this time till his death, a period of nearly fifty years, Hiero remained the firm and steadfast ally of the Romans.

Capture of Agrigentum.

The Romans, now freed from the hostility of Syracuse, laid siege to Agrigentum, the second of the Greek cities in Sicily, which was now held by the flower of the Carthaginian troops. They blockaded the town, but their supplies were in turn cut off by the Phoenician fleet, and the distress on both sides was great. At length a battle was fought, and the Romans, gaining a decisive victory over the Carthaginian army which had been sent to raise the siege, obtained possession of the town (262 B.C.).

Rome builds a fleet.

The first three years of the war had already made the Romans masters of the greater part of Sicily. But the coasts of Italy were exposed to the ravages of the Carthaginian fleet, and the Romans saw that they could not hope to bring the war to a successful termination so long as Carthage was mistress of the sea. To form a fleet in the ancient world was not the undertaking it is for a modern nation. It required a command of men, money, and materials—all of which Rome now possessed in abundance; for seamanship, which is a thing of gradual growth, was, in the coasting voyages of the time, a secondary consideration. The first necessity was to build ships of a heavier kind than the few triremes of which the Roman navy was composed; a Carthaginian quinquereme, which had been wrecked upon the coast of

Italy, served as a model. In the short space of sixty days from the time the trees were felled, 130 ships were launched, and while the ships were building, the rowers were trained on scaffolds placed upon the land like benches of ships at sea. As we may imagine, the sea-going power of these Roman ships was contemptible; all that they could boast was weight and size.

In the fifth year of the war (260 B.C.) one of the consuls, Cn. Cornelius, first put to sea with only seventeen vessels, but was surprised near Lipara, and taken prisoner, with the whole of his squadron. His colleague, C. Duilius, now took the command of the rest of the fleet. He saw that the only means of conquering the Carthaginians by sea was to deprive them of all the advantages of manœuvring, and to take their ships by boarding. For this purpose every ship was provided with a boarding-bridge, thirty-six feet in length, which was pulled up by a rope and fastened to a mast in the fore part of the ship. As soon as an enemy's ship came near enough, the rope was loosened, the bridge fell down, and became fastened by means of an iron spike in its under side. The boarders then poured down the bridge into the enemy's ship.

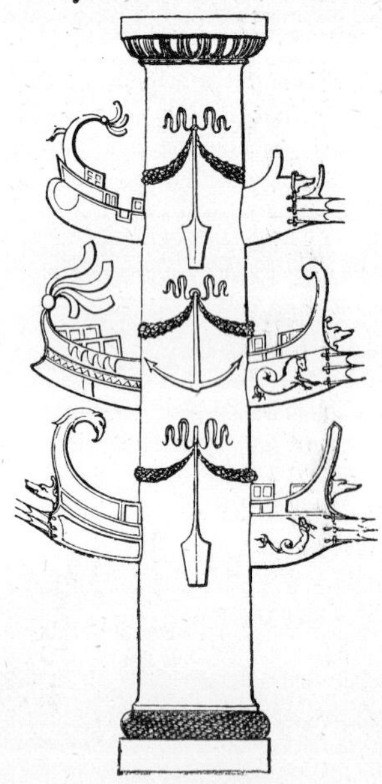
Columna Rostrata.

Thus prepared, Duilius boldly sailed out to meet the fleet of the enemy. He found them off the Sicilian coast, near Mylae. The Carthaginians hastened to the fight as if to a triumph, but their ships were rapidly seized by the boarding-bridges, and when it came to a close fight their crews were no match for the veteran soldiers of Rome. The victory of Duilius was complete. Thirty-one of the enemy's ships were taken, and fourteen destroyed; the

Victory at Mylae.

rest only saved themselves by an ignominious flight. On his return to Rome, Duilius celebrated a magnificent triumph. Public honours were conferred upon him; he was to be escorted home in the evening from banquets by the light of torches and the sound of the flute, and a column adorned with the beaks of the conquered ships, and thence called the Columna Rostrata, was set up in the forum.*

Regulus invades Africa.

For the next few years the war languished, and nothing of importance was effected on either side; but in the ninth year of the struggle (256 B.C.) the Romans resolved by strenuous exertions to bring it to an end. They therefore made preparations for invading Africa with a great force. The two consuls, M. Atilius Regulus and L. Manlius, set sail with 330 ships, took the legions on board in Sicily, and then put out to sea in order to cross over to Africa. The Carthaginian fleet, consisting of 350 ships, met them near Ecnomus, on the southern coast of Sicily. Never, perhaps, had the ancient world seen a battle in which such numbers were engaged. The boarding-bridges of the Romans again annihilated all the advantages of maritime skill. Their victory was decisive. They lost only twenty-four ships, while they destroyed twenty-four of the enemy's vessels, and took sixty-four with all their crews. The passage to Africa was now clear; and the remainder of the Carthaginian fleet hastened home to defend the capital. The Romans landed near the town of Clupea or Aspis, which they took, and there established their head-quarters. From thence they laid waste the Carthaginian territory with fire and sword, and collected an immense booty from the defenceless country. On the approach of winter, Manlius, one of the consuls, by order of the senate, returned to Rome with half of the army; while Regulus remained with the other half to prosecute the war. He carried on his operations with the utmost vigour, and was greatly assisted by the incompetency of the Carthaginian generals. The enemy had collected a considerable force; but the Carthaginian generals avoided the plains, where their cavalry and elephants would have given them an advantage over the Roman army, and withdrew into the mountains. There they were attacked by Regulus, and utterly defeated with great

* The inscription upon this column, or at any rate a very ancient copy of it, is still preserved in the Capitoline Museum at Rome.

loss: 15,000 men were killed in battle, and 5000 men, with eighteen elephants, were taken. The vanquished troops retired within the walls of Carthage; Regulus now overran the country without opposition, and began to plan the siege of the capital. Amongst other towns that fell into his power was Tunis, which was at the distance of only twenty miles from Carthage. The Numidians took the opportunity of recovering their independence, and their roving bands completed the devastation of the country. The Carthaginians in despair sent a herald to Regulus to solicit peace. But the Roman general, intoxicated with success, would only grant it on such intolerable terms that the Carthaginians resolved to continue the war, and hold out to the last.

In the midst of their distress and alarm, succour came to them from an unexpected quarter. Among the Greek mercenaries who had lately arrived at Carthage was a Lacedaemonian of the name of Xanthippus. He emphasized the folly of lurking in the hills and forests; and he inspired such confidence in the government, that he was placed at the head of their troops. Relying on his 4000 cavalry and 100 elephants, Xanthippus boldly marched into the open country to meet the enemy. Regulus, without even attempting to secure his retreat, readily accepted battle; but it ended in his total overthrow; 30,000 Romans were slain: scarcely 2000 escaped to Clupea, and Regulus himself with 500 more was taken prisoner (255 B.C.).

Defeat of Regulus. Loss of Roman fleets.

Another disaster awaited the Romans in this year. Their fleet, which had been sent to Africa to carry off the remains of the army of Regulus, had not only succeeded in their object, but had gained a victory over the Carthaginian fleet. They were returning home when they were overtaken off Camarina, in Sicily, by a fearful storm. Nearly the entire fleet was destroyed, and the coast was strewn for miles with wrecks and corpses.

The Romans, with undiminished energy, immediately set to work to build a new fleet, and in less than three months 220 ships were ready for sea. But the same fate awaited them. In 253 B.C. the consuls had ravaged the coasts of Africa, but on their return were again surprised by a fearful storm off Cape Palinurus. A hundred and fifty ships were wrecked. This blow, coming so soon after the other, damped the courage even of the Roman senate; it determined not to rebuild the fleet, and to keep only sixty ships for the defence of the coast of Italy and the protection of the transports.

Victory at Panormus.

The war was now confined to Sicily, but since the defeat of Regulus the Roman soldiers had been so greatly alarmed by the elephants, that their generals did not venture on attack. At length, in 250 B.C., the Roman pro-consul, L. Metellus, accepted battle under the walls of Panormus, and gained a decisive victory. The Carthaginians lost 20,000 men; thirteen of their generals adorned the triumph of Metellus; and 104 elephants were also led in the triumphal procession. This was the most important battle that had been yet fought in Sicily, and had a decisive influence upon the issue of the contest. It so raised the spirits of the Romans that they determined once more to build a fleet of 200 sail. The Carthaginians, on the other hand, were anxious to bring the war to an end, and accordingly sent an embassy to Rome to propose an exchange of prisoners, and to offer terms of peace.

Regulus.

Regulus, who had been now five years in captivity, was allowed to accompany the ambassadors, with the promise that he would return to Carthage if their proposals were declined. This embassy is the subject of one of the most celebrated stories in the Roman annals. The orators and poets relate how Regulus at first refused to enter the city as a slave of the Carthaginians; how afterwards he would not give his opinion in the senate, as he had ceased by his captivity to be a member of that illustrious body; how, at length, when induced by his countrymen to speak, he endeavoured to dissuade the senate from assenting to a peace, or even to an exchange of prisoners; and when he saw them wavering, from their desire to redeem him from captivity, how he told them that the Carthaginians had given him a slow poison, which would soon terminate his life; and how, finally, when the senate, through his influence, refused the offers of the Carthaginians, he firmly resisted all the persuasions of his friends to remain in Rome, and returned to Carthage, where a martyr's death awaited him. It is related that he was placed in a barrel covered over with iron nails, and thus perished; other writers state in addition, that, after his eyelids had been cut off, he was first thrown into a dark dungeon, and then suddenly exposed to the full rays of a burning sun. When the news of the barbarous death of Regulus reached Rome, the senate is said to have given two of the noblest Carthaginian prisoners to the family of Regulus, who revenged themselves by putting them to death with cruel torments.

Siege of Lilybaeum.

The Carthaginian dominion in Sicily was now confined to the north-western corner of the island; and Lilybaeum and Drepanum were the only two towns remaining in their hands. Lilybaeum, situated upon a promontory at the western extremity of the island, was the stronghold of the Carthaginian power; and accordingly the Romans determined to concentrate all their efforts, and to employ the armies of both consuls in attacking this city. This siege, which is one of the most memorable in ancient history, commenced in 250 B.C., and lasted till the termination of the war.

Defeat at Drepanum.

In the second year of the siege (249 B.C.) the Consul P. Claudius, tired of the delay before Lilybaeum, formed the design of attacking the Carthaginian fleet in the neighbouring harbour of Drepanum. In vain did the auguries warn him; the keeper of the sacred chickens told him that they would not eat. "At any rate," said he, "let them drink," and he ordered them to be thrown overboard. His impiety met with a meet reward. He was defeated with great loss; ninety-three of his ships were taken or destroyed, and only thirty escaped. Great was the indignation at Rome. He was recalled by the senate, ordered to appoint a dictator, and then to lay down his office. Claudius, in scorn, named M. Claudius Glycias, a son of one of his freedmen. But the senate would not brook this insult; they deprived the unworthy man of the honour, and caused A. Atilius Calatinus to be appointed in his place.

Destruction of the Roman fleet.

The other consul, C. Junius, was equally unfortunate. He was sailing along the coasts of Sicily with a convoy of 800 vessels, intended to relieve the wants of the army at Lilybaeum, when he was overtaken by one of those terrible storms which had twice before proved so fatal to the Roman fleets. The transports were all dashed to pieces, and of his 105 ships of war only two escaped. Thus the Roman fleet was a third time destroyed. These repeated misfortunes compelled the Romans to abandon any further attempts to contest the supremacy of the sea.

Hamilcar at Herctè and Eryx.

About this time a really great man was placed at the head of the Carthaginian army—a man who, at an earlier period of the war, might have brought the struggle to a very different termination. This was the celebrated Hamilcar Barca,* the father of the still more celebrated Hannibal. He was still a young man at the time of his appointment to the command in Sicily (247 B.C.). His very first operations were equally daring and successful. Instead of confining himself to the defence of Lilybaeum and Drepanum, with which the Carthaginian commanders had been hitherto contented, he made descents upon the coast of Italy, and then suddenly landed on the north of Sicily, and established himself with his whole army on a mountain called Herctè (the modern *Monte Pellegrino*), which overhung the town of Panormus (the modern *Palermo*), one of the most important of the Roman possessions. Here he maintained himself for nearly three years, to the astonishment alike of friends and foes; and from hence he made continual descents into the enemies' country, and completely prevented them from making any vigorous attacks either upon Lilybaeum or Drepanum. All the efforts of the Romans to dislodge him were unsuccessful; and he only quitted Herctè in order to seize Eryx, a town situated upon the mountain of this name, and only six miles from Drepanum. This position he held for two years longer, until the Romans realized that the only means of driving the Carthaginians out of Sicily was to recover their supremacy by sea.

Victory at the Aegates insulae.

In 242 B.C. the Consul Lutatius Catulus put out with a fleet of 200 ships, and in the following year he gained a decisive victory over the Carthaginian fleet, commanded by Hanno, off the group of islands called the Aegates.

This victory gave the Romans the desired control over the Carthaginian strongholds. Lilybaeum, Drepanum, and Eryx might

* *Barca* is the same as the Hebrew word *Barak*, "lightning."

now be reduced by famine. The Carthaginians, weary of the war, and indisposed to make any further sacrifices, sent orders to Hamilcar to make peace on the best terms he could, and it was at length concluded on the conditions: that Carthage should evacuate Sicily and the adjoining islands; that she should restore the Roman prisoners without ransom, and should pay the sum of 3200 talents within the space of ten years (241 B.C.).

Peace with Carthage.

The evacuation of Sicily brought Rome face to face with a new problem. She could not leave the Sicilian states, like those of Magna Graecia, bound to her by the loose ties of a military alliance; this was rendered impossible by the insular position of the new conquest and the danger from Carthage. So the whole of Sicily, with the exception of the territory of Hiero, was organized as a separate "department of administration" (*provincia*), and placed under the command of an annual praetor; and the first stone was laid in the foundation of an empire.

Sicily a province.

Fighting elephant making a prisoner (gem in "Cabinet de France," No. 1911 (Chabouillet)).

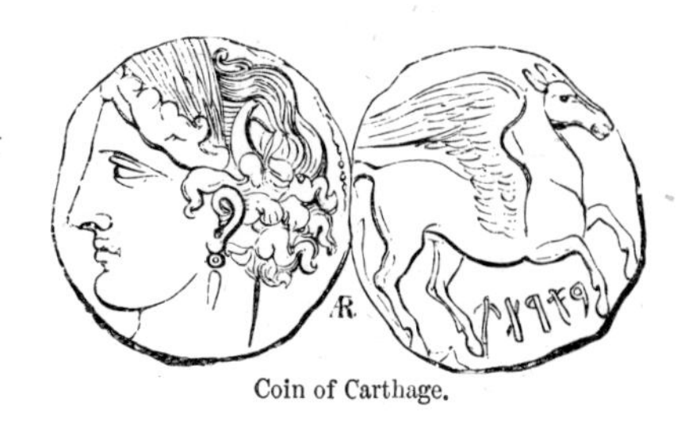

Coin of Carthage.

CHAPTER XI.

THE CONQUEST OF NORTHERN ITALY. THE CARTHAGINIANS IN SPAIN. 240–219 B.C.

Mercenary war at Carthage.

TWENTY-THREE years elapsed between the First and Second Punic Wars. The power of Carthage, though crippled, was not destroyed; and Hamilcar returned home, burning with hatred against Rome, and determined to renew the war upon a favourable opportunity. But a new and terrible danger threatened Carthage upon her own soil. The mercenary troops, who had been transported from Sicily to Africa at the conclusion of the war, being unable to obtain their arrears of pay, rose in open mutiny. Their leaders were Spendius, a runaway Campanian slave, and Matho, a Libyan. They were quickly joined by the native Libyans, and brought Carthage almost to the brink of destruction. They laid waste the whole country with fire and sword, made themselves masters of all the towns except the capital, and committed the most frightful atrocities. Carthage owed her safety to the genius and abilities of Hamilcar. The struggle was fierce and sanguinary, but was at length brought to a successful issue, after it had lasted more than three years, by the destruction of all the mercenaries. It was called the War without Peace, or the Inexpiable War (238 B.C.).

The Romans availed themselves of the exhausted condition of Carthage to demand from her the islands of Sardinia and Corsica, and the payment of a further sum of 1200 talents.

The mercenary troops in Sardinia, who had also revolted, had applied to Rome for assistance; and the senate menaced her rival with war unless she complied with these unjust demands. Resistance was impossible, and Sardinia and Corsica were soon formed into a Roman province, governed, like Sicily, by a praetor, sent annually from Rome. This is almost the only act of unjustifiable acquisition which we shall meet with in Roman annals. But the senate had made up its mind that the Tyrrhenian sea must belong to Rome, and did not shrink from robbery in pursuit of its narrow defensive policy (238 B.C.). Hamilcar, with his resentment against the grasping Republic deepened by this outrage, now departed for Spain, where, for many years, he steadily worked to lay the foundation of a new empire, which might not only compensate for the loss of Sicily and Sardinia, but enable him at some time to renew hostilities against Rome.

Rome seizes Sardinia and Corsica.

Rome was now at peace, and in 235 B.C. the temple of Janus, which had remained open since the days of Numa, was closed for a second time. Two new tribes were added to the Roman territory, making their total number thirty-five.

The temple of Janus did not long remain closed. The Illyrians, who dwelt near the head of the Adriatic upon its eastern side, were a nation of pirates, who ravaged the coasts of this sea. The senate having sent ambassadors to the Illyrian king Agron to complain of these outrages, he declined to attend to their complaints, and the ambassadors were murdered on their way home. War was straightway declared, and a Roman army for the first time crossed the Adriatic (229 B.C.). Demetrius of Pharos, an unprincipled Greek, who was the chief counsellor of Teuta, widow and successor of Agron, deserted his mistress, and surrendered to the Romans the important island of Corcyra. Teuta was obliged to yield to the Romans everything they demanded, and promised that the Illyrians should not appear south of Lissus with more than two vessels. The suppression of piracy in the Adriatic was hailed with gratitude by the Greek states, and deserves notice as the first occasion upon which the Romans were brought into immediate contact with Greece. The Consul Postumius, who had wintered in Illyria, sent envoys to Athens, Corinth, and other Greek cities, to explain what had been done.

Illyrian War.

The envoys were received with honour, and thanks were returned to Rome (228 B.C.).

Gallic wars.

The Romans had scarcely brought this trifling war to an end when they became involved in a formidable struggle with their old enemies the Gauls. Since the conquest of the Senones in 283 B.C., and of the Boii in 282 B.C., the Gauls had remained quiet. The Romans had founded the colony of Sena after the subjugation of the Senones; and in 268 B.C. they had still further strengthened their dominion in those parts by founding the colony of Ariminum. But the greater part of the soil from which the Senones were ejected became public land. In 232 B.C. the Tribune C. Flaminius carried an Agrarian Law to the effect that this portion of the public land, known by the name of the "Gallic Land," * should be distributed among the poorer citizens. This alarmed the Boii, who dwelt upon the borders of this district. They invoked the assistance of the powerful tribe of the Insubres, and being joined by them, as well as by large bodies of Gauls from beyond the Alps, they set out for Rome.

Battle of Telamon.

All Italy was in alarm. The Romans dreaded a repetition of the disaster of the Allia. The Sibylline books, when consulted, declared that Rome must be occupied twice by a foreign foe; whereupon the senate, to allay the superstitious fears of the people, ordered that two Gauls should be buried alive in the forum. The allies eagerly offered men and supplies to meet a danger which was common to the whole peninsula. An army of 150,000 foot and 6000 horse was speedily raised. A decisive battle was fought near Telamon, in Etruria. The Gauls were hemmed in between the armies of the two consuls. As many as 40,000 of their men were slain, and 10,000 taken prisoners (225 B.C.). The Romans followed up their success by invading the country of the Boii, who submitted in the following year (224 B.C.), and the plain as far as the Po was in the hands of Rome.

In 223 B.C. the Romans crossed the river, and the Consul C. Flaminius gained a brilliant victory over the Insubres. The consuls of the next year, Cn. Cornelius Scipio and M. Claudius Marcellus, continued the war against the Insubres, who called in to their aid a fresh body of Transalpine Gauls. Marcellus

* *Gallicus ager.*

slew with his own hand Viridomarus, the chief of the Insubrian Gauls, and thus gained the third *Spolia Opima*. At the same time, Scipio took Mediolanium (Milan), the chief town of the Insubres. This people now submitted without conditions, and the war was brought to an end. To secure their recent conquests, the Romans determined to plant two powerful Latin colonies at Placentia and Cremona, on opposite banks of the Po. These were founded in 218 B.C., and consisted each of 6000 men. The Via Flaminia, a road constructed by C. Flaminius from Rome to Ariminum (220 B.C.), secured the communication with the north of Italy.

Extension of Roman power beyond the Po.

The results of this war were of vast importance, for Italy had now reached her natural boundaries. Rome's dominion now extended to the Po, and, through the dependent Gallic tribes who dwelt beyond that river, her sphere of influence reached the Alps.

Meanwhile Hamilcar, as commander-in-chief of the Carthaginian army in Spain, with powers that rendered him almost entirely independent of the home government, had been steadily pursuing a career of conquest. The subjugation of this country was only a means to an end. His great object, as already stated, was to obtain the means of attacking, and, if possible, crushing, that hated rival who had robbed his country of Sicily, Sardinia, and Corsica. His implacable animosity against Rome is shown by the well-known tale, that when he crossed over to Spain in 236 B.C., taking with him his son Hannibal, then only nine years old, he made him swear at the altar eternal hostility to Rome. During the eight years that Hamilcar continued in Spain he carried the Carthaginian arms into the heart of the country. While he conquered several states in war, he gained over others by negotiation, and availed himself of their services as allies or mercenaries. He fell in battle in 228 B.C., and was succeeded in the command by his son-in-law Hasdrubal. His plans were ably carried out by his successor. The conciliatory manners of Hasdrubal gained him the affections of the Spaniards; and he consolidated the Carthaginian empire in Spain by the foundation of New Carthage, now Cartagena, in a situation admirably chosen on account of its excellent harbour and easy communication with

Hamilcar and Hasdrubal in Spain.

Africa, as well as from its proximity to the silver-mines, which supplied him with the means of paying his troops. His trusted lieutenant was the youthful Hannibal, who had been trained in arms under the eye of his father, and who already displayed that ability for war which Rome was so soon to feel. The successes of Hamilcar and Hasdrubal could not fail to attract the notice of the Romans; they did not understand the objects of the Phoenician generals, but, as it dawned on them that Spain might possibly be a battle-ground in the future, they concluded a treaty, by which the river Ibērus (Ebro) was fixed as the northern boundary of the Carthaginian empire in Spain (228 B.C.).

Hasdrubal was assassinated in 221 B.C. by a slave whose master he had put to death. Hannibal had now acquired such a remarkable ascendency over the army, that the soldiers unanimously proclaimed him commander-in-chief, and the government at Carthage hastened to ratify an appointment which they had not, in fact, the power to prevent. There can be no doubt that he already looked forward to the invasion and conquest of Italy as the goal of his ambition; but it was necessary for him first to complete the work which had been so ably begun by his two predecessors, and to establish the Carthaginian power as firmly as possible in Spain. This he accomplished in two campaigns, in the course of which he brought all the nations south of the Iberus into subjection to Carthage. His army was now in the highest degree of efficiency, and he felt that the time had come for the final move. All that was lacking was a pretext for war, and this he soon created.

Hannibal attacks Saguntum.

Early in the spring of 219 B.C. he proceeded to lay siege to Saguntum, a city of Greek origin founded by the Zacynthians. Though situated to the south of the Iberus, and therefore not included under the Roman protectorate established by the treaty with Hasdrubal, Saguntum had concluded an alliance with Rome. The excuse for this aggression was the same of which the Romans so often availed themselves—some injury inflicted by the Saguntines upon one of the neighbouring tribes under the protection of Carthage. The resistance of the city was long and desperate, and it was not till after a siege of nearly eight months that he made himself master of the place.

During all this period the Romans sent no assistance to their

War declared with Carthage.

allies. They had, indeed, as soon as they heard of the siege, despatched ambassadors to Hannibal, but he referred them for an answer to the government at home, and they could obtain no satisfaction from the Carthaginians, in whose councils the war party had now a decided predominance. A second embassy was sent, after the fall of Saguntum, to demand the surrender of Hannibal, in atonement for the breach of the treaty. After much discussion, Q. Fabius, one of the Roman ambassadors, holding up a fold of his toga, said, "I carry here peace and war; choose ye which ye will." "Give us which you will," was the reply. "Then take war," said Fabius, letting fall his toga. And the senators of Carthage cried, "We accept the gift."

Coin of Hiero.

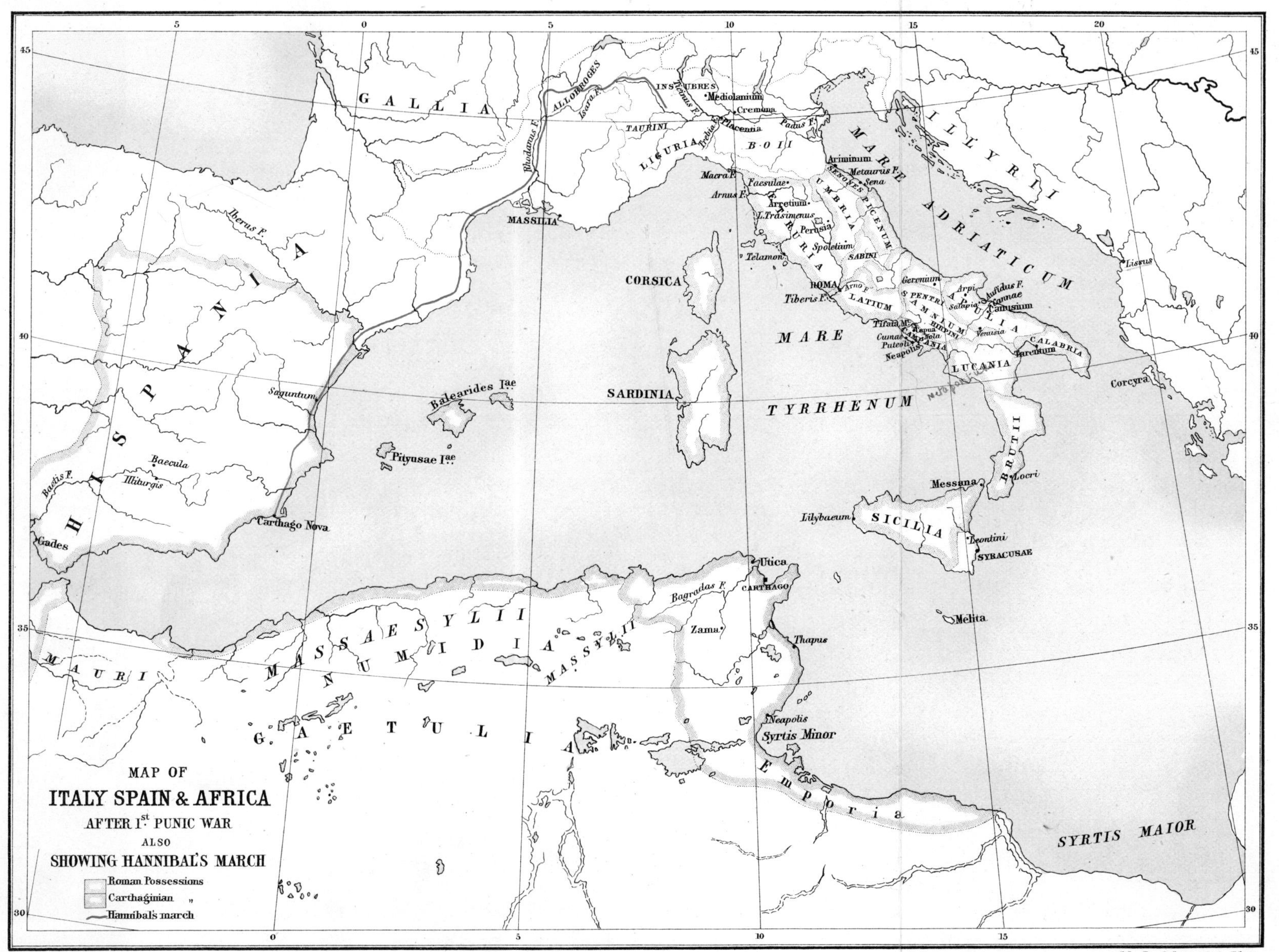

London. John Murray, Albemarle Street.

John Bartholomew & Co., Edinr.

Lake Trasimenus.

CHAPTER XII.

THE SECOND PUNIC WAR: FIRST PERIOD, DOWN TO THE BATTLE OF CANNAE. 218–216 B.C.

Hannibal's preparations for invading Italy.

In the Second Punic War we have no longer a distant contest between Carthaginians and Romans fought out on neutral ground; it is the struggle of Italy against the individual genius of a foreign invader. The position of Hannibal was indeed very peculiar. His command in Spain, and the powerful army there, which was entirely at his own disposal, rendered him in great measure independent of the government at Carthage, and the latter seemed disposed to devolve all responsibility upon him. Even now they did little themselves to prepare for the impending contest. All was left to Hannibal, who, after the conquest of Saguntum, had returned once more to New Carthage for the winter, and was there actively engaged in preparations for carrying the war into the enemy's country. At the same time, he did not neglect to provide for the defence of Spain and Africa during his absence. In the former country he placed his brother Hasdrubal, with a considerable army, great part of which was composed of Africans, while he sent over a large body of Spanish troops to contribute to the defence of Africa, and even of Carthage itself.

All his preparations being now completed, Hannibal quitted his winter quarters at New Carthage in the spring of 218 B.C., and crossed the Iberus with an army of 90,000 foot and 12,000 horse. The tribes between that river and the Pyrenees offered at first a vigorous resistance, and, though they were quickly subdued, Hannibal thought it necessary to leave behind him a force of 11,000 men under Hanno to maintain this newly acquired province. His forces were further thinned by desertion during the passage of the Pyrenees, which obliged him to send home a large body of his Spanish troops. With a greatly diminished army, but one on which he could securely rely, he now continued his march from the foot of the Pyrenees to the Rhone without meeting with any opposition; for the Gallic tribes through which he passed were favourably disposed to him, or had been previously gained over by his emissaries.

The Consul P. Cornelius Scipio had been ordered to proceed to Spain, but various causes had detained him in Italy, and upon landing at Massilia (Marseilles) he found that Hannibal was already advancing towards the Rhone. Meantime the Carthaginian general effected his passage across the river, notwithstanding the opposition of the Gauls; and when Scipio marched up the left bank of the river, he found that Hannibal had advanced into the interior of Gaul, and was already three days in advance of him. Despairing, therefore, of overtaking Hannibal, he determined to sail back to Italy and await him in Cisalpine Gaul. But as the Republic had already an army in that province, he sent the greater part of his own forces into Spain under the command of his brother Cn. Scipio. This prudent step probably saved Rome; for if the Carthaginians had maintained the undisputed mastery of Spain, they might have

Hannibal crosses the Rhone.

concentrated all their efforts to support Hannibal in Italy, and have sent him such strong reinforcements after the battle of Cannae as would have compelled Rome to submit.

Hannibal, after crossing the Rhone, continued his march up the left bank of the river as far as its confluence with the Isère. Here he interposed in a dispute between two rival chiefs of the Allobroges, and, by lending his aid to establish one of them firmly on the throne, secured the co-operation of an efficient ally, who greatly facilitated his farther progress. But in his passage across the Alps he was attacked by the barbarians, and as he struggled through the narrow and dangerous defiles the enemy destroyed numbers of his men. It was some days before he reached the summit of the pass. Thenceforth he suffered but little from hostile attacks, but the descent was difficult and dangerous. The natural difficulties of the road, enhanced by the lateness of the season (the beginning of September, at which time the snows had already commenced in the high Alps), caused him almost as much loss as the opposition of the barbarians on the other side of the mountains. So heavy were his losses from these combined causes that, when he at length emerged from the valley of Aosta into the plains of the Po, and encamped in the friendly country of the Insubres, he had with him no more than 20,000 foot and 6000 horse.* There were no Roman legions near to attack his thinned and exhausted troops; the blunder which had permitted the passage of the Alps left the frontier of Italy undefended.

The passage of the Alps.

Hannibal's first care was now to recruit the strength of his army, worn out as it was by the hardships and fatigues it had undergone. After a short interval of repose, he turned his arms against the Taurini (a tribe bordering on, and hostile to, the Insubres), whom he quickly reduced, and took their principal city (Turin). The news of the approach of P. Scipio next obliged him to turn his attention towards a more formidable enemy. In the first action, which took place in the plains westward of the Ticinus, the cavalry and light-armed troops of the two armies were alone engaged; and the superiority of Hannibal's

Battles of the Ticinus and Trebia.

* The pass of the Alps which Hannibal crossed was probably the Graian Alps, or *Little St. Bernard*. See note "On the Passage of Hannibal across the Alps," at the end of this chapter.

Numidian horse at once decided the combat in his favour. The Romans were completely routed, and Scipio himself severely wounded; in consequence of which he hastened to retreat beyond the Ticinus and the Po, under the walls of Placentia. Hannibal crossed the Po higher up, and, advancing to Placentia, offered battle to Scipio; but the latter declined the combat, and withdrew to the hills on the left bank of the Trebia. Here he was soon after joined by the other consul, Ti. Sempronius Longus, who had hastened from Ariminum to his support: their combined armies were greatly superior to that of the Carthaginians, and Sempronius, whose year of office was expiring, was eager to bring on a general battle, of which Hannibal, on his side, was not less desirous, notwithstanding the great inferiority of his force. The result was decisive: the Romans were completely defeated, with heavy loss; and the remains of their shattered army, together with the two consuls, took refuge within the walls of Placentia. The battles of the Ticinus and Trebia had been fought in December, and the winter had already begun with unusual severity, so that Hannibal's troops suffered severely from cold, and all his elephants perished except one. But his victory had caused all the wavering tribes of the Gauls to declare in his favour, and he was now able to take up his winter quarters in security, and to levy fresh troops among the Gauls, while he awaited the approach of spring.

Hannibal passes the Apennines.

As soon as the season permitted the renewal of military operations (217 B.C.), Hannibal entered the country of the Ligurian tribes, who had lately declared in his favour, and descended by the valley of the Macra into the marshes on the banks of the Arno. He had apparently chosen this route in order to avoid the Roman armies, which guarded the more obvious passes of the Apennines; but the hardships and difficulties which he encountered in struggling through the marshes were immense; great numbers of his horses and beasts of burthen perished, and he himself lost the sight of one eye by a violent attack of ophthalmia. At length, however, he reached Faesulae in safety, and was able to allow his troops a short interval of repose.

The consuls for this year were Cn. Servilius and C. Flaminius. The latter was the author of the celebrated Agrarian Law which occasioned the Gallic War, and in his first consulship he had gained a great victory over the Insubrian Gauls (see p. 97). He had been raised to his second consulship by popular favour, in spite of the opposition of the senate; and he hurried from Rome before the Ides of March,* lest the senate might throw any obstacle in the way of his entering upon his consulship. He was a man of great energy, but headstrong and reckless. When Hannibal arrived at Faesulae, Flaminius was with his army at Arretium.

Battle of the Trasimene lake.

It was always the object of Hannibal to bring the Roman commanders to a battle after himself choosing the ground, and therefore, in moving from Faesulae, he passed by the Roman general, and advanced towards Perusia, laying waste the fertile country on his line of march. Flaminius immediately broke up his camp, and, following the traces of Hannibal, fell into the snare which was prepared for him. He found himself in a narrow defile, both sides of which had been occupied by Hannibal's light troops; the outlet was barred by Hannibal's infantry, and the entrance was closed by the Trasimene lake. The destruction of the imprisoned army was almost complete. Thousands fell by the sword, among whom was the consul himself; thousands more perished in the lake, and no less than 15,000 prisoners fell into the hands of Hannibal, who on his side is said to have lost only 1500 men. Hannibal's treatment of the captives on this occasion, as well as after the battle of the Trebia, was marked by the same policy on which he afterwards uniformly acted: the Roman citizens alone were retained as prisoners, while their Italian allies were dismissed without ransom to their respective homes. By this means he hoped to excite the nations of Italy against their Roman masters, and to place himself in the position of the leader of a national movement rather than that of a foreign invader. It was in order to give time for this feeling to display itself that he did not, after the conquest of Etruria, push on towards Rome itself; but, after an unsuccessful attempt upon the Roman colony of Spoletium, he turned aside through the Apennines into Picenum, and thence into the northern part of Apulia. Here he spent a great part of the summer, and was able effectually to refresh his troops, who

* At this time the consuls entered upon their office on the Ides of March. It was not till 153 B.C. that the consulship commenced on the Kalends of January.

had suffered much from the hardships of their previous marches. But no symptoms appeared of the insurrections he had looked for; the Italians, who might have joined a Western leader, could not be brought to look on a Phoenician chief as their deliverer.

Policy of Fabius.

Meantime the Romans had collected a fresh army, which they placed under the command of Q. Fabius Maximus, who had, in consequence of the absence of the consuls from Rome, been *elected* dictator by the Comitia of the Centuries. Fabius formed a different plan for the campaign. He determined to keep the heights, and not to risk a battle, but at the same time to watch the Carthaginian army, cut off its supplies, and harass and annoy it in every possible way. From pursuing this policy he received the surname of *Cunctator*, or the *Lingerer*.

Hannibal now recrossed the Apennines, descended into the rich plains of Campania, and laid waste, without opposition, that fertile territory. But he was unable either to make himself master of any of the towns, or to draw the wary Fabius to a battle. The Roman general contented himself with occupying the mountain-passes leading from Samnium into Campania, by which Hannibal must of necessity retreat, and believed that he had caught him as it were in a trap; but Hannibal eluded his vigilance by an ingenious stratagem. He had faggots tied to the horns of 2000 oxen, which were amongst the booty: and when night was closing in, he had the faggots lit, and made his light-armed troops drive the cattle straight up the mountain slopes in the direction of the Roman ambush. The garrison, astonished at what they believed to be a night attack by torch-light from an unexpected quarter, hastily retreated, and Hannibal rapidly mounted the pass with his whole forces, passed the defiles of the Apennines without loss, and established himself in the plains of Apulia, where he collected supplies from all sides, in order to prepare for the winter.

Discontent of the popular party at Rome.

Meantime the popular party at Rome, impatient at the inactivity of Fabius, had raised Minucius, the Master of the Horse, to an equality in command. The rashness with which he sought to justify the popular choice very nearly gave Hannibal the opportunity, for which he was ever on the watch, to crush the Roman army by a decisive blow. One of his ambushes had taken the troops of Minucius by surprise, and the Roman army was being shut in on every side, when Fabius suddenly appeared upon the scene. The Phoenician forces retired before the combined armies, and took up their winter quarters at Geronium. Minucius acknowledged his error, and resumed his post of Master of the Horse.

During the winter the Romans made preparations for bringing an unusually large force into the field. The people thought that it needed only a man of energy and decision at the head of an overwhelming force to bring the war to a close. They therefore raised to the consulship C. Terentius Varro, said to have been the son of a butcher, who had been for some time regarded as the champion of the popular party. The senate regarded this election with dismay, as Varro possessed no military experience; and they therefore persuaded the people to appoint as his colleague L. Aemilius Paullus, who had distinguished himself by the way in which he had conducted the Illyrian War during his consulship.

Battle of Cannae.

Hannibal remained at Geronium until late in the spring (216 B.C.), when, compelled to move by the want of provisions, he surprised the Roman magazines at Cannae, a small town of Apulia, and established his head-quarters there until the harvest could be got in. Meanwhile the two Roman consuls arrived at the head of an army of 80,000 infantry and 6000 cavalry. Hannibal's infantry was but half the number of the Roman, but his cavalry numbered 10,000. He offered battle on the left, and, when this was declined, on the right bank of the Aufidus, in a wide plain eminently suited to the evolutions of cavalry. It was the cavalry that decided the day; the immense army of the Romans was not only defeated, but annihilated; and between 40,000 and 50,000 men are said to have fallen in the field, among whom was the Consul Aemilius Paullus, both the consuls of the preceding years, the late Master of the Horse, Minucius, above eighty senators, and a multitude of the knights who composed the Roman cavalry and mounted officers. The other consul, Varro, escaped with a few horsemen to Venusia, and a small band of resolute men forced their way from the Roman camp through the enemy's army to Canusium; all the rest were killed, dispersed, or taken prisoners. Hannibal has been generally blamed for not following up his advantage at once, after so decisive a victory, by an immediate advance upon Rome itself—a measure which was strongly urged upon him by Maharbal. "Only send me on with the cavalry," said this officer, "and within five days thou shalt sup in the Capitol." But his army was not skilled in siege operations, he had no means of investing the city, and an immediate attack on Rome might have involved a repulse which would have dimmed the glory of his recent victory.

He waited in Apulia to see the effect on Italy; and now the allies began to waver. The Hirpinians, all the Samnites (except the Pentrian tribe), and almost all the Apulians, Lucanians, and Bruttians, declared in favour of Carthage. The whole of the south of Italy seemed lost to the Romans, but the effect of these defections was not so decisive as might at first appear; for the Latin colonies, which still, without exception, remained faithful, gave the Romans a powerful hold upon the revolted districts; and the Greek cities on the coast, though mostly disposed to join the Carthaginians, were restrained by the presence of Roman garrisons. Hence it became necessary to support the insurrection in the different parts of Italy with a Carthaginian force.

Defection of the Italian allies.

Hannibal marched first into Samnium, and from thence into Campania, where he obtained possession of the important city of Capua, the gates of which were opened to him by the popular party. Here he established his army in winter quarters. Thus ends the first period of the war, in which Hannibal had met with uninterrupted success. Three great victories in three years, followed by the revolt of a city scarcely inferior to Rome itself in importance, seemed to promise a speedy termination of the war.

Loss of Capua.

NOTE ON HANNIBAL'S PASSAGE ACROSS THE ALPS.

(See p. 103.)

The narrative in the text is taken from that of the Greek historian Polybius, which is certainly by far the most trustworthy that has descended to us: but that author has nowhere clearly stated by which of the passes across the Alps Hannibal effected his march; and this question has given rise to much controversy both in ancient and modern times. Into this discussion our limits will not allow us to enter, but the following may be briefly stated as the general results:—1. That after a careful examination of the text of Polybius, and comparison of the different localities, his narrative will be found on the whole to agree best with the supposition that Hannibal crossed the Graian Alps (*Little St. Bernard*) by a pass which led into the territory of the Salassi and Insubres. 2. That Caelius Antipater certainly represented him as taking this route (Liv. xxi. 38); and as he is known to have followed the Greek history of Silenus, who is said to have accompanied Hannibal in many of his campaigns, his authority is of the greatest weight. 3. That Livy and Strabo, on the contrary, both suppose him to have crossed the Cottian Alps (*Mont Genèvre*) by a pass which led into the territory of the Taurini. But the main argument that appears to have weighed with Livy, as it has done with several modern writers on the subject, is the assumption that Hannibal descended in the first instance into the country of the Taurini, which is opposed to the direct testimony of Polybius, who says expressly that he descended among the Insubres, and *subsequently* mentions his attack on the Taurini. 4. That, as according to Livy himself (xxi. 29) the Gallic emissaries who acted as Hannibal's guides were Boii, it was natural that these should conduct him by the passage that led directly into the territory of their allies and brothers-in-arms the Insubres, rather than into that of the Taurini, a Ligurian tribe, who were at this very time in a state of hostility with the Insubres. And this remark will serve to explain why Hannibal chose apparently a longer route, instead of the more direct one of Mont Genèvre. Lastly, it is remarkable that Polybius, though he censures the exaggerations and absurdities with which earlier writers had encumbered their narrative, does not intimate that any doubt was entertained as to the line of march; and Pompey, in a letter to the senate, written in B.C. 73, alludes to the route of Hannibal across the Alps as something well known. Hence it appears clear that the passage by which he crossed them must have been one of those frequented in subsequent times by the Romans. This argument seems decisive against the claims of a third possible route, that by the *Mont Cenis*, which have been advocated by some modern writers, that pass having apparently never been used till the Middle Ages.—See *Dict. of Greek and Roman Biography*, vol. ii. pp. 334, 335.

Capua.

CHAPTER XIII.

SECOND PUNIC WAR: SECOND PERIOD, FROM THE REVOLT OF CAPUA TO THE BATTLE OF THE METAURUS. 215–207 B.C.

Hannibal at Capua.

CAPUA was celebrated for its wealth and luxury; and the enervating effect which these produced upon the army of Hannibal became a favourite theme of rhetorical exaggeration in later ages. The futility of such declamations is sufficiently shown by the simple fact that the superiority of that army in the field remained as decided as ever. Still it may be truly said that the winter spent at Capua (216–215 B.C.) was in great measure the turning-point of Hannibal's fortune, and from this time the war assumed an altered character. The experiment of what he could effect with his single army had now been fully tried, and, notwithstanding all his victories, it had decidedly failed; for Rome was still unsubdued, and still provided with the means of maintaining a protracted contest. But Hannibal had not relied on his own forces alone, and he now found himself, apparently at least, in a condition to commence the execution of his long-cherished plan—that of arming Italy itself against the Romans, and crushing the ruling power by means of her own subjects. It was to this object that his attention was henceforth mainly directed.

From this time, also, the Romans changed their plan of operations; and, instead of opposing to Hannibal one great army in the field, they hemmed in his movements on all sides, guarded all the most important towns with strong garrisons, and kept up armies all over Italy to thwart the operations of his lieutenants and check the rising disposition to revolt. It is impossible here to follow in detail the complicated operations of the subsequent campaigns, during which Hannibal himself frequently traversed Italy in all directions, appearing suddenly wherever his presence was called for, and astonishing and often baffling the enemy by the rapidity of his marches. All that we can do is to notice very briefly the leading events which distinguished each successive campaign.

Policy of Rome.

The campaign of 215 B.C. was not marked by any decisive events. The consuls were Q. Fabius Maximus (whose plan of conducting the war had been fully vindicated by the terrible defeat of Cannae) and Tiberius Sempronius Gracchus. With the advance of spring Hannibal took up his camp on Mount Tifata, where, while awaiting the arrival of reinforcements from Carthage, he was at hand to support his partisans in Campania and oppose the Roman generals in that province. But his attempts on Cumae and Neapolis were foiled; and even after he had been joined by a force from Carthage (very inferior, however, to what he had expected) he sustained a repulse before Nola, which was magnified by the Romans into a defeat. As the winter approached he withdrew into Apulia, and took up his quarters in the plains around Arpi.

But other prospects were already opening before him. In his camp on Tifata he had received embassies from Philip king of Macedon and Hieronymus of Syracuse, both of which he had eagerly welcomed, and thus sowed the seeds of two fresh wars, and raised up two formidable enemies against the Roman power.

Macedon and Syracuse negotiate with Hannibal.

These two collateral wars in some degree drew off the

attention of both parties from that in Italy itself; yet the Romans still opposed to the Carthaginian general a chain of armies which fettered all his operations; and though Hannibal was ever on the watch for the opportunity of striking a blow, the campaign of 214 B.C. was still less decisive than that of the preceding year. Fabius was again elected consul, and Marcellus was appointed his colleague. Early in the summer Hannibal advanced from Apulia to his former station on Mount Tifata to watch over the safety of Capua; from thence he had descended to the Lake Avernus, in hopes of making himself master of Puteoli, when a prospect was held out to him of surprising the important city of Tarentum. Thither he hastened by forced marches, but arrived too late; Tarentum had been secured by a Roman force. After this his operations were of little importance, until he again took up his winter quarters in Apulia.

Tarentum betrayed to Hannibal.

During the following summer (213 B.C.), while all eyes were turned towards the war in Sicily, Hannibal remained almost wholly inactive in the neighbourhood of Tarentum, still cherishing hopes of making himself master of that important city. Before the close of the ensuing winter he was rewarded with the long-looked-for prize, and Tarentum was betrayed into his hands by two of its citizens. The advantage, however, was incomplete, for a Roman garrison still held possession of the citadel, from which he was unable to dislodge them. The next year (212 B.C.) was marked by important events in Sicily and Spain, to which we must now direct our attention.

Sicily.

Hiero, so long the faithful ally of Rome, died shortly after the battle of Cannae (216 B.C.), and was succeeded by his grandson Hieronymus, a vain youth, who abandoned the alliance of Rome for that of Carthage. But he was assassinated after a reign of fifteen months, and a republican form of government was established in Syracuse. A contest ensued between the Roman and Carthaginian parties in the city, but the former ultimately prevailed, and Epicydes and Hippocrates, two brothers, whom Hannibal had sent as his agents to Syracuse, had to quit the town, and took refuge at Leontini. Such was the state of affairs when the Consul Marcellus arrived in Sicily (214 B.C.). He forthwith marched against Leontini, which Epicydes and Hippocrates defended with a considerable force. He took the city by storm; and, though he spared the inhabitants, executed in cold blood 2000 Roman deserters whom he found among the troops that had formed the garrison. This sanguinary act at once alienated the minds of the Sicilians, and alarmed the mercenary troops in the service of Syracuse.

Defection of Syracuse from Rome.

The latter immediately joined Hippocrates and Epicydes, who had made their escape; the gates of Syracuse were opened to them by their partisans within the walls, and the party hostile to Rome was thus established in the undisputed command of that city. Marcellus now appeared before Syracuse at the head of his army, and, after a fruitless summons to the inhabitants, proceeded to lay siege to the city both by sea and land. His attacks were vigorous and unremitting, and were directed especially against the quarter of Achradina from the side of the sea; but, though he brought many powerful military engines against the walls, these were rendered wholly unavailing by the superior skill and science of Archimedes, which were employed on the side of the besieged.

Siege and capture of Syracuse.

All the efforts of the assailants were baffled; and the Roman soldiers were inspired with so great a dread of Archimedes and his engines,* that Marcellus was compelled to give up all hopes of carrying the city by open force, and to turn the siege into a blockade. The siege was prolonged far on into the summer of 212 B.C., nor did there appear any prospect of its termination, as the communications of the besieged by sea were almost entirely open. In this state of things Marcellus fortunately discovered a part of the walls more accessible than the rest; and, having prepared scaling-ladders, effected an entrance at this point during the night which followed a great festival, and thus made himself master of Epipolai. The two quarters called Tycha and Neapolis were now at his mercy, and were given up to plunder; but Epicydes still held the main city, composed of the island-citadel and Achradina, which formed two separate and strong fortresses. Marcellus, however, made himself master of the fort of Euryelus,

* The story that Archimedes set the Roman ships on fire by the reflected rays of the sun is probably a fiction; though later writers give an account of this burning mirror.

and had closely invested Achradina, when the Carthaginian army under Himilco and Hippocrates advanced to the relief of the city. Their efforts were, however, in vain; all their attacks on the camp of Marcellus were repulsed, and they were unable to effect a junction with Epicydes and the Syracusan garrison. The swamps that had so often saved Syracuse gave rise to a pestilence which carried off both the generals of the Carthaginian army, and led to the entire break-up of their forces. Shortly afterwards the treachery of a leader of Spanish mercenaries in the Syracusan service gave Marcellus the possession of the island, and the citizens immediately threw open the gates of Achradina. The city was given up to plunder, and Archimedes was slain by a Roman soldier, being so intent upon a mathematical problem at the time that he did not answer a question that was asked him. He was deeply regretted by Marcellus, who gave orders for his burial, and befriended his surviving relatives.*

The booty found in the captured city was immense: besides the money in the royal treasury, which was set apart for the coffers of the state, Marcellus carried off many of the works of art with which the city had been adorned, to grace his own triumph and the temples at Rome. This was the first instance of that practice of violent art-collecting which afterwards became so general; and it gave great offence not only to the Greeks of Sicily, but to a large party at Rome itself.

The Scipios in Spain.

The fall of Syracuse was followed, though not immediately, by the subjugation of the whole island by the Romans; but these successes were counterbalanced by the defeat and death of the two Scipios in Spain. We have already seen that P. Scipio, when he landed at Massilia and found himself unable to overtake Hannibal in Gaul, sent his brother Cneius with the army into Spain, while he himself returned to Italy. In the following year (217 B.C.) Publius himself crossed over into Spain, where he found that his brother had already obtained a firm footing. They continued in Spain for several years, during which they gained many victories and prevented Hasdrubal from marching into Italy to

* Upon his tomb was placed the figure of a sphere inscribed in a cylinder. When Cicero was quaestor in Sicily (75 B.C.), he found his tomb near one of the gates of the city, almost hid among briars, and forgotten by the Syracusans.

support his victorious brother. When Hasdrubal was recalled to Africa to oppose Syphax, one of the Numidian kings, whom Rome had stirred up to war against Carthage, the Scipios availed themselves of his absence to extend their power. They gained

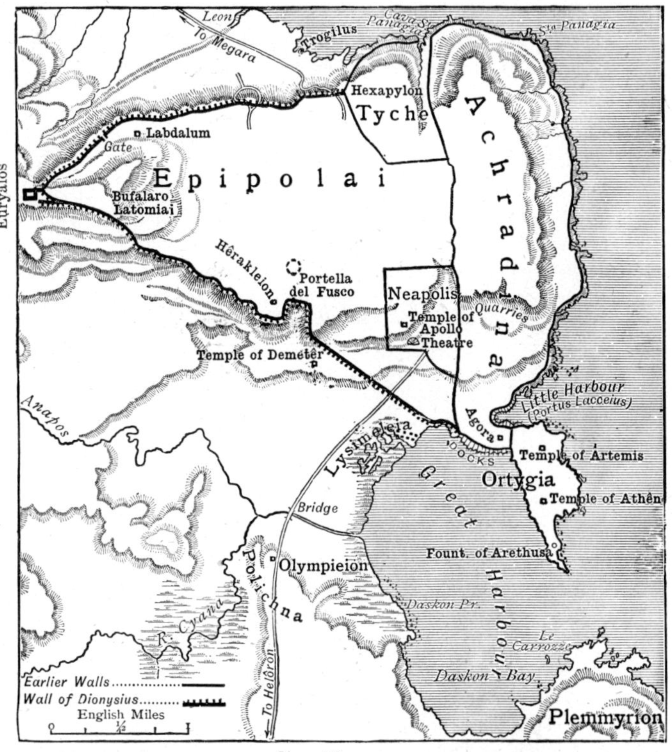

Plan of Syracuse.

over new tribes to the Roman cause, took 20,000 Celtiberians into their pay, and felt themselves so strong in 212 B.C. that they resolved to cross the Iberus and to make a vigorous effort to drive the Carthaginians out of Spain.

They accordingly divided their forces; but the result was fatal. Publius was destroyed, with the greater part of his troops; and Cneius was also defeated, and fell in battle, twenty-nine days after the death of his brother. These victories seemed to establish the superiority of Carthage in Spain, and open the way for Hasdrubal to join his brother in Italy.

Their defeat and death.

Here the two consuls Appius Claudius and Q. Fulvius began to draw together their forces for the purpose of besieging Capua (212 B.C.). Hannibal advanced to relieve it, and compelled the consuls to withdraw; but he was unable to force either of them to fight. Shortly afterwards he returned again to the south to urge on the siege of the citadel of Tarentum, which still held out; and he spent the winter and the whole of the ensuing spring (211 B.C.) in its immediate neighbourhood. But during his absence the consuls had renewed the siege of Capua, and prosecuted it with such activity, that they had succeeded in surrounding the city with a double line of entrenchments. The pressing danger once more summoned Hannibal to its relief. He accordingly presented himself before the Roman camp, and attacked their lines from without, while the garrison co-operated with him by a vigorous sally from the walls.

The Romans besiege Capua.

Both attacks were, however, repulsed, and Hannibal, foiled in his attempt to raise the siege by direct means, determined on the manœuvre of marching directly upon Rome itself, in hopes of thus compelling the consuls to abandon their designs upon Capua, in order to provide for the defence of the city. But this scheme failed in its effect; the appearance of Hannibal before the gates of Rome for a moment struck terror through the city; but a considerable body of troops was at the time within the walls; and the Consul Fulvius, as soon as he heard of Hannibal's march, hastened, with a portion of the besieging army, from Capua, while he still left with the other consul a force amply sufficient to carry on the siege. Hannibal was thus disappointed in the main object of his advance, and he had no means of effecting anything against Rome itself, where Fulvius and Fabius confined themselves strictly to the defensive, allowing him to ravage the whole country without opposition, up to the very walls.

Hannibal marches on Rome.

Nothing therefore remained for him but to retreat, and he accordingly recrossed the Anio, and marched slowly and sullenly through the land of the Sabines and Samnites. From thence he retired to the Bruttii, leaving Capua to its fate. The city soon after surrendered to the Romans. Its punishment was terrible. All the leaders of the insurrection were beheaded; the chief men were imprisoned; and the rest of the people were sold. The city became a village, its territory part of the Roman domain.

Capua recovered by Rome.

The commencement of the next season (210 B.C.) was marked by the fall of Salapia, which was betrayed by the inhabitants to Marcellus; but this loss was soon avenged by the total defeat and destruction of the army of the Proconsul Cn. Fulvius at Herdoniae. The Consul Marcellus, on his part, carefully avoided an action for the rest of the campaign, while he harassed his opponent by every possible means. Thus the rest of that summer too wore away without any important results. But this state of comparative inactivity was necessarily injurious to the cause of Hannibal; the nations of Italy that had espoused that cause when triumphant now began to waver in their attachment; and in the course of the following summer (209 B.C.) the Samnites and Lucanians submitted to Rome, and were admitted to favourable terms.

A still more disastrous blow to the Carthaginian cause was the loss of Tarentum, which was betrayed into the hands of Fabius, as it had been into those of Hannibal. In vain did the latter seek to draw the Roman general into a snare: the wary Fabius eluded his toils. The recovery of Tarentum was the last exploit in the military life of the aged general. From the time of the battle of Cannae he had directed almost exclusively the councils of his country, and his policy had been pre-eminently successful; but the times now demanded bolder measures, and something else was necessary than the caution of the Lingerer to bring the war to a close.

Recovery of Tarentum.

After the fall of Tarentum, Hannibal still traversed the open country unopposed, and laid waste the territories of his enemies. Yet we cannot suppose that he any longer looked for ultimate success from any efforts of his own: his object was doubtless now only to maintain his ground in the south until his brother Hasdrubal should appear in the north of Italy, an event to which he had long anxiously looked forward. Yet the following summer (208 B.C.) was marked by some brilliant achievements. The two consuls, Crispinus and Marcellus, who were opposed to Hannibal in Lucania, allowed themselves to be led into an ambush, in which Marcellus was killed, and Crispinus mortally wounded. Marcellus was one of the ablest of the Roman generals. Hannibal displayed a generous sympathy for his fate, and caused due honours to be paid to his remains.

The following year (207 B.C.) decided the issue of the war in Italy. The war in Spain during the last few years had been carried on with brilliant success by the young P. Scipio, of whose exploits we shall speak presently. But in 208 B.C., Hasdrubal, leaving his colleagues to make head against Scipio, resolved to join his brother in Italy. As Scipio was in undisputed possession of the province north of the Iberus, and had secured the passes of the Pyrenees on that side, Hasdrubal crossed these mountains near their western extremity, and plunged into the heart of Gaul. After spending a winter in that country, he prepared to cross the Alps in the spring of 207 B.C., and to descend into Italy. The two consuls for this year were C. Claudius Nero and M. Livius. Nero was in Southern Italy, keeping a watch upon Hannibal; Livius took up his quarters at Ariminum to oppose Hasdrubal. The latter experienced little loss or difficulty in crossing the Alps. The season of the year was favourable, and the Gauls were friendly to his cause. But instead of pushing on at once into the heart of Italy, he allowed himself to be engaged in the siege of Placentia, and lost much precious time in fruitless efforts to reduce that colony. When at length he abandoned the enterprise, he sent messengers to Hannibal to apprise him of his movements, and concert measures for their meeting in Umbria. But his despatches fell into the hands of the Consul Nero, who formed the bold design of instantly marching with a picked body of 7000 men to join his colleague, and fall upon Hasdrubal with their united forces before Hannibal could receive any tidings of his brother's movements.

Hasdrubal arrives in Italy.

The consul's march was rapid and silent. Hannibal knew nothing of his departure, and in a week Nero covered the 250 miles to Sena, where his colleague was encamped in presence of Hasdrubal. He entered the camp of Livius in the night, that

lius Caesar born B. C. 100 was
~~longed~~ the descendant to an old patrician
mily. He belonged to the
[m]arian party, which was
opposed to the aristocracy &
was then in power. When
still young he married
Cornelia, daughter of Cinna, the most distinguished Marian leader
refused to divorce her at
the command of Sulla, the
dictator. This was the first
proof he gave of the resolution
& determination for which
through life he was distinguished
. his first campaign in Asia
gained a civic crown for
saving the life of a fellow
soldier. In 77. he proved himself
an orator in his accusation of
Dolabella of extortion in Macedonia

his arrival might not be known to the Carthaginians. After a day's rest the two consuls proceeded to offer battle; but Hasdrubal, perceiving the augmented numbers of the Romans, and hearing the trumpet sound twice, felt convinced that the consuls had united their forces, and that his brother had been defeated. He therefore declined the combat, and in the following night commenced his retreat towards Ariminum.

Junction of the Roman armies.

The Romans pursued him, and he found himself compelled to give them battle on the right bank of the Metaurus. On this occasion Hasdrubal displayed all the qualities of a consummate general; but his forces were greatly inferior to those of the enemy, and his Gallic auxiliaries were of little service. The gallant resistance of the Spanish and Ligurian troops is attested by the heavy loss of the Romans; but all was of no avail, and seeing the battle irretrievably lost, he rushed into the midst of the enemy, and fell, sword in hand, in a manner worthy of the son of Hamilcar and the brother of Hannibal. The Consul Nero hastened back to Apulia almost as speedily as he had come, and announced to Hannibal the defeat and death of his brother, by throwing into his camp the severed head of Hasdrubal. "I recognize," said Hannibal, sadly, "the doom of Carthage."

Battle of the Metaurus.

The victory of the Metaurus was, as we have already said, decisive of the fate of the war in Italy; and the conduct of Hannibal shows that he felt it to be such. From this time he abandoned all thoughts of offensive operations, and, withdrawing his garrisons from Metapontum and other towns that he still held in Lucania, collected together his forces within the peninsula of the Bruttii. In the fastnesses of that wild and mountainous region he maintained his ground for nearly four years, while the towns that he still possessed on the coast gave him the command of the sea.

Hannibal.

CHAPTER XIV.

SECOND PUNIC WAR: THIRD PERIOD: FROM THE BATTLE OF THE METAURUS TO THE CONCLUSION OF THE WAR. 206–201 B.C.

AFTER the battle of the Metaurus, Italy was no longer the chief battle-ground, and the main interest of the war was transferred to Spain and Africa. Its conduct is associated with the name of P. Scipio, one of those exceptionally gifted men of whom Rome has so few to show, but whom fate seemed to reserve for her graver crises. The son of that P. Scipio who had fallen in Spain in 212 B.C., he had, even in his early years, acquired the confidence and admiration of his usually unenthusiastic countrymen. His devout Roman mind led him to believe that he was under the special protection of heaven; for all he proposed or executed he alleged the divine approval; and the extraordinary success which attended all his enterprises deepened in him this belief in his own destiny, and even imposed it on others.

Scipio.

P. Scipio is first mentioned in 218 B.C. at the battle of the Ticīnus, where he is reported to have saved the life of his father, though he was then only seventeen years of age. He fought at Cannae two years afterwards (216 B.C.), when he was already a tribune of the soldiers, and was one of the few Roman officers who survived that fatal day. He was chosen, with Appius Claudius, to command the remains of the army, which had taken refuge at Canusium; and it was owing to his youthful heroism and presence of mind that the Roman nobles, who had thought of leaving Italy in despair, were prevented from carrying their rash project into effect. After the death of Scipio's father and uncle, C. Nero was sent out as propraetor to supply their place; but shortly afterwards the senate resolved to increase the army in Spain, and to place it under the command of a proconsul.

Scipio as proconsul in Spain.

The dangerous post was not eagerly sought; and when Scipio, who was then barely twenty-four, presented himself as a candidate, his boldness and merit were held sufficient to counterbalance the illegality of his claim. As he was not invested with any magistracy which conferred the *imperium*, the new device was adopted of creating him Proconsul at the Comitia of the Centuries.*

Capture of New Carthage.

Scipio arrived in Spain in the summer of 210 B.C. He found that the three Carthaginian generals, Hasdrubal son of Barca, Hasdrubal son of Gisgo, and Mago, were not on good terms, and were at the time engaged in separate enterprises in distant parts of the peninsula. Instead of attacking any of them singly, he formed the project of striking a deadly blow at the Carthaginian power by a sudden and unexpected attack upon New Carthage. He gave the command of the fleet to his intimate friend Laelius, to whom alone he entrusted the secret of the expedition, while he led the land-forces by extremely rapid marches against the city. The project was crowned with complete success. The Carthaginian garrison did not amount to more than a thousand men, and before any succour could arrive New Carthage was taken by assault. The hostages who had been given by the various Spanish tribes to the Carthaginians, had been placed for security in the city. These now fell into the hands of Scipio, who treated them with kindness; and the hostages of those people who declared themselves in favour of the Romans were restored without ransom. Scipio also found in New Carthage magazines of arms, corn, and other necessaries; for the Carthaginians had there deposited their principal stores.

* A *consul* was usually, at this time, created *proconsul* by the senate.

The immediate effects of this brilliant success were immense. Many of the Spanish tribes deserted the Carthaginian cause; and when Scipio took the field in the following year (209 B.C.) Mandonius and Indibilis, two of the most powerful and hitherto the most faithful supporters of Carthage, quitted the camp of Hasdrubal Barca, and awaited the arrival of the Roman commander. Hasdrubal was encamped in a strong position near the town of Baecula, in the upper valley of the Baetis (Guadalquiver), where he was attacked and defeated by Scipio. But he succeeded in making good his retreat, and retired into Northern Spain. He subsequently crossed the Pyrenees, and, as we have already told, marched into Italy to the assistance of his brother Hannibal. Scipio, in spite of his brilliant successes, had not fulfilled his direct mission; he had initiated wonderful enterprises, but failed in defending Italy. His only plan now was to complete the conquest of Spain. This was practically effected in 206 B.C. by a second great battle at Baecula, in which a decisive victory was won over Hasdrubal son of Gisgo, and Mago.

Victories at Baecula, and conquest of Spain.

The Carthaginian generals took refuge within the walls of Gades, an old Phoenician settlement, which was almost the only place that now belonged to the Carthaginians; and all the native chiefs hastened to acknowledge the supremacy of Rome. But Spain had not been won by arms alone. The Spanish tribes, always strangely susceptible to personal influence, had felt the magnetic attraction of Scipio's character. His courage and energy, his humanity and his courtesy, had won him their admiration, their obedience, and even their love.

The subjugation of Spain was regarded by Scipio as only a means to an end. He had formed the project of correcting his great blunder by transferring the war to Africa, and thus compelling the Carthaginians to recall Hannibal from Italy. He therefore resolved, before returning to Rome, to cross over into Africa, and secure, if possible, the friendship and co-operation of some of the native princes. His personal influence had already secured the attachment of Masinissa, the son of the king of the Massylians, or Western Numidians, who was serving in the Carthaginian army in Spain; and he trusted that the same personal ascendency might gain the more powerful support of

Negotiations with African chiefs.

Syphax, the king of the Massaeylians, or Eastern Numidians. With only two quinqueremes he ventured to leave his province and repair to the court of Syphax. There he met his old adversary, Hasdrubal son of Gisgo, who had crossed over from Gades for the same purpose; and the two generals spent several days together in friendly intercourse. Scipio made a great impression upon Syphax; but the charms of Sophonisba, the daughter of Hasdrubal, whom the latter offered in marriage to Syphax, prevailed over the influence of Scipio. Syphax married her, and from that time became the zealous supporter and ally of the Carthaginians.

During Scipio's absence in Africa a formidable insurrection had broken out in Spain; but on his return it was speedily put down, and terrible vengeance was inflicted upon the town of Illiturgis, which had taken the principal share in the revolt. Scarcely had this danger passed away when Scipio was seized with a dangerous illness. Eight thousand of the Roman soldiers, discontented with not having received their usual pay, availed themselves of this opportunity to break out into open mutiny; but Scipio quelled it with his usual promptitude and energy.

He crushed the last remains of the insurrection; and to crown his other successes, Gades at last surrendered to the Romans. Mago had crossed over into Liguria, to effect a diversion in favour of his brother Hannibal, and there was therefore now no longer any enemy left in Spain.

Surrender of Gades.

Scipio returned to Rome in 206 B.C., and immediately offered himself as a candidate for the consulship. He was elected for the following year (205 B.C.) by the votes of the centuries, although he had not yet filled the office of praetor, and was only thirty years of age. His colleague was P. Licinius Crassus, the Pontifex Maximus, who could not, by the rules of his order, leave Italy. Consequently, if the war was to be carried on abroad, the conduct of it must of necessity devolve upon Scipio. The latter was anxious to land at once in Africa, and bring the contest to an end at the gates of Carthage; but the older members of the senate opposed the project, partly through timidity and partly through jealousy of the youthful conqueror.

All that Scipio could obtain was the province of Sicily, with permission to invade Africa if he should think it for the advantage of the Republic; but the senate resolutely refused him an army, thus making the permission of no practical use. The allies had a truer view of the interests of Italy than the Roman senate; from all the Italian towns volunteers flocked to join the standard of the youthful hero. The senate could not refuse to allow him to enlist these volunteers; and such was the enthusiasm in his favour that he was able to cross over to Sicily with an army and a fleet, contrary to the expectations and even the wishes of the senate.

Scipio in Sicily.

While busy with preparations in Sicily, he sent over Laelius to Africa with a small fleet to concert a plan of co-operation with Masinissa. But meantime his enemies at Rome had nearly succeeded in depriving him of his command. Although he had no authority in Lower Italy, he had assisted in the reduction of Locri, and after the conquest of the town had left Q. Pleminius in command. The latter had been guilty of such excesses against the inhabitants, that they sent an embassy to Rome to complain of his conduct. Q. Fabius Maximus eagerly availed himself of the opportunity to inveigh in general against the conduct of Scipio, and to urge his immediate recall. Scipio's magnificent style of living, and his love for Greek literature and art, were denounced by his enemies as dangerous innovations upon old Roman manners and frugality. It was asserted that the time which ought to be given to the exercise and the training of his troops was wasted in the Greek gymnasia or in literary pursuits. Though the senate lent a willing ear to these attacks, they did not venture upon his immediate recall, but sent a commission into Sicily to inquire into the state of the army. During the winter Scipio had been busy in completing his preparations; and by this time he had collected all his stores, and brought his army and navy into the most efficient state. The commissioners were astonished at what they saw. Instead of ordering him to return to Rome, they bade him cross over to Africa as soon as possible.

Scipio's campaign in Africa.

Accordingly, in 204 B.C., Scipio, who was now proconsul, sailed from Lilybaeum and landed in Africa, not far from Utica. He was immediately joined by Masinissa, who rendered him the most important services in the war. He commenced the campaign by laying siege to Utica, and took up his quarters on a projecting headland to the east of the town, on a spot which long bore the name of the Cornelian Camp. Meantime the Carthaginians had collected a powerful army, which they placed under the command of Hasdrubal son of Gisgo, Scipio's old opponent in Spain; and Syphax came to their assistance with a great force.

In the beginning of 203 B.C. Scipio planned a night attack upon the two camps occupied by Hasdrubal and Syphax. With the assistance of Masinissa, his enterprise was crowned with success; the two camps were burnt to the ground, and only a few of the enemy escaped the fire and the sword. Among these, however, were both Hasdrubal and Syphax; the former fled to Carthage, where he persuaded the senate to raise another army, and the latter retreated to his native dominions, where he likewise collected fresh troops. But their united forces were again defeated by Scipio. Hasdrubal did not venture to make his appearance again in Carthage; and Syphax once more fled into Numidia. Scipio did not give the Numidian prince any repose; he was pursued by Laelius and Masinissa, and finally taken prisoner. Among the captives who fell into their hands was Sophonisba, the wife of Syphax, whom Masinissa had long loved, and had expected to marry when she was given to his rival. Masinissa now not only promised to preserve her from captivity, but, to prevent her falling into the hands of the Romans, determined to marry her himself. Their nuptials were accordingly celebrated without delay, but Scipio, fearful of the influence which she might exercise over his ally, sternly upbraided him with his weakness, and insisted on the immediate surrender of the princess. Unable to resist this command, Masinissa spared her the humiliation of captivity by sending her a bowl of poison, which she drank without hesitation, and thus put an end to her own life.

Recall of Hannibal.

These repeated disasters so alarmed the Carthaginians that they resolved to recall Hannibal and Mago. Hannibal quitted Italy in 203 B.C., to the great joy of the Romans. For more than fifteen years had he carried on the war in that country, laying it waste from one extremity to another; and during all this period his superiority in the field had been uncontested. The Romans calculated that in these fifteen years their losses in the field alone had amounted to not less than 300,000 men—a statement which will hardly appear exaggerated when we consider the continual combats in which they were engaged by their ever-watchful foe.

As soon as Hannibal landed in Africa the hopes of the Carthaginians revived, and they looked forward to a favourable termination of the war. Hannibal, however, formed a truer estimate of the real state of affairs; he saw that the loss of a battle would be the ruin of Carthage, and he was therefore anxious to conclude a peace before it was too late. Scipio, who was eager to have the glory of bringing the war to a close, and who feared lest his enemies in the senate might appoint him a successor, was equally desirous of a peace. But the war-party had now the ascendency at Carthage; the terms proposed by Scipio, though moderate in themselves, were rejected; and as Hannibal, at a personal interview with the Roman general, could not obtain any abatement of the conditions, he was forced, against his will, to continue the war. Into the details of the campaign, which are related very differently, our limits will not permit us to enter.

Battle of Zama.

The decisive battle was at length fought on the 19th of October, 202 B.C., on the Bagradas, not far from the city of Zama; and Hannibal, according to the express testimony of his antagonist, displayed on this occasion all the qualities of a consummate general. But he was now particularly deficient in that formidable cavalry which had so often decided the victory in his favour; his elephants, of which he had a great number, were rendered unavailing by the skilful management of Scipio; and the battle ended in his complete defeat, notwithstanding the heroic exertions of his veteran infantry. Twenty thousand of his men fell on the field of battle, as many were made prisoners, and Hannibal himself with difficulty escaped the pursuit of Masinissa. Upon his arrival at Carthage he was the first to admit the magnitude of the disaster, and to point out the impossibility of the further prosecution of the war. The terms, however, now imposed by Scipio were much more severe than before. Carthage had no alternative but submission; but the negotiations were protracted for some time, and a final treaty was not concluded till the following year (201 B.C.). By this treaty it was agreed that the Carthaginians were to preserve their independence and territory in Africa, but to give up all claims to any foreign possessions; that they were to surrender all prisoners and deserters, all their ships of war except ten triremes, and all their elephants; that they were not to make war in Africa or out of Africa without the consent of Rome; that they were to acknowledge Masinissa as king of Numidia; and that they were to pay 10,000 talents in silver in the course of fifty years.

Terms of peace.

Soldiers blowing Tubae and Cornua (from Column of Trajan).

Coin of Antiochus the Great.

CHAPTER XV.

WARS IN THE EAST. THE MACEDONIAN, SYRIAN, AND GALATIAN WARS. 214–188 B.C.

Results of the Punic Wars.

THE Second Punic War made the Romans undisputed masters of the western shores of the Mediterranean. Sicily, Sardinia, and Corsica were Roman provinces; Spain owned the Roman supremacy, and Carthage was completely humbled. Rome's immediate object was secured, and here, had her own wishes been consulted, she might have paused; but it is the fate of a conquering nation not to be able to assign any precise limits to its power. The Roman Republic was now the most powerful state in the ancient world, and, as such, was necessarily drawn into the vortex of Eastern politics.

The kingdoms of Asia.

The Greek kingdoms in Asia, founded by the successors of Alexander the Great, bore within them the seeds of decay. The mighty kingdom of SYRIA, which had once extended from the Indus to the Aegean Sea, had now lost some of its fairest provinces. The greater part of Asia Minor no longer owned the authority of the Syrian kings. PONTUS was governed by its own rulers. A large body of Gauls, a portion of the migratory hordes which had burst on Greece and Asia in 280 B.C., had settled in the northern part of Phrygia, which district was now called GALATIA after them. A new kingdom was founded in Mysia, to which the name of PERGAMUS was given from its chief city; and Attalus, who was king of Pergamus during the Second Punic War, formed an alliance with Rome as a protection against Syria and Macedonia. The king of Syria at this time was Antiochus III., who, from his victory over the Parthians, had received the surname of the Great.

Egypt.

EGYPT was governed by the Greek monarchs, who bore the name of Ptolemy. They had, even as early as the time of Pyrrhus, formed an alliance with Rome (see p. 81). The kingdom had since declined in power, and upon the death of Ptolemy IV., surnamed Philopator, in 205 B.C., the ministers of his infant son Ptolemy Epiphănes, dreading the ambitious designs of the Macedonian and Syrian kings, placed him under the protection of the Roman senate, who consented to become his guardians.

Rhodes.

The Republic of RHODES was the chief maritime power in the Aegean Sea. It extended its dominion over a portion of the opposite coasts of Caria and Lycia, and over several of the neighbouring islands. Like the king of Pergamus, the Rhodians had formed an alliance with Rome as a protection against Macedonia.

Macedonia and Greece.

MACEDONIA was still a powerful kingdom, governed at this time by Philip V., a monarch of considerable ability, who ascended the throne in 220 B.C., at the early age of seventeen. His dominion extended over the greater part of Greece, but two new powers had sprung up since the death of Alexander, which served as some counterpoise to the Macedonian supremacy. Of these the most important was the ACHAEAN LEAGUE, which embraced the greater part of the Peloponnesus. The AETOLIAN LEAGUE included at this time a considerable portion of Central Greece. ATHENS and SPARTA still retained their independence, but with scarcely a shadow of their former greatness and power.

Such was the state of the Eastern world when it came into contact with the arms of Rome. The challenge came from Macedon.

First Macedonian War.

We have already seen that during the Second Punic War Philip had been engaged in hostilities with the Roman Republic. Demetrius of Pharos, twice a traitor to his masters, after he had been driven by the Romans from the Illyrian dominions which he had usurped, had taken refuge at the court of Philip, and soon acquired unbounded influence over the mind of the young king. This wily Greek urged him to take up arms against the grasping Republic; and the ambition of Philip was still further excited by the victories of Hannibal. After the battle of Cannae (216 B.C.) he concluded a treaty with Hannibal; but, instead of supporting the Carthaginian army and fleet, his proceedings were marked by an unaccountable degree of hesitation and delay. It was not till 214 B.C. that he appeared in the Adriatic with a fleet, and laid siege to Oricum and Apollonia, which the Romans had retained possession of at the close of the Illyrian War.* He succeeded in taking Oricum; but the arrival of a small Roman force, under the command of M. Valerius Laevinus, compelled him to raise the siege of Apollonia, and to burn his own ships to prevent their falling into the hands of the enemy. For the next three years the war was carried on with unaccountable slackness on both sides; but in 211 B.C. it assumed a new character after the Romans had formed with the Aetolian league an alliance which gave them their first footing in Greece. Into the details of the campaigns which followed it is unnecessary to enter; but the attention of the Romans was soon afterwards directed to affairs in Spain, and the Aetolians were left almost alone to cope with Philip. The Achaeans also joined Philip against the Aetolians, and the latter people were so hard pressed that they were glad to make peace with the Macedonian king. Shortly afterwards the Romans, who were desirous of turning their undivided attention to the invasion of Africa, also concluded peace with him (205 B.C.).

Philip renews hostilities.

The peace, which thus terminated the First Macedonian War, was probably regarded by both parties as little more than a suspension of hostilities. Philip even went so far as to send to the Carthaginians in Africa a body of 4000 men, who fought at Zama under the command of Hannibal. At the same time, he proceeded to carry out his plans for his own aggrandizement in Greece, without any regard to the Roman alliances in that country. In order to establish his naval supremacy in the Aegean Sea, he attacked the Rhodians and Attalus king of Pergamus, both of whom were allies of Rome. He had also previously made a treaty with Antiochus, king of Syria, for the dismemberment of the Egyptian

* See p. 96.

monarchy, which was placed under the guardianship of the Roman people.

It was impossible for the senate to pass over these acts of hostility, and accordingly, in the year after the conclusion of the Second Punic War, the Consul P. Sulpicius Galba proposed to the Comitia of the Centuries that war should be declared against Philip. But the people longed for repose, and rejected the proposition by the almost unanimous vote of every century. It was only by the most earnest remonstrance, and by alarming them with the picture of Philip, like another Hannibal, invading Italy, that they were induced to reverse their decision and declare war (200 B.C.).

Second Macedonian War.

Philip was at this time engaged in the siege of Athens, which had joined Attalus and the Rhodians. The Consul Galba crossed over to Epirus, and Athens was relieved by a Roman fleet; but before he withdrew, Philip, prompted by anger and revenge, displayed his barbarism by destroying the gardens and buildings in the suburbs, including the Lycēum and the tombs of the Attic heroes; and in a second incursion which he made with large reinforcements he committed still greater excesses. For some time, however, the war lingered on without any decided success on either side. The Consul Villius, who succeeded Galba in 199 B.C., effected nothing of importance; and it was not till the appointment of the Consul T. Quinctius Flamininus to the command that the war was carried on with energy and vigour (198 B.C.). He forced his way through the narrow pass of the Aous, which was occupied by the enemy, invaded Thessaly, and took up his winter quarters in Phocis and Locris.

In the following year (197 B.C.) the struggle was brought to a termination by the battle of Cynoscephalae (Dogs' Heads), a range of hills near Scotussa, in Thessaly. The Romans were at first in a dangerous position from which they were only saved by the excellent Aetolian cavalry; but, when once the rigid lines of the Macedonian phalanx had been broken, the slaughter was terrific: 8000 Macedonians were killed and 5000 taken prisoners, while Flamininus lost only 700 men. Philip was obliged to sue for peace, and in the following year (196 B.C.) a treaty was ratified

Battle of Cynoscephalae.

by which the Macedonians were compelled to withdraw their garrisons from the Greek towns, to surrender their fleet, to promise to conclude no foreign alliances without Rome's consent, and to pay 1000 talents for the expenses of the war, half at once, and half by annual instalments in the course of ten years.

The war left the cities of Greece at the mercy of Rome; but the senate shrank from undertaking permanent responsibilities even in Eastern Europe, and when at the ensuing Isthmian games Flamininus solemnly proclaimed the independence and freedom of Greece, this declaration was an outcome of policy as well as of the phil-Hellenic spirit of the Roman general, whom the throngs of Greeks that gathered round him hailed as their liberator.

Greece declared free.

Flamininus, who remained two years longer in the country, seems to have been actuated by a sincere desire to restore the internal peace and welfare of Greece; and whenever his actions appear at variance with this object, he was under the influence of the policy of the Republic. Thus, though he made war upon Nabis, the tyrant of Sparta, and deprived him of the southern portion of Laconia, he did not depose him, but retained him as a useful check upon the Achaeans. When Flamininus returned to Italy in 194 B.C., he withdrew the Roman garrisons from all the Greek towns, even from Corinth, Chalcis, and Demetrias, the three strongest fortresses in the country, which were called the Fetters of Greece. On his departure he convoked an assembly of the Greeks at Corinth, in which he exhorted them to use their freedom wisely, and to remain faithful to Rome. He then returned, after an absence of five years, with a reputation second only to that of Scipio Africanus, and celebrated a splendid triumph.

It has been already mentioned that Philip had formed an alliance with Antiochus III., king of Syria, surnamed the Great, for the dismemberment of the Egyptian monarchy. During the war between Philip and the Romans, Antiochus had occupied Asia Minor, and was preparing to cross into Greece. Upon the conclusion of this war Flamininus sternly forbade him to set foot in Europe, and for a time he shrank from a contest with the victorious arms of Rome. But the Aetolians, who had fought on the Roman side,

Antiochus of Syria.

were discontented with the arrangements of Flamininus. Their arrogance led them to claim the chief merit of the victory of Cynoscephalae, and their cupidity desired a larger share in the spoils of the war. Flamininus had scarcely quitted Greece before the Aetolians endeavoured to persuade Philip, Nabis, and Antiochus to enter into a league against the Romans. Philip at once refused, but Nabis took up arms, and Antiochus willingly entered into the designs of the Aetolians. At this time Hannibal appeared as an exile at the Syrian court. After the Second Punic War he had set himself to work, like his father Hamilcar at the end of the previous war, to prepare means for renewing the contest at no distant period. One of these means was a reform in the constitution of Carthage; to establish his power, he limited the term of office of the 104 to a year, and thus made the government more democratic; but the oligarchs avenged themselves by denouncing him to the Romans as engaged in negotiations with Antiochus to induce him to take up arms against Rome. The senate sent envoys to Carthage to inquire into these charges; and Hannibal, seeing that his enemies were too strong for him, secretly took flight, and reached the Syrian court in safety.

He was received with the highest honours, and urged the king to place an army at his disposal with which he might invade Italy. But Antiochus was persuaded by the Aetolians to cross over into Greece, and landed at Demetrias in Thessaly in 192 B.C. The Romans now declared war, and in the following year (191 B.C.) the Consul Acilius Glabrio marched into Thessaly. The king had entrenched himself in the passes of Thermopylae, that he might prevent the Romans from penetrating into Central Greece. But there was, as is well known, a difficult passage across Mount Oeta, by which the Persians had descended to fight with Leonidas.

Antiochus crosses to Greece.

This passage was now forced by M. Cato, who was serving as one of the consul's lieutenants, and, as soon as he appeared in the rear of the Syrian army, they fled in confusion, and the battle was won. Antiochus now hastened back to Asia, abandoning all further hopes of conquest in Greece. As soon as he had placed the sea between himself and the Romans, he thought that he was safe; but Hannibal warned him

His retreat.

of his error, and said that he wondered that the Romans had not already followed him.

Next year (190 B.C.) L. Cornelius Scipio, the brother of the great Africanus, and C. Laelius, the intimate friend of the latter, were consuls. L. Scipio was anxious to have the command of the war against Antiochus; but the senate had not much confidence in his ability, and it was only in consequence of his brother Africanus offering to serve under him as his lieutenant that he obtained the command which he desired.

Roman invasion of Asia.

Meantime Antiochus had collected a vast army from all parts of his dominions, and, advancing northwards from Ephesus, laid waste the kingdom of Pergamus. But upon the approach of the Roman army, which entered Asia by crossing the Hellespont, Antiochus retreated southwards; and the decisive battle was fought near Magnesia at the foot of Mount Sipylus. The Romans obtained an easy and bloodless victory over the vast but disorderly rabble of the Syrian monarch. Only 400 Romans fell, while Antiochus lost 53,000 men. He at once gave up the contest in despair, and humbly sued for peace. Rome left him his kingdom of Syria, but forced him to abandon all claim to the territories west of Mount Taurus with the exception of Cilicia (that is, nearly the whole of Asia Minor); he had besides to pay 15,000 Euboic talents within twelve years, to give up his elephants and ships of war, and to surrender to the Romans Hannibal and some others who had taken refuge at his court. Hannibal foresaw his danger, and made his escape to Crete, from whence he afterwards repaired to the court of Prusias, king of Bithynia.

Battle of Magnesia.

L. Scipio returned to Rome in the following year, bringing with him enormous treasures. In imitation of his brother, he assumed the surname of ASIATICUS.

The Romans were now at leisure to punish the Aetolians, who had to make head against the Romans by themselves. The consul M. Fulvius Nobilior (189 B.C.) took their most important town, Ambracia, after an obstinate resistance, and compelled them to sue for peace. This was granted, but on the most humiliating conditions. They were required to acknowledge the supremacy of Rome,

Subjection of the Aetolians.

to renounce all the conquests they had recently made, to pay an indemnity of 500 talents, and to engage in future to aid the Romans in their wars. The power of the Aetolian league was thus for ever crushed, though it seems to have existed, in name at least, till a much later period.

Victories over the Galatians.

The colleague of M. Fulvius Nobilior was Cn. Manlius Volso, who had received command in Asia that he might conclude the peace which had been made with Antiochus, and arrange the affairs of the surrendered territories. But Manlius was not content with the subordinate part allotted to him; and being anxious for booty as much as for glory, he attacked the Galatians in Asia Minor, without waiting for any instructions from the senate, and in direct opposition to the ten commissioners who had been sent to assist him in the work of organization. This was the first instance in which a Roman general had made war without the authority of the senate or the people—a dangerous precedent, which was afterwards only too faithfully followed. The Galatians or Gallograeci were a body of Gauls, who, after laying waste a great part of Asia Minor, had, as we saw, settled in the north of Phrygia, and had there acquired a semi-Greek culture. The assistance which they had given, as mercenary troops, to Antiochus at Magnesia supplied Manlius with a pretext for marching against them. He defeated them in two battles, and compelled them to sue for peace. The campaign greatly enriched Manlius and his legions, as the Gauls had accumulated enormous wealth by their many conquests.

Organization of Asia.

Manlius remained another year (188 B.C.) in the East as proconsul, and, in conjunction with the ten commissioners, formally concluded the peace with Antiochus, and settled the affairs of Asia. Here, as in Greece, Rome steadily refused to acquire territory for herself; the principle adopted was that which we now call the "balance of power," two existing governments being strengthened to check the ambition of the Syrian king. Eumenes, the king of Pergamus, received the Chersonnese, Mysia, Lydia, and part of Caria, and the Rhodians obtained the remaining portion of Caria, together with Lycia and Pisidia. Manlius returned to Rome in 187 B.C., and celebrated a magnificent triumph. But his soldiers, like those of Scipio, had been touched by the corrupting influence of the East. These campaigns, as we shall presently see, exercised a most injurious influence upon the character of the Roman nobles and people, teaching them to love war for the sake of acquiring wealth, and prompting them to acts of robbery and rapine.

"Dying Galatian" (so-called dying gladiator). From the Original in the Museum of the Capitol.

Roman Soldiers (from Column of Trajan).

CHAPTER XVI.

WARS IN THE WEST. THE GALLIC, LIGURIAN, AND SPANISH WARS. 200–175 B.C.

WHILE the Roman legions in the East were acquiring wealth and winning easy conquests, their less fortunate comrades in the West were carrying on a severe struggle with the warlike Gauls, Ligurians, and Spaniards. The Romans had hardly concluded the Second Punic War when they received intelligence that Hamilcar, a Carthaginian officer, had excited several tribes in Northern Italy to take up arms against Rome. These were the Gauls on both sides of the Po, and the Ligurians, a race of hardy mountaineers, inhabiting the upper Apennines and the Maritime Alps.* The Gauls commenced the war in 200 B.C. by the

* See p. 3.

capture and destruction of the Roman colony of Placentia, and by laying siege to that of Cremona, the two strongholds of the Roman dominion in Northern Italy.

Subjugation of the Gauls.

The Romans now set themselves to work, with the characteristic stubbornness of their nation, to reduce these tribes to a thorough subjection. The Insubres and the Cenomani, to the north of the Po, were the first to yield; but the Boii resisted for some years all the efforts of the Romans, and it was not till 191 B.C. that the Consul P. Cornelius Scipio Nasica received their final submission. His progress through their territory was a pitiless slaughter, and he made it one of the claims of his triumph that he had left only children and old men alive.

Organization of Cispadane Gaul.

This warlike people was now thoroughly subdued, and from henceforth Cisalpine Gaul became a Roman province, and gradually adopted the language and customs of Rome. The submission of the people was secured by the foundation of new colonies and the formation of military roads. In 189 B.C. a colony was established at Bononia, now Bologna, in the country of the Boii, and six years afterwards others were also founded at Mutina (Modena) and Parma. A military road made by M. Aemilius Lepidus, consul for 180 B.C., and called the Via Aemilia, was a continuation of the Via Flaminia, and ran from Ariminum past Bononia, Mutina, and Parma to Placentia.

Ligurian War.

The subjugation of the Ligurians was a longer and more difficult task. These hardy mountaineers continued the war, with intermissions, for a period of eighty years. The Romans, after penetrating into the heart of Liguria, were seldom able to effect more than the temporary dispersal of the tribes, which took refuge in their villages and castles—the latter being mountain-fastnesses, in which they were generally able to defy their pursuers. Into the details of these long-protracted and inglorious hostilities it is unnecessary to enter: but the result of these northern wars was of great importance. Roman influence and Italian civilization were firmly established up to the Po, which now practically replaced the Apennines as the boundary of Italy, while the subjection of the Transpadane Gauls closed the gates of the Alps to further Celtic immigrants.

The conquests of Scipio Africanus had driven the Carthaginians out of Spain, and established the Roman supremacy in that country. Accordingly, soon after the end of the Second Punic War (about 197 B.C.), the Romans proceeded to consolidate their dominion in Spain by dividing it into two provinces, each governed by a praetor, which were called Hispania Citerior, or Hither Spain, and Hispania Ulterior, or Further Spain, and divided from each other by the Iberus, or Ebro. But it was little more than the eastern part of the peninsula that was really subject to Rome. The powerful tribes of the Celtiberians in Central Spain, the Lusitanians in Portugal, and the Cantabrians and Gallaecians in the north-west, still maintained their independence. Rome had now for the first time to establish a permanent garrison in a dependency across the sea; for, in order to secure a semblance of tranquillity in Spain, four legions had to be kept in the country. Thus originated the principle of taxing a nation to defray the expenses of its military occupation. A direct tax was imposed on Spain, paid partly in money and partly in kind. The division of the country into two provinces, and the army of occupation, showed that the Romans intended to hold Spain permanently, and this conviction occasioned a general insurrection in both the provinces.

The Spanish provinces.

The Consul M. Porcius Cato, of whom we shall speak more fully presently, was sent to put down this rebellion (195 B.C.). The whole country was in arms; but his military genius and indefatigable industry soon re-established the superiority of Rome. He gained several decisive victories, contrived to set tribe against tribe, and took native mercenaries into his pay. The details of his campaign are full of horrors. We read of the wholesale slaughter of men who had laid down their arms, of multitudes sold as slaves, and of many more who put themselves to death to escape this fate. Cato was not the man to feel any compunctions of conscience in the performance of what he considered a rigorous public task. He boasted of having destroyed more towns in Spain than he had spent days in that country. When he had reduced the whole of Hither Spain to a hollow, sullen, and temporary submission, he returned to Rome, and was rewarded with a triumph.

Cato quells the Spanish insurrection.

The severe measures of Cato only exasperated the Spaniards. They again took up arms, and continued to resist the Roman praetors for the next sixteen years, till Tib. Sempronius Gracchus, the father of the celebrated tribunes, after gaining several brilliant victories over the Celtiberians, granted them an honourable peace. He gave equitable charters to the conquered tribes, while he tried to secure the interest of the Spanish chiefs by attaching them to the Roman military service, and to check the roving habits of the people by the founding of towns. By his wise measures and conciliatory conduct he won the affections of the natives, and induced them to regard the Roman supremacy with greater patience (179 B.C.).

Pacification of Spain by Gracchus.

Two petty wars in the West then engaged for a time the attention of Rome. The Sardinians and Corsicans revolted, and held out for two years against the conqueror of Spain (177–175 B.C.). But Gracchus effected their complete subjugation, and brought to Rome so large a number of captives for sale as to give rise to the proverb "Sardi venales" for anything that was cheap and worthless.

Sardinian and Istrian Wars.

The Istrians, near the head of the Adriatic Gulf, had been conquered by the Romans just before the Second Punic War. But their complete subjugation was now necessary, on account of their proximity to the newly-formed province of Cisalpine Gaul. Accordingly the consuls invaded Istria in 178 B.C., and in the following year the whole people was reduced to submission.

A Roman general addressing his soldiers.

Lictors.

CHAPTER XVII.

THE ROMAN CONSTITUTION AND ARMY.

THE career of foreign conquest upon which the Republic had now entered continued with little or no interruption till the establishment of the Empire. We may here pause to take a brief survey of the form of government, as well as of the military organization by which these conquests were effected.

Equality of the orders.

The earlier history of the Roman constitution has been already related. We have seen how, after a long struggle, the plebeians acquired more than political equality with the patricians. In the Second Punic War the antagonism between the two orders had almost disappeared, and the only mark of separation between them in political matters which was of material importance was the regulation, that, of the two consuls and two censors one must be a plebeian. The other patrician privileges were merely formal. The fictitious ratification of laws passed by the Comitia—the so-called *patrum auctoritas*—was in the hands of the patrician members of the senate; it was they, too, who appointed the interrex, who must himself be a patrician; while certain priestly offices of no political importance—those of the Rex Sacrorum and the three great Flamines—were closed to the plebeians.

The magistrates.

I. THE MAGISTRATES.—Every Roman citizen who aspired to the consulship had to pass through a regular gradation of public offices, and the earliest age at which he could become a candidate for them was fixed by a law passed in 179 B.C., and known by the name of the Lex Annalis. The earliest age for the quaestorship, which was the first of these magistracies, was 28 years; for the aedileship, 37; for the praetorship, 40; and for the consulship, 43.

All magistrates at Rome were divided into *curules* and those who were not curules. The Curule Magistrates were so called because they had the right of sitting upon the *Sella Curulis*, originally an emblem of kingly power, imported, along with other insignia of royalty, from Etruria. They were either (i.) ordinary magistrates, *e.g.* consuls, praetors, and curule aediles; or (ii.) extraordinary, *e.g.* the dictator, the magister equitum, and the interrex.

Quaestors.

1. The *quaestors* were the paymasters of the state. It was their duty to receive the revenues, and to make all the necessary payments for the military and civil services. There were originally only two quaestors, but their number was constantly increased with the conquests of the Republic. Besides two quaestors who always remained at Rome in charge of the treasury, every consul, praetor, or pro-magistrate who conducted a war or governed a province was attended by one of these officials.

Aediles.

2. The *aedileship* was originally a plebeian office, instituted at the same time as the tribunate of the plebs.* To the two plebeian aediles two curule aediles were added in 365 B.C. The four aediles in common had the charge of the public buildings,† the care of the cleansing and draining of the city, and the superintendence of the police. They had also the regulation of the public festivals; and the celebration of the Ludi Magni, or Great Games, was their especial function. Originally they received a sum of money from the state to defray the expenses of these games, but this grant was withdrawn about the time of the First Punic War—a measure

* See p. 38.

† Hence their name, from *aedes*, a temple.

attended with important consequences, since the higher magistracies were thus confined to the wealthy, who alone could defray the charges of these costly entertainments. After the Macedonian and Syrian wars the curule aediles often incurred a prodigious expense with the view of pleasing the people, and securing their votes in future elections.

Next come the magistrates with *imperium*—the praetors and consuls.

Praetors.

3. The institution of the *praetorship* in 366 B.C. has been already narrated. It was an office modelled closely on the consulship; the praetor had the *imperium*, with the attendant powers of summoning the senate and people, jurisdiction and military command; and he was attended by six lictors. There was originally only one praetor, subsequently called Praetor Urbanus, whose chief duty was the administration of civil justice. In 246 B.C. a second praetor was added, who had to decide cases in which foreigners were concerned, and who was hence called Praetor Peregrinus. When the territories of the state extended beyond Italy, new praetors were created to govern the provinces. Two praetors were appointed to take the administration of Sicily and Sardinia (227 B.C.), and two more were added when the two Spanish provinces were formed (197 B.C.). There were thus six praetors, two of whom stayed in the city while the other four went abroad.

Consuls.

4. The *consuls* were the highest ordinary magistrates at Rome, and were at the head both of the state and the army. They convoked the senate and the assemblies of the centuries and of the tribes; they presided in each, and had to see that the resolutions of the senate and the people were carried into effect. They had the supreme command of the armies in virtue of the *imperium* conferred upon them by a special vote of the people. At the head of the army, they had full power of life and death over their soldiers. They were preceded by twelve lictors, but this outward sign of power was enjoyed by them month by month in turn.

The magistrates above mentioned were elected annually, but it was usual to prolong the command of the consuls or praetors in the provinces under the titles of proconsuls or propraetors. In the later times of the Republic it was customary for both consuls and several praetors to remain at Rome during their year of office, and at its close to take the command of provinces, with the titles of proconsuls or propraetors.

Dictator.

5. The *dictatorship*, which occurs so often in the early history of the Republic, disappears altogether after the Second Punic War. As the Republic became powerful, and had no longer to dread any enemies in Italy, there was no necessity for such an extraordinary magistracy as the dictatorship, but whenever internal dangers seemed to require a stronger executive, the senate, with doubtful legality, invested the consuls with dictatorial power.*

Censors.

6. The *censors* were two in number, elected every five years, but holding their office for only eighteen months. The censorship was the crown of a political career, as the office was usually held by an ex-consul. The duties of the censors, which were very extensive and very important, may be divided into three classes, all of which, however, were closely connected.

(*a*) Their first and most important duty was to take the census. This was not simply a list of the population, according to the modern use of the word, but a valuation of the property of every Roman citizen. This valuation was necessary, not only for the assessment of the property-tax, but also for determining the position of every citizen in the state, which was regulated, in accordance with the constitution of Servius Tullius, by the amount of his property. Accordingly, the censors had to draw up lists of the classes and centuries. They also made out the lists of the senators and equites, striking out the names of all whom they deemed unworthy, and filling up all vacancies in both orders.

(*b*) The censors possessed a general control over the conduct and morals of the citizens. In the exercise of this important power they were not guided by any rules of law, but simply by their own sense of duty. They punished acts of private as well as public immorality, and visited with their censure, not only offences against the laws, but everything opposed to the old Roman character and habits, such as living in celibacy, extravagance, luxury, etc. They had the power of degrading every citizen to a lower rank, of expelling senators from the senate,

* This was done by the well-known formula, "Videant," or "Dent operam Consules, ne quid res publica detrimenti capiat."

of depriving the equites of their horses, and of removing ordinary citizens from their tribes, and thus excluding them from all political rights.

(*c*) The censors also had the administration of the finances of the state, under the direction of the senate. They let out the taxes to the highest bidders for the space of a lustrum, or five years.* They likewise received from the senate certain sums of money to keep the public buildings, roads, and aqueducts in repair,† and to construct new public works in Rome and other parts of Italy. Hence we find that many of the great public roads, such as the Via Appia and Via Flaminia, were made by censors.

The senate.

II. THE SENATE.—The senate, originally a mere advising body, had by this time become the real executive government of Rome, and the magistrates, of whom we have been speaking, were only its ministers. This was the result of the inherent weakness of the Roman constitution—the complete dependence of the comitia on a number of magistrates with clashing authority, which rendered popular government impossible. The growth of the senate's power was assisted by the long wars, in which it proved itself the most capable administrative authority, and its influence was strengthened by the mode in which its members were appointed. The senate consisted of 300 members, who held the dignity for life unless expelled by the censors for reasons already mentioned, but who could not transmit the honour to their sons. All vacancies in the body were filled up by the censors every five years, as a rule from those who had held the quaestorship or any higher magistracy, only in exceptional cases from nominees of their own; and, as the censors were thus practically confined in their selection to those who had already received the confidence of the people, the great majority of those who entered the senate already possessed considerable knowledge of political affairs.

The power of the senate was very great. It exercised a control over legislation, since custom dictated that no law should be proposed to the assemblies of the people unless it had first

* These farmers of the public revenues were called *publicani*.

† It is not easy to define with accuracy the respective duties of the censors and aediles in relation to the public buildings; but it may be stated in general that the superintendence of the aediles was more in the way of police, while that of the censors had reference to all financial matters.

received the approval of the senate. In many cases "Senatus Consulta" * came to usurp the place of laws, and there were some spheres of administration in which the senate's right to decide without reference to the people was unquestioned. This was especially the case in matters affecting finance, the provinces, and all foreign relations. It had usurped the direction of finance at an early period, and the quaestors were entirely under its control. The senate assigned the provinces into which the consuls and praetors were to be sent, it prolonged the command of a general or superseded him at its pleasure, and on his return it granted or refused him a triumph. It determined the manner in which a war was to be conducted, and the number of troops to be levied; it alone carried on negotiations with foreign states, and all ambassadors were appointed from its own body.

III. THE POPULAR ASSEMBLIES.—1. The *Comitia Curiata* had become a mere form as early as the First Punic War. The gradual decline of its power has been already traced. It continued to meet for the transaction of certain matters, such as the ratification of the *imperium*, but was represented simply by thirty lictors.

Comitia Curiata.

2. The constitution of the *Comitia Centuriata*, as established by Servius Tullius,† had undergone a great change between the time of the Licinian Rogations and the Punic Wars, the object of which appears to have been to give more power and influence to the popular element in the state. For this purpose the thirty-five tribes were taken as the basis of the new constitution of the centuries. Each tribe was divided into five property classes, and each classis was subdivided into two centuries, one of seniores and the other of juniores. Each tribe would thus contain ten centuries, and consequently the thirty-five tribes would have 350 centuries, so that, with the eighteen centuries of the knights, and five centuries of smiths, horn-blowers, and *capite censi*,‡ the total number of the centuries would be 373.

Comitia Centuriata.

The Comitia of the Centuries still retained the election of the magistrates with *imperium*, the power of declaring war and making peace, and also the highest judicial functions. Accusations

* A *Senatus consultum* was so called because the consul or other presiding magistrate who brought a matter before the senate was said *Senatum consulere*.

† See p. 25. ‡ See p. 24.

for treason were brought before the centuries, and appeals against capital sentences could be heard only by this body.*

3. The assembly of the plebs (*concilium plebis tributim*) obtained its superior influence and power mainly through its tribunes. The assembly of the whole people by tribes (*comitia tributa populi*), being summoned and presided over by consuls or praetors, was, like that of the centuries, to a great extent an instrument in the hands of the senate. But the plebeian assembly, being guided by its own magistrates, and representing the popular element, was frequently opposed to the senate, and took an active part in the internal administration of the state. The *plebiscita* of this assembly had the same force as the *leges* of the two assemblies of the populus. There were thus two legal sovereigns at Rome, the populus and the plebs, each independent of the other; but this dual control only strengthened the power of the actual sovereign, the senate.

The two assemblies of the tribes.

The tribunate had changed its character since its original institution, and, though it could still be held only by plebeians, it had practically become a magistracy of the state. The right of intercession possessed by the tribunes was extended to all matters; thus they could prevent the consuls from summoning the senate, and from proposing laws to the Comitia of the People. As their persons were sacred, the senate could exercise no control over them, while they, on the contrary, could seize even a consul or a censor and throw him into prison. But this vast power really worked in the interest of the senate; for out of the large college of ten tribunes it was certain that one at least could be found to put his veto upon the acts of his colleagues or other magistrates. It was, in fact, through the tribunate that the senate was able to keep all the magistrates in check.

The tribunate.

IV. FINANCE.—The ordinary expenditure of the Roman state was not large. All the magistrates discharged their duties without pay; and the allied troops, which formed so large a portion of a Roman army, were maintained by the allies themselves. The expenses of war were defrayed by a property-tax called *tributum*, which was usually one in a

Finance.

* The technical word for this appeal was *provocatio*. The word *appellatio* signified an appeal from one magistrate to another.

thousand, or one-tenth per cent., but after the last war with Macedonia the treasury received such large sums from the provinces that the tributum was abolished. From this time the expenses of the state were almost entirely defrayed by the taxes levied in the provinces. The other revenues of the state, which bore the general name of *vectigalia*, were common to Italy and the provinces. They consisted of the rents arising from public lands, forests, mines, salt-works, etc., and of harbour dues; but no direct taxation, and no indirect tax on private lands, was imposed on the Italian towns.

The provinces.

V. THE PROVINCES.—The provinces were territorial districts placed under the command of magistrates with *imperium*; those where large military forces were required were generally under proconsuls, the rest under propraetors. But it was the cities within the provinces rather than the provinces themselves which were the units of government. Some of these cities were free and paid no tribute, and these were entirely exempt from the governor's control. Far the greater part, however, paid tribute, either a direct tax (*stipendium*) paid generally in money, or a proportion of their produce (*vectigal*), such as the tithes collected in Sicily, Sardinia, and afterwards in Asia. Over these tributary states the governor possessed full criminal and civil jurisdiction, and in the winter months went on circuit, holding courts in the leading cities of his province. The summer months were, in the case of military provinces, usually spent in the camp. When it is remembered that none of the restraints on the *imperium* which existed at Rome—such as the veto of a colleague, the *provocatio* to the people, or the control of the senate—were to be found in the provinces, it is easy to understand the almost regal position held by the governor, and the evil effects of such uncontrolled power on the character of most of its possessors.

The army.

VI. THE ARMY.—The Roman army was originally called *legio*; and this name, which is coeval with the foundation of Rome, continued down to the latest times. The legion was, therefore, not equivalent to what we call a regiment, inasmuch as it contained troops of all arms, infantry, cavalry, and, when military engines were extensively employed, artillery also. The number of soldiers who, at different periods, were contained in a legion does not appear to have been absolutely fixed, but to have varied within moderate limits. Originally the legion contained 3000 foot-soldiers, and from the beginning of the Republic until the second year of the Second Punic War the regular number may be fixed at 4000 or 4200 infantry. From the latter period until the consulship of Marius the ordinary number was from 5000 to 5200. For some centuries after Marius the numbers varied from 5000 to 6200, generally approaching to the higher limit. Amid all the variations with regard to the infantry, 300 horsemen formed the regular complement of the legion. The organisation of the legion differed at different periods.

1. *First Period. Servius Tullius.*—The legion of Servius is so closely connected with the Comitia Centuriata that it has already been discussed,* and it is only necessary to state here that it was a phalanx equipped in the Greek fashion, the front ranks being furnished with a complete suit of armour, their weapons being long spears, and their chief defence the round Argolic shield (*clipeus*).

2. *Second Period. The Great Latin War*, 340 B.C.—The legion in 340 B.C. had almost entirely discarded the tactics of the phalanx. It was now drawn up in three lines. The soldiers of the first line, called Hastati, consisted of youths in the first bloom of manhood, distributed into fifteen companies or maniples (*manipuli*), a moderate space being left between each. The maniple contained sixty privates, two centurions (*centuriones*), and a standard-bearer (*vexillarius*). The second line, the Principes, was composed of men in the full vigour of life, divided, in like manner, into fifteen maniples, all heavily armed. The two lines of the Hastati and Principes taken together amounted to thirty maniples, and formed the Antepilani. The third line, the Triarii, composed of tried veterans, was also in fifteen divisions, but each of these was triple, containing three maniples.

3. *Third Period. During the Wars of the younger Scipio.*—Under ordinary circumstances four legions were levied yearly, two being assigned to each consul. But a regular consular army no longer consisted of Roman legions only, for, as Italy became gradually subjugated, the various states under the dominion of Rome were bound to furnish a contingent, and the

* See p. 24.

number of allies usually exceeded that of the citizens. They were, however, kept perfectly distinct, both in the camp and in the battle-field.

The men belonging to each legion were separated into four divisions. 1. 1000 of the youngest and poorest were set apart to form the Velites, the light-armed troops or skirmishers of the legion. 2. 1200 who came next in age (or who were of the same age with the preceding, but more wealthy) formed the Hastati. 3. 1200, consisting of those in the full vigour of manhood, formed the Principes. 4. 600 of the oldest and most experienced formed the Triarii. When the number of soldiers in the legion exceeded 4000, the first three divisions were increased proportionally, but the number of the Triarii remained always the same.

Armour, and mode of fighting.

All three classes wore a metal helmet, a leathern shield and breastplate, and all bore the short two-edged Spanish sword. But the Hastati and Principes carried the light pilum, which was hurled against the enemy, while the Triarii bore the long hasta, or thrusting-spear. The division into maniples was still continued, the advantage of this small tactical unit being that it encouraged an individual mode of fighting suited to any emergency, and that, unlike the unwieldy phalanx, it could manoeuvre on uneven ground. The battle opened with the advance of the Hastati, who hurled their pila at a distance of ten or twenty paces from the enemy, and then charged with the sword. If this charge was not decisive, the Principes advanced, the Hastati retiring through the divisions between the maniples. The Triarii acted as a reserve, to be called out only in the last resort.

Three hundred horse-soldiers were apportioned to each legion, divided into ten troops (*turmae*), out of which three officers were chosen named decuriones.

The infantry furnished by the Socii was for the most part equal in number to the Roman legions, the cavalry twice or thrice as numerous, and both were divided equally between the two consular armies. Each consul named twelve superior officers, who were termed Praefecti Sociorum, and corresponded to the Legionary Tribunes.

4. *Fourth Period. From the times of the Gracchi until the*

*downfall of the Republic.**—After the times of the Gracchi the following changes in military affairs may be noticed:—In the first consulship of Marius the legions were thrown open to citizens of all grades, without distinction of fortune. The legionaries, when in battle-order, were no longer necessarily arranged in three lines, each consisting of ten maniples with an open space between each maniple, but sometimes in two, sometimes in three lines, each consisting of cohorts, with a space between each division. The number of the cohorts, which now became the tactical units, was always ten, and, as the cohorts were always equal to one another, their strength varied with the strength of the legion. The younger soldiers were no longer placed in the front, but in reserve, the van being composed of veterans. As a necessary result of the above arrangements, the distinction between Hastati, Principes, and Triarii, ceased to exist, and the pilum was now made the common weapon of the whole army, the hasta being abolished. The skirmishers, included under the general term Levis Armatura, consisted for the most part of foreign mercenaries possessing peculiar skill in the use of some national weapon, such as the Balearic slingers, the Cretan archers (*sagittarii*), and the Moorish dartmen. When operations requiring great activity were undertaken, such as could not be performed by mere skirmishers, detachments of legionaries were lightly equipped, and marched without baggage, for these special services.† The cavalry of the legion underwent a change in every respect analogous to that which took place with regard to the light-armed troops. The Roman equites attached to the army were very few in number, and were chiefly employed as aides-de-camp, and on confidential missions. The bulk of the cavalry consisted of foreigners, and hence we find the legions and the cavalry spoken of as completely distinct from each other. After the termination of the Social War, when most of the inhabitants of Italy became Roman citizens, the ancient distinction between the Legionarii and the Socii disappeared, and all who had served as Socii became incorporated with the legions.

* We anticipate the course of events in order to give under one view the history of the Roman legion.

† Hence the frequent occurrence of such phrases as *expediti, expediti milites, expeditae cohortes*, and even *expeditae legiones*.

A Roman triumph.

In the course of the history the triumphs granted to victorious generals have been frequently mentioned, and therefore a brief description of them may appropriately close this sketch of the Roman army. A triumph was a solemn procession, in which a victorious general entered the city in a chariot drawn by four horses. He was preceded by the captives and spoils taken in war, was followed by his troops, and, after passing in state along the Via Sacra, ascended the Capitol to offer sacrifice in the Temple of Jupiter. From the beginning of the Republic down to the extinction of liberty, a triumph was recognized as the summit of military glory, and was the cherished object of ambition to every Roman general. After any decisive battle had been won, or a province subdued by a series of successful operations, the general forwarded to the senate a laurel-wreathed despatch containing an account of his exploits. If the intelligence proved satisfactory, the senate decreed a public thanksgiving.* After the war was concluded, the general with his army repaired to Rome, or ordered his army to meet him there on a given day, but did not enter the city. A meeting of the senate was held without the walls, that he might have an opportunity of urging his pretensions in person, and these were then scrutinized and discussed with the most jealous care. If the senate gave their consent, they voted a sum of money towards defraying the necessary expenses, and at the same time, if the general was a city magistrate such as a consul, recognized the full military *imperium*, which ceased at the gates of Rome, as vested in him for the single day. If, on the other hand, the triumphing general was only a pro-magistrate, one of the tribunes applied for a plebiscitum to enable him to hold the *imperium* for the single day; for such a commander possessed no *imperium* at all within the walls, and a special enactment was in this case necessary to render the military pageant possible.

* Called *supplicatio*.

Scipio Africanus.

CHAPTER XVIII.

INTERNAL HISTORY OF ROME DURING THE MACEDONIAN AND SYRIAN WARS. CATO AND SCIPIO.

Effects of Eastern conquests on Rome.

THE conquests of the Romans in the East had exercised a most pernicious influence upon the national character. They were originally a hardy, industrious, and religious race, distinguished by unbending integrity and love of order. They lived with great frugality upon their small farms, which they cultivated with their own hands. But they were stern and somewhat cruel, and cared little or nothing for literature and the arts. Upon such a people the sudden acquisition of wealth produced its natural effects. They employed it in the gratification of their appetites, and in coarse sensual pleasures. Some of the Roman nobles, such as Scipio Africanus, Flamininus (the conqueror of Philip), and others, acquired a love for Greek literature and art. But the great mass of the nation imitated only the vices of the Greeks. Cooks, who had formerly been the cheapest kind of slaves at Rome, now became the most valuable. A love of luxury and a general depravity gradually spread through all classes of society.

Bacchanalian conspiracy.

A striking instance of the growing licentiousness of the times was brought to light in 186 B.C. It was discovered that the worship of Bacchus had been introduced from Southern Italy into Rome and other towns, and that secret societies were formed, which, under the cloak of this worship, indulged in the most abominable vices. A stringent inquiry was made into these practices; the most guilty were put to death; and a decree of the senate was passed, forbidding the worship of Bacchus in Rome and throughout Italy.

Gladiatorial shows.

The increasing love of gladiatorial combats, the gratification of which was now rendered possible by the new wealth of the state, was an indication of the gloomier side of Roman character. These cruel sports are said to have taken their origin from the Etruscans, who were accustomed to kill slaves and captives at the funerals of their relatives. They were first exhibited at Rome in the beginning of the First Punic War (264 B.C.). At first confined to funerals, they were afterwards exhibited by the aediles at the public games, with the view of pleasing the people. The passion for this brutalizing amusement rose to a great height towards the end of the Republic and under the Empire. Great pains were taken with the training of gladiators, who were divided into different classes according to their arms and modes of fighting.

Rise of a new nobility.

Among many other important consequences of these foreign wars, two which exercised an especial influence upon the future fate of the Republic, were the rise of a new nobility and the disappearance of the peasant proprietors. The nobles became enormously rich, and the peasant proprietors almost entirely disappeared. This new nobility rested largely on wealth, and was composed alike of plebeian and patrician families; but it soon became hereditary. Every one whose ancestry had not held any of the curule magistracies * was called a New Man, and was branded as an upstart.† It became more and more difficult for a New Man to rise to office; and thus an aristocracy (hereditary but without primogeniture) was found in the exclusive possession of the government. The wealth its members had acquired in foreign commands enabled them not only to incur a prodigious expense in the celebration of the public games in their aedileship, with the view of gaining the votes of the people at future elections, but also to spend large sums of money in the actual purchase of votes. The first law against bribery ‡ was passed in 181 B.C., a sure proof of the growth of the practice.

Decay of peasant-proprietors.

The decay of the peasant proprietors was an inevitable consequence of these frequent and long-protracted wars. In the earlier times the citizen-soldier, after a few weeks' campaign, returned home to cultivate his land; but this became impossible when wars were carried on out of Italy. Moreover, the soldier, easily obtaining abundance of booty, found life in the camp more pleasant than the cultivation of the ground. He was thus as ready to sell his land as the nobles were anxious to buy it. But money acquired by plunder is soon squandered. The soldier, returning to Rome, swelled the ranks of the poor, and thus, while the nobles became richer and richer, the lower classes became poorer and poorer. In consequence of the institution of slavery there was little or no demand for free labour; and, as prisoners taken in war were sold as slaves, the slave-market was always well supplied. The estates of the wealthy were cultivated by large gangs of slaves; and even the mechanical arts which give employment to such large numbers in the modern towns of Europe, were practised in the

* See p. 142.

† The *Nobiles* were distinguished from the *Ignobiles*. The outward distinction of the former was the *Jus Imaginum*. These imagines were painted masks of wax, representing the ancestors who had held any of the curule magistracies. They were placed on busts in cases in the atrium or reception-hall of the house, and were carried in the funeral procession of a member of the family. Any one who first obtained a curule magistracy became the founder of the nobility of his family. Such a person was himself neither a *nobilis* nor an *ignobilis*. He was termed a *Novus Homo*, or a New Man.

‡ The Latin word for bribery is *ambitus*, literally canvassing. It must not be confounded with *repetundae*, the offence of extortion or pecuniary corruption committed by magistrates in the provinces or at Rome.

main by slaves or freedmen. The poor at Rome were thus left almost without resources; their votes in the popular assembly were nearly the only thing they could turn into money; and it is therefore not surprising that they were ready to sell them to the highest bidder.

Many distinguished men saw with deep regret the old Roman virtues disappearing, and strove vigorously against these corruptions of the national character. Of this party the most conspicuous member was M. Porcius Cato, who set himself up as a type of the old Roman character. He was born at Tusculum in 234 B.C. When a young man the death of his father put him in possession of a small hereditary estate in the Sabine territory, at a distance from his native town. It was here that he had passed the greater part of his early youth, hardening his body by healthful exercise, and superintending and sharing the operations of the farm. Near his estate was a humble cottage, which had been tenanted, after three triumphs, by its owner, M. Curius Dentatus, whose warlike exploits and simple character were often talked of with admiration in the neighbourhood. The ardour of the youthful Cato was kindled. He resolved to imitate the character, and hoped to rival the glory, of Dentatus. Opportunity was not wanting. He took his first military lessons in the campaigns against Hannibal, and gained the favour and friendship of Fabius Maximus. He was also patronized by L. Valerius Flaccus, a Roman noble in his neighbourhood, and a warm supporter of the old Roman manners, who had observed Cato's eloquence, as well as his martial spirit. Encouraged by Fabius and Flaccus, Cato became a candidate for office, and was elected quaestor in 204 B.C. He followed P. Scipio Africanus to Sicily, but there was not that cordiality of co-operation between Cato and Scipio which was supposed to subsist between a quaestor and his proconsul. Fabius had opposed the permission given to Scipio to carry the attack into the enemy's home, and Cato, whose appointment was intended to operate as a check upon Scipio, adopted the views of his friend. Cato was praetor in Sardinia in 198 B.C., where he took the earliest opportunity of illustrating his principles by his practice. He diminished official expenses, walked his circuits with a single attendant, administered justice with strict impartiality, and

Cato.

restrained usury with unsparing severity. He had now established a reputation for pure morality and strict old-fashioned virtue, and was looked upon as the living type and representative of the ideal ancient Roman. To the advancement of such a man opposition was vain. In 195 B.C. he was elected consul with his old friend and patron L. Valerius Flaccus.

During his consulship a strange scene took place peculiarly illustrative of Roman manners. In 215 B.C., at the height of the Punic War, a law had been passed, proposed by the Tribune Oppius, that no woman should possess more than half an ounce of gold, nor wear a garment of divers colours, nor drive a carriage with horses within a mile of the city, except for the purpose of attending the public celebration of religious rites. Now that Hannibal was conquered, and Rome abounded with Carthaginian wealth, there appeared to be no longer any necessity for women to contribute towards the exigencies of an impoverished treasury the savings spared from their ornaments and pleasures, and two tribunes thought it time to propose the abolition of the Oppian law; but they were opposed by two of their colleagues. The most important affairs of state excited far less interest and zeal than this singular contest. The matrons blockaded every avenue to the forum, and intercepted their husbands as they approached, beseeching them to restore the ancient ornaments of the Roman matrons. Even Flaccus wavered, but his colleague Cato was inexorable. Finally, the women carried the day. Worn out by their importunity, the two tribunes withdrew their opposition, and the hated law was abolished by the suffrage of the tribes.

Repeal of the Lex Oppia.

Cato's campaign in Spain during his consulship, which added greatly to his military reputation, has been already related. He afterwards served in Greece under M'. Glabrio, where he distinguished himself at the battle of Thermopylae fought against Antiochus (191 B.C.).

The victory of Zama had made P. Scipio Africanus the first man in the Republic, and for a time silenced all his enemies. They might have remained silenced, had Scipio known how to endure prosperity; but his obvious consciousness of his superiority invited attack from his old enemies, headed by Fabius, and supported by Cato. After the

Scipio.

return of P. Scipio and his brother Lucius from the war against Antiochus, they were charged with having been bribed to give favourable terms to the king, and of having appropriated to their own use a portion of the money which had been paid by Antiochus to the Roman state.

The first blow was directed against Lucius. At the instigation of Cato, the two Petillii, "Tribunes of the people," required him to render an account of all sums of money which he had received from Antiochus. Lucius prepared his accounts, but, as he was in the act of delivering them up, his brother indignantly snatched them from his hands, and tore them in pieces, saying "it was unworthy to call to account for a few thousands a man who had paid millions into the treasury." But this act of insolence appears to have produced an unfavourable impression, and his brother, when brought to trial in the course of the same year, was declared guilty, and sentenced to pay a heavy fine. The tribune ordered him to be dragged to prison, and there detained till security was furnished for the payment of the fine; whereupon Africanus, still more enraged at this fresh insult to his family, rescued his brother from the hands of the tribune's officer, and thus committed an act of treason. The contest would probably have been attended with fatal results had not the tribune, Tib. Gracchus, the father of the celebrated reformer, had the prudence, although he disapproved of the violent conduct of Africanus, to release his brother Lucius from the sentence of imprisonment.

Attack on the Scipios.

The successful issue of the prosecution of Lucius emboldened his enemies to bring the great Africanus himself before the people. His accuser was the Tribune M. Naevius. When the trial came on, Scipio did not condescend to say a single word in refutation of the charges that had been brought against him, but descanted long and eloquently upon the signal services he had rendered to the commonwealth. Having spoken till nightfall, the trial was adjourned till the following day. Early next morning, when the tribunes had taken their seats on the rostra, and Africanus was summoned, he contented himself with reminding the people that this was the anniversary of the day on which he had defeated Hannibal at Zama, and called upon them to neglect all disputes and lawsuits, and follow him to the Capitol, there to return thanks to the immortal gods, and pray that they would grant the Roman state other citizens like himself. Scipio struck a chord which vibrated in every heart; their veneration for the hero returned; and he was followed by such crowds to the Capitol, that the tribunes were left alone in the rostra.

Satisfied with this triumph over the laws of his country, Scipio quitted Rome, and retired to his country-seat at Liternum. The tribunes wished to renew the prosecution, but Gracchus wisely persuaded them to let it drop. There was no room in Rome for a man like Scipio Africanus; he would neither submit to the laws nor aspire to the sovereignty of the state: and he therefore resolved to expatriate himself for ever. He passed his remaining days in the cultivation of his estate at Liternum; and at his death is said to have requested that his body might be buried there, and not in his ungrateful country (183 B.C.).

P. Scipio leaves Rome.

Hannibal perished in the same year as his great opponent. Scipio was the only member of the senate who opposed the unworthy persecution which the Romans employed against their once dreaded foe. Each of these great men, possessing true nobility of soul, could appreciate the other's merits. A story is told that Scipio was one of the ambassadors sent to Antiochus at Ephesus, at whose court Hannibal was then residing, and that he there had an interview with the great Carthaginian, who half seriously declared him the greatest general that ever lived. Scipio had asked, "Who was the greatest general?" "Alexander the Great," was Hannibal's reply. "Who was the second?" "Pyrrhus." "Who the third?" "Myself," replied the Carthaginian. "What would you have said then, if you had conquered me?" asked Scipio in astonishment. "I should then have placed myself above Alexander, Pyrrhus, and all other generals."

Death of Hannibal.

After the defeat of Antiochus, Hannibal, as we have already seen, took up his abode with Prusias, king of Bithynia, and there found for some years a secure asylum. But the Romans could not rest so long as their old enemy remained alive; and T. Flamininus was at length despatched to the court of Prusias to demand the surrender of the fugitive. The Bithynian king was unable to resist; but Hannibal, who had long been in expectation of such an event, took poison to avoid falling into the hands of his implacable foes.

Cato's censorship.

The censorship had always been the organ for the expression of conservative opinion at Rome, and Cato's tenure of this office (184 B.C.) marked an epoch in his life. Reckless of the enemies he was making, he applied himself strenuously to reform. He repaired the water-courses, paved the reservoirs, cleansed the drains, raised the rents paid by the publicani for farming the taxes, and beat down the prices for the public contracts which they undertook. He attacked at once the capitalist class, which, represented by the equites, had now become a power, and the vicious members of the new nobility. His position as censor enabled him to check luxury by levying a heavy tax on costly and useless articles; and he cleansed the senate by the expulsion of worthless members, without regard to rank or name.

His attitude to the new culture.

The strong national prejudices of Cato appear to have diminished in force as he grew older and wiser. He applied himself in old age to the study of Greek literature, with which in youth he had no acquaintance, although he was not ignorant of the Greek language. Himself an historian and orator, the excellences of Demosthenes and Thucydides made a deep impression upon his kindred mind. But throughout life his conduct was guided by prejudices against classes and nations whose influence he deemed to be hostile to the simplicity of the old Roman character. When Eumenes, king of Pergamus, visited Rome after the war with Antiochus, and was received with honour by the senate, and splendidly entertained by the nobles, Cato was indignant at the respect paid to the monarch, refused to go near him, and declared that "kings were naturally carnivorous animals." He had an antipathy to physicians, because they were mostly Greeks, and therefore unfit to be trusted with Roman lives. He loudly cautioned his eldest son against them, and dispensed with their attendance. When Athens sent three celebrated philosophers, Carneades, Diogenes, and Critolaus, to Rome, in order to negotiate a remission of the 500 talents which the Athenians had been awarded to pay to the Oropians, Carneades excited great attention by his philosophical conversation and lectures, in which he preached the pernicious doctrine of an expediency distinct from justice, which he illustrated by the example of Rome herself: "If Rome were stripped of all that she did not justly gain, the Romans might go back to their huts." Cato, offended with his principles, and jealous of the attention paid to the Greek, gave advice which the senate followed: "Let these deputies have an answer, and a polite dismissal as soon as possible."

But the spirit which rejected Greek culture also scorned Greek humanism, and Cato the "old Roman" was an unfeeling and cruel master. His conduct towards his slaves was detestable. The law held them to be mere chattels, and he treated them as such, without any regard to the rights of humanity. After supper he often severely chastised them, thong in hand, for trifling acts of negligence, and sometimes condemned them to death. When they were worn out, or useless, he sold them, or turned them out of doors. He treated the lower animals no better. His war-horse, which bore him through his campaign in Spain, he sold before he left the country, that the state might not be charged with the expenses of its transport. As years advanced he sought gain with increasing eagerness, but never attempted to profit by the misuse of his public functions. He accepted no bribes; he reserved no booty to his own use; but he became a speculator, not only in slaves, but in buildings, artificial waters, and pleasure-grounds. In this, as in other points, he was a representative of the old Romans, who were a money-getting and money-loving people.

Head of Perseus. From a gem in the British Museum.

CHAPTER XIX.

THE THIRD MACEDONIAN, ACHAEAN, AND THIRD PUNIC WARS. 179-146 B.C.

Perseus.

THE Roman senate may have thought that, with an empire in the West and a protectorate over the East, the power of Rome was for a time consolidated. But a movement now began, the final issue of which was to extend far more widely the limits of imperial rule. Rome had really no hold over the irresponsible despots whom she still permitted to exist in the Eastern world, and the actions of the Macedonian king soon attracted her suspicions. The latter years of the reign of Philip had been spent in preparations for a renewal of war; and when, in 179 B.C., his son Perseus ascended the throne, he found himself amply provided with men and money for the impending contest. But, whether from a sincere desire of peace, or from irresolution of character, he sought to avert an open rupture as long as possible, and one of the first acts of his reign was to obtain from the Romans a renewal of the treaty which they had concluded with his father. It is probable that neither party was sincere in the conclusion of this peace, at least neither could entertain any hope of its duration; yet a period of seven years elapsed before the mutual enmity of the two powers broke out into open hostilities. Meanwhile, Perseus was not idle; he secured the attachment of his subjects by equitable and popular measures, and formed alliances not only with the Greeks and the Asiatic princes, but also with the Thracian, Illyrian, and Celtic tribes which surrounded his dominions. The Romans naturally viewed these proceedings with jealousy and suspicion; and at length, in 172, Perseus was formally accused before the Roman senate, by Eumenes, king of Pergamus, in person, of entertaining hostile designs against the Roman power. The attempt to murder Eumenes near Delphi, on his return homewards, of which Perseus was suspected, aggravated the feeling against him at Rome, and in the following year war was declared.

Perseus was at the head of a numerous and well-appointed army, but of all his allies, only Cotys, king of the Odrysians, ventured to support him against so formidable a foe. Yet the war was protracted three years without any decisive result; nay, the balance of success seemed on the whole to incline in favour of Perseus, and many states, which before were wavering, now showed a disposition to join his cause. But his ill-timed parsimony restrained him from taking advantage of their offers, and in 168 B.C. the arrival of the Consul L. Aemilius Paullus completely changed the aspect of affairs.

Third Macedonian War.

Perseus was driven from a strong position which he had taken up on the banks of the Enipeus, forced to retreat to Pydna, and, finally, to accept an engagement near that town. At first the serried ranks of the phalanx seemed to promise superiority; but its order having been broken by the inequalities of the ground, the Roman legionaries penetrated the disordered mass, and committed fearful carnage, to the extent, it is said, of 20,000 men. Perseus fled first to Pella, then to Amphipolis, and finally to the sanctuary of the sacred island of Samothrace, but was at length obliged to surrender himself to a Roman squadron. He was treated with courtesy, but was reserved to adorn the triumph of his conqueror.

Battle of Pydna.

Such was the ending of the Macedonian empire; but the Romans did not annex the territory, although they imposed, as a tribute, one-half of the land-tax that had been formerly paid to the Macedonian kings. The senate decreed that Macedonia should be divided into four independent districts, each under the jurisdiction of an oligarchical council.

Downfall of Macedonian monarchy.

Before leaving Greece, Paullus was commanded by the senate to inflict a terrible punishment upon the Epirotes, because they had favoured Perseus. Having placed garrisons in the seventy towns of Epirus, he razed them all to the ground in one day, and carried away 150,000 inhabitants as slaves. Epirus never recovered from this blow. In the time of Augustus the country was still a scene of desolation, and the inhabitants had only ruins and villages to dwell in.

Epirus ravaged.

Paullus arrived in Italy towards the close of 167 B.C. The booty which he brought with him from Macedonia, and which he paid into the Roman treasury, was of enormous value; and his triumph, which lasted three days, was the most splendid that Rome had yet seen. Before his triumphal car walked the captive monarch of Macedonia, and behind it, on horseback, were his two eldest sons, Q. Fabius Maximus and P. Scipio Africanus the younger, both of whom had been adopted into other families. But his glory was darkened by the death of his two younger sons, one dying a few days before, and the other a few days after, his triumph.

After the triumph Perseus was thrown into a dungeon, but, in consequence of the intercession of Paullus, he was released and permitted to end his days in an honourable captivity at Alba. His son Alexander learned the Latin language, and earned a living as a public clerk in Italy.

The fall of the Macedonian monarchy made Rome the real mistress of the eastern shores of the Mediterranean. The most haughty monarchs trembled before the Republic. Antiochus Epiphanes had invaded Egypt, and was marching upon Alexandria, when he was met by three Roman commissioners, who presented him with a decree of the senate, commanding him to abstain from hostilities against Egypt. The king, having read the decree, promised to take it into consideration with his friends, whereupon Popillius, one of the Roman commissioners, stepping forward, drew a circle round the king with his staff, and told him that he should not stir out of it till he had given a decisive answer. The king was so frightened by this boldness that he immediately promised to withdraw his troops. Eumenes, king of Pergamus, whose conduct during the war with Perseus had

Relations with Eastern powers.

excited the suspicion of the senate, hastened to make his submission in person, but was not allowed to enter Rome. Prusias, king of Bithynia, had the meanness to appear at Rome with his head shaven, and in the dress of a liberated slave. The Rhodians, who had offered their mediation during the war with Perseus, were deprived of Lycia and Caria.

The immediate question was whether the cities of Greece should be allowed to maintain their troublesome independence. Annexation was not immediately resolved on, and Rome contented herself with working through a party favourable to her interests in the cities, especially through Callicrates, a man of great influence among the Achaeans, who, for many years, had acted as the tool of the Roman government. He now denounced more than a thousand Achaeans as having favoured the cause of Perseus. Among them were the historian Polybius, and the most distinguished men in every city of the league. They were all seized and sent to Italy; but, without any judicial investigation, they were kept as hostages and distributed among the cities of Etruria. Polybius alone was allowed to reside at Rome in the house of Aemilius Paullus, where he became the intimate friend of his son Scipio Africanus the younger. The Achaean League continued to exist, but it was really subject to Callicrates. The Achaean exiles languished in confinement for seventeen years. Their request to be allowed to return to their native land had been more than once refused; but the younger Scipio Africanus at length interceded on their behalf, and prevailed upon Cato to advocate their return. The conduct of the aged senator was kinder than his words. He did not interpose till the end of a long debate, and then simply asked, "Have we nothing better to do than to sit here all day long debating whether a parcel of worn-out Greeks shall be carried to their graves here or in Achaia?" A decree of the senate gave the required permission; but when Polybius was anxious to obtain from the senate restoration to their former honours, Cato bade him, with a smile, beware of returning to the Cyclops' den to fetch away any trifles he had left behind him.

Control of the Achaean league.

The Achaean exiles, whose numbers were now reduced from 1000 to 300, landed in Greece (150 B.C.) with feelings exasperated by their long confinement, and ready to indulge in any rash enterprise against Rome. Polybius, who had returned with the other exiles, in vain exhorted them to peace and unanimity, and to avoid a hopeless struggle with the Roman power. Shortly afterwards an adventurer laid claim to the throne of Macedonia (149 B.C.). He was a man of low origin called Andriscus, but he pretended to be the son of Perseus, and assumed the name of Philippus. At first he met with some success, and defeated the Roman praetor Juventius; but, after reigning scarcely a year, he was conquered and taken prisoner by Q. Metellus.

Revolt of Andriscus.

The temporary success of Andriscus had encouraged the war-party in the Achaean League. Polybius had quitted the country to join his friend Scipio in Africa; and Diaeus and Critolaüs, the most violent enemies of Rome, had now undisputed sway in the league. Diaeus incited the Achaeans to attack Sparta, on the ground that, instead of appealing to the league respecting a boundary question, as they ought to have done, they had violated its laws by sending a private embassy to Rome. The Spartans, feeling themselves incompetent to resist this attack, appealed to the Romans for assistance; and in 147 B.C. two Roman commissioners were sent to Greece to settle these disputes. The commissioners decided that not only Sparta, but Corinth, and all the cities recently acquired, should be restored to independence. Serious riots broke out at Corinth, where the Diet was assembled; all the Spartans in the town were seized, and even the Roman commissioners narrowly escaped violence. On their return to Rome a fresh embassy was despatched to demand satisfaction for these outrages.

But the violent and impolitic conduct of Critolaüs, then strategus of the league, rendered all attempts at accommodation fruitless, and, after the return of the ambassadors, the senate declared war against the league. The cowardice and incompetence of Critolaüs as a general were only equalled by his previous insolence. On the approach of the Romans from Macedonia under Metellus, he did not even venture to make a stand at Thermopylae; and, being overtaken by them near Scarphēa in Locris, he was totally defeated, and never again heard of. Diaeus, who succeeded him as strategus, displayed rather more energy and courage, and made preparations to defend Corinth. Metellus had hoped to

The Achaean War.

have had the honour of bringing the war to a conclusion, and had almost reached Corinth when the Consul L. Mummius landed on the isthmus and assumed the command. The struggle was soon brought to a close. Diaeus was defeated in battle; and Corinth was immediately evacuated, not only by the troops of the league, but also by the greater part of the inhabitants.

On entering the city Mummius put to the sword the few males who remained; by orders from the government he sold the women and children as slaves; and, having carried away all its treasures, consigned the city to the flames (146 B.C.). Corinth was filled with masterpieces of ancient art; and Mummius, with an indistinct appreciation of their worth, stipulated with those who contracted to convey them to Italy, that, if any were lost in the passage, they should be replaced by others of equal value! He then employed himself in regulating the whole of Greece; and ten commissioners were sent from Rome to settle its future condition.

Destruction of Corinth.

The whole country, to the borders of Macedonia and Epirus, was formed into one district, under the name of Achaea, derived from that confederacy which had made the last struggle for political existence, but was united with Macedonia as a single province, and the independent history of Greece was at an end.

Province of Macedonia and Achaea.

Carthage, so long the rival of Rome, had fallen in the same year as Corinth. The reforms introduced by Hannibal after the battle of Zama had restored some degree of prosperity to the state; and, though the Roman party obtained the supremacy after he had been compelled to fly to Antiochus, the commercial activity of the Carthaginians restored to the city much of its former influence. Rome looked with a jealous eye upon its reviving power, and encouraged Masinissa to make repeated aggressions upon its territory.

At length the popular party, having obtained more weight in the government, made a stand against these repeated encroachments of Numidia. Thereupon Cato recommended an instant declaration of war against Carthage; but this met with considerable opposition in the senate, and it was at length arranged that an embassy should be sent to Africa to gain information as to the real state of affairs. The ten ambassadors, of whom Cato

Cato urges the destruction of Carthage.

was the chief, offered their arbitration, which was accepted by Masinissa, but rejected by the Carthaginians, who had no confidence in Roman justice. The deputies accurately observed the warlike preparations and the defences of the frontier. They then entered the city, and saw the strength and population it had acquired since the Second Punic War. Upon their return Cato was the foremost in asserting that Rome would never be safe as long as Carthage was so powerful, so hostile, and so near. One day he drew a bunch of early ripe figs from beneath his robe, and, throwing it upon the floor of the senate-house, said to the astonished fathers, "Those figs were gathered but three days ago at Carthage; so close is our enemy to our walls." From that time forth, whenever he was called upon for his vote in the senate, whatever the subject of debate might be, his closing words were, "Delenda est Carthago"—"Carthage must be destroyed." *

Cato's opinion prevailed, and the senate only waited for a favourable opportunity to destroy the city. This soon occurred.

Pretexts for war.

The popular party having driven into exile the powerful partisans of Masinissa, the old Numidian king invaded the Carthaginian territory, and defeated the army which had been raised to oppose him (151 B.C.). This led to a change in the government, and the aristocratical party, once more restored to power, hastened to make their submission to Rome. But the Romans had resolved upon war; and, when the Carthaginian ambassadors arrived at Rome, the two consuls were already levying troops. The ambassadors, knowing that resistance was hopeless, sought to appease the anger of the senate by unconditional obedience. They were ordered to send 300 youths of the noblest families to meet the consuls at Lilybaeum, and were told that the consuls would acquaint them with the further orders of the senate. At Lilybaeum the consuls found the hostages awaiting them, and then promised the Carthaginian envoys that the decision of the senate should be announced to them in Africa. Upon reaching Utica, which surrendered to them in despair, the consuls informed the

* This story appears a strange one until we remember that it was a custom for Roman senators, when called upon for their votes, to express—no matter what the question—any opinion which they deemed of great importance to the welfare of the state. It was, in fact, the only way in which the individual senator could gain the right of initiative.

Carthaginians that, as their state would henceforth be under the protection of Rome, they had no longer any occasion for arms, and must surrender all the munitions of war. Even this demand was complied with; and the Roman commissioners who were sent to Carthage brought to the Roman camp 200,000 stands of arms, and 2000 catapults. The consuls, thinking that the state was now defenceless, threw off the mask, and announced the final resolution of the senate: "That Carthage must be destroyed, and that its inhabitants must build another city ten miles distant from the coast."

Third Punic War.

When this terrible news reached Carthage, despair and rage seized all the citizens. They resolved to perish rather than submit to so perfidious a foe. All the Italians within the walls were massacred; the members of the former government took to flight, and the popular party once more obtained the power. Almost superhuman efforts were made to obtain means of defence; corn was collected from every quarter; arms were manufactured day and night; the women cut off their long hair to be made into strings for the catapults, and the whole city became one vast workshop. The consuls now saw that it would be necessary to have recourse to force; but they had no military ability, and their attacks were repulsed with great loss. The younger Scipio Africanus, who was then serving in the army as military tribune, displayed great bravery and military skill, and, on one occasion, saved the army from destruction. Still no permanent success was gained, and Scipio returned to Rome, accompanied by the prayers of the soldiers that he would come back as their commander. In the following year (148 B.C.) the new Consul L. Calpurnius Piso was even less successful than his predecessors. The soldiers became discontented; the Roman senate and people, who had anticipated an easy conquest, were indignant at their disappointment, and all eyes were turned to Scipio. Accordingly, when he became a candidate for the aedileship for the ensuing year (147 B.C.), he was elected consul, though he was only thirty-seven years old, and had not therefore attained the legal age for the office.

This remarkable man was, as we have already said, the son of L. Aemilius Paullus, the conqueror of Macedonia. He was adopted by P. Scipio, the son of the great Africanus, and is therefore called Scipio Africanus Minor, to distinguish him from his grandfather by adoption. To these names that of Aemilianus is sometimes added to mark the family of his birth, so that his full designation was P. Cornelius Scipio Africanus Aemilianus. His intimacy with the historian Polybius has been already mentioned. He appears from his earliest years to have devoted himself with ardour to the study of literature; and he eagerly availed himself of the superior knowledge of Polybius to direct him in his literary pursuits. He was accompanied by the Greek historian in almost all his campaigns, and, in the midst of his most active military duties, lost no opportunity of enlarging his knowledge of Greek literature and philosophy by constant intercourse with his friend. Nor did he neglect the literature of his own country, for Terence was admitted to his intimacy, and he is even said to have assisted him in the composition of his comedies. His friendship with Laelius, whose tastes and pursuits were so congenial to his own, has been immortalized by Cicero's celebrated treatise "On Friendship."

Scipio the younger.

Scipio landed in Africa in 147 B.C. His first step was to restore discipline to the army. He next took by storm Megara, a suburb of Carthage, and then proceeded to construct a work across the entrance of the harbour to cut off the city from all supplies by sea. But the Carthaginians defended themselves with a courage and an energy rarely paralleled in history. While Scipio was engaged in this laborious task, they built a fleet of fifty ships in their inner port, and cut a new channel communicating with the sea. Hence, when Scipio at length succeeded in blocking up the entrance of the harbour, he found all his labour useless, as the Carthaginians sailed out to sea by the new outlet. But this fleet was destroyed after an obstinate engagement which lasted three days. At length, in the following year (146 B.C.), Scipio had made all his preparations for the final assault. The Carthaginians defended themselves with the courage of despair. They fought from street to street, and from house to house, and the work of destruction and butchery went on for six days. The fate of this once magnificent city moved Scipio to tears, and, anticipating that a similar catastrophe might one day befall Rome, he is said to have repeated the lines of the "Iliad" over the flames

Siege of Carthage.

of Carthage: "The day shall come when sacred Troy shall perish, and Priam and his people shall be slain."

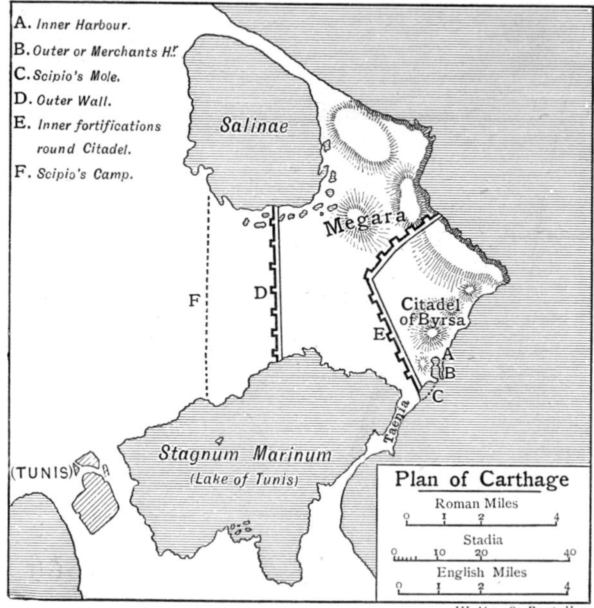

Walker & Boutall sc.

Scipio returned to Rome in the same year, and celebrated a splendid triumph on account of his victory. The surname of Africanus, which he had inherited by adoption, had now been acquired by his own exploits.

Carthage destroyed.

A portion of the Carthaginian dominions was assigned to Utica. The remainder was formed into a Roman province under the name of Africa. The city itself was levelled to the ground, and a curse pronounced upon any who should rebuild it.* Corinth and Carthage,

* C. Gracchus, however, only twenty-four years afterwards, attempted to found a new city upon the ancient site, under the name of Junonia; but evil prodigies at its foundation, and the subsequent death of Gracchus, interrupted this design. The project was revived by Julius Caesar, and was carried into effect by Augustus; and Roman Carthage, built at a short distance from the former city, became the capital of Africa, and one of the most flourishing cities in the ancient world.

the two great commercial cities of East and West, had now fallen; and perhaps in their overthrow we may see not merely the narrow jealousy of the Roman statesman, but the selfish interest of the capitalist class, which was already a power at Rome and aimed at a monopoly of commerce in the conquered world.

The year 146 B.C. marks the close of the second period of Roman imperial policy. The system of a protectorate had broken down in Eastern Europe, and been succeeded by direct imperial rule. It remained only to be seen how long the discredited system could be maintained in Asia; but dangers in the West and internal troubles deferred this question for a considerable period.

CHAPTER XX.

SPANISH WARS, 153-133 B.C. FIRST SERVILE WAR, 134–132 B.C.

THE next twenty years were occupied by serious disturbances in the West. The first trouble came from the indomitable province of Spain. Here the generous policy of Tib. Sempronius Gracchus in 179 B.C.* had secured a long period of tranquillity; but in 153 B.C. the inhabitants of Segeda having commenced rebuilding the walls of their town, which was forbidden by one of the articles in the treaty of Gracchus, a new war broke out, which lasted for many years. The Celtiberians in general espoused the cause of Segeda, and the Consul Q. Fulvius Nobilior made an unsuccessful campaign against them. His successor, the Consul M. Claudius Marcellus, grandson of the Marcellus who was celebrated in the Second Punic War, carried on the war with vigour, and concluded a peace with the enemy on very fair terms (152 B.C.).

Risings in Spain.

The war now took an aggressive turn; for the consul of the following year, L. Lucinius Lucullus, finding the Celtiberians at peace, turned his arms against the Vaccaei, Cantabri, and other nations as yet unknown to the Romans. At the same time, the Praetor Ser. Sulpicius Galba invaded Lusitania; but, though he met with some advantage at first, he was subsequently defeated with great loss, and escaped with only a few horsemen.

Invasion of Lusitania.

In the following year (150 B.C.) he again invaded the country from the south, while Lucullus attacked it from the north. The Lusitanians therefore sent ambassadors to Galba to make their submission. He received them with kindness, lamented the poverty of their country, and promised to assign them more fertile lands, if they would

Treachery of Galba.

* See p. 140.

meet him in three bodies, with their wives and children, in three places which he fixed upon. The simple people believed him. But he meditated one of the most atrocious acts of treachery and cruelty recorded in history. He fell upon each body separately, and butchered them, men, women, and children, without distinction. Among the very few who escaped was Viriathus, the future avenger of his nation. Galba was brought to trial on his return to Rome on account of his outrage; and Cato, then in the eighty-fifth year of his age, inveighed against his treachery and baseness. But Galba was eloquent and wealthy, and the liberal employment of his money, together with the compassion excited by his weeping children and ward, obtained his acquittal.

Viriathus.

Viriathus appears to have been one of those able guerilla chiefs whom Spain has produced at every period of her history. He is said to have been first a shepherd and afterwards a robber, but he soon acquired unbounded influence over the minds of his countrymen. After the massacre of Galba, those Lusitanians who had not left their homes rose as a man against the rule of such treacherous tyrants. Viriathus at first avoided all battles in the plains, and waged an incessant predatory warfare in the mountains; and he met with such continued good fortune, that numbers flocked to his standard. The aspect of affairs seemed at length so threatening that in 145 B.C. the Romans determined to send the Consul Q. Fabius Maximus into the country. In the following year Fabius defeated Viriathus with great loss; but this success was more than counterbalanced by the revolt of the Celtiberians, the bravest of the Spaniards. The war is usually known by the name of the Numantine, from Numantia, a town on the river Douro, and the capital of the Arevaci, the most powerful of the Celtiberian tribes.

Lusitanian War.

Henceforward two Roman armies were employed in Spain, one in the north against the Celtiberians, and the other in the south against Viriathus and the Lusitanians. The war against the Lusitanians was first brought to a conclusion. In 141 B.C. Viriathus surprised the Proconsul Fabius Servilianus in a narrow pass, where escape was impossible. He used his victory with moderation, and suffered the Romans to depart uninjured, on condition of their allowing the Lusitanians to retain undisturbed possession of their own territory, and recognizing him as a friend and ally of Rome. This treaty was ratified by the Roman people; but the Consul Q. Servilius Caepio, who succeeded Fabius in the command in Southern Spain, found some pretext for violating the peace, and renewed the war against Viriathus. The latter sent envoys to Caepio to propose fresh terms of peace; but the Roman consul persuaded them, by promises of large rewards, to murder their general. On their return they assassinated him in his own tent, and made their escape to the Roman camp before the Lusitanians were aware of the death of their chief. But, when the murderers claimed their reward, the consul coolly told them that the Romans did not approve of the murder of a general by his own soldiers. The Lusitanians continued in arms a little longer, but the war was virtually terminated by the death of Viriathus. Their country was finally reduced to subjection by the Consul D. Junius Brutus in 138 B.C., who also crossed the rivers Douro and Minho, and received the surname of Callaïcus in consequence of his receiving the submission of the Callaïci, or Gallaeci, a people in the north-west of Spain.

Numantine War. Defeat of Mancinus.

The war against the Celtiberians was at first conducted with success by the Consul Q. Metellus Macedonicus, who during his praetorship had defeated the pretender to the Macedonian throne. But the successors of Metellus experienced repeated disasters, and at length in 137 B.C. the Consul C. Hostilius Mancinus was entirely surrounded by the Celtiberians, and forced to sign a peace in which he recognized their independence. He only obtained these terms on condition that his quaestor, Tib. Sempronius Gracchus, who was greatly respected by the Spaniards for his father's sake, should become responsible for the execution of the treaty. The senate refused to ratify it, and went through the hypocritical ceremony of delivering over Mancinus bound and naked to the enemy. But the Numantines, like the Samnites in a similar case, declined to accept the offering.

Appointment of Scipio.

The war continued to drag on; and the people now called upon Scipio Africanus to bring it to a conclusion. We have already traced the career of this eminent man till the fall of Carthage. In 142 B.C. he was censor with L. Mummius. In the administration of the duties of his office he followed in the footsteps of Cato, and attempted to repress the growing luxury and immorality of his contemporaries; but his efforts were thwarted by his colleague. He vainly wished to check in the people the appetite for foreign conquests; and in the solemn prayer which he offered at the conclusion of the lustrum he changed the usual supplication for the enlargement of the Republic into one for its preservation. He was now elected consul a second time, and was sent into Spain in 134 B.C. In his camp before Numantia were two men who were soon destined to play a large part on the stage of history—the Arpinate peasant Marius, and the Numidian prince Jugurtha. Scipio's first efforts were directed, as in Africa, to the restoration of discipline in the army, which had become disorganized and demoralized by every kind of indulgence.

Close of the Spanish wars.

Having brought his troops into an effective condition, he proceeded, in the following year, to lay siege to the town. It was defended by its inhabitants with the courage and perseverance which has pre-eminently distinguished the Spaniards in all ages in the defence of their walled towns. It was not till they had suffered the most dreadful extremities of famine, eating even the bodies of the dead, that they surrendered the place (133 B.C.). Fifty of the principal inhabitants were selected to adorn Scipio's triumph, the rest were sold as slaves, and the town was levelled to the ground. As a result of the two wars, the whole of Spain, with the exception of the northern coast, was now nominally subject to Rome.

During the Numantine War Rome was menaced by a new danger, which revealed one of the plague-spots in the Republic.

Slavery.

We have already had occasion to describe the decay of the free population in Italy, and the great increase in the number of slaves from the foreign conquests of the state.* A system of plantation slavery now grew up, which presented all the worst features of that detestable system. The old domestic servitude of the Romans, in which the slave was a member of the family, had now given place to the plantation system, which left the slave to the mercy of the overseer. Sometimes, where under the changed economic conditions land could not be profitably cultivated, vast territories in Italy had been turned into sheep-walks, where the slave was

* See p. 155.

left to shift for himself, getting his food as best he could; and it required little to change these men, most of whom had known the gift of freedom, into brigands.

It was in Sicily, where the proportion of slaves to free labourers was greater even than in Italy, that the first Servile War broke out. Damophilus, a wealthy landowner of Enna, had treated his slaves with excessive barbarity. They entered into a conspiracy against their cruel master, and consulted a Syrian slave of the name of Eunus, who belonged to another lord. This Eunus pretended to the gift of prophecy, and appeared to breathe flames of fire from his mouth. He not only promised them success, but joined in the enterprise himself. Having assembled to the number of about 400 men, they suddenly attacked Enna, and, being joined by their fellow-sufferers within the town, quickly made themselves masters of it. Great excesses were committed, and almost all the freemen were put to death with horrid tortures. Eunus had, while yet a slave, prophesied that he should become king. He now assumed the royal diadem, and the title of king Antiochus. Sicily was at this time swarming with slaves, a great proportion of them Syrians, who flocked to the standard of their countryman and fellow-bondsman. The revolt now became general, and the island was delivered over to the murderous fury of men maddened by oppression, cruelty, and insult. The praetors, who first led armies against them, were totally defeated; and in 134 B.C. it was thought necessary to send the Consul C. Fulvius Flaccus to subdue the insurrection. But neither he, nor the consul of the following year, succeeded in this object; and it was not till 132 B.C. that the Consul P. Rupilius brought the war to an end by the capture of Tauromenium and Enna, the two strongholds of the insurgents. The life of Eunus was spared, probably with the intention of carrying him to Rome, but he died in prison at Morgantia.

First Servile War.

About the same time Rome obtained her first possession in Asia. Attalus Philometor, the last king of Pergamus, dying childless, bequeathed his kingdom and treasures to the Roman people (133 B.C.). A vigorous attempt was made by Aristonicus, a natural son of Eumenes, the father of Attalus, to resist the bequest. He even defeated the Consul P. Licinus Crassus, who was slain

Province of Asia.

(131 B.C.), but he was himself defeated and taken prisoner in the following year, and the kingdom of Pergamus was formed into a Roman province under the name of Asia (129 B.C.).

The Roman provinces.

Rome now exercised direct government in three continents over foreign domains which were divided into ten provinces. These provinces, with the date of their acquisition, were: 1. Sicily, 241 B.C. 2. Sardinia and Corsica, 238 B.C. 3, 4. The two Spains, Citerior and Ulterior, 205 B.C. 5. Gallia Cisalpina, 191 B.C. 6. Macedonia and Achaea, 146 B.C. 7. Illyricum, probably formed at the same time as Macedonia.* 8. Africa, consisting of the dominions of Carthage, 146 B.C. 9. Asia, including the kingdom of Pergamus, 129 B.C. To these a tenth was added in 118 B.C. by the conquest of the southern portion of Transalpine Gaul between the Alps and the Pyrenees. In contrast with the other portions of Gaul, it was frequently called simply the "Provincia," a name which has been retained in the modern "Provence.'

* Illyricum was, however, not yet treated as an independent province, but appears to have been regarded as an appendage to Cisalpine Gaul.

The Roman Forum, looking west.

CHAPTER XXI.

THE GRACCHI, AND THE ATTACK ON THE GOVERNMENT. 133–121 B.C.

WITH the year 133 begins the internal revolution at Rome which was to find no issue but in the establishment of an Empire. It took the form of an attempt by the people to regain the sovereignty usurped, and in their view misused, by the senate. The first point on which its authority was challenged was one of internal reform, and the first evil which seemed to call for reformation was the decay of the yeoman-farmer class.

Economic condition of Italy.

The more thoughtful Romans had long foreseen the danger with which Rome was menaced by the impoverishment of her free population, and the alarming increase in the number of slaves; but neither they nor the reformers of the present age seem to have understood its cause. It is true that the evil would never have reached its present height if the Licinian Law had been observed; but economic conditions were unfavourable to the existence of a class of peasant-proprietors. Through the importation of cheap grain from the provinces, corn could not be grown productively in Italy: the average Roman preferred to invest his capital in the provinces; and voluntary emigration, which accompanied the investment, was responsible for a great part of the depopulation of Italy which the would-be reformers deplored.

Still, the disappearance of the yeoman class, the backbone of the country, was an undoubted evil, and it was the desire for its restoration that wholly animated the policy of Tiberius Gracchus and partly that of his younger brother Caius. They perished in their attempt at reform, and their violent death may be regarded as the beginning of the Civil Wars which ended in the destruction of freedom, and the establishment of the despotism of the Empire.

The Gracchi.

Tiberius and Caius Gracchus were the sons of Tib. Sempronius Gracchus, whose prudent measures gave tranquillity to Spain for so many years.* They lost their father at an early age, but they were educated with the utmost care by their mother, Cornelia, the daughter of Scipio Africanus the elder, who had inherited from her father a love of literature, and united in her person the severe virtues of the ancient Roman matron with the superior knowledge and refinement which then prevailed in the higher classes at Rome. She engaged for her sons the most eminent Greek teachers; and it was mainly owing to the pains she took with their education that they surpassed all the Roman youths of their age.

Tiberius Gracchus.

Tiberius was nine years older than his brother Caius. The latter had more ability, but Tiberius was the more amiable, and won all hearts by the simplicity of his demeanour and his graceful and persuasive eloquence. So highly was Tiberius esteemed, that as soon as he reached the age of manhood he was elected augur, and at the banquet given at his installation Appius Claudius, then chief of the senate, offered him his daughter in marriage. When Appius returned home and informed his wife that he had just betrothed their daughter, she exclaimed, "Why in such a hurry, unless you

* See p. 140.

have got Tiberius Gracchus for her husband?" Sempronia, the only sister of Tiberius, was married to the younger Scipio Africanus. Tiberius was thus, by birth and marriage, connected with the noblest families in the Republic—the grandson of the conqueror of Hannibal, the son-in-law of the chief of the senate, and the brother-in-law of the destroyer of Carthage.

Tiberius served under his brother-in-law in Africa, and was the first who scaled the walls of Carthage. He was quaestor in 137 B.C., and accompanied the Consul Mancinus to Spain, where he saved the army by obtaining the treaty with the Numantines, which the senate refused to ratify.* In passing through Etruria, on his way to Spain, Tiberius had observed with grief and indignation the deserted state of that fertile country. Thousands of foreign slaves were tending the flocks and cultivating the soil of the wealthy landowners, while Roman citizens had not a clod of earth to call their own. He now conceived the design of applying a remedy to this state of things, and with this view became a candidate for the tribunate, and was elected for the year 133 B.C.

His agrarian law.

Tiberius, however, did not act with precipitation. The measure which he brought forward had previously received the approbation of some of the wisest and noblest men in the state; of his own father-in-law Appius Claudius; of P. Mucius Scaevola, the great jurist, who was then consul; and of Crassus, the Pontifex Maximus. It was proposed to re-enact the Licinian Law of 367 B.C.—which had, in fact, never been repealed—but with some modifications and additions. As in the Licinian Law, no one was to be allowed to possess more than 500 jugera of public land; but to relax the stringency of this rule, every possessor might hold in addition 250 jugera for each of two sons, and the land so retained was to become private property. All the rest of the public land was to be taken away from them and distributed, in lots of thirty jugera, among the poor citizens, who were not to be permitted to alienate these lots, in order that they might not be again absorbed into the estates of the wealthy. An indemnity was to be given from the public treasury for all buildings erected upon lands thus taken away. Three commissioners (triumviri) were to be elected annually by the people in order to carry this law into execution and to adjudicate on all disputes arising from it.

* See p. 175.

The law affected only public lands, but it was none the less regarded as a measure of confiscation. It is true that no prescription can, as a general rule, be pleaded against the rights of the state, but the possessors of the public lands had enjoyed them without question for so long a period that they had come to regard these lands as their private property. In many cases, as we have already said, they had been acquired by *bonâ fide* purchase, and the claim of the state, now advocated by Gracchus, was regarded as downright robbery. Attacks upon property have produced the greatest convulsions in all states, and the Roman landowners were ready to have recourse to any measures to defeat the law. But the thousands who would be benefited by it were determined to support Tiberius at any risk. He told them that "the wild beasts of Italy had their dens, and holes, and hiding-places, while the men who fought and bled in defence of Italy wandered about with their wives and children without a spot of ground to rest upon." It was evident that the law would be carried, and the government therefore resorted to the only means left to them.

Opposition of Octavius.

The senate, partly in the interest of its landowning members, partly because it objected to a measure of reform emanating from the people, induced M. Octavius, one of the tribunes, to put his veto upon the measure of his colleague. The contest was felt to be a duel between the senate and the people; and the immediate result was a political deadlock. Tiberius, after a vain attempt to induce Octavius to withdraw his veto, retaliated by forbidding the magistrates to exercise any of their functions, and by suspending, in fact, the entire administration of the government. But Octavius remained firm, and Tiberius therefore determined to depose him from his office.

Deposition of Octavius.

He summoned an Assembly of the Plebs and put the question to the vote. Seventeen out of the thirty-five tribes had already voted for the deposition of Octavius, and the addition of one tribe would reduce him to a private condition, when Tiberius stopped the voting, anxious, at the last moment, to prevent the necessity of so desperate a measure. Octavius, however, would not yield. "Complete what you have begun," was his only answer to the entreaties of his colleague. The eighteenth tribe voted, and

Tiberius ordered him to be dragged from the rostra. Octavius had only exercised his undoubted rights, and his deposition was clearly a violation of the spirit, if not of the letter, of the Roman constitution. This gave the enemies of Gracchus the handle which they needed. They could now justly charge him, not only with revolutionary measures, but with employing revolutionary means to carry them into effect.

Agrarian commission.

The Agrarian Law was passed without further opposition, and the three commissioners elected to put it in force were, unfortunately for its credit, a family party composed of Tiberius himself, his father-in-law Appius Claudius, and his brother Caius, then a youth of twenty, serving under P. Scipio at Numantia.

Attacks on the prerogatives of the senate.

Tiberius further proposed that the treasures acquired by the recent bequest of Attalus king of Pergamus should be distributed among the people who had received assignments of lands, to enable them to stock their farms and to assist them in their cultivation. He thus attacked two of the most fundamental prerogatives of the senate—its control of the provinces and its control of finance. The exasperation of the nobility was intense, and it was evident that his life would be no longer safe when he ceased to be protected by the sanctity of the tribune's office. Accordingly he became a candidate for the tribunate for the following year.

Attempt at re-election.

The tribunes did not enter upon their office till December, but the election took place in June, at which time the country-people, on whom he chiefly relied, were engaged in getting in the harvest. Still, two tribes had already voted in his favour, when the nobility interrupted the election by maintaining that it was illegal for a man to be chosen tribune for two consecutive years. After a violent debate, the Assembly was adjourned till the following day. Tiberius now became alarmed lest his enemies should get the upper hand, and he went round the forum with his child, appealing to the sympathy of the people and imploring their aid. They readily responded to his appeal, escorted him home, and a large crowd kept watch around his house all night.

Next day the adjourned Assembly met on the Capitol in the open space in front of the Temple of Jupiter. The senate also assembled in the Temple of Faith close by. Scipio Nasica, the leader of the more violent party in the senate, called upon the consul, Mucius Scaevola, to stop the re-election, but the consul declined to interfere. Fulvius Flaccus, a senator, and a friend of Tiberius, hastened to inform him of the speech of Nasica, and told him that his death was resolved upon. Thereupon the friends of Tiberius prepared to resist force by force; and as those at a distance could not hear him, on account of the tumult and confusion, the tribune pointed with his hand to his head, to intimate that his life was in danger. His enemies exclaimed that he was asking for the crown. The news reached the senate. Nasica appealed to the consul to save the Republic, but as Scaevola still refused to have recourse to violence, Nasica sprang up, and exclaimed, "The consul is betraying the Republic! let those who wish to save the state follow me." He then rushed out of the senate-house, followed by many of the senators. The terrified people made way for them; and the fathers, breaking up the benches, armed themselves with sticks, and rushed upon Tiberius and his friends. The tribune fled to the Temple of Jupiter, but the door had been barred by the priests, and in his flight he fell over a prostrate body. As he was rising he received the first blow from one of his colleagues, and was quickly despatched. Upwards of 300 of his partisans were slain on the same day. Their bodies were thrown into the Tiber. This was the first blood shed at Rome in civil strife since the expulsion of the kings, and it was the beginning of the Civil Wars.

Murder of Tiberius Gracchus.

Notwithstanding their victory, the nobles did not venture to propose the repeal of the Agrarian Law, and a new commissioner was chosen in the place of Tiberius. The popular indignation was so strongly excited against Scipio Nasica that his friends advised him to withdraw from Italy, though he was Pontifex Maximus, and therefore ought not to have quitted the country. He died shortly afterwards at Pergamus.

All eyes were now turned to Scipio Africanus, who returned to Rome in 132 B.C. When Scipio received at Numantia the news of the death of Tiberius, he is reported to have exclaimed, in the verse of Homer *—

"So perish all who do the like again!"

---

* *Od.*, i. 47.

The people may have thought that the brother-in-law of Tiberius would show some sympathy with his reforms and some sorrow for his fate. They were soon undeceived. Being asked in the Assembly of the Plebs by C. Papirius Carbo, the tribune, who was now the leader of the popular party, what he thought of the death of Tiberius, he boldly replied that "he was justly slain." The people, who had probably expected a different answer, loudly expressed their disapprobation; whereupon Scipio, turning to the mob, bade them be silent, since Italy was only their step-mother.* The people did not forget this insult; but for a time Scipio's unexpected adhesion to the nobility enabled them to prevent the Agrarian Law of Tiberius from being carried into effect. A chance was offered of checking the Agrarian Law on grounds that did not appear to represent the selfish interests of a class. The Italians settled on Roman public land were alarmed at the prospect of being dispossessed, and Scipio skilfully availed himself of the circumstance to propose in the senate (129 B.C.) that the judicial powers should be taken out of the hands of the commissioners and transferred to the consuls. This measure was equivalent to an abrogation of the laws, and excited fierce hatred against Scipio. In the forum he was attacked by Carbo, with the bitterest invectives, as the enemy of the people; and upon his again expressing his approval of the death of Tiberius, the people shouted out, "Down with the tyrant!" In the evening he went home accompanied by the senate and a great number of the Italians. He retired to his chamber, with the intention of composing a speech for the following day.

Scipio champions the Italians.

Next morning Rome was thrown into consternation by the news that Scipio had been found dead in his room. The most contradictory rumours were circulated, but it was the general opinion that he had been murdered. Suspicion fell upon various persons, but Carbo was most generally believed to have been the murderer. There was no inquiry into the cause of his death (129 B.C.).

Death of Scipio.

But, though the opposition leader was thus treacherously removed, the influence of Scipio's last action was permanent.

* It must be recollected that the mob at Rome consisted chiefly of the four city-tribes, and that slaves when manumitted could be enrolled in these four tribes alone.

The introduction of the question of the Italians disorganized the democratic party by creating a difference of opinion between the popular leaders and their following. The former, thinking they had made a tactical mistake in alienating the Italians from their cause, now attempted to secure their adhesion by offering them the Roman citizenship if they would support the Agrarian Law. As Roman citizens they would, of course, be entitled to the benefits of the law, while they would, at the same time, obtain what they had so long desired—an equal share in protection and political power. But the proposal was far from popular at Rome, for the existing citizens saw that their own importance would be diminished, and their benefits in the Empire lessened, by an increase in their numbers. So strong was this feeling that, when great numbers of the Italians had flocked to Rome in 126 B.C., the Tribune M. Junius Pennus carried a law that all aliens should quit the city. Caius Gracchus spoke against this law, and his friends still remained faithful to the cause of the Italians. In the following year (125 B.C.) M. Fulvius Flaccus, who was then consul, brought forward a Reform Bill, granting the Roman citizenship to all the Italain allies. But it was evident that the Assembly would reject this law, and the senate got rid of the proposer by sending him into Transalpine Gaul.

Proposal to enfranchise the Italians.

In the previous year Caius Gracchus had gone to Sardinia as quaestor, so that the senate had now removed from Rome two of their most troublesome opponents, and the Italians had lost their two most powerful patrons. Bitter was the disappointment of the Italians, who had been buoyed up by hopes and probably by injudicious promises. Fregellae, a town of Latium, and one of the eighteen Latin colonies which had remained faithful to Rome during the Second Punic War, took up arms; but its example was not followed, and it had to bear alone the brunt of the unequal contest. It was quickly reduced by the praetor, L. Opimius; the city was utterly destroyed, and the insurrection, which a slight success would have made universal, was thus nipped in the bud (125 B.C.).

Revolt of Fregellae.

Caius Gracchus had taken very little part in public affairs since his brother's death. He had spoken only twice on political matters; once in favour of a law of Carbo for the re-election of tribunes, and a second time in opposition to the Alien Act of Junius Pennus, as already mentioned. But the eyes of the people were naturally turned towards him. His abilities were known, and the senate dreaded his return to Rome. He had been already two years in Sardinia, and they now attempted to retain him there another year by sending fresh troops to the province without releasing his superior officer from his command. But Caius suddenly appeared at Rome, to the surprise of all parties (124 B.C.). His enemies brought him before the censors to account for his conduct, but he defended himself so ably that not only was no stigma put upon him, but he was considered to have been very badly used. He showed that he had served in the army twelve years, though required to serve only ten; that he had acted as quaestor two years, though the law demanded only one year's service; and, he added, that he was the only soldier who took out with him a full purse and brought it back empty. Caius now became a candidate for the tribunate, and was elected for the year 123 B.C. He was not, like his more single-minded brother, merely a social reformer. His laws, so far as they were not merely animated by revenge, were meant to weaken permanently the authority of the senate; and the democratic programme which he fixed became, without the change of a single item, the heritage of the popular leaders to the close of the Republic. To this main object even his social legislation was subsidiary, and his measures for the amelioration of the poor were but bribes given to the masses to secure their support in his vigorous campaign against the government.

Caius Gracchus.

I. His principal laws for improving the condition of the people were—

Leges Semproniae.

1. The renewal of his brother's Agrarian Law; and an extension of agrarian relief by planting new citizen-colonies in Italy and the provinces. This was the first attempt made at transmarine colonization and at the extension of citizenship to the provinces.

2. A state provision for the poor, enacting that corn should be sold to every citizen at a price much below its market value. This was the first of the *Leges Frumentariae*, which, although to some extent justified by the entire absence of any state provision for the poor, were attended with the most injurious effects.

They emptied the treasury, at the same time that they taught the lower classes to become state paupers, instead of depending upon their own exertions for a living.

3. Another law enacted that the soldiers should be equipped at the expense of the Republic, without the cost being deducted from their pay, as had hitherto been the case.

II. The most important laws designed to diminish the power of the senate were—

1. The law by which the judices were to be taken only from the equites, and not from the senators, as had been the custom hitherto. This was a very important enactment, and needs a little explanation. All offences against the state were originally tried in the Popular Assembly; but when special enactments were passed for the trial of particular offences, the practice was introduced of entrusting the trial to a standing commission formed by a body of judices. This was first done upon the passing of the Calpurnian Law (149 B.C.) for the punishment of provincial magistrates for extortion in their government (*De Repetundis*). Such offences had to be tried before the praetor and a jury of senators, but as these very senators either had been or hoped to be provincial magistrates, they were not disposed to visit with severity offences of which they themselves either had been or were likely to be guilty. The equites, to whom Gracchus now transferred these criminal courts, were not the military order of that name. The title had been extended to denote the upper middle class in the state,* composed of capitalists, publicani, and rich merchants. It was to this class, which was sharply contrasted with the senatorial nobility, that Gracchus gave political recognition; and from this time is dated the creation of a civil *Ordo Equester*, whose interests were frequently opposed to those of the senate, and who therefore served as a check upon the latter.

Lex Judiciaria.

2. Another law was directed against the arbitrary proceedings of the senate in the distribution of the provinces. Hitherto the senate had assigned the provinces to the consuls after their election, and thus had had it in their power to grant wealthy governments to their partisans, or unprofitable ones to those opposed to them. It was now enacted that, before the election of the

Lex de provinciis consularibus.

* See p. 54.

consuls, the senate should determine the two provinces which the consuls should have; and that they should, immediately after election, settle between themselves, by lot or otherwise, which province each should take.

These laws raised the popularity of Caius still higher, and he became for a time the absolute ruler of Rome. He was re-elected tribune for the following year (122 B.C.), for, in the interval that had elapsed between the death of his brother and his first tribunate, re-election to the office had been made possible. M. Fulvius Flaccus, who had been consul in 125 B.C., was also chosen as one of his colleagues. Flaccus, it will be recollected, had proposed in his consulship to give the Roman franchise to the Italian allies, and it was now determined to bring forward a similar measure. Caius therefore brought in a bill conferring the citizenship upon all the Latin colonies, and making the Italian allies occupy the position which the Latins had previously held. This wise measure was equally disliked in the forum and the senate. Neither the influence nor the eloquence of Gracchus could induce the people to view with satisfaction the admission of the Italian allies to equal rights and privileges with themselves.

Lex de civitate danda.

The senate, perceiving that the popularity of Gracchus had been somewhat shaken by this measure, employed his colleague, M. Livius Drusus—who was noble, well-educated, wealthy, and eloquent—to undermine his influence with the people. With the sanction of the senate, Drusus now endeavoured to outbid Gracchus. He played the part of a demagogue in order to supplant the true friend of the people. He gave to the senate the credit of every popular law which he proposed, and gradually impressed the people with the belief that the nobles were their best friends. Gracchus proposed to found two colonies at Tarentum and Capua, and named among the first settlers some of the most respectable citizens. Drusus introduced a law for establishing no fewer than twelve colonies, and for settling 3000 poor citizens in each. Gracchus, in the distribution of the public land, reserved a rent payable to the public treasury. Drusus abolished even this payment. He also gained the confidence of the people by asking no favour for himself; he took no part in the foundation of colonies, and left to others the management of business in which

Counter-proposals of Drusus.

any money had to be expended. Gracchus, on the other hand, superintended everything in person; and the people, always jealous in pecuniary matters, began to suspect his motives. During his absence in Africa, whither he had gone as one of the three commissioners for founding a colony upon the ruins of Carthage, Drusus was able to weaken his popularity still further.

On his return he endeavoured in vain to reorganize his party and recover his power. Both he and Flaccus failed in being re-elected tribunes; while L. Opimius and Q. Fabius, two personal enemies of Gracchus, were raised to the consulship. The two new consuls had no sooner entered upon office (121 B.C.) than they resolved to drive matters to extremities. One of the first measures of Opimius was a proposal to repeal the law for colonizing Carthage, because it had been established upon the site which Scipio had cursed. It was evident that a pretext was only sought for taking the life of Gracchus, and Flaccus urged him to repel violence by force. Caius shrank from this step, but an accident gave his enemies the pretext which they longed for. The tribes had assembled at the Capitol to decide upon the colony at Carthage, when a servant of the Consul Opimius, pushing against Gracchus, insolently cried out, "Make way for honest men, you rascals!" Gracchus turned round to him with an angry look, and the man was immediately stabbed by an unknown hand. The Assembly immediately broke up, and Gracchus returned home, foreseeing the advantage which this unfortunate occurrence would give to his enemies.

Failure of Gracchus.

The senate now resorted to its last weapon; it declared Gracchus and Flaccus public enemies, and invested the consuls with dictatorial powers. During the night Opimius took possession of the Temple of Castor and Pollux, which overlooked the forum, summoned a meeting of the senate for the following morning, and ordered all the partisans of the senate to be present, each with two armed slaves. Flaccus seized the Temple of Diana on the Aventine, and distributed arms to his followers: here he was joined by Gracchus. Civil war was thus declared. After some fruitless attempts at negotiation, the consul proceeded to attack the Aventine. Little or no resistance was made, and Flaccus and Gracchus took to flight, and crossed the Tiber by the Sublician

Death of Caius Gracchus.

bridge. Gracchus escaped to the Grove of the Furies, accompanied only by a single slave. When the pursuers reached the spot, they found both of them dead. The slave had first killed his master and then himself. The head of Gracchus was cut off, and carried to Opimius, who gave to the person who brought it its weight in gold. Flaccus was also put to death, together with numbers of his party. Their corpses were thrown into the Tiber, their houses demolished, and their property confiscated. Even their widows were forbidden to wear mourning. After the bloody work had been finished, the consul, by order of the senate, dedicated a temple to Concord!

Fate of the Gracchan legislation.

The measures of social reform projected by the Gracchi did not long survive their authors. In 121 B.C. the land-allotments were made alienable, and a great deal of the public land, which had been distributed, appears to have lapsed again into the hands of its original possessors; for a law of 111 B.C., passed under the auspices of the senate, declared all such land private property; the slave population did not diminish, nor did the yeoman class increase. But, if the final downfall of the Roman constitution was a worthy object of Roman ambition, C. Gracchus at least had not lived in vain.

A Roman trophy.

CHAPTER XXII.

THE JUGURTHINE WAR AND THE DEFEAT OF THE GOVERNMENT.

118–104 B.C.

Marius.

THE first attack on the senate's government had been foiled, and the failure and death of the Gracchi proved that internal reform could not be forced on the governing corporation. It was now to be assailed on a more vulnerable point—that of imperial administration; their conduct in the Jugurthine War raised against the nobility a more terrible opponent than the Gracchi had ever been, and showed that the leader of the popular party need not be a powerless tribune relying on the fickle votes of the Assembly, but might be an *imperator* at the head of an army. This military leader was found in C. MARIUS. He was a native of Arpinum, first saw service in Spain, and was present at the siege of Numantia in 134 B.C. Here he attracted the notice of Scipio Africanus, and received from him many marks of honour. Scipio, indeed, admitted him to his table; and on a certain occasion, when one of the guests asked where the Roman people would find such another general after his death, he is said to have laid his hand on the shoulder of Marius, and said, "Perhaps here." Through distinguished service in the army Marius reached the honours generally reserved for birth, and was at length raised to the Tribunate of the Plebs in 119 B.C., though not till he had attained the mature age of thirty-six. Only two years had elapsed since the death of C. Gracchus; and the nobles, flushed with victory, resolved to put down with a high hand the least invasion of their privileges and power. But Marius had the boldness to propose a law for the purpose of giving greater freedom at elections; and when the senate attempted to overawe him, he ordered one of his officers to carry the Consul Metellus to prison. Marius now became a marked man. He lost his election to the aedileship, and with difficulty obtained the praetorship (115 B.C.); but he added to his influence by his marriage with Julia, the sister of C. Julius Caesar, the father of the future ruler of Rome. His military abilities recommended him to the Consul Metellus (109 B.C.), who was anxious to restore discipline in the army and to retrieve the glory of the Roman name, which had been tarnished by the incapacity and corruption of the previous generals in the Jugurthine War.

Jugurtha.

The relations into which Rome had entered with the protected kings of Numidia had drawn her into a miserable dynastic quarrel. The aged Masinissa had died in 149 B.C., leaving three sons, Micipsa, Mastanabal, and Gulussa, among whom his kingdom was divided by Scipio Africanus, according to the dying directions of the old king. Mastanabal and Gulussa dying in their brother's lifetime, Micipsa became sole king. Jugurtha was a bastard son of Mastanabal; but Micipsa brought him up with his own sons, Hiempsal and Adherbal. Jugurtha's distinction and popularity excited the fears of the king, and in order to remove him to a distance, and not without a hope that he might perish in the war, Micipsa sent him, in 134 B.C., with an auxiliary force, to assist Scipio against Numantia; but this only proved to the young man a stepping-stone to success. By his zeal, courage, and ability he gained the favour, not only of his commander, but of all the leading nobles in the Roman camp, by many of whom he was secretly stimulated to nourish ambitious schemes for acquiring the sole sovereignty of Numidia; and notwithstanding the contrary advice of Scipio, the counsels seem to have sunk deep into Jugurtha's mind. On his return he was received with every demonstration of honour by Micipsa; nor did he allow his ambitious projects to break forth during the lifetime of the old man. Micipsa, on his deathbed, though but too clearly foreseeing what would happen, commended the two young princes to the care of Jugurtha; but fierce dissensions soon broke out.

Jugurtha seizes Numidia

Shortly afterwards Jugurtha found an opportunity to surprise and assassinate Hiempsal; whereupon Adherbal and his partisans rushed to arms, but were defeated in battle by Jugurtha. Adherbal himself fled for refuge to the Roman province, from whence he hastened to Rome to lay his cause before the senate. Jugurtha had now, for the first time, the opportunity of putting to the test the lessons learnt in the camp before Numantia. He sent ambassadors to Rome to counteract, by a lavish distribution of bribes, the effect of Adherbal's complaints; and by these means succeeded in averting the indignation of the senate; although, even without this inducement, the government would probably not have been unwilling to see the protected kingdom under an able ruler who had won the confidence of the people. Still, the forms of justice were preserved: a decree was passed for the division of the kingdom of Numidia between the two competitors, and a commission of senators sent out; but the commissioners were worked on by Jugurtha, who obtained, in the partition of the kingdom, the western division adjacent to Mauretania, by far the larger and richer portion of the two (116 B.C.).

Capture of Cirta, and massacre of Italians.

This advantage, however, was far from contenting him, and shortly afterwards he invaded the territories of his rival with a large army. Adherbal was defeated in the first engagement, his camp taken, and he himself with difficulty made his escape to the strong fortress of Cirta. Here he was closely blockaded by Jugurtha. The garrison surrendered on a promise of their lives being spared; but these conditions were shamefully violated by Jugurtha, who immediately put to death Adherbal and all his followers (112 B.C.).

Unfortunately, a number of Italian merchants were amongst the massacred, and a piercing cry went up from the all-powerful capitalists of Rome. With the equites on its side, the popular party had its chance, and one of the tribunes, C. Memmius, by bringing the matter before the people, compelled the senate to declare war. In 111 B.C. one of the consuls, L. Calpurnius Bestia, landed in Africa with a large army, and immediately proceeded to invade Numidia. But both Bestia and M. Scaurus, who acted as his principal lieutenant, are said to have been bribed by Jugurtha to grant him a favourable peace, on condition only of a pretended submission, together with the surrender of thirty elephants and a small sum of money. The scandal of this transaction was dwelt on by Memmius, and it was agreed to send the Praetor L. Cassius, a man of the highest integrity, to Numidia, in order to prevail on the king to repair in person to Rome, the popular party hoping to be able to convict the leaders of the nobility by means of his evidence.

Memmius and the opposition.

The safe conduct granted him by the state was religiously observed; but the scheme failed of its effect, for, as soon as Jugurtha was brought forward in an assembly of the People to make his statement, one of the tribunes, who had been previously gained over by the friends of Scaurus and Bestia, forbade him to speak. He, nevertheless, remained at Rome for some time longer, and engaged in secret intrigues, which would probably have been ultimately crowned with success, had he not in the mean time ventured to assassinate Massiva, son of Gulussa, who was putting in a claim to the Numidian throne. It was impossible to overlook so daring a crime, perpetrated under the very eyes of the senate. Jugurtha was ordered to quit Italy without delay. It was on this occasion that he is said, when leaving Rome, to have uttered the memorable words, "A city for sale, and destined to perish quickly, if it can find a purchaser."

Jugurtha at Rome.

War was now inevitable; but the incapacity of Sp. Postumius Albinus, who arrived to conduct it (110 B.C.), and still more that of his brother Aulus, whom he left to command in his absence when called away to hold the elections at Rome, proved as favourable to Jugurtha as the corruption of their predecessors. Aulus, having penetrated into the heart of Numidia, suffered himself to be surprised in his camp: great part of his army was cut to pieces, and the rest only escaped a similar fate by the ignominy of passing under the yoke. The disgrace at once roused all the spirit of the Roman people; the treaty concluded by Aulus was instantly annulled, immense exertions were made to raise troops, and one of the consuls for the new year (109 B.C.), Q. Caecilius Metellus, hastened to Numidia to retrieve the honour of the Roman arms.

War in Numidia. Defeat of Aulus Albinus.

But this did not satisfy the people. The scandalous conduct of so many of the nobles had given fresh life to the popular party; and the Tribune C. Mamilius carried a bill for the appointment of three commissioners to inquire into the conduct of all of those who had received bribes from Jugurtha. Scaurus, though one of the most guilty, managed to be put upon the commission. But he dared not shield his confederates. Many men of the highest rank were condemned, among whom were Bestia, Albinus, and Opimius. The last-named was the Opimius who acted with such ferocity towards Caius Gracchus and his party. He died in exile at Dyrrhacium some years afterwards, in great poverty.

Special commission.

The Consul Metellus, who was an able general and a man of the strictest integrity, landed in Africa, with Marius as his lieutenant, in 109 B.C. As soon as Jugurtha discovered the character of the new commander, he began to despair of success, and made overtures for submission in earnest. These were apparently entertained by Metellus, while he sought, in fact, to gain over the adherents of the king, and induce them to betray him to the Romans, at the same time that he continued to advance into the enemy's territories. Jugurtha, in his turn, detected his designs, attacked him suddenly on his march with a numerous force, but was, after a severe struggle, repulsed, and his army totally routed. Metellus ravaged the greater part of the country, but failed in taking the important town of Zama before he withdrew into winter quarters. But he had produced such an effect upon the Numidian king, that Jugurtha was induced, in the

Metellus prosecutes the war.

course of the winter, to make offers of unqualified submission, and even surrendered all his elephants, with a number of arms and horses, and a large sum of money, to the Roman general; but when called upon to place himself personally in the power of Metellus, his courage failed him, he broke off the negotiation, and once more had recourse to arms.

Marius had greatly distinguished himself in the preceding campaign. The readiness with which he shared the toils of the common soldiers, eating of the same food, and working at the same trenches with them, had endeared him to them, and through their letters to their friends at Rome his praises were in everybody's mouth. His increasing reputation and popularity induced him to aspire to the consulship. His hopes were increased by a circumstance which happened to him at Utica. While sacrificing at this place, the officiating priest told him that the victims predicted some great and wonderful events, and bade him execute whatever purpose he had in his mind. Marius thereupon applied to Metellus for leave of absence, that he might proceed to Rome and offer himself as a candidate. The consul, who belonged to the family which "Fate destined for the consulship," at first tried to dissuade Marius from his presumptuous attempt, by pointing out the certainty of failure; and when he could not prevail upon him to abandon his design, he civilly evaded his request by pleading the exigencies of the public service, which required his presence and assistance. Marius's insistence at last drew from him the impatient remark, "You need not hurry; it will be quite time enough for you to apply for the consulship along with my son." The latter, who was then serving with the army, was a youth of only twenty years of age, and could not, therefore, become a candidate for the consulship for more than twenty years. This insult was never forgotten by Marius. He now began to intrigue against his general, and to spread the absurd report that the war was purposely prolonged by Metellus to gratify his own vanity and love of military power. He openly declared that with one-half of the army he would soon have Jugurtha in chains; and, as all his remarks were carefully reported at Rome, the people began to regard him as the only person competent to finish the war.

Metellus at last allowed him to leave Africa, but only twelve days before the election. Meeting with a favourable wind, he arrived at Rome in time, and was elected consul with an enthusiasm which bore down all opposition. He received from the people the province of Numidia, although the senate had previously decreed that Metellus should continue in his command. The soldier-demagogue made the most of the situation. In his speeches to the public, he gloried in his humble origin. He upbraided the nobles with their effeminacy and licentiousness; he told them that he looked upon the consulship as a trophy of his conquest over them; and he proudly compared his own wounds and military experience with their indolence and ignorance of war. It was a great triumph for the people and a great humiliation for the aristocracy, and Marius made them drink to the dregs the bitter cup. While engaged in these attacks upon the nobility, he at the same time carried on a levy of troops with great activity, and formed the first mercenary army of Rome by enrolling any persons who chose to offer for the service, however poor and mean, instead of taking them from the five classes according to ancient custom.*

Marius elected consul. Appointed to Numidia.

Meantime Metellus had been carrying on the war in Africa as proconsul (108 B.C.). But the campaign was not productive of such decisive results as might have been expected. Jugurtha avoided any general action, and eluded the pursuit of Metellus by the rapidity of his movements. Even when driven from Thala, a stronghold which he had deemed inaccessible from its position in the midst of arid deserts, he only retired among the Gaetulians, and quickly succeeded in raising among those wild tribes a fresh army, with which he once more penetrated into the heart of Numidia. A still more important accession was that of Bocchus, king of Mauretania, who had been prevailed upon to raise an army and advance to the support of Jugurtha. Metellus, however, having now relaxed his own efforts, from disgust at hearing that C. Marius had been appointed to succeed him in the command, remained on the defensive, while he sought to amuse the Moorish king by negotiation.

The arrival of Marius (107 B.C.) infused fresh vigour into the Roman arms: he quickly reduced in succession almost all the strongholds that still remained to Jugurtha, in some of which the king had deposited his principal treasures; and the latter.

* On this important change in the Roman army, see p. 151.

seeing himself thus deprived step by step of all his dominions, at length determined on a desperate attempt to retrieve his fortunes by one grand effort. He with difficulty prevailed on the wavering Bocchus, by the most extensive promises in case of success, to co-operate with him in this enterprise; and the two kings with their united forces attacked Marius on his march, when he was about to retire into winter quarters. Though the Roman general was taken by surprise for a moment, his skill, the discipline of his troops, and the energy of Sulla, Marius's quaestor, who scattered the Mauri under Bocchus, proved triumphant; the Numidians were repulsed, and their army, as usual with them in case of a defeat, dispersed in all directions. Jugurtha himself, after displaying the greatest courage in the action, cut his way almost alone through a body of Roman cavalry, and escaped from the field of battle. He quickly again gathered round him a body of Numidian horse; but his only hope of continuing the war now rested on Bocchus.

Marius in Numidia.

The only hope of closing the war was to get possession of Jugurtha, for Marius's victories had been as nugatory as those of Metellus. Fortunately, Marius had in his camp a man of great diplomatic ability; it was his quaestor Sulla who enabled him to perform his rash promises to the people. After protracted negotiations, Bocchus was gained over to the Roman cause. Through his treachery Jugurtha was surprised and handed over to Sulla, who conveyed him to the Roman camp (early in 106 B.C.).

Capture of Jugurtha.

L. Cornelius Sulla, the quaestor of Marius, who afterwards plays such a distinguished part in Roman history, was descended from a patrician family which had been reduced to great obscurity. But his means were sufficient to secure him a good education. He studied the Greek and Roman writers with diligence and success, and early imbibed that love of literature and art by which he was distinguished throughout his life. But he was also fond of pleasure, and was conspicuous even among the Romans for licentiousness and debauchery. He was in every respect a contrast to Marius. He possessed all the accomplishments and all the vices which the old Cato had been most accustomed to denounce, and he was one of those advocates of Greek literature and of Greek

Sulla.

profligacy who had since Cato's time become more and more common among the Roman nobles. But Sulla's love of pleasure did not absorb all his time, nor enfeeble his mind; for no Roman during the latter days of the Republic, with the exception of Julius Caesar, had a clearer judgment, a keener discrimination of character, or a firmer will. Upon his arrival in Africa, Marius was not well pleased that a quaestor had been assigned to him who was known only for his profligacy, and who had had no experience in war; but the zeal and energy with which Sulla attended to his new duties soon rendered him a useful and skilful officer, and gained for him the unqualified approbation of his commander, notwithstanding his previous prejudices against him. He was equally successful in winning the affections of the soldiers. He seized every opportunity of conferring favours upon them, was ever ready to take part in all the jests of the camp, and at the same time never shrank from sharing in all their labours and dangers. The enemies of Marius claimed for Sulla (apparently with reason) the glory of the betrayal of Jugurtha, and Sulla himself took the credit of it by always wearing a signet-ring representing the scene of the surrender.

Triumph of Marius.

But the people were not to be baulked of their champion. Marius entered Rome on the first of January, 104 B.C., leading Jugurtha in triumph. The Numidian king was then thrown into a dungeon, and there starved to death. Marius, during his absence, had been elected consul a second time, and he entered upon his office on the day of his triumph. This signal honour was due to a panic which had seized on Italy at a great danger threatening from the north.

German priestess in chariot drawn by oxen (from Antonine column).

CHAPTER XXIII.

THE CIMBRI AND TEUTONES, B.C. 113–101.—SECOND SERVILE WAR IN SICILY, B.C. 103–101.

The Cimbri and Teutones.

A GREATER danger than Rome had experienced since the time of Hannibal now threatened the state. Two nations of barbarians, probably dislodged by some movement of peoples on the Baltic or the Lower Rhine, had gathered on the northern side of the Alps, and seemed ready to pour down upon Italy. They are spoken of as Cimbri and Teutones, and the traditions of their mode of fighting and religious rites seem to show that both nations were of Germanic origin, although they had probably gathered to themselves during their wanderings large numbers of the Celtic race. They came with all their belongings, their wagon-homes, their women and children, to seek new settlements in the south; and the whole host is said to have numbered 300,000 fighting men.

The alarm was still further increased by the disaster which had hitherto attended the attempts to repel these barbarians.

Defeat of Roman armies.

Army after army had fallen before them. The Cimbri were first heard of in 113 B.C., in Noricum, whence they descended into Illyricum, and defeated a Roman army under the command of Cn. Papirius Carbo. They then marched westward into Switzerland, where they were joined by the Tigurini and the Ambrones. They next poured over Gaul, which they plundered and ravaged in every direction. The Romans sent army after army to defend the south-western part of the country, which was now a Roman province; but all in vain. In 109 B.C. the Consul M. Junius Silanus was defeated by the Cimbri; in 107 B.C. the Tigurini cut in pieces, near the Lake of Geneva, the army of the Consul L. Cassius Longinus, the colleague of Marius, who lost his life in the battle; and shortly afterwards M. Aurelius Scaurus was also defeated and taken prisoner. But the most dreadful loss was still to come. In 105 B.C. two consular armies, commanded by the Consul Cn. Mallius Maximus and the Proconsul Cn. Servilius Caepio, consisting of 80,000 men, were completely annihilated by the barbarians: only ten men are said to have escaped the slaughter.

These repeated disasters hushed all party quarrels. Every one at Rome felt that Marius was the only man capable of saving the state, and he was accordingly elected consul by the consent of all parties while he was still absent in Africa. He entered Rome in triumph, as we have already said, on the 1st of January, 104 B.C., which was the first day of his second consulship. A breathing-space was granted by the erratic movements of the barbarians. Instead of crossing the Alps and pouring down upon Italy, as had been expected, the Cimbri marched into Spain, which they ravaged for the next two or three years. The interval was employed by Marius in training the new troops, and accustoming them to hardships and toil. It was probably during this time that he introduced the various changes into the organization of the Roman army which are usually attributed to him. Notwithstanding the sternness and severity with which he punished the

Marius appointed to command.

least breach of discipline, he was a favourite with his new soldiers, who learned to place implicit confidence in their general, and were delighted with the strict impartiality which recognized no distinctions of rank when punishments were to be inflicted.

As the enemy still continued in Spain, Marius was elected consul a third time for the year 103 B.C., and also a fourth time for the following year, with Q. Lutatius Catulus as his colleague. It was in this year (102 B.C.) that the long-expected barbarians arrived. The Cimbri, who had returned from Spain, united their forces with the Teutones. Marius first took up his position in a fortified camp upon the Rhone, probably in the vicinity of the modern Arles; and as the entrance of the river was nearly blocked up by mud and sand, he employed his soldiers in digging a canal from the Rhone to the Mediterranean, that he might the more easily obtain his supplies from the sea.* Meantime the barbarians had divided their forces. The Cimbri marched round the northern foot of the Alps, in order to enter Italy by the north-east, crossing the Tyrolese Alps by the defiles of Tridentum (*Trent*).

Movements of the barbarians.

The Teutones and Ambrones, on the other hand, marched against Marius, intending, as it seems, to penetrate into Italy by Nice and the Riviera of Genoa. Marius, anxious to accustom his soldiers to the savage and strange appearance of the barbarians, would not give them battle at first. The latter resolved to attack the Roman camp; but as they were repulsed in this attempt, they pressed on at once for Italy. So great were their numbers, that they are said to have been six days in marching by the Roman camp.

The Teutones march on Italy.

As soon as they had advanced a little way, Marius followed them; and thus the armies continued to march for a few days, the barbarians in the front and Marius behind, till they came to the neighbourhood of Aquae Sextiae (*Aix*). Here the decisive battle was fought. An ambush of 3000 soldiers, which Marius had stationed in the rear of the barbarians, and which fell upon them when they were

Battle of Aquae Sextiae.

* This canal continued to exist long afterwards, and bore the name of *Fossa Mariana*.

already retreating, decided the fortune of the day. Attacked both in front and rear, enervated by the unaccustomed heat, they at length broke their ranks and fled. The carnage was dreadful; the whole nation was annihilated, for those who escaped put an end to their lives, and their wives followed their example. Immediately after the battle, as Marius was in the act of setting fire to the vast heap of broken arms which was intended as an offering to the gods, horsemen rode up to him, and greeted him with the news of his being elected consul for the fifth time.

The Cimbri on the Padus.

The Cimbri, in the mean time, had forced their way into Italy. The colleague of Marius, Q. Lutatius Catulus, despairing of defending the passes of the Tyrol, had taken up a strong position on the Athesis (*Adige*); but in consequence of the terror of his soldiers at the approach of the barbarians, he was obliged to retreat even beyond the Po, thus leaving the whole of the rich plain of Lombardy exposed to their ravages. Marius was therefore recalled from the battle-field of *Aix* to join the army of Catulus on the Po (101 B.C.).

Battle of Vercellae.

The united forces of the consul and proconsul crossed the river, and hastened in search of the Cimbri, who had marched slowly up the stream, in search of a convenient crossing-place, and, perhaps, in hopes of being joined by the Teutones, of whose destruction they had not yet heard. They were now stationed to the west of Milan near Vercellae. The Cimbri met with the same fate as the Teutones; the whole nation was annihilated; and the women, like those of the Teutones, put an end to their lives. The first tide of Germanic invasion had been stemmed, and Marius was hailed as the saviour of the state; his name was coupled with the gods in the libations and at banquets; and he received the title of third founder of Rome. He celebrated his victories by a brilliant triumph, in which, however, Catulus was allowed to share.

Second Servile War in Sicily.

During the brilliant campaigns of Marius, Sicily had been exposed to the horrors of a second Servile War. The insurrection again broke out at Enna in the east of the island, where the slaves elected as their king one Salvius, a soothsayer. He displayed considerable abilities, and in a short time collected a force of 20,000 foot and 2000 horse. After defeating a Roman army, he assumed all the pomp of royalty, and took the surname of Tryphon, which had been borne by a usurper to the Syrian throne. The success of Salvius led to an insurrection in the western part of the island, where the slaves chose as their leader a Cilician named Athenio, who joined Tryphon, and acknowledged his sovereignty. Upon the death of Tryphon, Athenio became king. The insurrection had now assumed such a formidable aspect that, in 101 B.C., the senate sent the Consul M'. Aquillius into Sicily. He succeeded in subduing the insurgents, and killed Athenio with his own hand. The survivors were sent to Rome, and condemned to fight with wild beasts; but they disdained to minister to the pleasures of their oppressors, and slew each other with their own hands in the amphitheatre.

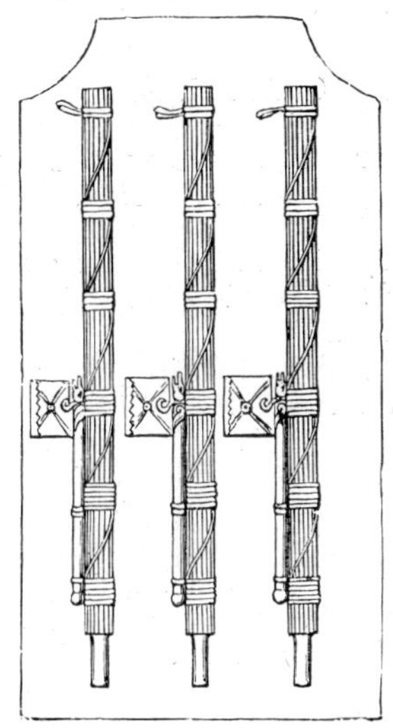

Fasces (from the original in the Capitol of Rome).

Caius Marius.

CHAPTER XXIV.

THE DOWNFALL OF THE OPPOSITION, AND THE ATTEMPT OF DRUSUS AT REFORM.

THE five consulships of Marius had been a gross violation of the constitution, only to be excused by the dangers of the times; but the democratic party had no hope except in the rule of a single man; and, as the time for the consular elections approached, Marius became again a candidate for the consulship. He wished to be first in peace as well as in war, and to rule the state as well as the army. But he did not possess the qualities requisite for a popular leader at Rome; he had no programme and no power of oratory, and he lost his presence of mind in the noise and shouts of the popular assemblies.

Marius and the extreme democrats.

To secure his election he entered into close connection with two of the most violent demagogues that ever appeared at Rome, Saturninus and Glaucia. The former was a candidate for the tribunate, and the latter for the praetorship; and by their means, as well as by bribing the tribes, Marius secured his election to the consulship for the sixth time. Glaucia also obtained the praetorship, but Saturninus was not equally successful. He lost his election

Glaucia and Saturninus.

chiefly through the exertions of A. Nonius, who was chosen in his stead. But assassination as a political weapon was coming into vogue; on the evening of his election Nonius was murdered, and next morning, at an early hour, before the forum was full, Saturninus was chosen to fill up the vacancy.

Laws of Saturninus.

As soon as Saturninus had entered upon his office (100 B.C.) he brought forward an Agrarian Law for dividing among the soldiers of Marius the lands in Gaul which had been lately occupied by the Cimbri, and to which the state had as little right as the Cimbri themselves. He added to the law a clause that, if it was enacted by the people, every senator should swear obedience to it within five days, and that whoever refused to do so should be expelled from the senate, and pay a fine of twenty talents. This clause, which completely reversed the established order of legislation, was employed by Marius to effect the ruin of Metellus. Marius rose in the senate, and declared that he would never take the oath, and Metellus made the same declaration; but when the law had been passed, and Saturninus summoned the senators to the rostra to comply with the demands of the law, Marius, to the astonishment of all, immediately took the oath, and advised the senate to follow his example. Metellus alone refused compliance; and on the following day Saturninus sent his beadle to drag him out of the senate-house.

Exile of Metellus.

Not content with this victory, Saturninus brought forward a bill to punish him with exile. The friends of Metellus were ready to take up arms in his defence; but he declined their assistance, and withdrew privately from the city. Saturninus brought forward other popular measures, such as had already figured in the Gracchan programme. He proposed a *Lex Frumentaria*, by which the state was to sell corn to the people at a very low price; and also a law for founding new colonies in Sicily, Achaia, and Macedonia. In the election of the magistrates for the following year Saturninus was again chosen tribune. Glaucia was at the same time a candidate for the consulship, the two other candidates being M. Antonius and C. Memmius. The election of Antonius was certain, and the struggle lay between Glaucia and Memmius. But this stumbling-block was also removed, and Memmius, murdered openly in the comitia, fell a victim to his own party. All sensible people had previously become alarmed at the mad conduct of Saturninus and his partisans; and the equites, who had hitherto supported Marius, swung over to the side of the government. The senate felt themselves now sufficiently strong to declare Glaucia and Saturninus public enemies, and invested the consuls with dictatorial power. Marius was unwilling to act against his associates, but he had no alternative, and his backwardness was compensated by the zeal of others.

End of the revolution.

Driven out of the forum, Saturninus, Glaucia, and the quaestor Saufeius, took refuge in the Capitol; but the partisans of the senate cut off the pipes which supplied the citadel with water before Marius began to move against them. Unable to hold out any longer, they surrendered to Marius. The latter did all he could to save their lives: as soon as they descended from the Capitol, he placed them, for security, in the Curia Hostilia, but the mob pulled off the tiles of the senate-house, and pelted them till they died. The senate gave their sanction to the proceeding, by rewarding with the citizenship a slave of the name of Scaeva, who claimed the honour of having killed Saturninus.

Marius goes to the East.

Marius had lost all influence in the state by allying himself with such unprincipled adventurers. In the following year (99 B.C.) he left Rome, in order that he might not witness the return of Metellus from exile—a measure which he had been unable to prevent. He set sail for Cappadocia and Galatia, under the pretence of offering services which he had vowed to the Great Mother. He had, however, a deeper purpose in visiting these countries. He longed for another military command that might restore him to power, and accordingly repaired to the court of Mithridates, king of Pontus, to discover the lengths to which that monarch was likely to go in his opposition to Rome, and to make hostilities more certain by exciting the fears of the king.

The mad scheme of Saturninus, and the discredit into which Marius had fallen, had given new strength to the senate. Unmindful of the fact that it was through the support of the equites that their recent victory had been won, they judged the opportunity favourable for depriving this order of the judicial power which they had enjoyed, with only a temporary cessation, since the time of C. Gracchus.

Abuse of power by the equites.

The equites had abused their power, as the senate had done before them. They were the capitalists who farmed the public revenues in the provinces, where they committed peculation and extortion with habitual impunity. Their possession of the courts gave them a complete control over provincial governors, and their unjust condemnation of Rutilius Rufus had shown how unfit they were to be entrusted with judicial duties. Rutilius was a man of spotless integrity, and while acting as lieutenant to Q. Mucius Scaevola, proconsul of Asia in 98 B.C., he displayed so much honesty and firmness in repressing the extortions of the farmers of the taxes, that he became an object of fear and hatred to the whole body. Accordingly, on his return to Rome, a charge of malversation was trumped up against him; he was found guilty, and compelled to withdraw into banishment (B.C. 92).

Reforms of Livius Drusus the younger.

The senate had learnt the lesson of the past ten years; that section of the order which was genuinely desirous of reform was strong, and its representative, M. Livius Drusus, the son of the celebrated opponent of C. Gracchus, and tribune for 91 B.C., was the Tory democrat of the day. Full of aristocratic prejudices, and a firm believer in the rule of the nobility, he condescended to take some items from the current democratic programme. Laws granting the distribution of corn at a low price, and the establishment of colonies in Italy and Sicily, were thrown as a sop to the people, and he was thus enabled to carry his measures for the reform of the judicia; which were that the senate should be increased from 300 to 600 by the addition of an equal number of equites, and that the judices should be taken from the senate thus doubled in numbers. Drusus aimed at a coalition government, which should keep the Radicals in check; but this measure of compromise was acceptable to neither party. The senators viewed with dislike the elevation to their own rank of 300 equites; while the equites, who had no desire to transfer to a select few of their own order the profitable share in the administration of justice which they all enjoyed, were hopelessly alienated.

Another measure of Drusus rendered him equally unpopular with the people. He had held out to the Latins and the Italian allies the promise of the Roman franchise. It may be doubtful what the intention of the similar proposal of C. Gracchus had been; but there can be no doubt that Drusus was firmly convinced that the enfranchisement of Italy, by widening the basis of government, would ensure the safety of the state. The Roman people, however, still looked askance at such a measure, and Drusus foundered on the rock which had proved fatal to C. Gracchus. But promises had been made to the allies; it was too late to retreat; and in order to oppose the formidable coalition against him, Drusus had recourse to a device which might easily be interpreted as treasonable. A secret society was formed, in which the members bound themselves by a solemn oath to have the same friends and foes with Drusus, and to obey all his commands. The ferment soon became so great that the public peace was more than once threatened. The allies were ready to take up arms at the first movement.

Assassination of Drusus.

The consuls, looking upon Drusus as a conspirator, resolved to meet his plots by counter-plots. But he knew his danger, and whenever he went into the city kept a strong body-guard of attendants close to his person. The end could not much longer be postponed; and the civil war was on the point of breaking out, when one evening Drusus was assassinated in his own house, while dismissing the crowds who were attending him. A leather-cutter's knife was found sticking in his loins. Turning round to those who surrounded him, he asked them, as he was dying, "Friends and neighbours, when will the Commonwealth have a citizen like me again?"

The Varian commission.

Even in the lifetime of Drusus the senate had, by the discovery of a technical flaw, repealed all his laws. The reaction after his death was terrible. The Tribune Q. Varius brought forward a law declaring all persons guilty of high treason who had assisted the cause of the allies. Many leading men fell victims to the criminal commission established by this law, and the measure, following the assassination of Drusus, roused the indignation of the allies to the highest pitch. They saw clearly that the Roman people would yield nothing except upon compulsion.

Coin of the eight Italian nations taking the Oath of Federation.

CHAPTER XXV.

THE SOCIAL OR MARSIC WAR, AND THE INCORPORATION OF ITALY.
90–89 B.C.

THE issue of the impending war was to decide whether Rome was to remain a dominant city in Italy, or to become merged as a subordinate state in an Italian confederation. Alone she could hardly have resisted the whole of Italy; but the insurrection was confined almost exclusively to the Sabellians and their kindred races. The Etruscans and Umbrians, where the capitalist class preponderated, stood aloof; while the tribes or cities which had received the Roman franchise in whole or in part, such as the Sabines and Volscians, with the Latin colonies and the Greek towns such as Neapolis and Rhegium, were in the main faithful to the Republic, and furnished the materials of her armies. The nations which composed the formidable conspiracy against Rome were originally eight in number,—the Marsians, Paelignians, Marrucinians, Vestinians, Picentines, Samnites, Apulians, and Lucanians. Of these the Marsians were particularly distinguished for their courage and skill in war; and from the prominent part which they took in the struggle, it was frequently termed the Marsic as well as the Social War.

The revolted communities.

The war broke out at Asculum in Picenum. The Proconsul Q. Servilius, who had the charge of this part of Italy, hearing that the inhabitants of Asculum were organizing a revolt, entered the town, and endeavoured to persuade them to lay aside their hostile intentions. But he was murdered, together with his legate, by the exasperated

The Italian confederation.

citizens, and all the Romans in the place were likewise put to death. This was the signal for a general insurrection. Corfinium, a strong city of the Paeligni, to which the name of Italica was given, was fixed upon as the new capital of the Italian Confederation. The government of the new Italian Republic was modelled on that of Rome; it was to have two consuls, twelve praetors, and a senate of 500 members. But if, as is probable, magistrates and senate were elected from all the confederate tribes and cities, Italica was not like Rome a city state, but the head of a federal government. Q. Pompaedius Silo, a Marsian, one of the chief instigators of the war, and C. Papius Mutilus, a Samnite, who cherished the hereditary hatred of his countrymen against the Romans, were chosen consuls. Under them were many able lieutenants, who had learnt the art of war under the best Roman generals. Their soldiers had served in the Roman armies, the weapons and discipline of the contending parties were the same, and the struggle presented many of the features of a civil war. But the Romans had the advantage of unity of council, which a single state always possesses over a confederation.

First year of the war.

Our information of the details of the war is very meagre. But in the military operations we clearly see that the allies formed two principal groups; the one composed of the Marsians, with their neighbours the Marrucinians, Paelignians, Vestinians, and Picentines,—the other of the Samnites, with the Lucanians and Apulians. The two Roman consuls, L. Julius Caesar and P. Rutilius Lupus, took the field with powerful armies, and under them served Marius, Sulla, and the most experienced generals of the time. The Romans were fully aware of the formidable nature of the struggle, which was one for existence, and not for victory. In the first campaign the advantage was on the side of the allies. The Samnites, under their consul Papius, overran Campania, took most of the towns, and laid siege to Acerrae, into which Caesar threw himself. The Italian army in Central Italy was still more successful. There the Marsians under Cato defeated the Roman Consul P. Rutilius Lupus with great slaughter at the Tolenus, between Tibur and Alba, and Rutilius himself was slain in the battle. This disaster was to some extent repaired by Marius, who commanded a separate army in the neighbourhood, and compelled the victorious allies to retire. The old general then intrenched himself in a fortified camp, and neither the stratagems nor the taunts of the Samnites could entice him from his advantageous position. "If you are a great general," said the Italian consul Pompaedius, "come down and fight;" to which the veteran replied, "Nay, do *you*, if you are a great general, compel me to fight against my will." The Romans considered that Marius was over-cautious and too slow; and Plutarch says that his age and corpulence rendered him incapable of enduring the fatigue of very active service. But it is more probable that he was not very willing to destroy the allies, who had been among his most active partisans, and to whom he still looked for support in his future struggles with the nobility.

The Romans now saw the necessity of making some concessions. The Lex Julia, proposed by the consul Julius Caesar (90 B.C.), granted the franchise to those of the allies who had up to that time remained faithful to Rome. The effects of this concession were immediately seen. Several of the allied cities hastened to avail themselves of it, and disunion and distrust were produced among the rest.

Lex Julia.

The next campaign (89 B.C.) was decidedly favourable to the Romans. The consuls were Cn. Pompeius Strabo, the father of the great Pompey, and L. Porcius Cato. The latter, it is true, was slain at the commencement of the campaign; but his loss was more than compensated by his lieutenant Sulla obtaining, in consequence, the supreme command in the south. He carried on the war with the utmost vigour, and completely eclipsed his old commander Marius. He drove the enemy out of Campania, subdued the Hirpini, and then penetrated into the very heart of Samnium. Here he defeated Papius Mutilus, the Samnite consul, and followed up his victory by the capture of the strong town of Bovianum.

Second year of the war.

Meanwhile Pompeius Strabo had been equally successful in the north. Asculum was reduced after a long and obstinate siege. The Marrucinians, Vestinians, Paelignians, and finally the Marsians, laid down their arms before the end of the year. Their submission was facilitated by the Lex Plautia Papiria, proposed by the tribunes M. Plautius Silvanus and C. Papirius Carbo (89 B.C.),

Lex Plautia Papiria.

which completed the arrangements of the Lex Julia, and granted, in fact, everything which the allies had demanded before the war. All citizens of a town in alliance with Rome could obtain, by this law, the Roman franchise, provided they were at the time resident in Italy, and registered their names with the praetor within sixty days.*

The war, which had cost the lives of 300,000 men, the flower of Rome and Italy, was virtually concluded within two years, although the Samnites and Lucanians still maintained a guerilla warfare in their mountains, and continued to keep possession of the strong fortress of Nola in Campania, from which all the efforts of Sulla failed to dislodge them. The result was to merge Italy in Rome, and to give the city-state a territory which stretched from the Padus to the Straits of Messina. But the franchise was grudgingly accorded; and the incorporation granted was, in deference to popular opinion at Rome, still very incomplete. The allies were enrolled in only eight of the thirty-five tribes, to prevent their outnumbering the old citizens; nor could the suffrage be effectively exercised in the absence of representative institutions. But the value of the Roman citizenship was not to be measured by the voting power it conferred. The allies had gained the protection of the *provocatio* and the sanctity with which the Roman name invested them in the eyes of Roman proconsuls and barbarian kings.

The incorporation of Italy.

Roman in toga.

* A law of the consul Pompeius bestowed the Latin franchise upon all the citizens of the Gallic towns between the Po and Alps, the chief right so conferred being the attainment of Roman citizenship by any one who had held a magistracy in his native town.

Terracina.

CHAPTER XXVI.

FIRST CIVIL WAR. 88-86 B.C.

Contest between Marius and Sulla.

ONE reason which induced the senate to bring the Social War to a conclusion was the necessity of attacking Mithridates, king of Pontus, one of the ablest monarchs with whom Rome ever came into contact. It was this foreign war, the origin and history of which will be narrated in the following chapter, that was the occasion of the first armed struggle of factions at Rome, from the dispute it aroused between Marius and Sulla as to which should have the command against Mithridates. The ability which Sulla had displayed in the Social War, and his well-known attachment to the senatorial party, naturally marked him out as the man to whom this important dignity was to be granted. He was accordingly elected consul for the year 88 B.C., with Q. Pompeius Rufus as his colleague; and he forthwith received the command of the Mithridatic War. But Marius had long coveted this distinction; he quitted the magnificent villa which he had built at Misenum, and took up his residence at Rome; and, in order to show that neither his age nor his corpulence had destroyed his vigour, he repaired daily to the Campus Martius, and went through the usual exercises with the young men. He was determined not to yield without a struggle to his hated rival. As he had formerly employed the Tribune Saturninus to carry out his designs, so now he found an able instrument for his purpose in the Tribune P. Sulpicius Rufus.

Sulpicius was one of the greatest orators of the age, and had acquired great influence by his splendid talents. He was an intimate friend of the Tribune M. Livius Drusus, and had been himself elected tribune for 88 B.C., through the influence of the senatorial party, who placed great hopes in him; it has been suspected that his sudden defection to the democratic party was due to his being overwhelmed with debt, and to his having been promised by Marius a liberal share of the spoils of the Mithridatic War. Sulpicius now brought forward a law by which the Italians were to be distributed among the thirty-five tribes. As they far outnumbered the old Roman citizens, they would have an overwhelming majority in each tribe, and would certainly confer upon Marius the command of the Mithridatic War. To prevent the tribune from putting these rogations to the vote, the consuls declared a *justitium*, during which no business could be legally transacted. But Sulpicius was resolved to carry his point; with an armed band of followers he entered the forum, and called upon the consuls to withdraw their prohibition; and upon their refusal to comply with his demand, he ordered his satellites to draw their swords and fall upon them. Pompeius escaped, but his son Quintus, who was also the son-in-law of Sulla, was killed. Sulla himself took refuge in the house of Marius, which was close to the forum, and in order to save his life he was obliged to remove the *justitium*.

Sulpicius.

Sulla quitted Rome and hastened to his army, then besieging Nola, which was still held by the Samnites (see p. 214). The city was now in the hands of Sulpicius and Marius, and the Redistribution Bill passed into law without opposition, as well as a further decree conferring upon Marius the command of the Mithridatic War. Marius lost no time in sending some officers of the legions to assume on his behalf the command of the army at Nola; but the soldiers, who loved Sulla, and who feared that Marius might lead another army to Asia, and thus deprive them of their anticipated plunder, stoned his deputies to death.

Passing of the Sulpician laws.

Sulla found his soldiers ready to respond to his wishes; they called upon him to lead them to Rome, and deliver the city from the tyrants. He therefore hesitated no longer, but at the head of six legions broke up from his encampment at Nola, and marched towards the city. His officers, however, refused to serve against their country, and all quitted him, with the exception of one quaestor. This was the first time that a Roman had ever marched at the head of Roman troops against the city. Marius was taken by surprise. Such was the reverence that the Romans entertained for law, that it seems never to have occurred to him or to his party that Sulla would venture to draw his sword against the state. Marius attempted to gain time for preparations by forbidding Sulla, in the name of the Republic, to advance any further; but the praetors who carried this command narrowly escaped being murdered by the soldiers; and Marius, as a last resource, offered liberty to the slaves who would join him.

Sulla marches on Rome.

But it was all in vain. Sulla forced his way into the city, and Marius took to flight with his son and a few followers. Sulla used his victory with moderation. He protected the city from plunder; and only Marius, Sulpicius, and ten others of his bitterest enemies, were declared public enemies by the senate. Sulpicius was betrayed by one of his slaves, and put to death; but Marius and his son succeeded in making their escape. Marius himself embarked on board a ship at Ostia, with a few companions, and then sailed southward along the coast of Italy. At Circeii he and his companions were obliged to land on account of the violence of the wind and the want of provisions. After wandering about for a long time they learnt from some peasants that a number of horsemen had been in search of them; and they accordingly turned aside from the road, and passed the night in a deep wood in great want. But the indomitable spirit of the

Flight of Marius.

old man did not fail him; and he consoled himself and encouraged his companions by the assurance that he should still live to see his seventh consulship, in accordance with a prediction that had been made to him in his youth. Shortly afterwards, when they were near to Minturnae, they descried a party of horsemen galloping towards them. In great haste they hurried down to the sea, and swam off to two merchant-vessels, which received them on board. The horsemen bade the crew bring the ship to land or throw Marius overboard; but, moved by his tears and entreaties, they refused to surrender him. The sailors soon changed their minds; and, fearing to keep Marius, they cast anchor at the mouth of the Liris, where they persuaded him to disembark, and rest himself from his fatigues till a wind should rise; but they had no sooner landed him than they immediately sailed away. Marius was now quite alone amid the swamps and marshes through which the Liris flows. With difficulty he reached the hut of an old man, who concealed him in a hole near the river, and covered him with reeds; but hearing shortly afterwards the noise of his pursuers, he crept out of his hiding-place and threw himself into the marsh. He was discovered, and dragged out of the water; and, covered with mud and with a rope round his neck, was delivered up to the authorities of Minturnae. The magistrates then deliberated whether they should comply with the instruction that had been sent from Rome to all the municipal towns to put Marius to death as soon as they found him. After some consultation they resolved to obey it, and sent a Cimbrian slave to carry out their orders. The room in which the old general was confined was dark; and, to the frightened barbarian, the eyes of Marius seemed to dart forth fire, and from the darkness a terrible voice shouted out, "Man! durst thou slay Caius Marius?" The barbarian immediately threw down his sword, and rushed out of the house, exclaiming, "I cannot kill Caius Marius!" Straightway there was a revulsion of feeling among the inhabitants of Minturnae. They repented of their ungrateful conduct towards a man who had saved Rome and Italy. They got ready a ship for his departure, provided him with everything necessary for the voyage, and, with prayers and wishes for his safety, placed him on board. The wind carried him to the island of Aenaria (now Ischia), where he found the rest of his friends; and from thence he set sail for Africa, which he reached in safety. He landed near the site of Carthage, but he had scarcely put his foot on shore before the praetor Sextilius sent an officer to bid him leave the country, or else he would carry into execution the decree of the senate. This last blow almost unmanned Marius. Grief and indignation for a time deprived him of speech, and his only reply was, "Tell the praetor that you have seen Caius Marius a fugitive sitting on the ruins of Carthage." Shortly afterwards Marius was joined by his son, and they crossed over to the island of Cercina, where they remained unmolested.

Meantime a revolution had taken place at Rome, which prepared the way for the return of Marius to Italy. Sulla's soldiers were impatient for the plunder of Asia, and he had abruptly to interrupt his great work of the reform of the constitution, which he had already commenced. After securing the repeal of the Sulpician laws, he sent forward his legions to Capua, that they might be ready to embark for Greece; he himself remained in Rome till the consuls were elected for the following year, to secure if possible the support of his interests in the capital during his absence in Asia. But the candidates whom he recommended were rejected, and the choice fell on Cn. Octavius, who belonged to the aristocratical party, but was a weak and irresolute man, and on L. Cinna, a professed champion of the popular side.

Repeal of the Sulpician laws.

Sulla did not attempt to oppose their election: to have recalled his legions to Rome would have been a dangerous experiment when the soldiers were so eager for the spoils of the East; and he only took the vain precaution of making Cinna promise that he would make no attempt to disturb the existing order of things. But as soon as Sulla had quitted Italy, Cinna again brought forward the law for incorporating the new Italian citizens among the thirty-five tribes. The two consuls had recourse to arms—Octavius to oppose, and Cinna to carry the law. A dreadful conflict took place in the forum. The party of Octavius obtained the victory, and Cinna was driven out of the city with great slaughter. But in spite of this repulse, he was soon at the head of a formidable army composed chiefly of the new citizens, whose cause he had espoused.

Sulla quits Italy.

As soon as Marius heard of these changes he set sail from

Africa, and offered to serve under Cinna, who gladly accepted his proposal, and named him proconsul; but Marius refused all marks of honour. The sufferings and privations he had endured had exasperated his proud and haughty spirit almost to madness, and nothing but the blood of his enemies could appease his resentment. He continued to wear a mean and humble dress, and his hair and beard had remained unshorn from the day he had been driven out of Rome. After joining Cinna, Marius prosecuted the war with great vigour. He first captured the corn-ships, and thus cut off Rome from its usual supply of food. He next took Ostia and the other towns on the sea-coast; then, marching northward, he encamped on the Janiculum. Famine began to rage in the city, and the senate were obliged to yield. They sent a deputation to Cinna and Marius, inviting them into the city, but entreating them to spare the citizens. Cinna received the deputies sitting in his chair of office, and gave them a kind answer. Marius stood in silence by the side of the consul, but his looks spoke louder than words.

Marius and Cinna.

After the audience was over they entered the city. The most frightful scenes followed. The Consul Octavius was slain while seated in his curule chair. The streets ran with the noblest blood of Rome. Every one whom Marius hated or feared was hunted out and put to death; and no consideration, either of rank, talent, or former friendship, induced him to spare the victims of his vengeance. The great orator, M. Antonius, fell by the hands of his assassins; and his former colleague, Q. Catulus, who had triumphed with him over the Cimbri, was obliged to put an end to his own life. Cinna was soon tired of the butchery; but the appetite of Marius seemed only whetted by the slaughter, and daily required fresh victims for its gratification.

Massacres at Rome.

Without going through the form of an election, Marius and Cinna named themselves consuls for the following year (86 B.C.), and thus was fulfilled the prediction that Marius should be seven times consul. But he did not long enjoy the honour: he was now in his seventy-first year; his body was worn out by the fatigues and sufferings he had recently undergone; and on the eighteenth day of his consulship he died of an attack of pleurisy, after a few days' illness.

Death of Marius.

Mount Argaeus in Cappadocia.

CHAPTER XXVII.

FIRST MITHRIDATIC WAR. 88–84 B.C.

The kingdom of Pontus.

THE kingdom of Pontus, which derived its name from being on the coast of the Pontus Euxinus, or Black Sea, was originally a satrapy of the Persian Empire, extending from the river Halys on the west to the frontiers of Colchis on the east. Even under the later Persian kings the rulers of Pontus were really independent; and in the wars of the successors of Alexander the Great it became a separate kingdom. Most of its kings bore the name of Mithridates; and the fifth monarch of this name formed an alliance with the Romans, and was rewarded with the province of Phrygia for the services he had rendered them in the war against Aristonicus (p. 177).

He was assassinated about 120 B.C., and was succeeded by his son Mithridates VI., commonly called the Great, who was then only about twelve years of age. The young monarch grew up to be the type of ruler which is the ideal of the Eastern mind. His vast strength and powers of endurance, his matchless skill in arms and the restless vigour of his mind were emblems of that power under which the Oriental loves to be crushed, and whose guidance he will ever follow. A careful training had still further developed these natural gifts. As a boy, Mithridates had been brought up at Sinope, where he had probably received the elements of a Greek education, and so powerful was his memory that he is said to have learnt not less than twenty-five languages, and to have been able, in the days of his greatest power, to transact business with the deputies of every tribe subject to his rule in their own peculiar dialect.

Mithridates.

As soon as he was firmly established on the throne, he began to turn his arms against the neighbouring nations. On the west his progress was hemmed in by the power of Rome, and the minor sovereigns of Bithynia and Cappadocia enjoyed the all-powerful protection of the Republic. But on the east his ambition found free scope. He subdued the barbarian tribes between the Euxine and the confines of Armenia, including the whole of Colchis and the province called Lesser Armenia; and he even added to his dominions the Tauric Chersonesus, now called the *Crimea.* The Greek kingdom of Bosporus, which formed a portion of the Chersonesus, likewise submitted to his sway. He further strengthened himself by alliances with Tigranes, king of Greater Armenia, to whom he gave his daughter Cleopatra in marriage, and with the warlike nations of the Parthians and Iberians. He thus found himself in possession of power and resources sufficient to make him deem himself equal to a contest with Rome itself.

Extension of the Pontic power.

Many causes of dissension had already arisen. Shortly after his accession the Romans had taken advantage of his minority to wrest from him the province of Phrygia. In 93 B.C. they resisted his attempt to place upon the throne of Cappadocia one of his own nephews, and appointed a Cappadocian named Ariobarzanes to be king of that country. For a time Mithridates submitted,

Mithridates in conflict with Rome.

but the death of Nicomedes II. king of Bithynia brought matters to a crisis. That monarch was succeeded by his eldest son Nicomedes III., but Mithridates took the opportunity to set up a rival claimant, whose pretensions he supported with an army, and quickly drove Nicomedes out of Bithynia (90 B.C.). About the same time his generals openly invaded Cappadocia, and expelled Ariobarzanes from his kingdom, establishing the Pontic pretender Ariarathes in his place. Both the fugitive princes had recourse to Rome, where they found ready support: a decree was passed that Nicomedes and Ariobarzanes should be restored to their respective kingdoms, and the execution of it was confided to M'. Aquillius and L. Cassius.

Mithridates again yielded, and the two fugitive kings were restored to their dominions; but no sooner was Nicomedes replaced on the throne of Bithynia than he was urged by the Roman legates to invade the territories of Mithridates, into which he made a predatory incursion. Mithridates offered no resistance, but sent to the Romans to demand satisfaction, and it was not until his ambassador was dismissed with an evasive answer that he prepared for immediate hostilities (88 B.C.). His first step was to invade Cappadocia, from which he easily expelled Ariobarzanes once more. His generals drove Nicomedes out of Bithynia, and defeated Aquillius.

Mithridates invades "Asia."

Mithridates, following up his advantage, not only made himself master of Phrygia and Galatia, but invaded the Roman province of Asia. Here the universal discontent of the inhabitants, caused by the oppression of the Roman governors, enabled him to overrun the whole province almost without opposition. The Roman officers, who had imprudently brought this danger upon themselves, were unable to collect any forces to oppose his progress; and Aquillius himself, the chief author of the war, fell into the hands of the king of Pontus.

Massacre of Romans and Italians.

Mithridates took up his winter quarters at Pergamus, where he issued the sanguinary order to all the cities of Asia to put to death on the same day all the Roman and Italian citizens who were to be found within their walls. So hateful had the Romans rendered themselves during the short period of their dominion, that these commands were obeyed with alacrity by almost all the cities of Asia. Eighty thousand persons are said to have perished in this fearful massacre.

The success of Mithridates encouraged the Athenians to join the liberator of the East; and the king accordingly sent his general Archelaus with a large army and fleet into Greece. Most of the Greek states had declared for the king when Sulla landed in Epirus in 87 B.C. He immediately marched southwards, and laid siege to Athens and the Piraeus. For many months all his attacks were resisted; but Athens at last surrendered in the spring of the following year; and Archelaus, despairing of defending the Piraeus, withdrew into Boeotia, where he received some powerful reinforcements from Mithridates.

Greek cities revolt.

The Roman army now captured the Piraeus, and Athens and her seaport were given up to plunder. This, however, was the only penalty which the Athenians suffered for their treachery; their state, in virtue of the memories of the past, was still allowed to remain a free city.

Capture of Athens.

Sulla then turned against Archelaus in Boeotia, and defeated him with enormous loss at Chaeronea. Out of the 110,000 men of which the Pontic army consisted, Archelaus assembled only 10,000 at Chalcis in Euboea, where he had taken refuge. Mithridates, on receiving news of this great disaster, immediately set about raising fresh troops, and was soon able to send another army of 80,000 men to Euboea. But he now found himself threatened with danger from a new and unexpected quarter. While Sulla was still occupied in Greece, the party of Marius at Rome had sent a fresh army to Asia under the Consul L. Valerius Flaccus, to carry on the war at once against their foreign and domestic enemies. Flaccus was murdered by his troops at the instigation of Fimbria, who now assumed the command, and gained several victories over Mithridates and his generals in Asia (85 B.C.).

Battle of Chaeronea.

About the same time the new army, which the king had sent to Archelaus in Greece, was defeated by Sulla in the neighbourhood of Orchomenus. These repeated disasters made Mithridates anxious for peace, but it was not granted by Sulla till the following year (84 B.C.), when, unmoved by the triumph of his enemies at

Battle of Orchomenus.

home, he resolved to finish the work by carrying the war into Asia.

Peace with Mithridates.

The terms of peace were definitely settled at an interview which the Roman general and the Pontic king had at Dardanus in the Troad. Mithridates consented to abandon all his conquests in Asia, to restrict himself to the dominions which he held before the commencement of the war, to pay a sum of 2000 talents, and to surrender to the Romans his present fleet of seventy ships fully equipped.

Return of Sulla.

Sulla was now at liberty to turn his arms against Fimbria, who was with his army at Thyatira. His name was sufficient to cause the troops of Fimbria to desert their general, who put an end to his own life. Sulla now prepared to return to Italy. After exacting enormous sums from the wealthy cities of Asia, he left his legate, L. Licinius Murena, in command of that province, with two legions, and set sail with his own army to Athens. While preparing for his deadly struggle in Italy, he did not lose his interest in literature. He carried with him from Athens to Rome the valuable library of Apellicon of Teos, which contained most of the works of Aristotle and Theophrastus.

Coin of Nicomedes III. King of Bithynia.

Brundusium.

CHAPTER XXVIII.

SECOND CIVIL WAR — SULLA'S DICTATORSHIP, LEGISLATION, AND DEATH. 83–78 B C.

Fruitless negotiations of the senate.

SULLA landed at Brundusium in the spring of 83 B.C., in the consulship of L. Scipio and C. Norbanus. During the preceding year he had written to the senate, recounting the services he had rendered to the commonwealth, complaining of the ingratitude with which he had been treated, announcing his speedy return to Italy, and threatening to take vengeance upon his enemies and those of the Republic. The senate, in alarm, sent an embassy to Sulla to endeavour to bring about a reconciliation between him and his enemies, and meantime ordered the consuls Cinna and Carbo to desist from levying troops and making further preparations for war.

Cinna and Carbo gave no heed to this command; they knew that a reconciliation was impossible, and resolved to cross the Adriatic with an army in order to oppose Sulla in Greece; but, after one detachment of their troops had embarked, the rest of the soldiers rose in mutiny, and murdered Cinna. The Marian party had thus lost their chief leader, but continued nevertheless to make every preparation to resist Sulla, for they were well aware that he would never forgive them, and that their only choice lay between victory and destruction.

Murder of Cinna.

Besides this the Italians were ready to support them, as these new citizens feared that Sulla would deprive them of the rights which they had lately obtained after so much bloodshed. The Marian party had every prospect of victory, for their troops far exceeded those of their opponent. They had 200,000 men in arms, while Sulla landed at Brundusium with only 30,000, or at the most 40,000 men. But, on the other hand, the popular party had no one of sufficient influence and military reputation to take the supreme command in the war; their vast forces were scattered about Italy, in different armies, under different generals; the soldiers had no confidence in their commanders, and no enthusiasm in their cause; and the consequence was, that whole hosts of them deserted to Sulla on the first opportunity. Sulla's soldiers, on the contrary, were veterans, who had frequently fought by each other's sides, and had acquired that confidence in themselves and in their general which frequent victories always give. Still, if the Italians had remained faithful to the cause of the Marian party, Sulla would hardly have conquered, and therefore one of his first cares after landing at Brundusium was to detach them from his enemies.

Preparations for war.

For this purpose he would not allow his troops to do any injury to the towns or fields of the Italians in his march from Brundusium through Calabria and Apulia, and he formed separate treaties with many of the Italian towns, by which he secured to them all the rights and

Sulla's return.

privileges of Roman citizens which they then enjoyed. Among the Italians the Samnites continued to be the most formidable enemies of Sulla. They had joined the Marian party, not simply with the design of securing the supremacy for the latter, but with the hope of conquering Rome by their means, and then destroying for ever their hated oppressor. Thus this civil war became merely another phase of the social war, and the struggle between Rome and Samnium for the supremacy of the peninsula was renewed after the subjection of the latter for more than two hundred years.

Desertion of Scipio's army.

Sulla marched from Apulia into Campania without meeting with any resistance. In Campania he gained his first victory over the consul Norbanus, who was defeated with great loss, and obliged to take refuge in Capua. His colleague Scipio, who was at no great distance, willingly accepted a truce which Sulla offered him, although Sertorius, the ablest of the Marian generals, warned him against entering into any negotiations. His caution was justified by the event. By means of his emissaries Sulla seduced the troops of Scipio, who at length found himself deserted by all his soldiers, and was taken prisoner in his tent. Sulla dismissed him uninjured under the pretence that the convention now concluded bound the whole of the revolutionary party, which should lay down its arms immediately or become public enemies of Rome. This suborning of Scipio's troops led Carbo to observe "that he had to contend in Sulla both with a lion and a fox, but that the fox gave him more trouble." Many distinguished Romans meantime had taken up arms on behalf of Sulla. Cn. Pompeius, the son of Cn. Pompeius Strabo, then only twenty-three years of age, levied three legions in Picenum and the surrounding districts; and Q. Metellus Pius, M. Crassus, M. Lucullus, and several others offered their services as legates. It was not, however, till the following year (82 B.C.) that the struggle was brought to a decisive issue. The consuls of this year were Cn. Papirius Carbo and the younger Marius; the former of whom was entrusted with the protection of Etruria and Umbria, while the latter had to guard Rome and Latium. Sulla appears to have passed the winter at Campania.

At the commencement of spring he advanced against the younger Marius, who had concentrated all his forces at

Sacriportus, and defeated him with great loss. Marius took refuge in Praeneste; and Sulla, after leaving Q. Lucretius Ofella with a large force to blockade the town, marched with the main body of his army to Rome. Marius was resolved not to perish unavenged, and accordingly, before Sulla could reach Rome, he sent orders to L. Damasippus, the praetor, to put to death all his leading opponents. His orders were faithfully obeyed. Q. Mucius Scaevola, the Pontifex Maximus and jurist, P. Antistius, L. Domitius, and many other distinguished men were butchered, and their corpses thrown into the Tiber. Sulla entered the city without opposition, and marched against Carbo, who had been previously opposed by Pompey and Metellus. The history of this part of the war is involved in great obscurity. Carbo made two efforts to relieve Praeneste, but failed in each; and, after fighting with various fortune against Pompey, Metellus, and Sulla, he at length embarked for Africa, despairing of further success in Italy.

Siege of Praeneste.

Meantime Rome had nearly fallen into the hands of the enemy. The Samnites under Pontius Telesinus and the Lucanians under M. Lamponius, after attempting to relieve Praeneste, resolved to march straight upon Rome, which had been left without any army for its protection. Sulla arrived barely in time to save the city. The battle was fought before the Colline Gate; it was a long and obstinate contest, the issue of which was not merely the supremacy of a party: for the very existence of Rome was at stake, and Pontius had declared that he would raze the city to the ground. The left wing, where Sulla commanded in person, was driven off the field by the vehemence of the enemy's charge; but the success of the right wing, which was commanded by Crassus, enabled Sulla to restore the battle, and at length gain a complete victory. Fifty thousand men are said to have fallen on each side. All the most distinguished leaders of the Marian party either perished in the engagement, or were taken prisoners and put to death. Among these was the brave Samnite Pontius, whose head was cut off and carried under the walls of Praeneste, thereby announcing to the younger Marius that his last hope of succour was gone. To the Samnite prisoners Sulla showed no mercy. He was resolved to root out of the peninsula those heroic enemies of Rome. On the third day after the battle he

Battle of the Colline Gate.

collected all the Samnite and Lucanian captives in the Campus Martius, and ordered his soldiers to cut them down. The dying shrieks of so many victims alarmed the senators, who had been assembled by Sulla in the neighbouring temple of Bellona; but he bade them attend to what he was saying, and not mind what was taking place outside, as he was only chastising some rebels.

Surrender of Praeneste. Sulla master of Italy.

Praeneste surrendered soon afterwards. The Romans in the town were pardoned; but the Samnites and Praenestines were massacred without mercy. The younger Marius put an end to his own life. The war in Italy was now virtually at an end, for the few towns which still held out had no prospect of offering any effectual opposition, and were reduced soon afterwards. In other parts of the Roman world the war continued still longer, and Sulla did not live to see its completion. The armies of the Marian party in Sicily and Africa were subdued by Pompey in the course of the same year; but Sertorius in Spain continued to defy all the attempts of the senate till 72 B.C.

Sulla was now master of Rome. He had not commenced the civil war, but had been driven to it by the mad ambition of Marius. His enemies had attempted to deprive him of the command in the Mithridatic War, which had been legally conferred upon him by the senate; and, while he was fighting the battles of the Republic, they had declared him a public enemy, confiscated his property, and murdered the most distinguished of his friends and adherents. For all these wrongs Sulla had threatened to take the most ample vengeance; and he more than redeemed his word. He resolved to extirpate the popular party root and branch, and renew in a legalized form the indiscriminate massacres of his Marian rivals.

The proscription.

One of his first acts was to draw up a list of his enemies who were to be put to death, which list was exhibited in the forum to public inspection, and called a *proscriptio*.* It was the first instance of the kind in Roman history. All persons in this list were outlaws, who might be killed by any one with impunity; their property was confiscated to the state; their children and grandchildren were for ever excluded from all public offices. Further, all who

* *Proscriptio* means literally the "notice of sale" of the goods of outlawed persons. It was here extended to include the act of outlawry.

killed a proscribed person, or indicated the place of his concealment, received two talents as a reward, and whoever sheltered such a person was punished with death. Terror now reigned, not only at Rome, but throughout Italy. Fresh lists of the proscribed constantly appeared. No one was safe; for Sulla gratified his friends by placing in the fatal lists their personal enemies, or individuals whose property was coveted by his adherents. An estate, a house, or even a piece of plate, was to many a man, who belonged to no political party, his death-warrant; for, although the confiscated property belonged to the state, and had to be sold by public auction, the friends and dependents of Sulla purchased it at a nominal price, as no one dared to bid against them. Oftentimes Sulla did not require the purchase-money to be paid at all, and in many cases he gave such property to his favourites without even the formality of a sale. Four thousand seven hundred names are said to have found their way into the Sullan proscription-lists.

Sulla appointed dictator.

At the commencement of these horrors Sulla had been appointed dictator. As there were no consuls, he caused the senate to elect Valerius Flaccus interrex, and the latter brought before the people a *rogatio*, conferring the dictatorship upon Sulla, for the purpose of restoring the Republic, and for as long a time as he judged to be necessary, and giving a retrospective sanction to his acts (81 B.C.). This dictatorship had little resemblance to the occasional office of the early Republic. It was practically a restoration of the monarchy, and foreshadowed the autocratic power of Caesar in later times. But the new ruler did not mean to be king. His dictatorship was only a provisional government by which he meant to place the government of the Republic on a firm and secure basis. Consuls were chosen for the following year (81 B.C.), and Sulla was elected to the office himself in 80 B.C., while he continued to be dictator.

At the beginning of 81 B.C. Sulla celebrated a splendid triumph on account of his victory over Mithridates. In a speech which he delivered to the people at the close of the gorgeous ceremony, he claimed for himself the surname of *Felix*, as he attributed his success in life to the favour of the gods. All ranks in Rome bowed in awe before their master; and among other marks of distinction which were voted to him by the obsequious senate, a gilt equestrian statue was erected to his honour before the Rostra, bearing the inscription, "Cornelio Sullae Imperatori Felici."

Treatment of Italy.

During the years 80 and 79 B.C. Sulla completed his various reforms in the constitution, of which an account is given at the end of this chapter. Two questions which immediately engaged his attention were the punishment of the rebel communities in Italy, and the rewards to his soldiers. Both were settled by the same means. Although he wisely upheld the distribution of the new Italian citizens in the thirty-five tribes, the inhabitants of those Italian towns which had fought against him were deprived of the full Roman franchise which had been lately conferred upon them, while their lands were confiscated and given to the soldiers who had fought under him.

Settlement of veterans.

A great number of these colonists were settled in Etruria. They had the strongest interest in upholding the new institutions, since any attempt to invalidate the latter would have endangered their newly acquired possessions. But, though they were a support to the power of Sulla, they hastened the fall of the commonwealth; nothing could change the idle and licentious soldiery into agriculturists; and Catiline found nowhere more adherents than among the Sullan veterans. While Sulla thus established throughout Italy a population devoted to his interests, he created at Rome a kind of body-guard for his protection by giving the citizenship to a great number of slaves belonging to the proscribed. The slaves thus rewarded are said to have been as many as 10,000, and were called Cornelii after him as their patron.

Sulla resigns his dictatorship.

Sulla had completed his reforms by the beginning of 79 B.C.; and as he longed for the undisturbed enjoyment of his pleasures, he resigned his dictatorship, and declared himself ready to render an account of his conduct while in office. This voluntary abdication by Sulla of the sovereignty of the Roman world has excited the astonishment and admiration of both ancient and modern writers. But it is evident that Sulla never contemplated, like Julius Caesar, the establishment of a monarchical form of government; and both his life and his institutions were strongly guarded against attack. The 10,000 Cornelii at Rome, and his veterans stationed throughout Italy, as well as the whole strength of the aristocratical party, secured him against all danger. Even in his retirement his will was law, and shortly before his death he ordered his slaves to strangle a magistrate of one of the towns in Italy, because he was a public defaulter.

After resigning his dictatorship, Sulla retired to his estate at Puteoli, and there, surrounded by the beauties of nature and art, he passed the remainder of his life in those literary and sensual enjoyments in which he had always taken so much pleasure. He died in 78 B.C., in the sixtieth year of his age, of apoplexy brought on by a fit of passion. The senate, faithful to the last, resolved to give him the honour of a public funeral. This was, however, opposed by the Consul Lepidus, who had resolved to attempt the repeal of Sulla's laws; but the dictator's power continued unshaken even after his death. The veterans were summoned from their colonies, and Q. Catulus, L. Lucullus, and Cn. Pompeius placed themselves at their head. Lepidus was obliged to give way, and allowed the funeral to take place without interruption. It was a gorgeous pageant. The magistrates, the senate, the equites, the priests, and the Vestal virgins, as well as the veterans, accompanied the funeral procession to the Campus Martius, where the corpse was burnt according to the wish of Sulla himself, who feared that his enemies might insult his remains, as he had done those of Marius, which had been taken out of the grave and thrown into the Anio at his command. It had been previously the custom of the Cornelia gens to bury and not burn their dead. A monument was erected to Sulla in the Campus Martius, the inscription on which he is said to have composed himself. It stated that none of his friends ever did him a kindness, and none of his enemies a wrong, without being fully repaid.

His death.

All the reforms of Sulla were effected by means of *leges*, which were proposed by him in the Comitia Centuriata, and bore the general name of *Leges Corneliae*. The main object of his reforms was to restore the senate's power and to set it on a legal basis; and, in order to secure its permanence, to weaken the authority both of the magistrates and of the people.

Reform of the constitution.

His efforts were primarily directed against the tribunate. This magistracy, which had first served the interests of the plebs, and afterwards those of the senate, had now degenerated into a weapon which was used by powerful party-leaders for their own aggrandizement. Sulla took away from the tribunes their right of initiative in legislation, by prohibiting them from proposing measures except on the request of the senate. He also subordinated their power of veto to a similar control. To degrade the tribunate still further, he made the holding of this office a bar to all further advancement in the state; it ceased to be a stepping-stone and became a stumbling-block in the path to the higher magistracies.

Changes in the magistracy,

The danger of prolonged and unusual commands had recently been exhibited; Sulla consequently re-enacted the *Leges Annales*, making it necessary to hold the quaestorship before the praetorship, and the praetorship before the consulship; and he also forbade the same magistracy to be held a second time until after the expiration of ten years. But it was military command in the provinces, and its frequent combination with a home magistracy, that chiefly threatened danger to the state. Sulla secured a complete separation between home and foreign command. After his time the consul or praetor no longer takes the field. He is confined to civil duties during his year of office, and only then goes out as proconsul or propraetor.

The priestly colleges (especially those of the pontiffs and augurs) were of hardly less political importance than the magistracies. By a Lex Domitia of 104 B.C. the right of filling up these corporations had been given to an assembly of seventeen out of the thirty-five tribes. Sulla restored the old principle of *co-optatio*, by which the members of these bodies added to their own numbers, and thus rendered these corporations more aristocratic.

in the priestly colleges,

The popular voice was necessarily restricted by the limitations on the tribunate; for the Assembly of the Plebs could now only ratify the decrees of the senate; it still, however, elected the plebeian magistrates. The power of the Assembly of the Centuries was left technically unimpaired, but Sulla abolished the democratic system of tribe-

in the comitia,

voting,* and restored the old arrangement of the centuries on the Servian basis.

The senate, reduced in numbers by the late proscription, was recruited by the addition of 300 members from the equestrian order; and a permanent change was made in its constitution. The principle was now fixed by which the quaestorship was made the only stepping-stone to senatorial dignity; henceforth the personal choice by the censor ceases, and the senate is recruited in a purely automatic manner. The increase of the quaestors to twenty permanently doubled the number of its members, which from this time was about 600.

in the senate,

A thorough reform was also undertaken in the administration of justice. In place of the criminal jurisdiction of the comitia, or of the occasional commissioners which it appointed, Sulla established permanent courts (*quaestiones perpetuae*), each of which was to try a definite crime. A precedent for this change had been given by the Lex Calpurnia of 149 B.C., by which a standing commission was appointed for all trials *repetundarum*. Since that date the court for the trial of extortion had been frequently reconstituted, and another for the trial of bribery (*ambitus*) had been added. The number of *quaestiones* was greatly increased by Sulla; and treason, murder, breach of the peace, peculation, and forgery were made the subjects of the new criminal commissions.

in jurisdiction.

These new courts, consisting each of a definite number of jurors (*judices*), were presided over by those praetors who were not engaged in civil jurisdiction; as the praetors were now raised to eight, six were available as criminal judges; but the courts exceeded this number, and consequently they were sometimes presided over by a foreman chosen from the jury (*judex quaestionis*). Their establishment by Sulla was made the occasion of a *Lex Judiciaria* enacting that the *judices* should be taken exclusively from the senators and not from the equites, the latter of whom had possessed this privilege, with one brief interruption, from the time of C. Gracchus. The dependence of the senate on the equestrian order was thus removed, and the aristocracy was armed with a weapon by which it could defend its privileges and abuses and hold its enemies in check.

* p. 146.

General view of the Sullan constitution.

Such are the outlines of one of the most extraordinary attempts at reactionary legislation that history records. The new constitution contained within itself the germs of dissolution; for it invited attack from every side. The senate's power had formerly rested on public opinion, and for this coercive laws are a poor substitute. The shackles imposed on the tribunate made the restoration of the powers of this magistracy a popular party cry. The knights, whose support might have bolstered up the constitution, were hopelessly alienated by the loss of the judicia. The senate, still bent on plundering the provinces, showed no tendency to reform; and the censorship, which had kept the order comparatively pure, was practically abolished. We are not surprised, therefore, to find that in a few years Sulla's bulwarks were swept away. Those portions of his constitution alone were permanent that were not marked by a partisan spirit. His reconstruction of the senate, his regulation of provincial commands, and his criminal courts remained proofs of his genius for organization.

Coin of Sulla.

Cn. Pompeius Magnus.

CHAPTER XXIX.

FROM THE DEATH OF SULLA TO THE CONSULSHIP OF POMPEY AND CRASSUS. 78–70 B.C.

Revolt of Lepidus.

SULLA was scarcely dead before an attempt was made to overthrow the aristocratical constitution which he had established. The Consul M. Lepidus had already, as we have seen, endeavoured to prevent the burial of Sulla in the Campus Martius. He now proposed to repeal the dictator's laws; but the other consul, Q. Catulus, remained firm to the aristocracy, and offered the most strenuous opposition to the measures of his colleague. Faesulae in Etruria was soon the scene of a revolt of the proletariate which had been dispossessed by Sulla. When the consuls were ordered to suppress it, Lepidus seized the opportunity of putting himself at the head of the insurgents in the revolted district and marching straight upon Rome. The senate assembled an army, which they placed under the command of Q. Catulus, with Pompey as his lieutenant. A battle was fought near the Mulvian bridge, in which Lepidus was defeated, and, finding it impossible to maintain his footing in Italy, he sailed with the remainder of his forces to Sardinia, where he died soon afterwards.

Sertorius in Spain.

Meantime the remains of the Marian party had found refuge in Spain. Q. Sertorius, one of the ablest of their generals, had received the government of this country in the year 82 B.C. He soon acquired an extraordinary ascendency over the minds of the natives, and flattered them with the hope of establishing an independent state which might bid defiance to Rome. His influence was enhanced by the superstition of the people. He was accompanied on all occasions by a tame fawn, which they believed to be a familiar spirit. So attached did they become to his person, that he found no difficulty in collecting a formidable army, which for some years successfully opposed all the power of Rome. Sulla's generals had forced him for a time to quit Spain for Africa; but he soon returned, consolidated his power afresh, and was reinforced in 78 B.C. by a considerable body of troops which Perperna carried with him into Spain after the defeat of Lepidus. In 79 B.C. Metellus, who had been consul the previous year with Sulla, was sent against him; but, though an able general, he was baffled by the unexpected nature of a war, which was no longer a revolt, but a struggle for national independence; and the senate sent Pompey to aid in the reduction of the power, half Roman, half Spanish, of which Sertorius was the head. Pompey, though only thirty years of age, was already regarded as the ablest general of the Republic; and as he played such a prominent part in her later history, we may here pause to give a brief account of his early career.

Pompey.

POMPEY was born in 106 B.C., and was, as we have already seen, the son of Cn. Pompeius Strabo, who fought against the Italians in his consulship, 89 B.C. The young Pompey served under his father in this war, when he was only seventeen years of age, and continued with him till his death two years afterwards. Subsequently he was obliged to fight in the ranks of the democrats, when Cinna forced his way into Rome (87 B.C.); but Pompey was no democrat at heart. As soon as Sulla had finished the Mithridatic War, and was on his way to Italy, instead of waiting, like the other leaders of the aristocracy, for the arrival of their chief, he resolved to share with him the glory of crushing the Marian party. Accordingly he proceeded to levy troops in Picenum without holding any public office; and such was his personal influence that he was able to raise an army of three legions. Before joining Sulla he gained a brilliant victory over the Marian generals, and was received by Sulla with the greatest distinction. Upon the conclusion of the war in Italy, Pompey was sent first into Sicily, and afterwards into Africa, where the Marian party still held out. His success was rapid and decisive. In a few months he reduced the whole of Numidia, and, unlike other Roman governors, abstained from plundering the province. His military achievements and his incorruptibility procured him the greatest renown, and he returned to Rome covered with glory (80 B.C.). Numbers flocked out of the city to meet him; and the dictator himself, who formed one of the crowd, greeted him with the surname of MAGNUS or the GREAT, which he bore ever afterwards. Sulla at first refused to let him triumph, for he had held no magistracy: but as Pompey insisted upon the honour, Sulla gave way, and the young general entered Rome in triumph as a simple eques, and before he had completed his twenty-fifth year.

Pompey again exhibited his power, in promoting, in 79 B.C., the election of M. Aemilius Lepidus to the consulship, in opposition to the wishes of Sulla. The latter had now retired from public affairs, and contented himself with warning Pompey, as he met him returning from the comitia in triumph, "Young man, it is time for you not to slumber, for you have strengthened your rival against yourself." Lepidus seems to have reckoned upon the support of Pompey; but in this he was disappointed, for Pompey remained faithful to the aristocracy, and, after the struggle with Lepidus, crushed the remains of the revolutionary party in Cisalpine Gaul. The senate, who now began to dread Pompey, ordered him to disband his army; but he found various excuses for evading this injunction, as he was anxious to obtain the command of the war against Sertorius in Spain. They hesitated, however, to give him this opportunity for gaining fresh distinction and additional power; and it was only in consequence of the continuous success of Sertorius that they at length unwillingly determined to send Pompey to Spain, with the title of proconsul, and with powers equal to Metellus.

Pompey commands against Sertorius.

Pompey arrived in Spain in 76 B.C. He soon found that he had a more formidable enemy to deal with than he had yet encountered. He suffered several defeats, and, though he gained some advantages, yet such were his losses that at the end of two years he was obliged to send to Rome for reinforcements. The war continued three years longer; but Sertorius, who had lost some of his influence over the Spanish tribes, and who had become an object of jealousy to M. Perperna and his principal Roman officers, was unable to carry on operations with the same vigour as during the two preceding years. Pompey accordingly gained some advantages over him, but the war was still far from a close; and the genius of Sertorius would probably have soon given a very different aspect to affairs, had he not been assassinated by Perperna in 72 B.C.

Murder of Sertorius. Conquest of Spain.

Perperna had flattered himself that he should succeed to the power of Sertorius; but he soon found that he had murdered the only man who was able to save him from ruin. In his first battle with Pompey he was completely defeated, his principal officers slain, and himself taken prisoner. Anxious to save his life, he offered to deliver up to Pompey the papers of Sertorius, containing letters from many of the leading men at Rome. But Pompey refused to see him, and commanded the letters to be burnt. The war was now virtually at an end, and the remainder of the year was employed in subduing the towns which still held out. Metellus had taken no part in the final struggle with Perperna; and Pompey thus obtained the credit of bringing the war to a conclusion. The people longed for his return, that he might deliver Italy from Spartacus and his horde of gladiators, who had defeated the consuls, and were in possession of a great part of the peninsula.

Spartacus.

A righteous retribution had overtaken the Romans for their love of the cruel sports of the amphitheatre. The gladiators were generally prisoners taken in war and sold to persons who trained them in schools for the

Roman games. There was such a school at Capua, and among the gladiators was a Thracian of the name of Spartacus, originally a chief of banditti, who had been taken prisoner by the Romans, and was now destined to be butchered for their amusement. Having prevailed upon about seventy of his comrades, he burst out of the school with them, succeeded in obtaining arms, and took refuge on Vesuvius, at that time an extinct volcano (73 B.C.). Here he was soon joined by large numbers of slaves, who flocked to him from all quarters. He was now at the head of a formidable army. The desolation of the social and civil wars had depopulated Italy, while the employment of slave-labour furnished Spartacus with an endless supply of soldiers. In addition to this, the war with Sertorius was not yet finished, and that with Mithridates, of which we shall speak presently, had already commenced. For upwards of two years Spartacus was master of Italy, which he laid waste from the foot of the Alps to the southernmost corner of the peninsula. In 72 B.C. he found himself at the head of 100,000 men, and defeated both consuls.

Crassus.

As the consuls of the following year had no military reputation, the conduct of the war was entrusted to the praetor, M. Licinius Crassus, who had greatly distinguished himself in the wars of Sulla. He had been rewarded by the dictator with donations of confiscated property, and had accumulated an immense fortune. Six legions were now given him in addition to the remains of the consular armies already in the field. The Roman troops were disheartened and disorganized by defeat, but Crassus restored discipline by decimating the soldiers. Spartacus was driven to the extreme point of Bruttium; his design was to pass over to Sicily, where he would have been welcomed by thousands of followers. But he failed in his attempt to cross the straits, and Crassus drew strong lines of circumvallation across Bruttium to cut off his retreat. Spartacus broke through the lines and again entered Lucania.

Defeat of Spartacus.

The Roman general hastened in pursuit, and fell in with the main body of the fugitives. A desperate battle ensued, in which Spartacus perished, with the greater part of his followers. About 6000 were taken prisoners, whom Crassus impaled on each side of the Appian road between Rome and Capua. A body of 5000 made their way northwards, whom Pompey met as he was returning from Spain, and cut to pieces. Crassus had in reality brought the war to an end; but Pompey took the credit to himself, and wrote to the senate, saying, "Crassus, indeed, has defeated the enemy, but I have extirpated them by the roots."

Pompey and Crassus now approached the city at the head of their armies, and each laid claim to the consulship. Neither of them was qualified by the laws of Sulla. Pompey was only in his thirty-fifth year, and had not even held the office of quaestor. Crassus was still praetor, and two years ought to elapse before he could become consul. A compromise was come to between the generals, and, in order to win support from the democratic party within the city, Pompey declared himself the advocate of the popular rights, and promised to restore the tribunician power. The senate dared not offer opposition, and accordingly they were elected consuls for the following year. Pompey entered the city in triumph on the 31st of December, 71 B.C., and Crassus enjoyed the honour of an ovation.

Coalition of Pompey and Crassus.

The consulship of Pompey and Crassus (70 B.C.) was memorable for the downfall of the most important portions of Sulla's constitutional reforms. The law making the tribunate a bar to higher offices had already been repealed by a Lex Aurelia of 75 B.C.; but Pompey now removed the disabilities on its right of initiative and on the intercession. He also struck another blow at the aristocracy. By one of Sulla's laws the judices during the last ten years had been chosen from the senate. The corruption and venality of the latter in the administration of justice had excited the general indignation which finds expression in Cicero's Verrines, and some change was clamorously demanded by the people.

Downfall of the Sullan constitution.

Accordingly, the Praetor L. Aurelius Cotta, with the approbation of Pompey, proposed a law by which the judices were to be taken in future from the senate, equites, and Tribuni Aerarii, the latter probably representing the order which came next to the equites in the census. This law was likewise carried; but, though it rendered the courts less of a political weapon, it did not improve the purity of the administration of justice, since corruption was not confined to the

Lex Aurelia.

senators, but pervaded all classes of the community alike. Pompey had thus broken with the aristocracy, and had become the great popular hero. In carrying both these measures he was strongly supported by Caesar, who, though he was rapidly rising in popular favour, could as yet only hope to weaken the power of the aristocracy through Pompey's means. The democratic programme was again allied with the military power, and both were paving the way for absolutism.

Coin of Mithridates.

CHAPTER XXX.

THIRD OR GREAT MITHRIDATIC WAR. 74–61 B.C.

Second Mithridatic War.

WHEN Sulla returned to Italy after the first Mithridatic War, he left L. Murena, with two legions, to hold the command in Asia. Murena, who was eager for some opportunity of earning the honour of a triumph, pretending that Mithridates had not yet evacuated the whole of Cappadocia, not only marched into that country, but even crossed the Halys, and laid waste the plains of Pontus itself (83 B.C.). To this flagrant breach of the treaty so lately concluded the Roman general was in great measure instigated by Archelaus, who, finding himself regarded with suspicion by Mithridates, had consulted his safety by flight, and was received with the utmost honour by the Romans.

Defeat of Murena.

Mithridates, who was wholly unprepared to renew the contest with Rome, offered no opposition to the progress of Murena; but finding that general disregard his remonstrances, he sent to Rome to complain of his aggression. When, in the following spring (82 B.C.), he saw Murena preparing to renew his hostile incursions, he at once determined to oppose him by force, and assembled a large army, with which he met the Roman general on the banks of the Halys. The action that ensued terminated in the complete victory of the king; and Murena with difficulty effected his retreat into Phrygia, leaving Cappadocia at the mercy of Mithridates, who quickly overran the whole province.

Shortly afterwards A. Gabinius arrived in Asia, bringing

peremptory orders from Sulla to Murena to desist from hostilities; whereupon Mithridates once more consented to evacuate Cappadocia, and the peace with Rome was renewed.

Renewal of the peace.

Notwithstanding the interposition of Sulla, Mithridates was well aware that the peace between him and Rome was in fact only a suspension of hostilities; and that the haughty Republic would never suffer the massacre of her citizens in Asia to remain unpunished. Hence all his efforts were directed towards the formation of an army capable of contending, not only in numbers but in discipline, with the legions of Rome. With this view he armed his barbarian troops after the Roman fashion, and endeavoured to train them in that discipline the effect of which he had so strongly felt in the preceding contest. In these attempts he was, doubtless, assisted by the refugees of the Marian party, who had accompanied Fimbria into Asia, and, on the defeat of that general by Sulla, had taken refuge with the king of Pontus. At their instigation also Mithridates sent an embassy to Sertorius, who was still maintaining his ground in Spain, and concluded an alliance with him against their common enemies.

Preparations of Mithridates.

But it was the death of Nicomedes III., king of Bithynia, in 75 B.C., that brought matters to a crisis, and became the immediate occasion of the war which both parties had long felt to be inevitable. That monarch left his dominions by will to the Roman people; and Bithynia was accordingly declared a Roman province. But Mithridates asserted that the late king had left a legitimate son by his wife Nysa, whose pretensions he immediately prepared to support by arms.

Bithynia bequeathed to Rome.

The forces with which Mithridates was now prepared to take the field were such as might inspire him with no unreasonable confidence of victory. He had assembled an army of 120,000 foot-soldiers, armed and disciplined in the Roman manner, and 16,000 horse, besides a hundred scythed chariots. His fleet also was so far superior to any that the Romans could oppose to him, as to give him the almost undisputed command of the sea. These preparations, however, appear to have delayed him so long that before he was able to take the field the season was far advanced,

Success of Mithridates.

and both the Roman consuls, L. Licinius Lucullus and M. Aurelius Cotta, had arrived in Asia. Neither of them, however, was able to oppose his first irruption; he traversed almost the whole of Bithynia without encountering any resistance; and when at length Cotta ventured to give him battle under the walls of Calchedon, his army and fleet were totally defeated. Mithridates now proceeded to lay siege to Cyzicus both by sea and land. But Lucullus, who had advanced from Phrygia to the relief of Cotta, and followed Mithridates to Cyzicus, took possession of an advantageous position near the camp of the king, where he almost entirely cut him off from receiving supplies by land, while the storms of the winter prevented him from depending on those by sea. Hence it was not long before famine began to make itself felt in the camp of Mithridates; and all his assaults upon the city having been foiled by the courage and resolution of the besieged, he was at length compelled (early in the year 73 B.C.) to abandon the enterprise and raise the siege.

Victories of Lucullus.

In his retreat he was repeatedly attacked by the Roman general, and suffered very heavy loss at the passage of the Aesepus and Granicus. By the close of the year the great army with which he had commenced the war had been almost annihilated; and he was not only compelled to retire into his own dominions, but was without the means of opposing the advance of Lucullus into the heart of Pontus itself. But he now again set to work with indefatigable activity to raise a fresh army; and while he left the whole of the sea-coast of Pontus open to the invaders, he established himself in the interior at Cabira. Here he was again defeated by Lucullus; and despairing of opposing the further progress of the Romans, he fled into Armenia to claim the protection and assistance of his son-in-law Tigranes.

War with Tigranes.

Tigranes was at this moment the most powerful monarch of Asia, but he appears to have been unwilling to engage openly in war with Rome; and on this account, while he received the fugitive monarch in a friendly manner, he refused to admit him to his presence, and showed no disposition to attempt his restoration. But the arrogance of the Romans brought about a change in his policy; and Tigranes, offended at the haughty conduct of Appius Claudius, whom Lucullus had sent to demand the surrender of Mithridates, not only refused this request, but determined at once to prepare for war.

While Lucullus was waiting for the return of Claudius, he devoted his attention to the settlement of the affairs of Asia, which was suffering severely from the oppressions of the farmers of the public taxes. By various judicious regulations he put a stop to their exactions, and earned the gratitude of the Asiatic cities; but at the same time he brought upon himself the enmity of the equites, who were the farmers of the revenue. They were loud against him in their complaints at Rome, and by their continued clamours undoubtedly prepared the way for his ultimate recall.

Meanwhile community of interests between Mithridates and Tigranes had led to a complete reconciliation between them; and the Pontic king, who had spent a year and eight months in the dominions of his son-in-law without being admitted to a personal interview, was now made to participate in all the councils of Tigranes, and commissioned to raise an army to unite in the war. But it was in vain that in the ensuing campaign (69 B.C.) he urged upon his son-in-law the lessons of his own experience, and advised him to shun a regular action with Lucullus: Tigranes, confident in the multitude of his forces, gave battle at Tigranocerta, and was defeated, before Mithridates had been able to join him. But this disaster, so precisely in accordance with the warnings of Mithridates, served to raise the latter so high in the estimation of Tigranes, that from this time forward the whole conduct of the war was entrusted to the direction of the king of Pontus.

Defeat of Tigranes.

In the following summer (68 B.C.) Lucullus crossed the Taurus, penetrated into the heart of Armenia, and again defeated the allied monarchs near the city of Artaxata. But the early severity of the season, and the discontent of his own troops, checked the further advance of the Roman general, who turned aside into Mesopotamia. Here Mithridates allowed him to lay siege to the fortress of Nisibis, which was supposed to be impregnable, while he himself took advantage of his absence to invade Pontus, at the head of a large army, and endeavour to regain possession of his former dominions. The defence of Pontus was confided to Fabius, one of the lieutenants of Lucullus, but the oppression of

Defeat of Roman armies.

the Romans had excited a general spirit of disaffection, and the people crowded around the standard of Mithridates. Fabius was totally defeated, and compelled to shut himself up in the fortress of Cabira. In the following spring (67 B.C.) Triarius, another of the Roman generals, was also defeated with immense loss at Zela. The blow was one of the severest which the Roman arms had sustained for a long period: 7000 of their troops fell, among whom were an unprecedented number of officers, and their camp itself was taken.

The advance of Lucullus himself from Mesopotamia prevented Mithridates from following up his advantage, and he withdrew into Lesser Armenia, where he took up a strong position to await the approach of Tigranes. But the further proceedings of Lucullus were paralyzed by the mutinous and disaffected spirit of his own soldiers. Their discontents were fostered by P. Clodius, whose turbulent and restless spirit already showed itself in its full force, and were encouraged by reports from Rome, where the demagogues who were favourable to Pompey, or had been gained over by the equestrian party, were loud in their clamours against Lucullus. They accused him of protracting the war for his own personal objects, either of ambition or avarice; and the soldiery, whose appetite for plunder he had often checked, readily joined in the outcry. Accordingly, on the arrival of Tigranes, the two monarchs found themselves able to overrun almost the whole of Pontus and Cappadocia without opposition.

Disaffection in Lucullus' army.

Such was the state of affairs when ten legates arrived in Asia to reduce Pontus to the form of a Roman province; and they had in consequence to report to the senate that the country supposed to be conquered was again in the hands of the enemy. The adversaries of Lucullus naturally availed themselves of so favourable an occasion, and a decree was passed transferring to M'. Acilius Glabrio, one of the consuls for the year (67 B.C.), the province of Bithynia, and the command against Mithridates.

Glabrio appointed.

But Glabrio was wholly incompetent for the task assigned to him. On arriving in Bithynia he made no attempt to assume the command, but remained within the confines of his province, while he still further embarrassed the position of Lucullus by issuing proclamations to his soldiers, announcing to them that their general was superseded, and releasing them from their obedience. Before the close of the year (67 B.C.) Lucullus had the mortification of seeing Mithridates established once more in the possession of his hereditary dominions. But it was still more galling to his feelings when, in the spring of the following year (66 B.C.), he was called upon to resign the command to Pompey, who had just brought to a successful termination the war against the pirates.

Fruitless result of the war.

The Mediterranean had long been swarming with robbers. From the earliest times piracy has more or less prevailed in this sea, which, lying between three continents, and abounding in numerous creeks and islands, presents the greatest temptations and the greatest facilities for piratical pursuits. In consequence of the social and civil wars, and the absence of any united fleet to preserve order upon the sea, the evil had reached an alarming height, and the governors of the separate provinces, with the few ships at their command, found themselves quite unable to cope with this predatory organization. The pirates possessed fleets in all parts of the Mediterranean, were in the habit of plundering the most wealthy cities on the coasts, and had at length carried their audacity so far as to make descents upon the Appian road, and carry off Roman magistrates, with their lictors. All communication between Rome and the provinces was cut off, or rendered extremely dangerous; the fleets of corn-vessels, upon which Rome to a great extent depended for its subsistence, could not reach the city, and provisions rose to famine prices.

The pirates.

The ruin of trade and the scarcity of food united the equites and the masses against the government. At the beginning of 67 B.C. the tribune A. Gabinius, brought forward a bill which was intended to give a delegate of the people almost absolute authority over the greater part of the Roman world. It proposed that a man of consular rank should be chosen, who should possess command over the whole of the Mediterranean with an *imperium* equal to that of other provincial governors whose provinces he touched; he was to be given a fleet of 200 ships, with 15 senatorial legates, as many soldiers and sailors as he thought necessary, and 6000 Attic talents. The bill did not name Pompey, but it was clear who

Lex Gabinia.

was meant. The aristocracy were in the utmost alarm, and in the senate Caesar was almost the only person who came forward in its support. Party spirit ran to such a height that the most serious riots ensued. Even Pompey himself was threatened by one of the consuls, "If you emulate Romulus, you will not escape the end of Romulus." Q. Catulus and Q. Hortensius spoke against the bill with great eloquence, but to no effect. On the day that it became law the price of provisions at Rome immediately fell—a fact which showed the immense confidence which all parties placed in Pompey's military capacity.

Pompey subdues the pirates.

The admiral's plans were formed with great skill, and were crowned with complete success. He stationed his lieutenants with different squadrons in various parts of the Mediterranean to prevent the pirates from uniting, and to hunt them out of various bays and creeks in which they concealed themselves; while, at the same time, he swept the middle of the sea with the main body of his fleet, and chased them eastwards. In forty days he drove the pirates out of the western seas, and restored communication between Spain, Africa, and Italy. After then remaining a short time in Italy, he sailed from Brundusium; cleared the seas as he went along; and forced the pirates to the Cilician coast. Here the decisive action was fought; the pirates were defeated; and more than 20,000 prisoners fell into his hands. Those on whom most reliance could be placed were distributed among the small and depopulated cities of Cilicia, and a large number were settled at Soli, which was henceforward called Pompeiopolis. The second part of this campaign occupied only forty-nine days, and the whole war was brought to a conclusion in the course of three months. Pompey remained in Cilicia during the remainder of this year and the beginning of the one following.

Lex Manilia.

Meanwhile the tribune C. Manilius brought forward a bill (66 B.C.) giving to Pompey the command of the war against Mithridates, with a command unlimited by time or place over the army and the fleet in the East, and with rights equal to those of the ordinary provincial governors (*imperium infinitum aequum*). As his proconsular power already extended over all the coasts and islands of the Mediterranean in virtue of the Gabinian law, this new measure virtually placed almost the whole of the transmarine provinces in his hands. But there was no power, however excessive, which the enthusiasm of the people and the anger of the equites were not ready to entrust to the new hero; and the bill was accordingly passed, notwithstanding the opposition of Hortensius, Catulus, and the aristocratical party. Cicero, the spokesman of the equestrian order, advocated the measure in an oration which has come down to us (*Pro Lege Manilia*), and Caesar likewise supported it with his growing popularity and influence.

On receiving intelligence of this new appointment, Pompey immediately crossed the Taurus, and took the command of the army from Lucullus. The power of Mithridates had been broken by the previous victories of Lucullus, and the successes which the king had gained lately were only occasional and were mainly due to the disorganization of the Roman army. In the plan of the campaign Pompey displayed great military skill. One of his first measures was to secure the alliance of the Parthian king, which not only deprived Mithridates of all hopes of succour from that quarter, but likewise cut him off from all assistance from the Armenian king Tigranes, who was now obliged to look to the safety of his own dominions. Pompey next stationed his fleet in different squadrons along the coasts of Asia Minor, in order to deprive Mithridates of all communication from the sea, and he then proceeded in person at the head of his land forces against the king. Thus thrown back upon his own resources, Mithridates sued for peace, but, as Pompey would hear of nothing but unqualified submission, the negotiation was broken off. The king was still at the head of 30,000 foot and 3000 horse, but he knew too well the strength of a Roman army to venture an engagement with these forces, and accordingly withdrew gradually to the frontiers of Armenia.

Appointment of Pompey.

For a long time he succeeded in avoiding a battle, but he was, at length, surprised by Pompey in Lesser Armenia as he was marching through a narrow pass. The battle was soon decided; the king lost the greater number of his troops, and escaped with only a few horsemen to the fortress of Synorium, on the borders of the Greater Armenia. Here he again collected a considerable force; but as Tigranes refused to admit him into his dominions, because he suspected him of fomenting the intrigues of his son against him,

Defeat of Mithridates.

Mithridates had no alternative but to take refuge in his own distant dominions in the Cimmerian Bosporus. To reach them he had to march through Colchis, and to fight his way through the wild and barbarous tribes that occupied the country between the Caucasus and the Euxine. He succeeded, however, in this arduous enterprise, and reached the Bosporus in safety in the course of the next year (65 B.C.). Pompey abandoned at present all thoughts of following the fugitive king, and resolved at once to attack Tigranes, who was now the more formidable of the two monarchs.

Conquest of Armenia.

On entering Armenia Pompey met with no opposition. He was joined by the young Tigranes, who had revolted against his father, and all the cities submitted to them on their approach. When the Romans drew near to Artaxata, the king, deserted by his army and his court, went out to meet Pompey, and threw himself before him as a suppliant. Pompey received him with kindness, acknowledged him as king of Armenia, and demanded only the payment of 6000 talents. His foreign possessions, however, in Syria, Phoenicia, Cilicia, and Cappadocia, which had been conquered by Lucullus, were to belong to the Romans. To his son Tigranes, Sophene and Gordyene were given as an independent kingdom; but as the young prince was discontented with this arrangement, and even ventured to utter threats, Pompey had him arrested, and kept him in chains to grace his triumph.

Iberians and Albanians.

After thus settling the affairs of Armenia, Pompey proceeded northwards in pursuit of Mithridates. Conflicts ensued with the Iberians and Albanians, and, after the defeat of the latter, all the tribes south of the Caucasus were formally admitted into alliance with Rome (65 B.C.). But Pompey did not continue his projected march to the Crimea further than the Phasis. Here he obtained more certain information of the movements of Mithridates, and learning the wild and inaccessible nature of the country through which he would have to march in order to reach the king, he retraced his steps, and led his troops into winter-quarters at Amisus, on the Euxine. He now reduced Pontus to the form of a Roman province.

In 64 B.C. Pompey marched into Syria, where he deposed Antiochus Asiaticus, and made the country a Roman province.

He likewise compelled the neighbouring princes, who had established independent kingdoms on the ruins of the Syrian empire, to submit to the Roman dominion. The whole of this year was occupied with the settlement of Syria and the adjacent provinces.

Syria.

Next year (63 B.C.), Pompey advanced further south, in order to establish the Roman supremacy in Phoenicia, Coele-Syria, and Palestine. The latter country was at this time distracted by a civil war between the priest-kings Hyrcanus and Aristobulus. Pompey espoused the side of Hyrcanus; and Aristobulus surrendered himself to Pompey, when the latter had advanced near to Jerusalem. But the Jews refused to follow the example of their king; and it was not till after a siege of three months that the city was taken. Pompey entered the holy of holies, the first time that any human being, except the high priest, had penetrated into this sacred spot. He reinstated Hyrcanus in the high priesthood, but compelled him to pay a war indemnity to Rome: Aristobulus accompanied him as a prisoner. It was during this war in Palestine that Pompey received intelligence of the death of Mithridates.

Palestine.

During the last two years Mithridates had been making the most extensive preparations for the renewal of the contest. He had conceived the daring project of marching round the north and west coasts of the Euxine, and emulating Hannibal by penetrating into Italy, and was busily engaged in assembling an enormous fleet and army. But his proceedings were delayed by a long and painful illness, which incapacitated him for any personal exertion. At length, however, his preparations were completed, and he found himself at the head of an army of 36,000 men and a considerable fleet. But during his illness disaffection had made rapid progress among his followers. The full extent of his schemes was probably communicated to few; but enough had transpired to alarm the multitude; and a formidable conspiracy was organized by Pharnaces, the monarch's favourite son.

Last efforts of Mithridates.

He was quickly joined both by the whole army and the citizens of Panticapaeum, who unanimously proclaimed him king; and Mithridates saw that no choice remained to him but death or captivity. Hereupon he took

His death.

poison, which he constantly carried with him ; but his constitution had been so long inured to antidotes, that it did not produce the desired effect, and he was compelled to call in the assistance of one of his Gallic mercenaries to despatch him with his sword.

Pompey's organization of the East.

Pompey now devoted his attention to the settlement of affairs in Asia. His organization of the East marks the close of the third period of the extension of the Roman empire. The Protectorate system, so long clung to in the East, had now been given up, and the acquisition of the provinces of Pontus, Bithynia, and Syria made direct imperial rule extend to the Black Sea and the Euphrates. But a chain of client-states was still kept along the frontier. Pharnaces, the son of Mithridates, was confirmed in the possession of the kingdom of Bosporus; Deiotarus, tetrarch of Galatia, was rewarded with an extension of territory; and Ariobarzanes, king of Cappadocia, was restored to his kingdom. Great efforts were made to cultivate in the new provinces the Greek civic organization; and thirty-nine new towns are said to have sprung into life at Pompey's bidding.

Coin of Tigranes.

Cicero.

CHAPTER XXXI.

INTERNAL HISTORY, FROM THE CONSULSHIP OF POMPEY AND CRASSUS TO THE RETURN OF POMPEY FROM THE EAST.—THE CONSPIRACY OF CATILINE. 69–61 B.C.

DURING the five years of Pompey's absence in the East (67–62 B.C.) he had been the uncertain element in the politics of the Roman world; and both parties watched anxiously to see to what purpose he would use his vast military power. The senate had been beaten by the Gabinian and Manilian laws, and felt their position insecure. The popular party was still crushed and humiliated, and for their recent success had been forced to lean on P. Crassus and the equites. Meanwhile a new leader of the popular party had been rapidly rising into notice, who was destined not

State of parties.

only to crush the aristocracy, but to overthrow the Republic and become the undisputed master of the Roman world.

Caesar.

C. JULIUS CAESAR, who was descended from an old patrician family, was six years younger than Pompey, having been born in 100 B.C. He was connected with the popular party by the marriage of his aunt Julia with the great Marius, and he himself married, at an early age, Cornelia, the daughter of Cinna, the most distinguished of the Marian leaders. Sulla commanded him to divorce his wife, and on his refusal his life was for a time in danger. The vestal virgins and his friends with difficulty obtained his pardon from the dictator, who observed, when they pleaded his youth and insignificance, "that that boy would some day or another be the ruin of the aristocracy, for that there were many Mariuses in him."

This was the first proof which Caesar gave of the resolution and decision of character which distinguished him throughout life. His first campaign was fought under M. Minucius Thermus, in Asia, where he was rewarded, at the siege of Mitylene, with a civic crown for saving the life of a fellow-soldier. His political career commenced with the accusation of Cn. Dolabella for extortion in his province of Macedonia (77 B.C.). Dolabella was acquitted by the senatorial judges; but Caesar gained great reputation by this prosecution, and showed that he possessed powers of oratory which bade fair to place him among the foremost speakers at Rome. To render himself still more perfect, he sought the school of rhetoric at Rhodes, then frequented by Roman nobles; but on his voyage thither he was captured by pirates, with whom the seas of the Mediterranean then swarmed. They detained him until he could obtain fifty talents from the neighbouring cities for his ransom. Immediately on obtaining his liberty, he manned some Milesian vessels, overpowered the pirates, and conducted them as prisoners to Pergamus, where he shortly afterwards crucified them—a punishment he had frequently threatened in sport when he was their prisoner. He then repaired to Rhodes, where he studied for a short time under Apollonius, but soon afterwards crossed over into Asia, on the outbreak of the Mithridatic War in 74 B.C. Here, although he held no public office, he collected troops on his own authority, and repulsed the commander of the king, and then returned to Rome to receive from the people his first public appointment as a military tribune. His affable manners, and still more his unbounded liberality, won the hearts of the people.

Caesar obtained the quaestorship in 68 B.C. In this year he lost his aunt Julia, the widow of Marius, and his own wife Cornelia. He pronounced orations over both of them in the forum, in which he took the opportunity of passing a panegyric upon the former leaders of the popular party. At the funeral of his aunt he caused the images of Marius to be borne in the procession; they were welcomed with loud acclamations by the people, who were delighted to see their former favourite brought, as it were, into public again.

Caesar warmly supported the Gabinian and Manilian laws, which bestowed upon Pompey the command against the pirates and Mithridates: for to support these laws was to weaken the power of the senate. In 65 B.C. he was curule aedile, and still further increased his popularity by the splendid games which he exhibited. He now took a step which openly proclaimed him the leader of the Marian party. He caused the statues of Marius and the Cimbrian trophies, which had been all destroyed by Sulla, to be privately restored and placed at night in the Capitol. In the morning the city was in the highest state of excitement; the veterans of Marius wept with joy at beholding once more the features of their leader and the trophies of their victories, and greeted Caesar with shouts of applause. Q. Catulus brought the conduct of Caesar before the notice of the senate, but the popular excitement was so great that they thought it better to let the matter drop. This year brought Caesar into the full current of home politics, and into contact with a man of very different birth, temperament, and political views.

Cicero.

M. TULLIUS CICERO was born at Arpinum in 106 B.C., and consequently in the same year as Pompey. His father was of the equestrian order, and lived upon his hereditary estate near Arpinum, but none of his ancestors had ever held any of the offices of Rome. Cicero was, therefore, according to the Roman phraseology, a New Man (see p. 155). He served his first and only campaign in the social war (89 B.C.), and in the troubled times which followed he gave himself up with indefatigable perseverance to those studies which were essential to his success as a lawyer and orator. When tranquillity was restored by the final discomfiture of the Marian party he came forward as a pleader at the age of twenty-five. The young orator was not lacking in courage; the first important speech which he delivered upon a criminal trial was that in defence of Sex. Roscius of Ameria, who was charged with parricide by Chrysogonus, a freedman of Sulla, supported, as it was understood, by the influence of his patron. The speech contained a terrible invective against the creatures of the dictator, and, though kindly exempting their master from any active participation in their frauds, was the first strong protest raised against the iniquities of the Sullan *régime*. In consequence of the failure of his health Cicero quitted Rome in 79 B.C., and spent two years in study in the philosophical and rhetorical schools of Athens and Asia Minor. On his return to the city he took his station in the foremost rank of forensic orators, and ere long stood alone in acknowledged pre-eminence; his most formidable rivals—Hortensius, eight years his senior, and C. Aurelius Cotta, who had long been kings of the bar—having been forced, after a short but sharp contest for supremacy, to yield.

Cicero's reputation and popularity already stood so high that he was elected quaestor (76 B.C.), although, comparatively speaking, a stranger, and certainly unsupported by any powerful family interest. He served in Sicily as quaestor of Lilybaeum under the propraetor Sex. Peducaeus. In 70 B.C. he gained great renown by his impeachment of Verres for his oppression of the Sicilians, whom he had ruled as propraetor of Syracuse for the space of three years (73-71 B.C.). The most strenuous exertions were made by Verres, backed by some of the most powerful families, to wrest the case out of the hands of Cicero, who, however, defeated the attempt; and having demanded and been allowed 110 days for the purpose of collecting evidence, he instantly set out for Sicily, which he traversed in less than two months, and returned attended by all the necessary witnesses. Another desperate effort was made by Hortensius, now consul-elect, who was counsel for the defendant, to raise up obstacles which might have the effect of delaying the trial until the commencement of the following year; but here again he was defeated by the promptitude and decision of his opponent, who opening the case very briefly, proceeded at once to the examination of the witnesses and the production of the depositions and other papers, which taken together constituted a mass of testimony so decisive that Verres gave up the contest as hopeless, and retired at once into exile without attempting any defence. In the course of his accusation, Cicero pointed out that senatorial juries themselves were on their trial—a warning all the more significant as the judiciary law of Aurelius * had already been proposed.

In 69 B.C. Cicero was aedile and in 66 praetor. In the latter year he delivered his celebrated address to the people in favour of the Manilian law. Having now the consulship in view, and knowing that, as a new man, he must expect the most determined opposition from the nobles, he resolved to throw himself into the arms of the popular party, and to secure the friendship of Pompey, now certainly the most important person in the Republic.

First Catilinarian conspiracy.

The same year (66 B.C.) was marked by the first conspiracy of Catiline: a plot of such obscurity that its very existence has been doubted; yet it seems certain that the movement which culminated two years later must have already commenced. The circumstances of the times were favourable to a bold and unprincipled adventurer. A widespread feeling of disaffection extended over the whole of Italy. The veterans of Sulla had already squandered their ill-gotten wealth, and longed for a renewal of those scenes of blood which they had found so profitable. The multitudes whose estates he had confiscated and whose relations he had proscribed were eagerly watching for any movement which might give them a chance of becoming robbers and murderers in their turn. The evil of debt was at its height, and the lower classes in Rome and Italy had real grievances which called for settlement. Nor were leaders wanting; the younger nobility, as a class, were thoroughly demoralized, for the most part bankrupts in fortune as well as in fame, and eager for any change which might relieve them from their embarrassments. The rabble were restless and discontented, filled with envy and hatred against the rich and powerful. The time seemed favourable for revolution; for never was the executive weaker. The senate and magistrates were wasting their energies in petty disputes,

* Page 242.

indifferent to the wider interests of the state. Pompey, at the head of all the best troops of the Republic, was prosecuting a long-protracted war in the East; there was no army in Italy, where all was hushed in a treacherous calm.

Catiline.

Few of the nobles at this time were the subjects of darker rumours than L. SERGIUS CATILINA. He was the descendant of an ancient patrician family which had sunk into poverty, and he first appears in history as a zealous partisan of Sulla. During the horrors of the proscription he killed his brother-in-law, Q. Caecilius; he was suspected of an intrigue with a vestal virgin; and it was rumoured that he had made away with his first wife and afterwards with his son in order that he might marry the profligate Aurelia Orestilla, who objected to the presence of a grown-up step-child. Such is the incredibly black picture which two contemporaries, Sallust and Cicero, have painted of a man who moved in the best society, enjoyed great popularity among the younger nobles, and was a successful candidate in the race for honours. It is more certain that he possessed extraordinary powers of mind and body, and that all who came in contact with him submitted more or less to the charm of his manner and his many-sided genius. He was praetor in 68 B.C.; was governor of Africa during the following year; and returned to Rome in 66 B.C. in order to press his suit for the consulship. The election for 65 B.C. was carried by P. Autronius Paetus and P. Cornelius Sulla, both of whom were soon after convicted of bribery, and their places supplied by their competitors and accusers, L. Aurelius Cotta and L. Manlius Torquatus. Catiline, who was desirous of becoming a candidate, had been disqualified in consequence of an impeachment for extortion in his province preferred by P. Clodius Pulcher. Exasperated by their disappointment, Autronius and Catiline are said to have formed a project to murder the new consuls upon the first of January when offering up their vows in the Capitol, after which the conspirators were to seize the fasces. This extraordinary design is said to have been frustrated solely by the impatience of Catiline, who gave the signal prematurely before the whole of the armed agents had assembled.

Catiline was soon afterwards left unfettered by his acquittal on the charge of extortion—a result secured by collusion with his prosecutor—and his mind was again bent on securing the highest dignity of the state. Had he become consul for 63 B.C., there would have been no Catilinarian conspiracy, but probably a very violent financial revolution conducted on the lines of the constitution. He planned an abolition of all existing debts and wholesale measures of confiscation; and his agents were already chosen. They were men of broken fortunes; chief amongst them were Lentulus, an ex-consul who had been struck out of the list of the senate, and Cethegus, a violent and sanguinary revolutionist.

Designs of Catiline.

Catiline's competitors at the consular elections in 64 B.C. were Cicero and C. Antonius. Antonius he had already secured as an ally, and the struggle lay between himself and Cicero. The government, half conscious of his plans, was in the utmost alarm. There was no senatorial candidate who stood a chance of success, and, therefore, throwing its prejudices against a new man to the winds, it warmly supported Cicero. The orator, who already had the support of the equites and of a large section of the municipal voters of Italy, was returned at the head of the poll with Antonius as his colleague.

Cicero consul.

When Cicero assumed the consulship in 63 B.C. the democratic party was in great straits. A fragment of it was struggling for revolution with Catiline. The larger and more respectable portion now strove to gain for its leaders a position in the state which might balance that of Pompey in the East. An agrarian law was introduced by the tribune Rullus which, under the pretext of providing land by purchase for the poorer citizens, aimed at establishing a commission of ten men, with vast powers at home and abroad. If the democrats relied on Cicero's support, they were mistaken. The orator paid his debt to the aristocracy and to Pompey, whose position the law imperilled, by opposing and defeating Rullus' bill.

Agrarian law of Rullus.

The democrats were outwitted; but Cicero had now to meet the plots of the revolutionists. The safety of the state depended on his watchfulness, and he showed consummate skill in baffling what had now become a formidable conspiracy.

Cicero detects the conspiracy.

He gained over his colleague Antonius by resigning to him the province of Macedonia. Meantime he became acquainted with every detail of the plot through Fulvia, the mistress of Q. Curius, one of Catiline's intimate associates.

Second Catilinarian conspiracy.

Thus informed, Cicero called a meeting of the senate on the 21st of October, when he openly denounced Catiline, charged him broadly with treason, and asserted that the 28th was the period fixed for the murder of the leading men in the Republic. The senate thereupon invested the consuls with dictatorial power. The comitia for the election of the consuls was now held. Catiline, again a candidate, was again rejected. Driven to despair by this fresh disappointment, he resolved at once to bring matters to a crisis. On the night of the 6th of November he summoned a meeting of the ringleaders at the house of M. Porcius Laeca, and made arrangements for an immediate outbreak. Cicero, being immediately informed of what took place, summoned, on the 8th of November, a meeting of the senate in the temple of Jupiter Stator, and there delivered the first of his celebrated orations against Catiline. Catiline, who upon his entrance had been avoided by all, and was sitting alone upon a bench from which every one had shrunk, rose to reply, but had scarcely commenced when his words were drowned by the shouts of "enemy" and "parricide" which burst from the whole assembly, and he rushed forth with threats and curses on his lips. He now resolved to strike some decisive blow before troops could be levied to oppose him, and accordingly, leaving the chief control of affairs at Rome in the hands of Lentulus and Cethegus, he set forth in the dead of night, and proceeded to join Manlius, an old soldier who was mustering the troops of the revolutionists at Faesulae.

Shortly afterwards fresh evidence came into Cicero's hands which, he thought, justified prompter action. Ambassadors from the Gallic tribe of the Allobroges, who were now at Rome, had been tampered with by the conspirators. They thought fit to reveal the communication to Q. Fabius Sanga, the patron of their state, who in his turn acquainted Cicero. By the instructions of the latter the ambassadors affected great zeal in the undertaking, and obtained a written agreement signed by Lentulus, Cethegus,

Catiline quits Rome.

and others. They quitted Rome soon after midnight on the 3rd of December, accompanied by one T. Volturcius, who was charged with despatches for Catiline. The ambassadors were seized as they were crossing the Mulvian bridge by two of the praetors who had been stationed in ambush to intercept them.

The conspirators arrested.

Cicero instantly summoned Lentulus, Cethegus, and the other conspirators to his presence. Lentulus being praetor, the consul led him by the hand to the Temple of Concord, where the senate was already met; the rest of the accused followed closely guarded. Volturcius, finding escape impossible, agreed, upon his own personal safety being insured, to make a full confession. His statements were confirmed by the Allobroges, and the testimony was rendered conclusive by the signatures of the ringleaders, which they were unable to deny. The guilt of Lentulus, Cethegus, and seven others being thus established, Lentulus was forced to abdicate his office, and then with the rest was consigned to the charge of certain senators, who became responsible for their appearance.

Execution of the conspirators.

These circumstances, as they had occurred, were then narrated by Cicero in his third oration, delivered in the forum. On the nones (5th) of December the senate was again summoned to determine upon the fate of the conspirators. The feeling of the senate was in favour of their execution until the resolution of many was weakened by a vigorous speech from Caesar. While expressing horror of the conspiracy, he deprecated the death-penalty as unconstitutional, and proposed, as an alternative, that the property of the prisoners should be confiscated, and that they should be kept in perpetual confinement in municipal towns in Italy. But the scale was turned again by Cato's speech. He strongly advocated that the conspirators should be put to death, and his view found favour with the consul, who put his opinion to the vote. It was carried, and on the same night Lentulus and his associates were strangled by the common executioner in the Tullianum, a loathsome dungeon on the slope of the Capitol.

While things went thus at Rome Catiline had collected a force amounting to two legions, although not above one fourth part were fully equipped. When the news of the failure of the plot at Rome reached his camp many deserted. He thereupon attempted to cross the Apennines and take refuge in Cisalpine Gaul, but the passes were strictly guarded by Metellus Celer with three legions. Finding, therefore, that escape was cut off in front while Antonius was pressing on his rear, Catiline determined as a last resource to hazard an engagement. Antonius, in consequence of real or pretended illness, resigned the command to M. Petreius, a skilful soldier. The battle was obstinate and bloody. The rebels fought with the fury of despair; and when Catiline saw that all was lost he charged headlong into the thickest of the fight and fell sword in hand (62 B.C.).

Catiline defeated.

Although it is impossible to say how dangerous the Catilinarian movement really was, Cicero seemed for the moment to have rendered important services to the state. Catulus in the senate and Cato in the forum hailed him as the "Father of his Country;" thanksgivings in his name were voted to the gods; and all Italy joined in testifying enthusiastic admiration and gratitude. Cicero's elation knew no bounds; he fancied that his political influence was now supreme, and looked upon himself as a match even for Pompey. But his splendid achievement contained the germ of his humiliation and downfall. There could be no doubt that the punishment inflicted by the senate upon Lentulus and his associates was a violation of the fundamental principles of the Roman constitution, which declared that no citizen could be put to death until sentenced by the whole body of the people assembled in their comitia, and for this act Cicero, as the presiding magistrate, was held responsible. It was in vain to urge that the consuls had been armed with dictatorial power; the senate, in the present instance, assuming to themselves judicial functions which they had no right to exercise, gave orders for the execution of a sentence which they had no right to pronounce. Nor were Cicero's enemies long in discovering this vulnerable point. On the last day of the year, when, according to established custom, he ascended the Rostra to give an account to the people of the events of his consulship, Metellus Nepos, one of the new tribunes, forbade him to speak, exclaiming that the man who had put Roman citizens to death without granting them a hearing was himself unworthy of being heard. But this attack was premature. The audience had not yet forgotten their recent escape; so that,

Illegality of the execution.

when Cicero swore with a loud voice that "he had saved the Republic and the city from ruin," the crowd with one voice responded that he had sworn truly.

Rumoured complicity of the democratic leaders.

It was rumoured that many other eminent men had been privy to Catiline's conspiracy. Among others the names of Crassus and Caesar were mentioned in connection with the first conspiracy of 66 B.C., but the participation of either of these men in such an enterprise seems most improbable. The interests of Crassus were opposed to such an adventure; his vast wealth was employed in a variety of speculations which would have been ruined in a general overthrow; while he had not the energy or ability to seize and retain the helm in the confusion that would have ensued. Of Caesar's guilt there is no satisfactory evidence, and it is improbable that so keen-sighted a man would have leagued with such a desperate adventurer as Catiline. It is true that Caesar was suspected by some of the leading optimates; but then to men of this stamp all "radicals" (*improbi*), as Caesar and Catiline were indifferently called, are alike. It is impossible to say how much complicity there must be between the two extremes of the same party; but it is certain that in the next year (62 B.C.), when a suspicion of Caesar's guilt was raised, he challenged with success Cicero's testimony that he had of his own accord given the consul evidence concerning the conspiracy.

Coin of Pompey.

C. Julius Caesar.

CHAPTER XXXII.

FROM POMPEY'S RETURN FROM THE EAST TO CICERO'S BANISHMENT AND RECALL. 62–57 B.C.

Pompey's return and triumph.

POMPEY reached Italy in 62 B.C. To the astonishment and relief of all parties, he disbanded his army immediately after landing at Brundusium. He did not, however, enter Rome in triumph till the 30th of September, 61 B.C. The triumph lasted two days, and surpassed in splendour every spectacle that Rome had yet seen. The tablets carried in the procession, on which his victories were emblazoned, declared that he had subdued 14 nations, taken 1000 strong fortresses, 900 towns, and 800 ships; that he had founded 39 cities; that he had increased the revenue of the Roman people by 85 million sesterces; and that he had brought into the public treasury 20,000 talents. Before his triumphal car walked a crowd of piratical chieftains, Eastern princes, and hostages from Albania and Iberia.

With this triumph the first and most glorious part of Pompey's life may be said to have ended. Hitherto he had been employed almost exclusively in war; but now he was called upon to play a prominent part in the civil commotions of the Republic—a part for which neither his natural talents nor his previous habits had in the least fitted him.

His position at Rome.

From the death of Sulla to the present time, a period of nearly twenty years, he had been unquestionably the first man in the Roman world, and it is certain that, down to the outbreak of the civil war, he was still looked on as the leading man in the state, although he must himself have felt that the real power was centering in Caesar's hands. Pompey, on his return to Rome, hardly knew to which party he might have to attach himself. He had been appointed to the command against the pirates and Mithridates in opposition to the aristocracy, and they still regarded him with jealousy and distrust. At the same time he seems to have been indisposed to unite himself to the popular party, now more than ever discredited by the rash proceedings of Catiline. But the object which engaged the immediate attention of Pompey was to obtain from the senate a ratification of his acts in Asia, and an assignment of lands which he had promised to his veterans. In order to secure this object, he had purchased the consulship for one of his officers, L. Afranius, who was elected with Q. Metellus for 60 B.C. But L. Afranius was a man of slender ability; and the senate, glad of an opportunity to put an affront upon a person whom they both feared and hated, resolutely refused to sanction Pompey's measures in Asia.

Junction with Caesar and Crassus.

This was the deciding point; it is probable that, even before his return, overtures had been made to him by the democratic party. They were now accepted; the short-sighted policy of the optimates threw Pompey into Caesar's arms, and thus sealed the downfall of their party. Pompey was resolved to fulfil, at all costs, the promises which he had made to his Asiatic clients and his veteran troops.

Caesar had returned from Spain in the middle of this year. He had been in that province for one year as propraetor, during which time he displayed some military ability and a capacity for enriching himself at the expense of the provincials. For some successes gained in Lusitania his troops had saluted him as imperator, and the senate had honoured him by a public thanksgiving. He now laid claim to a triumph, and at the same time wished to become a candidate for the consulship. For the latter purpose his presence in Rome was necessary; but as he could not enter the city without relinquishing his triumph, he applied to the senate to be exempted from the usual law, and to become a candidate in his absence. As this was refused, he at once relinquished his triumph, entered the city, and stood for the consulship. He was elected without difficulty, but the aristocracy succeeded in associating with him in the consulship M. Bibulus, who belonged to the opposite party, and who had likewise been his colleague in the aedileship and praetorship.

The first triumvirate.

The coalition still lacked the support of the capitalist class; but this was soon supplied by M. Crassus, who, by his connexions and immense wealth, possessed great political influence. Pompey and Crassus had for a long time past been deadly enemies, but Caesar effected a reconciliation, and the three entered into an agreement to divide the power between themselves. This first triumvirate, as it is called, was therefore merely a private arrangement between the three most powerful men at Rome, which remained a secret till the proceedings of Caesar in his consulship showed that he was supported by a power against which it was in vain for his enemies to struggle.

Caesar's consulship.

As soon as Caesar had entered upon his consulship he fulfilled part of his compact with Pompey, and at the same time attracted the sympathy of the masses by proposing an agrarian law for the division of the rich Campanian land—a portion of the public domain which had been exempted even from the legislation of the Gracchi. The opposition of the aristocratical party was in vain, and Pompey and Crassus both spoke in favour of the law. On the day on which it was put to the vote Bibulus and the other members of the aristocracy were driven out of the forum by force of arms: the law was carried, the commissioners appointed, and about 20,000 citizens, comprising of course a great number of Pompey's veterans, subsequently received allotments. Bibulus, despairing of being able to offer any further resistance to Caesar, shut himself up in his own house, and attempted to interrupt public business by the announcement of omens, which were consistently disregarded by his colleague.

Caesar obtained from the people a ratification of all Pompey's acts in Asia; and, to cement their union more closely, gave him his only daughter Julia in marriage. His next step was to gain over the equites, who had rendered efficient service to Cicero in his consulship, and had hitherto supported the aristocratical party. An excellent opportunity now occurred for accomplishing this object. In their eagerness to obtain the farming of the public taxes in Asia, the equites had agreed to pay too large a sum, and accordingly petitioned the senate for more favourable terms. This, however, had been opposed by Metellus Celer, Cato, and others of the aristocracy; and Caesar therefore now carried a law to relieve the equites from one-third of the sum which they had agreed to pay. Having thus gratified the people, the equites, and Pompey, he was easily able to obtain for himself the provinces which he wished.

It is not attributing any extraordinary foresight to Caesar to suppose that he already saw that the struggle between the different parties at Rome must eventually be terminated by the sword. The same causes were still in operation which had led to the civil wars between Marius and Sulla; and he was well aware that the aristocracy would not hesitate to call in the assistance of force if they should ever succeed in detaching Pompey from his interests.

It was therefore of the first importance for him to obtain an army which he might attach to himself by victories and rewards. Accordingly he induced the tribune Vatinius to propose a bill to the people granting him the provinces of Cisalpine Gaul and Illyricum for five years (58–54 B.C.). Transalpine Gaul was shortly afterwards added. Caesar chose the Gallic provinces, as he would thus be able to pass the winter in Italy, and keep up his communication with the city, while the disturbed state of Further Gaul promised him sufficient materials for engaging in a series of wars in which he might employ an army that would afterwards

Gaul assigned to Caesar.

be devoted to his purposes. In addition to these considerations, Caesar was also actuated by the ambition of subduing for ever that nation which had once sacked Rome, and which had been, from the earliest times, an object of dread to the Roman state.

Cicero, in spite of earnest invitations, had held aloof from the triumvirate; and Caesar felt that it would be unsafe to leave Rome unless a man with a large Italian following, and whose matchless oratory was now at the service of the senatorial party, was in some way silenced. It was needless to devise means for Cicero's banishment; it was only necessary to refuse him protection against the attacks of Clodius.

Cicero's position.

P. Clodius Pulcher was the darling of the city mob, and represented their views as to the illegality of the execution of the Catilinarian conspirators. His hostility to Cicero was increased by a private grudge. In 62 B.C., while the wife of Caesar was celebrating in the house of her husband, then praetor and Pontifex Maximus, the rites of the Bona Dea, from which all male creatures were excluded, it was discovered that Clodius had found his way into the mansion disguised in women's apparel, and, having been detected, had made his escape by the help of a female slave. The matter was laid before the senate, and by them referred to the members of the Pontifical College, who passed a resolution that sacrilege had been committed. Caesar forthwith divorced his wife. Clodius was impeached and brought to trial. In defence he pleaded an alibi; but Cicero came forward as a witness, and swore that he had met and spoken to Clodius in Rome on the day in question. In spite of this decisive testimony, and the evident guilt of the accused, the judices pronounced him innocent by a majority of voices (61 B.C.). Clodius now vowed deadly vengeance against Cicero. To accomplish his purpose more readily, he determined to become a candidate for the tribunate, but for this it was necessary that he should be adopted into a plebeian family. This, after protracted opposition, was at length accomplished through the interference of the triumvirs, and he was elected tribune for 58 B.C.

Clodius.

One of the first acts of Clodius, after entering upon office, was to propose a bill interdicting from fire and water any one who should be found to have put a Roman citizen to death untried.

Cicero changed his attire, and, assuming the garb of one accused, went round the forum soliciting the compassion of all whom he met. For a brief period public sympathy was awakened. A large number of the senate and the equites appeared also in mourning, and the better portion of the citizens seemed resolved to espouse his cause. But all demonstrations of such feelings were promptly repressed by Piso and Gabinius, the consuls for the year, who were both creatures of the triumvirs; and Cicero was left to his fate. Giving way to despair, he quitted Rome at the beginning of April (58 B.C.), and reached Brundusium about the middle of the month. From thence he crossed over to Greece. The instant that the departure of Cicero became known, Clodius passed a law pronouncing his banishment, forbidding any one to entertain or harbour him, and denouncing as a public enemy whosoever should take any steps towards procuring his recall. His mansion on the Palatine, and his villas at Tusculum and Formiae, were at the same time given over to plunder and destruction.

Banishment of Cicero.

Clodius, having thus gratified his hatred, did not care to consult any longer the views of the triumvirs. He restored Tigranes to liberty, whom Pompey had kept in confinement, ridiculed the great imperator before the people, and was accused of making an attempt upon his life. Pompey in revenge resolved to procure the recall of Cicero from banishment, and probably Caesar, who never ceased to court the orator's support, thought that the lesson had been sufficient. The new consuls (57 B.C.), too, were favourable to Cicero; but though Clodius was no longer in office, he had several partisans among the tribunes who offered the most vehement opposition to the restoration of his great enemy.

Clodius opposes Pompey.

One of the chief supporters of Cicero was the tribune T. Annius Milo, a man as unprincipled and violent as Clodius himself. He opposed force to force, and at the head of a band of gladiators attacked the hired ruffians of Clodius. The streets of Rome were the scenes of almost daily conflicts between the leaders of these assassins.

Milo.

At length the senate, with the full approbation of Pompey, determined to invite the voters from the different parts of Italy to repair to Rome and assist in carrying a law for the recall of Cicero. Accordingly, on the 4th of August, the bill was passed by an overwhelming majority. On the same day Cicero quitted Dyrrachium, and crossed over to Brundusium. He received deputations and congratulatory addresses from all the towns on the line of the Appian Way; and having arrived at Rome on the 4th of September, a vast multitude poured forth to meet him, while the crowd rent the air with acclamations as he passed through the forum and ascended the Capitol to render thanks to Jupiter (57 B.C.).

Cicero's recall.

Temple of Nemausus (*Nîmes*), now called the *Maison Carrée.*

CHAPTER XXXIII.

CAESAR'S CAMPAIGNS IN GAUL. 58-50 B.C.

Caesar set out for his province immediately after Cicero had gone into exile (58 B.C.). During the next nine years he was occupied with the subjugation of Gaul. In this time he conquered the whole of Transalpine Gaul, which, with the exception of the province of Narbonensis, had hitherto been independent of Rome. Twice he crossed the Rhine, and carried the terror of the Roman arms beyond that river. Twice he landed in Britain, which had been hitherto unknown to the Romans. We can only offer a very brief sketch of the principal events of each year.

First Campaign, 58 B.C.—Caesar left Rome towards the latter end of April, and arrived at Genăva in eight days. His first campaign was against the Helvetii, a Gallic people situated to the north of the Lake of Geneva, and between the Rhine and Mount Jura. This people, quitting their homes under pressure from the Germans, had passed through the country of the Sequani, and were plundering the territories of the Aedui. Three out of their four clans had already crossed the Arar (*Saône*); but the fourth, which was still on the eastern side of the river, was surprised by Caesar and cut to pieces. He then threw a bridge across the Arar, followed them cautiously for some days, and at length fought a pitched battle with them near the town of Bibracte (*Autun*). The Helvetii were defeated with great slaughter, and the remnant compelled to return to their former homes.

Defeat of the Helvetii.

This great victory roused the Gauls to ask Caesar's assistance against the Germans; and the Aedui, with the consent of the central Gallic tribes, solicited his help against Ariovistus, a German king who had invaded Gaul, and was constantly bringing over the Rhine fresh swarms of Germans. Caesar commanded Ariovistus to abstain from introducing any more of his countrymen into Gaul, to restore the hostages to the Aedui, who were clients of Rome, and not to attack the latter or their allies. A haughty answer was returned to these commands, and both parties prepared for war. Caesar advanced northwards through the country of the Sequani, took possession of Vesontio (*Besançon*), an important town on the Dubis (*Doubs*), and some days afterwards fought a decisive battle with Ariovistus, who suffered a total defeat, and fled with the remains of his army to the Rhine, a distance of fifty miles. Only a very few, and amongst others Ariovistus himself, crossed the river; the rest were cut to pieces by the Roman cavalry. The Rhine had now become, what it afterwards remained, the boundary of the Roman empire against the Germans.

Ariovistus and the Germans.

Second Campaign, 57 B.C.—Central Gaul was for the moment pacified; but the northern tribes had not sought Caesar's help, and now the cantons of the Belgae, who dwelt between the Sequana (*Seine*) and the Rhine, alarmed at his success, had entered into a confederacy

Subjugation of the Belgae.

to oppose him, and had raised an army of 300,000 men. Caesar opened the campaign by marching into the country of the Remi, who submitted at his approach. He then crossed the Axona (*Aisne*), and pitched his camp in a strong position on the right bank. The enemy soon began to suffer from want of provisions, and they came to the resolution of breaking up their vast army, and retiring to their own territories. Hitherto Caesar had remained in his entrenchments, but he now broke up from his quarters, and resumed the offensive. The Suessiones, the Bellovaci, and the Ambiani were subdued in succession, or surrendered of their own accord; but a more formidable task awaited him when he came to the Nervii, the most warlike of all the Belgic tribes. In their country, near the river Sabis (*Sambre*), the Roman army was surprised by the enemy while engaged in fortifying the camp. The attack of the Nervii was so unexpected that before the Romans could form in rank the enemy was in their midst: the Roman soldiers began to give way, and the battle seemed entirely lost. Caesar freely exposed his own person in the first line of the battle, and discharged alike the duties of a brave soldier and an able general. His exertions and the discipline of the Roman troops at length triumphed; and the Nervii were defeated with such immense slaughter, that out of 60,000 fighting-men only 500 remained in the state. The Belgae were subdued, and the Remi, as the clients of Rome, made the leading canton in the district.

Third Campaign, 56 B.C.—In the third campaign Caesar completed the subjugation of Gaul. He conducted in person a naval war against the Veneti, the inhabitants of the modern Brittany, and by means of his lieutenants conquered the remaining tribes who still held out.

War with the Veneti.

In the later part of the summer Caesar marched against the Morini and Menapii (in the neighbourhood of Calais and Boulogne), who retired into their forest fastnesses. Thus all Gaul had been reduced in three years to an outward show of obedience, which ill expressed the yet unbroken spirit of the people.

Fourth Campaign, 55 B.C.—But Caesar felt that the conquest of Gaul was useless unless measures were taken to check the tide of German immigration from across the Rhine; for it was this that caused the movement of the Celtic nations which had so often threatened the safety of Italy. Two German tribes, the Usipetes and the Tencteri, had just been driven out of their own country by the Suevi, and had crossed the Rhine with the intention of settling in Gaul. This, however, Caesar was resolved to prevent, and accordingly prepared to attack them. The Germans opened negotiations with him, but while these were going on, a body of their cavalry defeated Caesar's Gallic horse. On the next day all the German chiefs came into Caesar's camp to apologise for what had been done; but Caesar detained them, and straightway led his troops to attack the enemy. Deprived of their leaders and taken by surprise, the Germans, after a feeble resistance, took to flight, and were almost all destroyed by the Roman cavalry.

Renewed conflicts with the Germans.

After this victory Caesar resolved to cross the Rhine in order to strike terror into the Germans. In ten days he built a bridge of boats across the river, probably in the neighbourhood of Cologne; and after spending eighteen days on the eastern side of the Rhine, and ravaging the country of the Sugambri, he returned to Gaul and broke down the bridge.

Cæsar crosses the Rhine.

Although the greater part of the summer was now gone, Caesar resolved to invade Britain. His object in undertaking this expedition at such a late period of the year was rather to inspire the natives with the fear of attack, and to force them to desist from their communications with Gaul, than with any view to permanent conquest. He accordingly took with him only two legions, with which he sailed from the port Itius (probably Wissant, between Calais and Boulogne), and effected a landing somewhere near the South Foreland, after a severe struggle with the natives. Several of the British tribes hereupon sent offers of submission; but, in consequence of the loss of a great part of the Roman fleet a few days afterwards, they took up arms again. Defeated, they renewed their offers of submission to Caesar, who simply demanded double the number of hostages he had originally required, as he was anxious to return to Gaul before the autumnal equinox.

First invasion of Britain.

The news of these victories over the Germans and far-distant Britons was received at Rome with the greatest enthusiasm.

The senate voted a public thanksgiving of twenty days, notwithstanding the opposition of Cato, who declared that Caesar ought to be delivered up to the Usipetes and Tencteri, to atone for his treachery in seizing the sacred persons of ambassadors.

Fifth Campaign, 54 B.C.—The greater part of Caesar's fifth campaign was occupied with his second invasion of Britain. He sailed from the port Itius with an army of five legions, and landed without opposition at the same place as in the former year. The British states had entrusted the supreme command to Cassivellaunus, a chief who ruled Middlesex and the surrounding districts to the north of the Thames (*Tamĕsis*). The Britons bravely opposed the progress of the invaders, but were defeated in a series of engagements. Caesar crossed the Thames above London, probably in the neighbourhood of Kingston, took the town of Cassivellaunus, and conquered great part of the counties of Essex and Middlesex. In consequence of these disasters, Cassivellaunus sued for peace; and after demanding hostages, and settling the tribute which Britain should pay yearly to the Roman people, Caesar returned to Gaul towards the end of the summer. Nothing was gained by this invasion in the way of a permanent occupation of the island; but this was, perhaps, not intended. Caesar's immediate and professed object—to prevent the Celts of Britain from furnishing assistance to disaffected Gallic chiefs across the Channel—was possibly attained.

Second invasion of Britain.

In consequence of the great scarcity of corn in Gaul, Caesar was obliged to divide his forces, and station his legions for the winter in different parts. This seemed to the Gauls a favourable opportunity for recovering their lost independence, and destroying their conquerors. The Eburones, a Gallic people between the Meuse and the Rhine, near the modern *Tongres*, destroyed the detachment under the command of T. Titurius Sabinus and L. Aurunculeius Cotta. They next attacked the camp of Q. Cicero, the brother of the orator, who was stationed among the Nervii. Cicero repulsed the enemy in all their attempts, till a mounted messenger was able to steal through their lines and bring the news to Caesar. He rapidly approached with two legions to the aid of his beleaguered legate. The siege was raised; Caesar defeated the forces of the enemy,

Revolt of the Eburones and Nervii.

which amounted to 60,000 men, and the insurgents rapidly dispersed.

Sixth Campaign, 53 B.C.—In the next year the Gauls again took up arms, and entered into a most formidable conspiracy to recover their independence. The destruction of the Roman troops under Sabinus and Cotta, and the unsettled state of Gaul during the winter, had led Caesar to apprehend a general rising of the natives; and he had accordingly levied two new legions in Cisalpine Gaul, and obtained one from Pompey, who was remaining in the neighbourhood of Rome as proconsul with the imperium. Being thus at the head of a powerful army, he was able to subdue the tribes that revolted, and soon compelled the Nervii, Senones, Carnutes, Menapii, and Treviri to return to obedience.

Renewed outbreaks.

But as the Treviri had been supported by the Germans, he crossed the Rhine again a little above the spot where he had passed over two years before; and after receiving the submission of the Ubii, ravaged the country of the Suevi. On his return to Gaul he laid waste the country of the Eburones with fire and sword. At the conclusion of the campaign he prosecuted a strict inquiry into the revolt of the Senones and Carnutes; and caused Acco, who had been the chief ringleader in the conspiracy, to be put to death.

Second passage of the Rhine.

Seventh Campaign, 52 B.C.—The unsuccessful issue of last year's revolt had not yet damped the spirits of the Gauls. The execution of Acco had alarmed all the chiefs, as every one feared that his turn might come next; the hatred of the Roman yoke was intense; and thus all the materials were ready for a general conflagration. It was first kindled by the Carnutes, and in a short time it spread from district to district till almost the whole of Gaul was in flames. Even the Aedui, who had been hitherto the faithful allies of the Romans, and had assisted them in all their wars, subsequently joined the general revolt.

General insurrection in Gaul.

At the head of the insurrection was Vercingetorix, a young man of noble family belonging to the Arverni, and by far the ablest general that Caesar had yet encountered. Never before had the Gauls been so united: Caesar's conquests of the last six years seemed to be now

Vercingetorix.

entirely lost. The campaign of this year, therefore, was by far the most arduous that he had yet conducted; but his genius triumphed over every obstacle, and rendered it the most brilliant of all. He concentrated his forces with incredible rapidity, and lost no time in attacking the chief towns in the hands of the enemy. Vellaunodunum (in the country of *Château-Landon*), Cenabum (*Orléans*), and Noviodunum (*Nouan*, between Orleans and Bourges) fell into his hands without difficulty. Alarmed at his rapid progress, Vercingetorix persuaded his countrymen to lay waste their country and destroy their towns. This plan was accordingly carried into effect; but, contrary to the wishes of Vercingetorix, Avaricum (*Bourges*), the chief town of the Bituriges, and a strongly fortified place, was spared from the general destruction. This town Caesar accordingly besieged; and, notwithstanding the heroic resistance of the Gauls, it was at length taken, and all the inhabitants, men, women, and children, were indiscriminately butchered.

Caesar now divided his army into two parts: one division, consisting of four legions, he sent, under the command of T. Labienus, against the Senones and Parisii; the other, comprising six legions, he led in person into the country of the Arverni, and with them laid siege to Gergovia (near *Clermont*). The revolt of the Aedui shortly afterwards compelled him to raise the siege, and inspired the Gauls with fresh courage.

Vercingetorix retired to Alesia (*Alise* in Burgundy), which was considered impregnable, and resolved to wait for succours from his countrymen. Caesar immediately laid siege to the place, and drew lines of circumvallation around it. The Romans, however, were in their turn soon surrounded by a vast Gallic army which had assembled to raise the siege. Caesar's army was thus placed in imminent peril, and on no occasion in his whole life was his military genius so conspicuous. He was between two great armies. Vercingetorix had 80,000 infantry alone in Alesia, and the Gallic army without consisted of between 250,000 and 300,000 men. Still he would not raise the siege. He prevented Vercingetorix from breaking through the lines, entirely routed the Gallic army without, and finally compelled Alesia to surrender. Vercingetorix himself fell into his hands. The fall of Alesia was followed by the submission of the Aedui and

Siege of Alesia.

Arverni. Caesar then led his troops into winter quarters. After receiving his despatches, the senate voted him a public thanksgiving of twenty days, as in the year 55 B.C.

Eighth Campaign, 51 B.C.—The victories of the preceding year had determined the fate of Gaul; but many states still remained in arms, and entered into fresh conspiracies during the winter. This year was occupied in the reduction of these states, into the particulars of which we need not enter. During the winter Caesar employed himself in the pacification of Gaul; and, as he already saw that his presence would soon be necessary in Italy, he was anxious to remove all causes for future wars. While fixing the tribute for each community, he treated the states with honour and respect, and even bestowed Roman citizenship upon some of their chiefs. The experience of the last two years had taught the Gauls that they had no hope of contending successfully against Caesar, and even in the great turmoil of the ensuing civil wars their loyalty to Rome remained unshaken.

Final pacification of Gaul.

So ended the nine years' war, which, though it appears as a long series of aggressions on Caesar's part, was really waged in a defensive spirit. It gave the Roman Empire a northern frontier, and saved the civilized world from barbarian invasions for more than four hundred years.

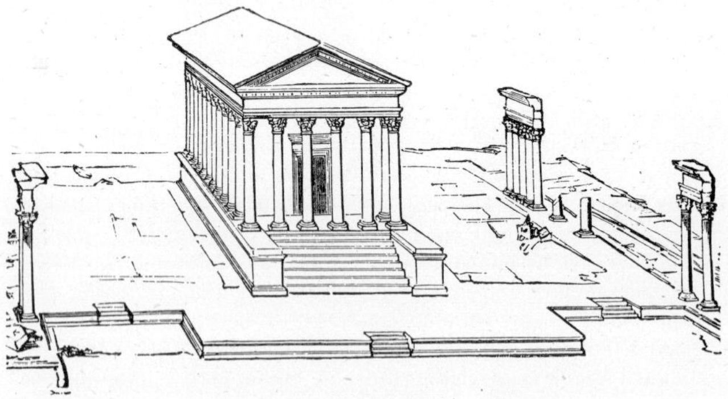

Outline view of the Maison Carrée at Nîmes.

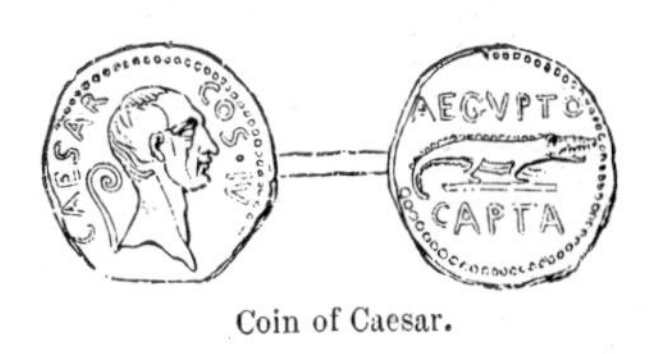

Coin of Caesar.

CHAPTER XXXIV.

INTERNAL HISTORY, FROM THE RETURN OF CICERO FROM BANISHMENT TO THE COMMENCEMENT OF THE CIVIL WAR.—EXPEDITION AND DEATH OF CRASSUS. 57–50 B.C.

CICERO returned from banishment an altered man. Though his return had been glorious, he saw that his position was entirely changed, and he was forced to yield to a power which he no longer dared to resist. He even lent his support to the triumvirs, and praised in public those proceedings which he had once openly and loudly condemned. Meantime the power of Pompey had been shaken at Rome. A misunderstanding had sprung up between him and Crassus; and Cato and the other leaders of the aristocracy attacked him with the utmost vehemence. The senate began to entertain hopes of recovering their power. They determined to support L. Domitius Ahenobarbus, who, in 56 B.C., had become a candidate for the consulship for the following year, and who threatened to deprive Caesar of his provinces and armies. Even Cicero was encouraged to join in the attack, and to propose in the senate a reconsideration of Caesar's distribution of the Campanian land.

Opposition to the triumvirs.

But these attacks only served to draw the triumvirs together. Caesar invited Pompey and Crassus to meet him at Luca (*Lucca*) in the spring of 56 B.C.; and the conference was largely attended by the partisans of the coalition. It was arranged that Pompey and Crassus should be consuls for the next year, and obtain provinces and armies, while Caesar was to have his government prolonged for another five years, and to receive pay for his troops. On their return

Conference of Luca.

to Rome Pompey and Crassus became candidates for the consulship; but the aristocratic opposition was so strong that it was found impossible to carry their election that year. By the help of the tribunician veto the consular comitia were prorogued, and the elections did not take place till the beginning of 55 B.C., under the presidency of an interrex. Even then Ahenobarbus and Cato did not relax in their opposition; and it was not till the armed bands of Pompey and Crassus had cleared the Campus Martius of their adversaries that they were declared consuls for the second time (55 B.C.).

Second consulship of Pompey and Crassus.

They forthwith proceeded to carry into effect the compact that had been made at Luca. They induced the Tribune C. Trebonius to bring forward a bill which gave the province of the two Spains to Pompey, and that of Syria to Crassus; another law proposed by the consuls prolonged Caesar's government for five years more, namely, from the 1st of March, 54 B.C., to the 1st of March, 49 B.C.* Pompey was again in command of the home government; and at the expiration of his year of office would no longer be a private man, but with the command of an army and in possession of the imperium. He had, however, no intention of quitting Rome; and after his year of office, while he sent an army into Spain under the command of his lieutenants, L. Afranius and M. Petreius, he himself remained in the neighbourhood of Rome as proconsul. During his consulship he opened the theatre he had just built with an exhibition of games of unparalleled splendour and magnificence. The building itself was worthy of the conqueror of the East. It was the first stone theatre that had been erected at Rome, and was sufficiently large to accommodate 40,000 spectators. The games exhibited lasted many days. Five hundred African lions and eighteen elephants were killed; and even the hardened Roman mob were satiated and disgusted with the wholesale slaughter.

Before the end of the year, 54 B.C., Crassus set out for Syria, with the intention of attacking the Parthians. He burnt to share in the military distinction of Pompey and Caesar; and, though upwards of sixty years of age, chose to enter upon an

* March 1st was the beginning of the official year in the provinces, as January 1st was at Rome.

undertaking for which he had no genius rather than continue the pursuit of wealth and influence at home. He crossed the Euphrates in 54 B.C., but, hesitating to proceed at once against Parthia, he gave the enemy time to assemble his forces, and returned to Syria without accomplishing anything of importance. He spent the winter in Syria, where, instead of exercising his troops and preparing for the ensuing campaign, he plundered the temples, and employed his time in collecting money from every quarter. In the following spring (53 B.C.) he again crossed the Euphrates, and with seven legions plunged into the sandy deserts of Mesopotamia. He trusted to the guidance of an Arabian chieftain, who promised to lead him by the shortest way to the enemy. But this man was in the pay of the "Surenas," as the Parthian general was entitled; and when he had brought the Romans into the open plains of Mesopotamia, he seized a frivolous pretext, and rode off to inform the Surenas that the Roman army was delivered into his hands. The Parthians soon appeared. They worried the densely marshalled Romans with showers of arrows; and by feigned retreats, during which they continued their desultory attack, they led the Romans into disadvantageous positions. The son of Crassus, who had distinguished himself as one of Caesar's lieutenants in Gaul, was slain; and the Romans, after suffering great loss, retreated to Carrhae, the Biblical Haran. On the following day they continued their retreat; and the Parthian general, fearing that Crassus might after all make his escape, invited him to an interview. He was treacherously seized, and in the scuffle which ensued was slain by some unknown hand. His head was carried to the Parthian king Orodes, and exhibited to the court, while an actor chanted the words of Agave from the Bacchae of Euripides—

Defeat and death of Crassus.

"We bear a fresh-cut tendril from the mountains to the hall." *

Twenty thousand Roman troops were slain, and ten thousand taken prisoners, in this expedition, one of the most disastrous in which the Romans were ever engaged. Only a small portion of the Roman army escaped to Syria under the command of L. Cassius Longinus, afterwards one of Caesar's assassins, who had displayed considerable ability during the war, but whose advice Crassus had constantly refused to follow.

* l. 1171.

The death of Crassus left Pompey and Caesar alone at the head of the state; and it became evident that sooner or later a struggle would take place between them for the supremacy. The death of Julia, in 54 B.C., to whom both her father and husband were strongly attached, broke a link which might have united them much longer. Pompey considered that he had been the chief means of raising Caesar to power, and he appeared long to have deemed it impossible that the conqueror of Mithridates could be thrown into the shade by any popular leader. Such a result, however, was now imminent. Caesar's brilliant victories in Gaul were in everybody's mouth; and Pompey saw with ill-disguised mortification that he was becoming the second person in the state. Though this did not lead him to break with Caesar at once, it made him anxious to increase his power and influence, and he therefore now resolved, if possible, to obtain the dictatorship.

Estrangement of Pompey and Caesar.

He accordingly used no effort to put an end to the disturbances at Rome between Milo and Clodius in this year, in hopes that all parties would be willing to accede to his wishes in order to restore peace to the city. Milo was a candidate for the consulship and Clodius for the praetorship. Each was attended by a band of hired ruffians; battles took place between them daily in the forum and the streets; all order and government were at an end. In such a state of things no elections could be held; and the confusion at length became downright anarchy, when Milo murdered Clodius on the 18th of January in the following year (B.C. 52). The two rivals had met on the Appian way near Bovillae, accompanied, as usual, by their armed followers. A fray ensued. The party of Milo proved the stronger, and Clodius took refuge in a house. But Milo attacked the house, dragged out Clodius, and having despatched him, left him dead upon the road. His body was found by a senator, carried to Rome, and exposed to the eyes of the people. Their excitement at the death of their favourite was still further inflamed by the harangues of the tribunes. The benches and tables of the senate-house were seized to make a funeral pile; and the senate-house with several other public buildings were reduced to ashes. As the riots still continued, the senate had no longer any choice but to

Milo and Clodius.

call in the assistance of Pompey. They therefore commissioned him to collect troops and put an end to the disturbances.

Pompey sole consul.

Pompey, who had obtained the great object of his desires, obeyed with alacrity; he was invested with the supreme power in the state by being elected sole consul at the close of the winter; and in order to deliver the city from Milo and his myrmidons, he brought forward laws against violence and bribery at elections. Milo was put upon his trial; the court was surrounded with soldiers; Cicero, who defended him, was intimidated, and Milo was condemned, and went into exile at Massilia.* Others shared the same fate, and peace was once more restored.

Measures taken against Caesar.

The fear of Caesar's possible designs now weighed heavily on the aristocratic party, and the approaches which they made to Pompey were met halfway. After Julia's death he had married Cornelia, the daughter of Metellus Scipio, whom he made his colleague on the 1st of August. His next step was to strike a blow at Caesar. He brought forward an old law that no one should become a candidate for a public office while absent, in order that Caesar might be obliged to resign his command, and to place himself in the power of his enemies at Rome, if he wished to obtain the consulship a second time. But the renewal of this enactment was so manifestly aimed at Caesar that his friends insisted he should be specially exempted from it; and, as Pompey was not yet prepared to break openly with him, he thought it more expedient to yield. At the same time, Pompey provided that he himself should remain in command of an army after his rival had ceased to have one, by obtaining a senatus-consultum, by which his government of the Spains was prolonged for another five years. And, in case Caesar should obtain the consulship, he caused a law to be enacted, in virtue of which no one could have a province till five years had elapsed from the time of his holding a public office. For the next five years the senate was to fill up commands at the earliest date at which they were legally vacant.†

* Cicero sent to Milo at Massilia the oration which he meant to have delivered, the one which we still have. Milo, after reading it, remarked, "I am glad it was not delivered, for I should then have been acquitted, and never known the delicate flavour of these Massilian mullets."

† Caesar's command technically expired on March 1st, 49; but, in accordance with the invariable custom, he claimed to continue it until January 1st, 48, when he would be succeeded by one of the consuls of 49.

In the following year (51 B.C.) Pompey declared himself still more openly on the side of the senate; but still he shrank from supporting all the violent measures of the Consul M. Claudius Marcellus, who proposed to send a successor to Caesar, on the plea that the war in Gaul was finished, and to deprive him of the privilege of becoming a candidate for the consulship in his absence. The consuls for the next year (50 B.C.), L. Aemilius Paullus and C. Claudius Marcellus, and the powerful tribune C. Curio, were all reckoned devoted partisans of Pompey and the senate. Caesar, however, gained over Paullus and Curio by large bribes, and with a lavish hand distributed immense sums of money among the leading men of Rome. It was proposed in the senate that Caesar should lay down his command on March 1st, 49 B.C. The consular elections were in July; and if Caesar came to Rome as a private man to sue for the consulship, there could be no doubt that his life or liberty would be sacrificed. Cato had declared that he would bring Caesar to trial for the illegalities committed during his consulship; but the trial would have been only a mockery, for Pompey was in the neighbourhood of the city at the head of an army, and would have overawed the judges by his soldiery as at Milo's trial. The tribune Curio consequently interposed his veto upon the proposal. The senate, anxious to diminish the number of his troops, had, under pretext of a war with the Parthians, ordered that Pompey and Caesar should each furnish a legion to be sent into the East. The legion which Pompey intended to devote to this service was the one which he had lent to Caesar in 53 B.C., and which he now accordingly demanded back; and, although Caesar saw that he should thus be deprived of two legions, which would probably be employed against himself, he complied with the request. Upon their arrival in Italy, they were not sent to the East, but were ordered to pass the winter at Capua. Caesar took up his quarters at Ravenna, the town in his province which bordered closest upon Italy.

Negotiations between Caesar and the senate.

Though war seemed inevitable, Caesar still showed himself willing to enter into negotiations with the aristocracy, and accordingly sent Curio with a letter addressed to the senate, in which he expressed his readiness to resign his command if Pompey would do the same. Curio arrived at Rome on the 1st of January,

49 B.C., the day on which the new consuls, L. Cornelius Lentulus and C. Claudius Marcellus, entered upon their office. It was with great difficulty that the tribunes, M. Antonius, afterwards the well-known triumvir, and Q. Cassius Longinus, forced the senate to allow the letter to be read. After a violent debate the motion of Scipio, Pompey's father-in-law, was carried, "that Caesar should disband his army by a certain day, and that if he did not do so he should be regarded as an enemy of the state." On the 6th of January the senate passed the decree investing the consuls with dictatorial power. Antonius and Cassius, considering their lives no longer safe, fled from the city in disguise to Caesar's army, and called upon him to protect the inviolable persons of the tribunes.

Preparations for war.

This was the crisis. The senate intrusted the management of the war to Pompey, determined that fresh levies of troops should be held, and voted him a sum of money from the public treasury. Both the senate and Pompey seem to have relied on an imagined disaffection amongst Caesar's troops, and grossly miscalculated their own military resources. It is true that Pompey commanded legions in Spain through his legates, and his personal influence could secure him almost unbounded resources in the East; but these would be of no avail against a direct attack from Gaul. He had boasted that he had only to stamp his foot, and armed men would spring from the soil of Italy; but, when the critical moment came, almost his only serviceable troops were the two legions taken from Caesar, and therefore of doubtful fidelity, and Italy was left defenceless.

Brutus.

CHAPTER XXXV.

FROM THE BEGINNING OF THE CIVIL WAR TO CAESAR'S DEATH. 49–44 B.C.

As soon as Caesar learnt at Ravenna the last resolution of the senate, he assembled his soldiers, informed them of the wrongs he had sustained, and called upon them to support him. Finding them quite willing to follow him, he crossed the Rubicon,* which separated his province from Italy, and occupied Ariminum. He commenced his march with only one legion, consisting of

Caesar advances through Italy.

* The crossing of this stream was in reality a declaration of war against the Republic, and later writers relate that upon arriving at the Rubicon Caesar long hesitated whether he should take this irrevocable step, and that, after pondering many hours, he at length exclaimed, "The die is cast," and plunged into the river. But there is not a word of this in Caesar's own narrative.

5000 foot-soldiers and 300 horse, but others had orders to follow him from Transalpine Gaul, and he knew the importance of speed that might anticipate the enemy's plans, and of successes at the outset that might turn the hearts of waverers. Though it was the middle of winter, he pushed on with the utmost rapidity, and such was the popularity of his cause, or the defencelessness of Italy, that city after city opened its gates to him, and his march was like a triumphal progress. Ancona, Arretium, Iguvium, and Auximum fell into his hands. These successes caused the utmost consternation at Rome; it was reported that Caesar's cavalry were already at the gates; a general panic seized the senate, and they fled from the city without even taking with them the money from the public treasury. Caesar continued his victorious march through Picenum till he came to Corfinium, which L. Domitius Ahenobarbus held with a strong force; but, as Pompey did not march to his assistance, Domitius was unable to maintain the place, and fell himself into Caesar's hands, together with several other senators and distinguished men. Caesar, with the same clemency which he displayed throughout the whole of the Civil War, dismissed them all uninjured. He then hastened southward in pursuit of Pompey, who had now resolved to abandon Italy. He reached Brundusium before Caesar, but had not sailed when the latter arrived before the town.

Pompey embarks for Greece.

Caesar straightway laid siege to the place, but Pompey skilfully evacuated it on the 17th of March, and embarked for Greece. Caesar was unable to follow him for want of ships. He accordingly marched back from Brundusium, and repaired to Rome, having thus in three months become the master of the whole of Italy.

Caesar at Rome.

Caesar was now in possession of the capital and of the machinery of government, and the only opposition which he met with in Rome was from L. Metellus the tribune, who attempted to prevent him from entering the "more sacred treasury," which contained the reserve destined for defence against a Gallic invasion—a resistance which drew from the professed champion of the tribunate the caustic remark: "War is no time for words; when I have laid down my arms, I shall listen to your arguments." After remaining in the neighbourhood of Rome for a short time, he set out for Spain, leaving M. Lepidus in charge of the city and M. Antonius in command of the troops in Italy. Pompey had threatened to starve Italy into surrender; hence it was all-important to get possession of the corn-supplying provinces. Caesar, therefore, sent Curio to drive Cato out of Sicily, and Q. Valerius to take possession of Sardinia. Curio and Valerius obtained possession of their respective islands without opposition; and the former then passed over into Africa, which was in possession of the Pompeian party. Here, however, he encountered strong opposition, and at length was defeated, and lost his life, in a battle with Juba, king of Mauretania, who supported P. Atius Varus, the Pompeian commander. But this disaster was more than counterbalanced by Caesar's victories in the mean time in Spain.

Caesar conquers Spain.

Leaving Rome about the middle of April, he found, on his arrival in Gaul, that Massilia refused to submit to him. He besieged the place forthwith, but, unable to take it immediately, he left C. Trebonius and D. Brutus with part of his troops to prosecute the siege, and continued his march to Spain. On the approach of Caesar, L. Afranius and M. Petreius, the lieutenants of Pompey in Spain, united their forces, and took up a strong position near the town of Ilerda (*Lerida* in Catalonia), on the right bank of the Sicoris (*Segre*). After experiencing great difficulty at first and some reverses, Caesar at length reduced Afranius and Petreius to such straits that they were obliged to surrender. They themselves were dismissed uninjured, part of their troops disbanded, and the remainder incorporated among Caesar's forces. The conqueror then proceeded to march against Varro, who commanded two legions in the Further Province; but, after the victory over Afranius and Petreius, there was no army in Spain capable of offering resistance, and Varro accordingly surrendered to Caesar on his arrival at Corduba (*Cordova*). Having thus subdued all Spain in forty days, he returned to Gaul. Massilia had not yet yielded; but the siege had been prosecuted with so much vigour, that the inhabitants were compelled to surrender the town soon after he appeared before the walls.

During his absence in Spain Caesar was appointed dictator by the praetor M. Lepidus, who had been empowered to do so by a law passed for the purpose. On his return to Rome, Caesar assumed the new dignity, but laid it down again at the end of eleven days, after holding the consular comitia, in which he himself and P. Servilius Vatia were elected consuls for the next year. But during these eleven days he caused some very important laws to be passed. The first was intended to relieve debtors, but at the same time to protect to a great extent the rights of creditors. He next restored the exiles banished under the exceptional legislation of 52 B.C., and removed the disabilities imposed by Sulla on the children of the proscribed; finally he conferred the full citizenship upon the Transpadani, who had hitherto held only the Latin franchise, and thus made Italy Roman up to the Alps.

Caesar created dictator.

After laying down the dictatorship Caesar went in December to Brundusium, where he had previously ordered his troops to assemble. He had lost many men in the long march from Spain, and also from sickness arising from their passing the autumn in the south of Italy. Pompey during the summer had raised a large force in Greece, Egypt, and the East, the scene of his former glory. He had collected an army consisting of nine legions of Roman citizens, and an auxiliary force of cavalry and infantry; and his forces far surpassed in number those which Caesar had assembled at Brundusium. Moreover Pompey's fleet, under the command of Bibulus, Caesar's colleague in his first consulship, completely commanded the sea. Still Caesar ventured to set sail from Brundusium on the 4th of January, and he arrived the next day in safety on the coast of Epirus. In consequence, however, of the small number of his ships, he was able to carry over only seven legions, which had been so thinned as to amount only to 15,000 foot and 500 horse. After landing this force he sent back his ships to bring over the remainder; but part of the fleet was intercepted in its return by M. Bibulus, who kept up such a strict watch along the coast that the rest of Caesar's army was obliged for the present to remain at Brundusium. Caesar was thus in a critical position, in the midst of the enemy's country, and cut off from the rest of his army; but he knew that he could thoroughly rely on his men, and therefore immediately commenced acting on the offensive. After gaining possession

Crosses to Epirus.

of Oricum and Apollonia, he hastened northwards, in hopes of surprising Dyrrhachium, where all Pompey's stores were deposited; but Pompey, by rapid marches, reached this town before him, and both armies then encamped opposite to each other, Pompey on the right, and Caesar on the left bank of the river Apsus. Caesar was now greatly in want of reinforcements, and such was his impatience that he attempted to sail across the Adriatic in a small boat. The waves ran so high that the sailors wanted to turn back, till Caesar discovered himself, telling them that they carried Caesar and his fortunes. They then toiled on, but the storm at length compelled them to return, and with difficulty they reached again the coast of Greece. Shortly afterwards M. Antonius succeeded in bringing over the remainder of the army.

Campaign near Dyrrhachium.

Pompey meantime had retired to some high ground near Dyrrhachium, and, as he would not venture a battle with Caesar's veterans, Caesar, in spite of the inferiority of his own forces, began to blockade him in his position, and to draw lines of circumvallation of an extraordinary extent. It was an error of judgment; Pompey forced a passage through Caesar's lines before they were completed, and drove back his legions with considerable loss. Caesar thus found himself compelled to retreat from his present position, and commenced a march on Thessaly. Pompey's policy of avoiding a general engagement with Caesar's veterans till he could place more reliance upon his own troops was undoubtedly a wise one, and had been hitherto crowned with success; but his hand was forced by the ignorance and impatience of his aristocratic supporters.

Battle of Pharsalus.

Stung by the reproaches with which they assailed him, and elated in some degree by his victory at Dyrrhachium, he resolved to bring the contest to an issue. Accordingly he offered battle to Caesar in the plain of Pharsalus, or Pharsalia, in Thessaly. The numbers on either side were very unequal: Pompey had 47,000 foot-soldiers and 7000 horse, Caesar 22,000 foot-soldiers and 1000 horse. The battle, which was fought on the 9th of August, 48 B.C., according to the old calendar,* ended in the total defeat of Pompey's army.

* In reality, on the 6th of June.

The Republic was not yet lost, but Pompey's hopes were at an end. He made no attempt to rally his forces, though he might still have collected a considerable army; but, regarding everything as lost, he hurried to the sea-coast with a few friends. He embarked on board a merchant-ship at the mouth of the river Penēus, and first sailed to Lesbos, where he took on board his wife Cornelia, and from thence made for Cyprus. He now determined to seek refuge in Egypt, as he had been the means of restoring to his kingdom Ptolemy Auletes, the father of the young Egyptian monarch. On his death in 51 B.C. Ptolemy Auletes had left directions that his son should reign jointly with his elder sister Cleopatra. But their joint reign did not last long, for Ptolemy, or rather Pothinus and Achillas, his chief advisers, expelled his sister from the throne. Cleopatra collected a force in Syria, with which she invaded Egypt. The generals of Ptolemy were encamped opposite her, near Alexandria, when Pompey arrived off the coast and craved the protection of the young king. This request threw Pothinus and Achillas into great difficulty, for there were many of Pompey's old soldiers in the Egyptian army, and they feared he would become master of Egypt. They therefore determined to put him to death. Accordingly they sent out a small boat, took Pompey on board with three or four attendants, and rowed for the shore. His wife and friends watched him from the ship, anxious to see in what manner he would be received by the king, who was standing on the edge of the sea with his troops. Just as the boat reached the shore, and Pompey was in the act of rising from his seat, in order to step on land, he was stabbed in the back by Septimius, who had formerly been one of his centurions.

Flight of Pompey.

Achillas and the rest then drew their swords; whereupon Pompey, without uttering a word, covered his face with his toga, and calmly submitted to his fate. He had just completed his 58th year. His head was cut off, and his body, which was cast upon the shore, was buried by his freedman Philippus, who had accompanied him from the ship. The head was brought to Caesar when he arrived in Egypt soon afterwards, but he turned away from the sight, shed tears at the untimely end of his rival, and put his murderers to death.

His death.

When news of the battle of Pharsalus reached Rome, various laws were passed which conferred supreme power upon Caesar. Though absent, he was nominated dictator a second time, and for a whole year. He appointed M. Antonius his master of the horse, and entered upon the office in September of this year (48 B.C.). He was also nominated to the consulship for the next five years, though he did not avail himself of this privilege; and he was invested with the tribunician power for life.

Alexandrine War.

Caesar had followed closely in pursuit of Pompey, and upon his arrival in Egypt he became involved in a war, which detained him several months, and gave the remains of the Pompeian party time to rally and to make fresh preparations for continuing the struggle. The war in Egypt, usually called the Alexandrine War, arose from Caesar's resolving to settle the disputes respecting the succession to the kingdom. He determined that Cleopatra, whose fascinations completely won his heart, and her brother Ptolemy should reign in common, according to the provisions of their father's will; but as this decision was opposed by the guardians of the young king, a war broke out between them and Caesar, in which he was for some time exposed to great danger on account of the small number of his troops. But, having received reinforcements, he finally prevailed, and placed Cleopatra and her younger brother on the throne, the elder having perished in the course of the contest.

Battle of Zela.

After bringing the Alexandrine War to a close, towards the end of March, 47 B.C., Caesar marched through Syria into Pontus in order to attack Pharnaces, the son of the celebrated Mithridates, who had defeated Cn. Domitius Calvinus, one of Caesar's lieutenants. This war, however, did not detain him long; for Pharnaces, venturing to come to an open battle with the dictator, was utterly defeated, on the 2nd of August, near Zela. It was in reference to this victory that Caesar sent the celebrated laconic despatch to the senate, *Veni, vidi, vici,* "I came, I saw, I conquered." He then proceeded to Rome, caused himself to be appointed dictator for the remainder of the year, and nominated M. Aemilius Lepidus his master of the horse. At the same time he quelled a formidable mutiny of his troops which had broken out in Campania.

Caesar did not remain in Rome more than two or three months. With his usual activity and energy he set out for Africa before the end of the year (47 B.C.), in order to carry on the war against Scipio and Cato, who had collected a large army in that country. Their forces were far greater than those which Caesar could bring against them; but he had too much reliance on his own genius to be alarmed by mere disparity of numbers.

War in Africa.

At first he was in considerable difficulties; but, having been joined by some of his other legions, he was able to prosecute the campaign with more vigour, and finally brought it to a close by the battle of Thapsus, on the 6th of April, 46 B.C., in which the Pompeian army was completely defeated.

Battle of Thapsus.

All Africa now submitted to Caesar, with the exception of Utica, which Cato commanded. The inhabitants saw that resistance was hopeless; and Cato, who was a sincere Republican, resolved to die rather than submit to Caesar's despotism. After spending the greater part of the night in perusing Plato's *Phaedo*, a dialogue on the immortality of the soul, he stabbed himself. His friends, hearing him fall, ran up, found him bathed in blood, and, while he was fainting, dressed his wounds. When, however, he recovered consciousness, he tore open the bandages, and so died.

Death of Cato.

Caesar returned to Rome by the end of July. Great apprehensions were entertained by his enemies, lest, notwithstanding his former clemency, he should imitate Marius and Sulla, and proscribe all his opponents. But these fears were perfectly groundless. A love of cruelty was no part of Caesar's nature; and, with a magnanimity which victors rarely show, and least of all those in civil wars, he freely forgave all who had borne arms against him, and declared that he should make no difference between Pompeians and Caesarians. His object was now to allay animosities, and to secure the lives and property of all the citizens of his empire.

As soon as the news of his African victory reached Rome, a public thanksgiving of forty days was decreed in his honour; the dictatorship was bestowed upon him for ten years; and the censorship, under the new title of "Praefectus Morum," for three years. Caesar had never

Honours voted to Caesar.

yet enjoyed a triumph; and, as he had now no further enemies to meet, he availed himself of the opportunity of celebrating his victories in Gaul, Egypt, Pontus, and Africa, by four magnificent triumphs. None of these, however, were in honour of his successes in the civil war, although, in the African triumph which celebrated his victory over Juba, the deaths of Scipio and Cato were depicted. These triumphs were followed by largesses of corn and money to the people and the soldiers, by public banquets, and all sorts of entertainments.

Measures of reform.

Caesar now proceeded to correct the various evils which had crept into the state, and to obtain the enactment of several laws suitable to the altered condition of the commonwealth. He attempted, by severe sumptuary laws, to restrain the extravagance which pervaded all classes of society. But the most important of his changes this year (46 B.C.) was the reformation of the calendar, which was a real benefit to his country and the civilized world, and which he accomplished in his character of Pontifex Maximus. The old Roman year had only 355 days, and the regulation of the Roman calendar had always been entrusted to the college of pontiffs; they had been accustomed to insert intercalary months at their pleasure for political purposes, and the confusion had at length become so great that the Roman year was three months behind the real time. To remedy this serious evil, Caesar added 90 days to the current year, and thus made it consist of 445 days; and he guarded against a repetition of similar errors for the future by creating a year of 365 days 6 hours, and thus adapting the calendar to the sun's course.

War in Spain.

The Pompeians were now preparing to make their last stand in Spain, where a formidable army had been collected under the command of Pompey's sons, Cneius and Sextus. Caesar left Rome at the end of 46 B.C., and with his usual activity arrived at Obulco near Corduba in 27 days.

Battle of Munda.

He found the enemy able to offer stronger opposition than he had anticipated; but he brought the war to a close by the battle of Munda, on the 17th of March, 45 B.C. It was a hard-fought battle: Caesar's troops were at first driven back, and were only rallied by their general's exposing his own person, like a common soldier, in the front line of the battle; but at last victory declared for the dictator. Cn. Pompeius was killed shortly afterwards, but Sextus made good his escape. The settlement of the affairs in Spain detained Caesar in the province some months longer, and he consequently did not reach Rome till September.

At the beginning of October he entered the city in triumph on account of his victories in Spain, although the victory had been gained over Roman citizens. The senate received him with the most servile flattery. They had in his absence voted a public thanksgiving of fifty days, and they now vied with each other in paying him every kind of adulation and homage. He was to wear, on all public occasions, the triumphal robe; he was to receive the title of "Father of his Country;" his statue was to be placed amongst those of the seven kings in the Capitol; his portrait was to be struck on coins; the month of Quintilis was to receive the name of Julius in his honour, and he was to be raised to a rank among the gods. But there were still more important decrees than these, which were intended to legalize his power, and confer upon him the whole government of the Roman world. He received the title of Imperator for life; he was nominated consul for the next ten years, and dictator for life; his person was declared sacred; a guard of senators and knights was offered for his protection; and the whole senate took an oath to watch over his safety.

New honours voted to Caesar.

If we now look at the way in which Caesar exerted his sovereign power, it cannot be denied that he used it in the main for the good of his country. He still pursued his former merciful course: no proscriptions or executions took place; and he took the first steps in a projected reform of the constitution which he did not live to carry out. He raised the senate to 900 members by the introduction of Gauls and Spaniards, on whom he had conferred the franchise, and Romans of the lowest class; there was a corresponding increase in the magistrates, the quaestors being raised to 40 and the praetors to 16. By swamping the senate Caesar was breaking the spirit of the republic and preparing the way for the monarchy, in which this body, now including representatives from the provinces, was to be only a council of advisers. A more distinctly regal act was his creation of new patrician families: for the patriciate had never been increased since the

Caesar's rule.

downfall of the monarchy at Rome. It was now whispered that Caesar, a king in fact, meant also to be a king in name. The popular sentiment was tested when in the next year (44 B.C.) the consul Antonius offered him the diadem, the symbol of Oriental royalty, at the festival of the Lupercalia. It was declined; and the shouts of the people showed that, though they could submit to the reality of monarchy, they could not endure the name.

Caesar's mental activity at this time was prodigious. One of its products was a comprehensive municipal law, by which uniform regulations were made for the towns possessing Roman citizenship in Italy and in the provinces. He also planned a codification of the existing Roman law, and material improvements, such as the draining of the Pomptine marshes and the enlargement of the harbour of Ostia. Amongst his immediate cares was the protection of the frontiers of the empire; he planned expeditions against the Parthians and the barbarous tribes on the Danube, and had already begun to make preparations for his departure to the East. In the midst of these vast projects he entered upon the last year of his life (44 B.C.), and his fifth consulship and dictatorship, with M. Antonius as his colleague in the consulship and M. Lepidus as his master of the horse.

The conspiracy.

A conspiracy against Caesar's life had been formed as early as the beginning of the year. It had been set on foot by a personal enemy, C. Cassius Longinus, and more than sixty persons were privy to it. Private hatred alone seems to have been the motive of Cassius, and probably of several others. Many of them had taken an active part on the Pompeian side, and had not only been forgiven by Caesar, but raised to offices of rank and honour. Among others was M. Junius Brutus, whom he had pardoned after the battle of Pharsalus, and had since treated almost as his son. In this very year Caesar had made him praetor, and held out to him the prospect of the consulship. Brutus, like Cato, seems to have been a sincere Republican, and Cassius persuaded him to join the conspiracy, and imitate his great ancestor who freed them from the Tarquins. It was now arranged to assassinate the dictator in the senate-house on the Ides or 15th of March. Rumours of the plot got abroad, and

Caesar was strongly urged not to attend the senate. But he disregarded the warnings which were given him.

As he entered, the senate rose to do him honour; and when he had taken his seat, the conspirators pressed around him as if to support the prayer of one Tillius Cimber, who entreated the dictator to recall his brother from banishment. When Caesar began to show displeasure at their importunity, Tillius seized him by his toga, which was the signal for attack. Casca, one of the tribunes of the Plebs, struck the first blow, and the other conspirators bared their weapons. Caesar defended himself till he saw Brutus had drawn his sword, and then, exclaiming, "And thou, too, Brutus!" he drew his toga over his head, and fell pierced with three and twenty wounds at the foot of Pompey's statue.

Murder of Caesar.

Caesar's death was undoubtedly a loss not only for the Roman people, but the whole civilized world. The Republic was utterly lost. The Roman world was now fated to go through many years of disorder and bloodshed, till it rested again under the supremacy of Augustus. The last days of the Republic had come, and its only hope of peace and security was under the strong hand of military power.

Caesar was in his 56th year at the time of his death. Sculptures and coins still preserve his noble and commanding presence. They show a clear-cut face, worn with thought and toil, but serene and benign; and we are told that he was tall in stature, and that his dark eyes were full of expression. His constitution was originally delicate, and he was twice attacked by epilepsy while transacting public business; but, by constant exercise and abstemious living, he had acquired strong and vigorous health, and could endure almost any amount of exertion. He took great pains with his person, was considered to be effeminate in his dress, and in his later years strove to conceal his increasing baldness with the golden laurel crown.

Caesar was probably the greatest man of antiquity. He was at one and the same time a general, a statesman, a lawgiver, a jurist, an orator, and an historian; his idler moments were devoted to philology and the general culture of the day, while, like most Roman nobles of the time, he dabbled in poetry. He was a perfect example of the Roman genius for practical life, combining great conceptions

Character of Caesar.

with an extraordinary command of detail. As a general he possessed some of the rarest military gifts: a mastery over men, a capacity for setting routine at defiance and adapting means to ends at the shortest notice, and an unequalled power of rapidity of movement. To estimate his military genius, one has only to remember that till his 40th year, when he went as propraetor into Spain, he had been almost entirely engaged in civil life, and his experience of war must have been of the most limited kind. Most of the greatest generals in the history of the world have been distinguished at an early age: Alexander the Great, Hannibal, Frederick of Prussia, and Napoleon Bonaparte, gained some of their most brilliant victories under the age of 30; but Caesar from the age of 23 to 40 had seen nothing of war, which he took up as a subordinate instrument to be used in his task of reforming the Roman world.

Statue of a Roman, representing the Toga (from the Louvre).

London. John Murray, Albemarle Street.
John Bartholomew & Co. Edinr.

M. Antonius.

CHAPTER XXXVI.

FROM THE DEATH OF CAESAR TO THE BATTLE OF PHILIPPI.
44–42 B.C.

Compromise agreed on; amnesty to Caesar's murderers.

WHEN the bloody deed had been finished, Brutus and his fellow-liberators rushed into the forum, proclaiming that they had killed the tyrant, and calling the people to join them. But they met with no response, and, finding alone averted looks, they retired to the Capitol. Here they were joined by Cicero, who had not been privy to the conspiracy, but was now one of the first to justify the murder. Meantime the friends of Caesar were not idle. Lepidus, the master of the horse, who was in the neighbourhood of the city, marched into the forum in the night; and Antony hastened to the house of the dictator, and took possession of his papers and treasures. But both parties feared to come to blows. A compromise was agreed to; and at a meeting of the senate it was determined that Caesar's murderers should not be punished, but on the other hand that all his regulations should remain in force, that the provisions of his will should be carried into effect, and that he should be honoured with a public funeral. The conspirators then descended from the Capitol; and, as a proof of reconciliation, Cassius supped with Antony and Brutus with Lepidus.

This reconciliation was only a pretence. Antony aspired to succeed to the power of the dictator; and to rouse the popular fury against the conspirators Caesar's will was immediately made public. He left as his heir his great-nephew Octavius, a youth of eighteen, the son of Atia, the daughter of his sister Julia. He bequeathed considerable legacies to his murderers. He gave his magnificent gardens beyond the Tiber to the public, and to every Roman citizen he bequeathed the sum of 300 sesterces (rather less than £3 sterling). When this became known, a deep feeling of sorrow for the untimely fate of their benefactor seized the minds of the people. Their feelings were raised to the highest point two or three days afterwards, when the funeral took place. The body was to be burnt in the Campus Martius, but it was previously carried to the forum, where Antony, according to custom, pronounced the funeral oration over it. After relating the exploits of the great dictator, reciting his will, and describing his terrible death, he lifted up the blood-stained robe which Caesar had worn in the senate-house, and which had hitherto covered the corpse, and pointed out the numerous wounds which disfigured the body. At this sight a yell of indignation was raised, and the mob rushed in every direction to tear the murderers to pieces. The liberators fled for their lives from the city, and the poet Helvius Cinna, being mistaken for the praetor Cinna, one of the assassins, was torn in pieces before the mistake could be explained.

Antony rouses the people.

Antony was now master of Rome. Being in possession of Caesar's papers, he was able to plead the authority of the dictator for everything which he pleased. The conspirators hastened to take possession of the provinces which Caesar had assigned to them. D. Brutus repaired to Cisalpine Gaul, M. Brutus

Arrangement of the provinces.

to Macedonia, and Cassius to Syria. Antony now procured a new disposition of the provinces, which gave Cisalpine Gaul to himself, Macedonia to his brother C. Antonius, and Syria to Dolabella.

Meantime a new actor appeared upon the stage. Octavius was at Apollonia, a town on the coast of Illyria, at the time of his uncle's death. Caesar had determined to take his nephew with him in his expedition against the Parthians, and had accordingly sent him to Apollonia, where a camp had been formed, that he might pursue his military studies. The soldiers now offered to follow him to Italy and avenge their leader's death, but he did not yet venture to take this decisive step. He determined, however, to sail at once to Italy, accompanied by only a few friends. Upon arriving at Brundusium he heard of the will of the dictator, and was saluted by the soldiers as Caesar. As the adopted heir of his uncle, his proper name was now C. Julius Caesar Octavianus, and by the last of these names we shall henceforth call him. He now made up his mind to proceed to Rome and claim his uncle's inheritance, in opposition to the advice of his mother, who dreaded this dangerous honour for her son. Upon arriving at Rome, he declared before the praetor in the usual manner that he accepted the inheritance, and he then promised the people to pay the money bequeathed to them. He even ventured to claim of Antony the treasures of his uncle; but, as the latter refused to give them up, he sold the other property, and even his own estates, to discharge all the legacies. Antony threw every obstacle in his way; but the very name of Caesar worked wonders, and the liberality of the young man gained the hearts of the people. He had indeed a difficult part to play. He could not join the murderers of his uncle; and yet Antony, their greatest enemy, was also his most dangerous foe. In these difficult circumstances the youth displayed a prudence and a wisdom which baffled the most experienced politicians. Without committing himself to any party, he professed a warm attachment to the senate. Cicero had once more taken an active part in public affairs; and Octavian, with that dissimulation which he practised throughout his life, completely deceived the veteran orator.

Octavian comes to Rome.

On the 2nd of September Cicero delivered in the senate the

first of his orations against Antony, which, in imitation of those of Demosthenes against Philip, are known by the name of the *Philippics*. Antony was absent at the time, but shortly afterwards attacked the orator in unmeasured terms. Cicero replied in the Second Philippic, one of the most violent invectives ever written. It was not spoken, but was published soon after Antony had quitted Rome.

Cicero opposes Antony.

Meantime the emissaries of Octavian had been sounding the disposition of the soldiers, and had already enlisted for him a considerable number of troops in various parts of Italy. Antony saw that the power was slipping from under his feet. Two of the legions which he had summoned from Epirus passed over to Octavian; and, in order to keep the remainder under his standard, and to secure the north of Italy to his interests, Antony now proceeded to Cisalpine Gaul, which had been previously granted to him by the people. Upon entering the province towards the end of December, D. Brutus threw himself into Mutina (*Modena*), to which Antony laid siege.

Octavian raises troops.

Soon after Antony's departure Cicero prevailed upon the senate to declare him a public enemy, and to intrust to the young Octavian the conduct of the war against him. Cicero was now at the height of his glory. His activity was unceasing, and in the twelve remaining "Philippics" he encouraged the senate and the people to prosecute the war with vigour. The two new consuls (43 B.C.) were A. Hirtius and C. Vibius Pansa, both of whom had been designated by the late dictator. As soon as they had entered upon their office, Hirtius, accompanied by Octavian, marched into Cisalpine Gaul, while Pansa remained in the city to levy troops.

War declared against Antony.

For some weeks no movement of importance took place in either army, but, when Pansa set out to join his colleague and Octavian, Antony marched southward, and on the 15th of April attacked him at Forum Gallorum near Bononia (*Bologna*). A fierce battle ensued, in which Pansa was mortally wounded; success at first declared for Antony, but the timely arrival of the other consul, Hirtius, forced him to retire to his camp before Mutina.

Battles of Forum Gallorum and Mutina.

A few days afterwards a more decisive battle took place. Antony was defeated with great loss, and forced to raise the siege of Mutina; but Hirtius fell in leading an assault on the besieger's camp. The death of the two consuls left Octavian the sole command; and so timely was their removal that he was accused by many of causing their death.

Antony, although he had found it impossible to continue the siege of Mutina, retreated in good order northwards, crossed the Alps, and was well received in Further Gaul by Lepidus, who had promised him support. Meantime the good understanding between Octavian and the senate had come to an end. The latter, being resolved to prevent him from obtaining any further power, gave the command of the consular armies to D. Brutus; and Cicero talked of removing the boy.

Octavian consul.

But the "boy" soon showed the senate that he was their master. He gained the confidence of the soldiers, who gladly followed the heir of Caesar to Rome. Though only twenty years of age, he demanded of the senate the consulship. At first they attempted to evade his demand; but his soldiers were encamped in the Campus Martius, and in the month of August he was elected consul with his cousin Q. Pedius. The first act of his consulship showed that he had completely broken with the senate. His colleague proposed a law declaring all the murderers of Caesar to be outlaws.

Junction with Antony and Lepidus.

Octavian then quitted Rome to march professedly against Antony, leaving Pedius in charge of the city; but it soon appeared that he had come to an understanding with Antony, for he had hardly entered Etruria before the unwilling senate were compelled, upon the proposal of Pedius, to repeal the sentence of outlawry against Antony and Lepidus. These two were now descending the Alps at the head of seventeen legions. Octavian was advancing northwards with a formidable army. Between two such forces the situation of D. Brutus was hopeless. He was deserted by his own troops, and fled to Aquileia, intending to cross over to Macedonia, but was put to death in the former place by order of Antony.

Lepidus, who acted as mediator between Antony and Octavian, now arranged a meeting between them on a small island near

Bononia, formed by the waters of the river Rhenus, a tributary of the Po. The interview took place near the end of November. It was arranged that the government of the Roman world should be divided between the three for a period of five years, under the title of "Triumvirs for settling the affairs of the Republic." * Octavian received Sicily, Sardinia, and Africa; Antony the two Gauls, with the exception of the Narbonese district, which, with Spain, was assigned to Lepidus. Octavian and Antony were to prosecute the war against M. Brutus and Cassius, who were in possession of the eastern provinces. Lepidus was to receive the consulship for the following year, with the charge of Italy.

The second triumvirate.

The triumvirs next proceeded to imitate the example of Sulla by drawing up a proscription—a list of persons whose lives were to be sacrificed and property confiscated. But they had not Sulla's excuse. He returned to Italy exasperated to the highest degree by the murder of his friends and the personal insults he had received. The triumvirs, out of a cold-blooded policy, resolved to remove every one whose opposition they feared or whose property they coveted. In drawing up the fatal list they sacrificed, without scruple, their nearest relatives and friends. To please Antony, Octavian gave up Cicero; Antony in return surrendered his own uncle, L. Caesar; and Lepidus sacrificed his own brother Paullus. As many as 300 senators and 2000 equites were entered in the lists.

Proscription.

As soon as the triumvirs had made their secret arrangements they marched towards Rome. Hitherto they had published the names of only seventeen of the proscribed; but the city was in a state of the utmost alarm, and it was with difficulty that Pedius could preserve the peace. So great was his anxiety and fatigue that he died the night before the entry of the triumvirs into the city. They marched into Rome at the head of their legions, and filled all the public places with their soldiery. No attempt at resistance was made. A law was proposed and carried conferring upon the triumvirs the title and powers they had assumed. The work of butchery then commenced. Lists after lists of the proscribed were published, each more numerous than the former. The soldiers hunted after the victims, cut off their

* *Triumviri Reipublicae constituendae.*

heads, and brought them to the authorities to prove their claims to the blood-money. Slaves were rewarded for betraying their masters, and whoever harboured any of the proscribed was punished with death. Terror reigned throughout Italy. No one knew whose turn would come next.

Death of Cicero.

Cicero was included in the first seventeen victims of the proscription. He was residing in his Tusculan villa with his brother Quintus, who urged him to escape to Brutus in Macedonia. They reached Astura, a small island off Antium, when Quintus ventured to Rome to obtain a supply of money, of which they were in need. Here he was apprehended, together with his son, and both were put to death. The orator again embarked, and coasted along to Formiae, where he landed at his villa, resolving no longer to fly from his fate. After he had spent a night in his own house, his attendants, hearing that the soldiers were close at hand, forced him to enter a litter, and hurried him through the woods towards the shore, distant a mile from his house. As they were passing onwards they were overtaken by their pursuers, and were preparing to defend their master with their lives, but Cicero commanded them to desist; and, stretching his head out of the litter, called upon his executioners to strike. They instantly cut off his head and hands, which were carried to Rome. Fulvia, the widow of Clodius and now the wife of Antony, gloated her eyes with the sight, and even thrust a hair-pin through his tongue. Antony ordered the head to be nailed to the Rostra, which had so often witnessed the triumphs of the orator. Thus died Cicero, in the sixty-fourth year of his age. He had not sufficient firmness of character to cope with the turbulent times in which his lot was cast; but as a man he deserves our admiration and love. In the midst of almost universal corruption he remained uncontaminated. He was an affectionate father, a faithful friend, and a kind master.

Sextus Pompeius.

Many of the proscribed escaped from Italy, and took refuge with Sextus Pompeius in Sicily, and with Brutus and Cassius in the East. After the death of Caesar the senate had appointed Sextus to the command of the Republican fleet. He had become master of Sicily; his fleet commanded the Mediterranean; and Rome began to suffer from want of its usual supplies of corn. It was arranged that Octavian should attempt the conquest of Sicily, while Antony was preparing for the campaign in the East. A fleet under Salvidienus Rufus was sent against Pompeius, but was worsted by the latter in the Straits of Sicily, in sight of Octavian. The war against Brutus and Cassius was more urgent; and accordingly Octavian and Antony sailed shortly afterwards to the East, leaving Pompeius undisputed master of the sea.

Brutus and Cassius in the East.

M. Brutus had gained secure possession of Macedonia. The remains of the Pompeian legions, which had continued in Greece after the battle of Pharsalus, gathered round him; and C. Antonius, whom his brother had sent over to take the command of the province, was obliged to become his prisoner. His colleague had been equally fortunate in Syria. Dolabella, to whom Antony had given this province, was besieged in Laodicea by Cassius, and put an end to his own life (43 B.C.).

Brutus and Cassius were now masters of the Roman world east of the Adriatic. It was evident that their enemies before long would cross over into Greece; but instead of concentrating their forces in that country, they began to plunder the cities of Asia Minor, in order to obtain money for their troops. Brutus pillaged Lycia, and Cassius Rhodes. The inhabitants of the Lycian town of Xanthus refused to submit to the exactions of Brutus, made an heroic defence when they were attacked, and preferred to perish in the flames of their city rather than to yield. Brutus and Cassius were thus engaged when the news of the triumvirate and the proscription reached them; but they continued some time longer plundering in the East, and it was not till the spring of 42 B.C. that the Republican chiefs at length assembled their forces at Sardis, and prepared to march into Europe.

Arrival of Antony and Octavian.

So much time, however, had now been lost, that Antony and Octavian had landed without opposition upon the coast of Greece, and had already commenced their march towards Macedonia before Brutus and Cassius had quitted Asia.

Brutus seems to have had dark forebodings of the approaching struggle. He continued his studious habits during the campaign, and limited his hours of sleep. On the night before his army crossed over into Europe he was sitting in his tent, the lamp burning dim, and the whole camp in deep silence, when he saw a gigantic and terrible figure standing by him. He had the courage to ask, "Who art thou, and for what purpose dost thou come?" The phantom replied, "I am thy evil genius, Brutus; we shall meet again at Philippi!" and vanished.

Battles at Philippi.

Brutus and Cassius now marched through Thrace and Macedonia to Philippi, where they met the army of the triumvirs. The Republican leaders took up their positions on two heights distant a mile from each other, Brutus pitching his camp on the northern, and Cassius on the southern near the sea. The camps, though separate, were enclosed within a common entrenchment, and midway between them was the pass which led like a gate from Europe to Asia. The enemy was on the lower ground in a less favourable position; Octavian opposed Brutus and Antony Cassius. The numbers that met in this last struggle for the Republic were enormous, and nineteen legions were counted on either side. The triumvirs, whose troops began to suffer from want of provisions, now endeavoured to force the Republican leaders to an engagement. Cassius was unwilling to quit his strong position, and recommended that they should wait for their fleet; but Brutus was anxious to put an end to this state of suspense, and persuaded the council to risk an immediate battle. Brutus himself defeated the army opposite to him, and penetrated into the camp of Octavian, who was lying ill and unable to take part in the battle. His litter was seized, and brought forth covered with blood, and a report spread that he had been killed.

Death of Cassius and Brutus.

Meantime, on the other side of the field, Cassius had been driven back by Antony. Retiring to a neighbouring hill with some of his men, he saw a large body of cavalry approaching. Thinking that they belonged to the enemy and that everything was lost, he ordered one of his freedmen to put an end to his life. In reality Brutus had sent the cavalry to obtain news of Cassius; and when he heard of the death of his colleague he wept over him as "the last of the Romans," an eulogy which Cassius had done nothing to deserve.

Twenty days after the first battle Brutus again led out his

forces; but this time he was completely defeated, and with difficulty escaped from the field. He withdrew into a wood, and in the night-time fell upon his sword, which Strato, who had been his teacher in rhetoric, held for him. Philippi was the last—perhaps the only—contest in which the existence of the Republic was the stake; with Brutus it perished, and indeed it would have been strange had its salvation been due to him. He was doubtless a sincere believer, but he was a man of weak judgment, deficient in knowledge of mankind, and more fitted for a life of study than the command of armies and the government of men.

Coin of Antony and Cleopatra.

Coin of Augustus with head of M. Agrippa on the reverse.

CHAPTER XXXVII.

FROM THE BATTLE OF PHILIPPI TO THE BATTLE OF ACTIUM.
41–30 B.C.

Antony in the East.

AFTER the battle the victors separated. Antony remained in the East to collect money for the soldiers. Octavian, who was in ill-health, returned to Italy to give the veterans the lands which had been promised them. Antony traversed Asia Minor, plundering the unfortunate inhabitants, who had already suffered so severely from the exactions of Brutus and Cassius. In the voluptuous cities of Asia he surrendered himself to every kind of sensual enjoyment. He entered Ephesus in the character of Bacchus, accompanied by a wild procession of women dressed like Bacchantes, and men and youths disguised as Satyrs and Fauns.

Influence of Cleopatra.

At Tarsus in Cilicia, whither he had gone to prepare for the war against the Parthians, he was visited by Cleopatra, whom he had summoned to his presence to answer for her conduct in supplying Cassius with money and provisions. She was now in her twenty-eighth year, and in the full maturity of her charms. In her fifteenth year her beauty had made an impression on the heart of Antony, when he was at Alexandria with Gabinius; and she now trusted to make him her willing slave. She sailed up the Cydnus to Tarsus in a magnificent vessel with purple sails propelled by silver oars to the sound of luxurious music. She herself reclined under an awning spangled with gold, attired as Venus and fanned by Cupids. The most beautiful of her female slaves held the rudder and the ropes. The perfumes burnt upon the vessel filled the banks of the river with their fragrance. The inhabitants cried that Venus had come to revel with Bacchus. Antony accepted her invitation to sup on board her galley, and was completely subjugated. Her wit and vivacity surpassed even her beauty. He followed her to Alexandria, where he forgot everything in luxurious dalliance, and the charms of her society.

Meantime important events had been taking place in Italy. Octavian found immense difficulties in satisfying the demands of the veterans. All Italy was thrown into confusion. Though he expelled thousands from their homes in Cisalpine Gaul, in order to give their farms to his soldiers, they still clamoured for more. Those who had obtained assignments of land seized upon the property of their neighbours, and those who had not were ready to rise in mutiny. The country people, who had been obliged to yield their property to the rude soldiery, filled Italy with their complaints, and flocked to Rome to implore in vain the protection of Octavian. Even if he had the wish, he had not the power to control his soldiers.

Octavian in Italy.

Fulvia, the wife of Antony, who had remained behind in Italy, resolved to avail herself of these elements of confusion, and crush Octavian. She was a bold and ambitious woman; she saw that sooner or later the struggle must come between her husband and Octavian; and by precipitating the war she hoped to bring her husband to Italy, and thus withdraw him from the influence of Cleopatra. L. Antonius, the brother of the triumvir, who was consul this year (41 B.C.), entered into her views. They proclaimed themselves the patrons of the unfortunate Italians, and also promised to the discontented soldiery that the triumvir would recompense them with the spoils of Asia. By these means they soon saw themselves at the head of a considerable force, and even obtained possession of Rome.

Revolt of L. Antonius and Fulvia.

But Agrippa, the ablest general of Octavian, forced them to quit the city, and pressed them so hard that they were obliged to take refuge in Perusia (*Perugia*), one of the most powerful cities of Etruria. Here they were besieged during the winter, and suffered so dreadfully from famine that they found themselves compelled to

Siege of Perusia.

capitulate in the following spring. The lives of L. Antonius and Fulvia were spared, but the chief citizens of Perusia itself were put to death, and the town burnt to the ground.

While Antony's friends were thus unfortunate in Italy, his own forces experienced a still greater disaster in the East. Q. Labienus, the son of Caesar's old lieutenant in Gaul, had been sent by Brutus and Cassius to seek aid from Orodes, the king of Parthia. He was in that country when the news arrived of the battle of Philippi, and had remained there up to the present time.

Parthian invasion of Syria.

The war in Italy, and Antony's indolence at Alexandria, held out a favourable opportunity for the invasion of the Roman provinces. Orodes placed a large army under the command of Labienus and his own son Pacorus. They crossed the Euphrates in 40 B.C., and carried everything before them. Antony's troops were defeated; the two powerful cities of Antioch and Apamea were taken; and the whole of Syria overrun by the Parthians. Pacorus penetrated as far south as Palestine, and Labienus invaded Cilicia. Such alarming news, both from Italy and the East, at length aroused Antony from his voluptuous dreams. Leaving his lieutenant Ventidius in Syria, to conduct the war against the Parthians, Antony sailed to Athens, where he met his brother and wife. He now formed an alliance with Sextus Pompeius, sailed to Italy, and laid siege to Brundusium.

Peace of Brundusium.

Another civil war seemed inevitable; but the soldiers on both sides were eager for peace; and mutual friends persuaded the chiefs to be reconciled, which was the more easily effected in consequence of the death of Fulvia at Sicyon. A new division of the Roman world was now made. Antony was to have all the eastern provinces, and Octavian the western, the town of Scodra in Illyricum forming the boundary between them. Italy was to belong to them in common. Lepidus was allowed to retain possession of Africa, which he had received after the battle of Philippi, but he had ceased to be of any political importance. It was agreed that Antony should carry on the war against the Parthians, and that Octavian should subdue Pompeius, whom Antony readily sacrificed. The consuls were to be selected alternately from the friends of each. To cement the alliance, Antony was to marry

Octavia, the sister of Octavian and widow of C. Marcellus, one of the noblest women of her age. The two triumvirs then repaired to Rome to celebrate the marriage (close of 40 B.C.).

Discontent, however, prevailed at Rome. Sextus Pompeius, who had been excluded from the peace, still continued master of the sea, and intercepted the ships which supplied the city with corn. The people were in want of bread, and became so exasperated that Octavian and Antony found it necessary to enter into negotiations with the enemy. An interview took place between the chiefs at Cape Misenum. It was agreed that Pompeius should receive Sicily, Sardinia, Corsica, and Achaia, and that he should send to Rome an immediate supply of corn. The chiefs then feasted one another, and Pompeius entertained Octavian and Antony on board his own galley. When the banquet was at its height, a Greek named Menas or Menodorus, one of Pompeius' captains, whispered to him, "Shall I cut off the anchors of the ship, and make you lord of the Roman world?" To which his master made the well-known reply, "You ought to have done it without asking me." The two triumvirs, on their return to Rome, were received with shouts of applause. The civil wars seemed to have come to an end (39 B.C.).

Treaty of Misenum.

Antony, with Octavia, returned to the East, where he found that his legate Ventidius had gained the most brilliant success over the Parthians. This man was a native of Picenum, and originally a mule-driver. He was taken prisoner in the Social War, and walked in chains in the triumphal procession of Pompeius Strabo. He was made tribune of the Plebs by Julius Caesar, and was raised to the consulship in 43 B.C. In the Parthian War he displayed military abilities of no ordinary kind. He first defeated Labienus, took him prisoner in Cilicia, and put him to death. He then entered Syria, and drove Pacorus beyond the Euphrates. In the following year (38 B.C.) the Parthians again entered Syria, but Ventidius gained a signal victory over them, and Pacorus himself fell in the battle.

Victories of Ventidius over the Parthians.

The treaty between Sextus Pompeius and the triumvirs did not last long. Antony refused to give up Achaia, and Pompeius therefore recommenced his piratical excursions. The price of provisions at Rome immediately rose, and Octavian found it necessary to commence war immediately; but his fleet was twice defeated by Pompeius, and was at last completely destroyed by a storm (38 B.C.). This failure only proved the necessity of making still more extensive preparations to carry on the war with success. The power of Octavian was insecure as long as Pompeius was master of the sea, and could deprive Rome of her supplies of corn. Nearly two years were spent in building a new fleet, and exercising the newly raised crews and rowers. The command of the fleet and the superintendence of all the necessary preparations for the war were entrusted to Agrippa. In order to obtain a perfectly secure and land-locked basin for his fleet, and thus secure it against any sudden surprise, he constructed the celebrated Portus Julius on the coast of Campania near Baiae, by connecting the inland Lake Avernus, by means of a canal, with the Lake Lucrinus, and by strengthening the latter lake against the sea by an artificial dyke or dam. While he was engaged in these great works, Antony sailed to Tarentum, in 37 B.C., with 300 ships. Maecenas hastened thither from Rome, and succeeded once more in concluding an amicable arrangement. He was accompanied on this occasion by Horace, who has immortalized, in a well-known satire, his journey from Rome to Brundusium.

War with Sextus Pompeius.

Octavian and Antony met between Tarentum and Metapontum; the triumvirate was renewed for another period of five years; Antony agreed to leave 120 ships to assist in the war against Pompeius; and Octavian promised to send a land-force to the East for the campaign against the Parthians.

Renewal of the triumvirate.

Octavian, now relieved of all anxiety on the part of Antony, urged on his preparations with redoubled vigour. By the summer of 36 B.C. he was ready to commence operations. He had three large fleets at his disposal: his own, stationed in the Julian harbour; that of Antony, under the command of Statilius Taurus, in the harbour of Tarentum; and that of Lepidus, off the coast of Africa. His plan was for all three fleets to set sail on the same day, and make a descent upon three different parts of Sicily; but a fearful storm marred this project. Lepidus alone reached the coast of Sicily, and landed at Lilybaeum; Statilius Taurus was able to put back to Tarentum; but

Octavian, who was surprised by the storm off the Lucanian promontory of Palinurus, lost a great number of his ships, and was obliged to remain in Italy to repair his shattered fleet.

Battle of Naulochus.

As soon as the ships had been refitted, Octavian again set sail for Sicily. Agrippa defeated Pompeius' fleet off Mylae, destroying thirty of his ships; but the decisive battle was fought on the 3rd of September (36 B.C.), off Naulochus, a seaport between Mylae and the promontory of Pelorus. Agrippa gained a brilliant victory; most of the Pompeian vessels were destroyed or taken. Pompeius himself fled to Lesbos with a squadron of seventeen ships.

Retirement of Lepidus.

Octavian did not pursue him, as Lepidus, who was at the head of a considerable force, now claimed Sicily for himself, and an equal share as triumvir in the government of the Roman world; but Octavian found means to seduce his soldiers from their allegiance; and Lepidus was at last obliged to surrender to Octavian, and to throw himself upon his mercy. His life was granted, but he was deprived of his triumvirate, his army, and his provinces, and was compelled to retire to Italy as a private person. He was allowed, however, to retain his property and the dignity of Pontifex Maximus. He lived till 12 B.C.

Death of Sextus Pompeius.

In 35 B.C. Pompeius crossed over from Lesbos to Asia, with the view of seizing that province; but he was easily crushed by the lieutenants of Antony, was taken prisoner as he attempted to escape to Armenia, and was put to death at Miletus. By the death of Pompeius and the deposition of Lepidus, Antony and Octavian were now left without a rival; and Antony's mad love for Cleopatra soon made Octavian the undisputed master of the Roman world.

After Antony's marriage with Octavia, in 40 B.C., he seems for a time to have forgotten or at least conquered the fascinations of the Egyptian queen. For the next three years he resided at Athens with his wife; but after his visit to Italy, and the renewal of the triumvirate in 37 B.C., he left Octavia behind at Tarentum, and determined to carry out his long-projected campaign against the Parthians.

As he approached Syria, "that great evil," as Plutarch calls it, his passion for Cleopatra, burst forth with more vehemence than ever. From this time she appears as his evil genius. He summoned her to him, and loaded her with honours and favours. He added to her dominions Phoenicia, Coele-Syria, Cyprus, a large part of Cilicia, Palestine, and Arabia, and publicly recognized the children she had borne him. Although he had collected a large army to invade the Parthian empire, he was unable to tear himself away from the enchantress, and did not commence his march till late in the year. The expedition proved most disastrous; the army suffered from want of provisions; and Antony found himself compelled to retreat. He narrowly escaped the fate of Crassus; and it was with the utmost difficulty that he succeeded in reaching the Armenian mountains after losing the best part of his troops.

Renewed influence of Cleopatra.

Antony returned to Alexandria, and surrendered himself entirely to Cleopatra. In 34 B.C. he made a short campaign into Armenia, and succeeded in obtaining possession of Artavasdes, the Armenian king. He carried him to Alexandria, and, to the great scandal of all the Romans, entered the city in triumph, with all the pomp and ceremonial of the Roman pageant. He now laid aside entirely the character of a Roman citizen, and assumed the state and dress of an Eastern monarch. Instead of the toga he wore a robe of purple, and his head was crowned with a diadem. Sometimes he assumed the character of Osiris, while Cleopatra appeared at his side as Isis. He gave the title of kings to Alexander and Ptolemy, his sons by Cleopatra. The Egyptian queen already dreamed of reigning over the Roman world.

Antony in Egypt.

While Antony was disgusting the Romans and alienating his friends and supporters by his senseless follies, Octavian had been restoring order to Italy; and, by his wise and energetic administration, was slowly repairing the evils of the civil wars. In order to give security to the frontiers and employment to the troops, he attacked the barbarians on the north of Italy and Greece, and subdued the Iapydes, Pannonians, and Dalmatians. He carried on these wars in person, and won the affection of the soldiers by sharing their dangers and hardships.

The contrast between the two triumvirs was sufficiently striking, but Octavian called attention to the follies of Antony.

Letters passed between them full of mutual recriminations, and both parties began to prepare for the inevitable struggle.

War declared against Cleopatra.

Towards the end of 32 B.C. the senate declared war against Cleopatra,* since there was no ground for treating Antony as a public enemy. The five years of the triumvirate had expired on the last day of this year; and on the 1st of January, 31 B.C., Octavian, as Consul of the Republic, proceeded to carry on the war against the Egyptian queen. The hostile fleets and armies assembled on the western coasts of Greece. Antony's fleet was superior both in the number and size of the ships, but they were clumsy and unmanageable. They were anchored in the Ambraciot Gulf in the modern *Bay of Prevesa*. (See Plan, P.) The army was encamped on the promontory of Actium (Plan, 3), which has given its name to the battle. The fleet of Octavian consisted of light Liburnian vessels, manned by crews which had gained experience in the wars against Sextus Pompeius. It was under the command of the able Agrippa, who took up his station at Corcyra, and swept the Adriatic Sea.

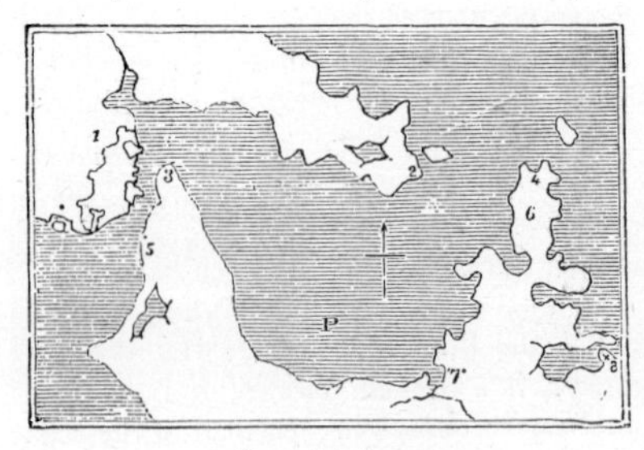

Plan of Actium.

1. Nicopolis. | 3. Prom. Actium.
2. *C. La Scara.* | 5. Temple of Apollo.
P. *Bay of Prevesa.*

Battle of Actium.

Octavian in person took the command of the land-forces, which were encamped on the coast of Epirus opposite Actium, on the spot where Nicopolis afterwards stood. (Plan, 1.) The generals of Antony strongly urged him to fight on land; but the desertions among his troops were numerous; Cleopatra became alarmed for her safety; and it was therefore resolved to sacrifice the army, and retire with the fleet to Egypt. But Agrippa was on the watch, and Antony had no sooner sailed outside the strait than he was compelled to fight. The battle was still undecided and equally

* Antony retaliated by sending Octavia a bill of divorce.

favourable to both parties, when Cleopatra, whose vessels were at anchor in the rear, taking advantage of a favourable breeze which sprung up, sailed through the midst of the combatants with her squadron of sixty ships, and made for the coast of Peloponnesus. When Antony saw her flight, he hastily followed her, forgetting everything else, and shamefully deserting those who were fighting and dying in his cause. The remainder of the fleet was destroyed before night-time, and the army, after a few days' hesitation, surrendered. The battle of Actium was fought on the 2nd of September, 31 B.C., from which day the sole rule of Octavian may be dated, although his constitutional position as Princeps was not secured until four years later (27 B.C.).

Octavian did not follow Antony to Alexandria for nearly twelve months after the battle of Actium. He sent Agrippa to Italy with his veteran troops, and himself passed the winter at Samos; but he could not satisfy the demands of the soldiers, who broke out into open mutiny. Octavian hastened to Brundusium, and with difficulty raised a sufficient sum of money to calm their discontent.

Octavian goes to Egypt.

This respite was of no service to Antony and Cleopatra. They knew that resistance was hopeless, and therefore sent ambassadors to Octavian to solicit his favour. To Antony no answer was given, but to Cleopatra hopes were held out if she would betray her lover. She began to flatter herself that her charms, which had fascinated both Caesar and Antony, might conquer Octavian, who was younger than either. Octavian at length appeared before Pelusium, which surrendered to him without resistance. He then marched upon Alexandria. Antony, encouraged by some slight success in an action with the cavalry, prepared to resist Octavian both by sea and land; but as soon as the Egyptian ships approached those of Octavian, the crews saluted them with their oars and passed over to their side. Antony's cavalry also deserted him; his infantry was easily repulsed; and he fled to Alexandria, crying out that he was betrayed by Cleopatra.

The queen had shut herself up in a mausoleum which she had built to receive her body after death, and where she had collected her most valuable treasures. Hearing of Antony's defeat, she sent persons to inform him that she was dead. He fell into the snare; they had promised not to survive one another; and Antony stabbed himself. He was drawn up into the mausoleum, and died in her arms. She was apprehended by the officers of Octavian, and a few days afterwards had an interview with the conqueror. Her charms, however, failed in softening the colder heart of Octavian. He only "bade her be of good cheer and fear no violence." Soon afterwards she learnt that she was to be sent to Rome in three days' time. This news decided her. On the following day she was found lying dead on a golden couch in royal attire, with her two women lifeless at her feet. The manner of her death was unknown. It was generally believed that she had died by the bite of an asp, which a peasant had brought to her in a basket full of figs. She was thirty-nine years of age at the time of her death. Egypt became a Roman possession. Octavian did not return to Rome till 29 B.C., when he celebrated a threefold triumph over the Pannonians, Dalmatians, and Egypt. The temple of Janus was closed for the third time in Roman history, and the exhausted Roman world, longing for repose, gladly acquiesced in the sole rule of Octavian.

Death of Antony and Cleopatra.

Thus ended the Roman Republic, an end to which it had been tending for the last hundred years. The corruption and demoralization of all classes had rendered a Republic almost an impossibility; and the civil dissensions of the state had again and again invested one or more persons with despotic authority. The means which Augustus employed to strengthen and maintain his power belong to a history of the Empire. He proceeded with the caution which was his greatest characteristic. He refused the names of king and dictator, and was contented with the simple appellation of *Princeps*, or "chief citizen," which had long been used to designate any one eminent in the service of the Republican government. He received, however, in 27 B.C., the novel title of *Augustus*, that is, "the sacred," or "the venerable," which was afterwards assumed by all the Roman emperors as a surname. His authority was secured by the assumption of two extraordinary powers—the *Proconsulare imperium*, which made him commander-in-chief of the Roman armies; and the *Tribanicia potestas*, which gave him pre-eminence over the civil magistrates of the state. He made a new division of the provinces, allowing the senate to appoint the governors of those which were

The Principate.

quiet and long-settled, like Sicily, Achaia, and Asia, but retaining for himself such as required the presence of an army, which were governed by means of his Legati. On the death of Lepidus in 12 B.C., he succeeded him as Pontifex Maximus, and thus became the head of the Roman religion. While he thus united in his own person all the great offices of state, he still allowed the consuls, praetors, and other magistrates of the Republic to be annually elected, and to perform their normal functions, while he restored the senate to the numbers fixed by Sulla, and to its Republican character of a body of Italian nobles. "In a few words, the system of Imperial government, as it was instituted by Octavian, and maintained by those princes who understood their own interest and that of the people, may be defined as an absolute government disguised by the form of a commonwealth. The masters of the Roman world surrounded their throne with darkness, concealed their irresistible strength, and humbly professed themselves the accountable ministers of the senate, whose supreme decrees they dictated and obeyed." *

* Gibbon.

Coin of Augustus commemorating the conquest of Egypt.

Medal of Horace.

CHAPTER XXXVIII.

SKETCH OF THE HISTORY OF ROMAN LITERATURE, FROM THE EARLIEST TIMES TO THE DEATH OF AUGUSTUS.

Folk-songs.

For many centuries after the foundation of the city the Romans can hardly be said to have had any literature at all. There may have existed, at an early period, some songs or ballads, recounting, in rude strains,* the exploits of the heroes of Roman story, but all trace of these has disappeared. It was not till the conquest of the Greek cities in Southern Italy, shortly before the First Punic War, that we can date the commencement of a true literature.

Early dramatic art.

It began with the Drama. The earliest dramatic exhibitions at Rome had been introduced from Etruria in 364 B.C.; they had a religious significance, and were intended to avert the anger of the gods on the occasion of a severe pestilence. But these exhibitions were only pantomimic scenes to the music of the flute, without any dialogue. It was not till 240 B.C. that a drama with a regular plot was performed at Rome.

* These were probably composed in the Saturnian metre, the oldest species of versification among the Romans, the freedom of which, with regard to the laws of quantity, gave greater play to the genius of the Latin language than the dactylic hexameter borrowed from the Greeks.

Its author was M. LIVIUS ANDRONICUS, a native of Magna Graecia, who was taken prisoner at the capture of Tarentum, and carried to Rome, where he became the slave of M. Livius Salinator. He was afterwards set free, and, according to Roman practice, took the gentilic name of his master. He acquired at Rome a perfect knowledge of the Latin language; and wrote both tragedies and comedies, which were borrowed or rather translated from the Greek. He also wrote an Odyssey in the Saturnian metre, and some hymns. He may be regarded as the first Roman poet. His works were read in schools in the time of Horace.

Livius Andronicus.

CN. NAEVIUS, the second Roman poet, was a Campanian by birth. He served in the First Punic War, and, like Livius, wrote dramas borrowed from the Greek. His first play was performed in 235 B.C. He was attached to the plebeian party; and, with the licence of the old Attic comedy, he made the stage a vehicle for assailing the aristocracy. In consequence of his attacks upon the Metelli he was thrown into prison. He obtained his release through the tribunes, but was soon compelled to expiate a new offence by exile. He retired to Utica, where he died about 204 B.C. In his exile he wrote, in the Saturnian metre, an epic poem on the First Punic War, in which he introduced the celebrated legends connected with the foundation of Rome. This poem was extensively copied both by Ennius and Vergil.

Naevius.

Q. ENNIUS, however, may be regarded as the real founder of Roman literature. Like Livius, he was a native of Magna Graecia. He was born at Rudiae, in Calabria, 239 B.C. Cato found him in Sardinia in 204 B.C., and brought him in his train to Rome. He dwelt in a humble house on the Aventine, and maintained himself by acting as preceptor to the youth of the Roman nobility. He lived on terms of the closest intimacy with the elder Scipio Africanus, and died in the year 169 B.C., at the age of seventy. He was buried in the sepulchre of the Scipios, and his bust was allowed a place among the effigies of that noble house. His most important work was an epic poem, entitled the "Annals of Rome," in eighteen books, written in dactylic hexameters, which, through his example, supplanted the old Saturnian metre. This poem commenced with the story of Aeneas, and contained a

Epic poetry Ennius.

chronological record of events down to the writer's own time. Vergil borrowed largely from it; and, down to his time, it was regarded as *the* great epic poem of the Latin language. He also wrote numerous tragedies, a few comedies, and several other works, such as *Saturae*, miscellaneous poems composed in a great variety of metres, from which circumstance they probably received their name.

Comedy: Plautus.

The comic drama of Rome, though it continued to be more or less a translation or an imitation of the Greek, was cultivated with distinguished success by two writers of genius, several of whose plays are still extant.

T. MACCIUS PLAUTUS was a native of Sarsina, a small village in Umbria, and was born about 254 B.C. He probably came to Rome at an early age, and was first employed in the service of the actors. With the money he had saved in this inferior station he left Rome, and set up in business: but his speculations failed: he returned to the capital, and his necessities obliged him to enter the service of a baker, who employed him in turning a hand-mill. While in this degrading occupation he wrote three plays, the sale of which to the managers of the public games enabled him to quit his drudgery, and begin his literary career. He was then about thirty years of age (224 B.C.), and continued to write for the stage for about forty years. He died in 184 B.C., when he was seventy years of age. The comedies of Plautus enjoyed unrivalled popularity among the Romans, and continued to be represented down to the time of Diocletian. Though they were founded upon Greek models, the characters in them act, speak, and joke like genuine Romans, and the poet thereby secured the sympathy of his audience more completely than Terence. It was not only with the common people that Plautus was a favourite; educated Romans read and admired his works down to the latest times. Cicero places his wit on a level with that of the old Attic comedy; and St. Jerome used to console himself with the perusal of the poet, after spending many nights in tears on account of his past sins. The favourable opinion which the ancients entertained of the merits of Plautus has been confirmed by the judgment of modern critics, and by the fact that several of his plays have been imitated by many of the best modern poets. Twenty of his comedies are extant.

Terence.

P. TERENTIUS AFER, usually called TERENCE, was born at Carthage, 195 B.C. By birth or purchase he became the slave of P. Terentius, a Roman senator, who afforded him the best education of the age, and finally gave him his freedom. The *Andria*, the first play of Terence placed on the stage (166 B.C.), was the means of introducing him to the most refined and intellectual circles of Rome. His chief patrons were Laelius and the younger Scipio, both of whom treated him as an equal, and are said even to have assisted him in the composition of his plays. He died in the thirty-sixth year of his age, in 159 B.C. Six comedies are all that remain to us. The ancient critics are unanimous in ascribing to Terence immaculate purity and elegance of language. Although a foreigner and a freedman, he divides with Cicero and Caesar the palm of pure Latinity.

There were two other comic poets, whose works are lost, but who enjoyed a great reputation among the Romans. STATIUS CAECILIUS was a native of Milan, and, like Terence, came to Rome as a slave. He was the immediate predecessor of Terence, and died 168 B.C., two years before the representation of the *Andria*. L. AFRANIUS flourished 100 B.C., and wrote comedies describing Roman scenes and manners, called *Comoediae Togatae*, to distinguish them from those depicting Grecian life, which were termed *Palliatae*, from *pallium*, the national dress of the Greeks.

Tragedy: Pacuvius.

There were two tragic poets contemporary with Terence, who also enjoyed great celebrity, though their works have likewise perished. M. PACUVIUS, son of the sister of Ennius, was born about 220 B.C., and died in the ninetieth year of his age. He is praised by the Latin writers for the loftiness of his thoughts, the vigour of his language, and the extent of his knowledge. Hence we find the epithet *doctus* frequently applied to him. Most of his tragedies were taken from the Greek writers; but some belonged to the class called *Praetextatae*, in which the subjects were taken from Roman story. One of these, entitled *Paullus*, had as its hero L. Aemilius Paullus, the conqueror of Perseus, king of Macedonia.

Accius.

L. ACCIUS, a younger contemporary of Pacuvius, was born 140 B.C., and lived to a great age. Cicero, when a young man, frequently conversed with him. His tragedies, like those of Pacuvius, were chiefly imitations of the Greek; but he also wrote some on Roman subjects, one of which was entitled *Brutus*.

Though the Roman drama, properly so called, was derived from the Greeks, there were some kinds of dramatic exhibitions which were of Italian origin. The first of these were the *Atellanae Fabulae*, or Atellane Plays, which took their name from Atella, a town in Campania. They were at first rude extemporaneous farces, but were afterwards divided into acts like a regular drama. They were originally composed in the Oscan dialect; but, when cultivated by the youth of Rome, who readily assumed parts in these pieces, they must have been acted in Latin.

Native drama.

The *Mimes* were another species of comedy, of which only the name seems to have been derived from the Greek. They were a species of low comedy, in which the dialogue was subordinate to mimicry and gesture. The Dictator Sulla was very fond of these performances. The two most distinguished writers of Mimes were D. LABERIUS, a knight, and P. SYRUS, a freedman, and originally a Syrian slave, both of whom were contemporaries of Julius Caesar. At Caesar's triumphal games in October, 45 B.C., P. Syrus challenged all his craft to a trial of wit in extemporaneous farce, and Caesar offered Laberius 500,000 sesterces to appear on the stage. Laberius was sixty years old, and the profession of a mimus was infamous, but the wish of the dictator was equivalent to a command, and he reluctantly complied. He had, however, revenge in his power, and took it. His prologue awakened compassion, and perhaps indignation; and during the performance he adroitly availed himself of his various characters to point his wit at Caesar. In the person of a beaten Syrian slave he cried out, "Marry! Quirites, but we lose our freedom," and all eyes were turned upon the dictator: and in another mime he uttered the pregnant maxim, "Needs must he fear who makes all else adread." Caesar, impartially or vindictively, awarded the prize to Syrus.

Mimes.

The *Fescennine Songs* were probably the origin of the *Satire*, the only important species of literature not derived from the Greeks, and altogether peculiar to Italy. These Fescennine Songs were rude dialogues, in which the country people assailed and ridiculed one another in

Satire.

extempore verses, and which were introduced as an amusement into various festivals.

Lucilius.

Saturae,* although the name was given to certain poems of Ennius, first assumed definite literary shape from the hands of C. LUCILIUS, who wrote in hexameter verse, and attacked the follies and vices both of distinguished persons and of mankind in general. He was born 180 B.C., at Suessa Aurunca, and died at Naples in 103 B.C. He lived upon terms of intimacy with the younger Scipio and Laelius; and was the great-uncle of Pompey on his mother's side. Lucilius continued to be admired in the Augustan age; and Horace, while he censures the harsh versification and the slovenly haste with which Lucilius threw off his compositions, acknowledges with admiration the fierceness and boldness of his attacks upon the vices and follies of his contemporaries.

Between Lucilius and the poets of the Augustan age lived Lucretius and Catullus, two of the greatest—perhaps the greatest—of all the Roman poets.

Poets of the later Republic: Lucretius.

T. LUCRETIUS CARUS was born 96 B.C., and died in 55 B.C. He is said to have been driven mad by a love-potion, and to have perished by his own hand. The work which has immortalized his name is a philosophical didactic poem, in heroic hexameters, entitled *De Rerum Natura*, divided into six books, and addressed to C. Memmius Gemellus, who was praetor in 58 B.C. Its object is to state clearly the leading principles of the Epicurean philosophy in such a form as might render the study attractive to his countrymen. He attempts to show that there is nothing in the history or actual condition of the world which does not admit of explanation without having recourse to the active interposition of divine beings. The work has been admitted by all modern critics to be the greatest of didactic poems. The most abstruse speculations are clearly explained in majestic verse; while the subject, which in itself is dry and dull, is enlivened by digressions of matchless power and beauty.

VALERIUS CATULLUS was born at Verona or in its immediate vicinity, in 87 B.C. He inherited considerable property from his father, who was the friend of Julius Caesar; but he squandered

* The name signifies a mixture or medley. Hence a *lex per saturam lata* is a law which contained several distinct regulations at once.

a great part of it by indulging freely in the pleasures of the metropolis. In order to better his fortunes he went to Bithynia in the train of the praetor Memmius, but it appears that the speculation was attended with little success. It was probably during this expedition that his brother died in the Troad, a loss which he deplores in the affecting elegy to Hortalus. On his return he continued to reside at Rome, or at his country-seats on the promontory of Sirmio and at Tibur. He died about 54 B.C. His poems are on a variety of topics, and composed in different styles and metres. Some are lyrical, others elegies, others epigrams; while the Nuptials of Peleus and Thetis is an heroic poem. Catullus adorned all he touched, and his shorter poems are characterized by original invention and felicity of expression. His *Atys* is one of the most remarkable poems in the whole range of Latin literature, distinguished by wild passion and the noblest diction.

Catullus.

Among the poets of the Augustan age Vergil and Horace stand forth pre-eminent.

The Augustan age: Vergil.

P. VERGILIUS MARO was born, 70 B.C., at Andes, a small village near Mantua in Cisalpine Gaul. His father left him a small estate, which he cultivated. After the battle of Philippi (42 B.C.) his property was among the lands assigned by Octavian to the soldiers. Through the advice of Asinius Pollio, who was then governor of Cisalpine Gaul, and was himself a poet, Vergil applied to Octavian at Rome for the restitution of his land, and obtained his request. The first Eclogue commemorates his gratitude. Vergil lived on intimate terms with Maecenas, whom he accompanied in the journey from Rome to Brundusium, which forms the subject of one of the Satires of Horace. His most finished work, the *Georgics*, was undertaken at the suggestion of Maecenas.* The poem was completed after the battle of Actium, 31 B.C., while Octavian was in the East.† The *Aeneid* was the occupation of his latter years. His health was always feeble, and he died at Brundusium in 19 B.C., in his fifty-first year. His remains were transferred to Naples, which had been his favourite residence, and placed on the road from Naples to Puteoli (*Pozzuoli*), where a monument is still shown, supposed to be the tomb of the poet. It is said that in his last

* *Georg.* iii. 41.

† Comp. *Georg.* iv. 560, and ii. 171.

illness he wished to burn the *Aeneid*, to which he had not given the finishing touches, but his friends would not allow him. He was an amiable good-tempered man, free from the mean passions of envy and jealousy. His fame, which was established in his lifetime, was cherished after his death as an inheritance in which every Roman had a share; and his works became school-books even before the death of Augustus, and continued such for centuries after. He was also the great poet of the Middle Ages. To him Dante paid the homage of his superior genius, and owned him for his master and his model. The ten short poems called *Bucolics*, or *Eclogues*, were the earliest works of Vergil, and probably all written between 41 B.C. and 39 B.C. They have all a Bucolic form and colouring, but some of them have nothing more. Their merit consists in their versification, and in many natural and simple touches. The *Georgics* is an "Agricultural Poem" in four books. Vergil treats of the cultivation of the soil in the first book, of fruit-trees in the second, of horses and other cattle in the third, and of bees in the fourth. This poem shows a great improvement both in his taste and in his versification. Neither in the *Georgics* nor elsewhere has he the merit of striking originality; his chief excellence consists in the skilful handling of borrowed materials. The *Aeneid*, or adventures of Aeneas after the fall of Troy, is an epic formed on the model of the Homeric poems. It was founded upon an old Roman tradition that Aeneas and his Trojans settled in Italy, and were the founders of the Roman name. In the first six books the adventures of Ulysses in the Odyssey are the model, and these books contain more variety of incident and situation than those which follow. The last six books, the history of the struggles of Aeneas in Italy, are based on the plan of the battles of the Iliad. Latinus, the king of the Latini, offers in marriage to the Trojan hero his daughter Lavinia, who had been betrothed to Turnus, the warlike king of the Rutuli. The contest is ended by the death of Turnus, who falls by the hand of Aeneas. The fortunes of Aeneas and his final settlement in Italy are the subjects of the *Aeneid*, but the glories of Rome and of the Julian house, to which Augustus belonged, are indirectly the poet's theme. In the first book the foundation of Alba Longa is promised by Jupiter to Venus, and the transfer of empire from Alba to Rome; from the line of Aeneas will descend the

"Trojan Caesar," whose empire will only be limited by the ocean, and his glory by the heavens. The ultimate triumphs of Rome are predicted.

Horace.

Q. HORATIUS FLACCUS, usually called HORACE, was born at Venusia in Apulia, 65 B.C. His father was a freedman. He had received his manumission before the birth of the poet, who was, therefore, of ingenuous origin, but who did not altogether escape the taunt which adhered to persons even of remote servile descent. His father's occupation was that of a collector (*coactor*) of taxes. With the profits of his office he had purchased a small farm in the neighbourhood of Venusia. Though by no means rich, he declined to send the young Horace to the common school, kept in Venusia by one Flavius, to which the children of the rural aristocracy resorted. Probably about his twelfth year his father carried him to Rome to receive the usual education of a knight's or senator's son. He frequented the best schools in the capital. One ot these was kept by Orbilius, a retired military man, whose flogging propensities have been immortalized by his pupil. The names of his other teachers he has not recorded. He was instructed in the Greek and Latin languages: the poets were the usual school-books—Homer in the Greek, and the old tragic writer, Livius Andronicus, in the Latin. In his eighteenth year Horace proceeded to Athens, in order to continue his studies at that seat of learning. When Brutus came to Athens after the death of Caesar, Horace joined his army, and received at once the rank of a military tribune. He was present at the battle of Philippi, and shared in the flight of the republican army. In one of his poems he playfully alludes to his flight and throwing away his shield. He now resolved to devote himself to more peaceful pursuits; and having obtained his pardon, he ventured at once to return to Rome. He had lost all his hopes in life; his paternal estate had been swept away in the general forfeiture; but he was enabled to obtain sufficient money to purchase a clerkship in the quaestor's office; and on the profits of that place he managed with the utmost frugality to live. Meantime some of his poems attracted the notice of Varius and Vergil, who introduced him to Maecenas (38 B.C.) Horace soon became the friend of Maecenas, and this friendship quickly ripened into intimacy. In the year following the commencement of their friendship (37 B.C.) Horace accompanied his patron on the journey to Brundusium already alluded to. About the year 32 B.C. Maecenas bestowed upon the poet a Sabine farm, sufficient to maintain him in ease, comfort, and even in content, during the rest of his life. Besides this estate, his admiration of the beautiful scenery in the neighbourhood of Tibur inclined him either to hire or to purchase a small cottage in that romantic town; and all the later years of his life were passed between the metropolis and these two country residences. He died in 8 B.C., in his fifty-seventh year. He was buried on the slope of the Esquiline Hill, close to his friend and patron Maecenas, who had died before him in the same year. Horace has described his own person. He was of short stature, with dark eyes and black hair, early tinged with grey. In his youth he was tolerably robust, but suffered from a complaint in his eyes. In more advanced life he grew fat, and Augustus jested about his corpulence. His health was not always good, and he seems to have inclined to be a valetudinarian. In dress he was rather careless. His habits, even after he became richer, were generally frugal and abstemious; though on occasions, both in youth and maturer age, he seems to have indulged in conviviality. He liked choice wine, and in the society of friends scrupled not to enjoy the luxuries of his time. He was never married. The *Odes* of Horace want the higher inspirations of lyric verse. His amatory verses are exquisitely graceful, but they have no strong ardour, no deep tenderness, nor even much of light and joyous gaiety; but as works of refined art, of the most skilful felicities of language and of measure, of translucent expression, and of agreeable images embodied in words which imprint themselves indelibly on the memory, they are unrivalled. In the *Satires* of Horace there is none of the lofty moral indignation, the fierce vehemence of invective, which characterized the later satirists. It is the folly rather than the wickedness of vice which he touches with such playful skill. In the *Epodes* there is bitterness provoked, it should seem, by some personal hatred or sense of injury. But the *Epistles* are the most perfect of the Horatian poetry, the poetry of manners and society, the beauty of which consists in its common sense and practical wisdom. The Epistles of Horace are, with the Poem of Lucretius, the Georgics of Vergil, and perhaps the Satires of Juvenal, the most perfect and most original form of Roman verse. The *Art of Poetry* was probably intended to dissuade one of the younger Pisos from devoting himself to poetry, for which he had little genius, or at least to suggest the difficulties of attaining to perfection.

Three celebrated Elegiac poets—Tibullus, Propertius, and Ovid—also belong to the Augustan age.

Tibullus.

ALBIUS TIBULLUS was of equestrian family, and possessed an hereditary estate between Tibur and Praeneste. His great patron was Messala, whom he accompanied in 31 B.C. to Aquitania, whither Messala had been sent by Augustus to suppress a formidable insurrection which had broken out in this province. In the following year (30 B.C.) Messala, having pacified Gaul, was sent into the East. Tibullus set out in his company, but was taken ill, and obliged to remain in Corcyra, from whence he returned to Rome. So ceased the active life of Tibullus. He died at an early age soon after Vergil. The poetry of his contemporaries shows Tibullus as a gentle and singularly amiable man. To Horace especially he was an object of warm attachment. His Elegies, which are exquisite small poems, celebrate the beauty and cruelty of his mistresses.

Propertius.

SEXTUS PROPERTIUS was a native of Umbria, and was born about 51 B.C. He was deprived of his paternal estate by an agrarian division, probably that in 36 B.C., after the Sicilian War. He began to write poetry at a very early age, and the merit of his productions soon attracted the attention and patronage of Maecenas. The year of his death is altogether unknown. As an elegiac poet a high rank must be awarded to Propertius, and among the ancients it was a disputed point whether the preference should be given to him or to Tibullus. To the modern reader, however, the elegies of Propertius are not nearly so attractive as those of Tibullus. This arises partly from their obscurity, but in a great measure also from a certain lack of natural inspiration. The fault of Propertius was too pedantic an imitation of the Greeks. His whole ambition was to become the Roman Callimachus, whom he made his model. He abounds with obscure Greek myths, as well as Greek forms of expression, and the same pedantry infects even his versification.

P. OVIDIUS NASO, usually called OVID, was born at Sulmo, in

the country of the Paeligni, on the 20th March, 43 B.C. He was descended from an ancient equestrian family, and was destined to be a pleader. But the bent of his genius showed itself very early. The hours which should have been spent in the study of jurisprudence were employed in cultivating his poetical talent. It is a disputed point whether he ever actually practised as an advocate after his return to Rome. The picture Ovid himself draws of his weak constitution and indolent temper prevents us from thinking that he ever followed his profession with perseverance, if indeed at all. He became, however, one of the *Triumviri Capitales*; and he was subsequently made one of the *Centumviri*, or judges who tried testamentary causes. Till his fiftieth year he continued to reside at Rome, where he had a house near the Capitol, occasionally taking a trip to his Paelignian farm. He not only enjoyed the friendship of a large circle of distinguished men, but the regard and favour of Augustus and the imperial family; notwithstanding which, in 9 A.D. he was suddenly commanded by an imperial edict to transport himself to Tomi, a town on the Euxine, near the mouths of the Danube, on the very border of the empire. He underwent no trial, and the sole reason for his banishment stated in the edict was his having published his poem on the Art of Love (*Ars Amatoria*). The real cause of his exile is unknown, for the publication of the Art of Love, demoralizing as the poem might be held to be, was certainly a mere pretext. Ovid draws an affecting picture of the miseries to which he was exposed in his place of exile. He complains of the inhospitable soil, of the severity of the climate, and of the perils to which he was exposed, when the barbarians plundered the surrounding country, and insulted the very walls of Tomi. In the midst of all his misfortunes he sought some relief in the exercise of his poetical talents. He died in exile in the sixtieth year of his age, 18 A.D. Besides his amatory poems, Ovid wrote the *Metamorphoses* in fifteen books, which consist of such legends or fables as involved a transformation, from the Creation to the time of Julius Caesar, the last being that emperor's change into a star—the *Fasti*, intended to extend to twelve books, of which only the first six are extant, a sort of poetical Roman calendar, with its appropriate festivals and mythology—and the *Elegies*, written during his banishment. Ovid undoubtedly possessed a great poetical

Ovid.

genius, which makes it the more to be regretted that it was not always under the control of a sound judgment. He exhibits great vigour of fancy and warmth of colouring, but he was the first to depart from that pure and correct taste which characterizes the Greek poets and their earlier Latin imitators.

We now turn to the history of prose literature among the Romans. The earliest prose works were Annals containing a meagre account of the principal events in Roman history, arranged under their respective years. The earliest annalists who obtained reputation were Q. FABIUS PICTOR and L. CINCIUS ALIMENTUS, both of whom served in the Second Punic War, and drew up an account of it, but they wrote in the Greek language.

Annalists.

The first prose writer in the Latin language, of whom any considerable fragments have been preserved, is the celebrated censor, M. PORCIUS CATO, who died 149 B.C., and of whose life an account has already been given. He wrote an important historical work entitled *Origines*. The first book contained the history of the Roman kings; the second and third treated of the origin of the Italian towns, and from these two books the whole work derived its title; the fourth book treated of the First Punic War, the fifth book of the Second Punic War, and the sixth and seventh continued the narrative to the year 149 B.C. There is still extant a work on agriculture (*De Re Rustica*) bearing the name of Cato, which is probably substantially his, though it is certainly not exactly in the form in which it proceeded from his pen. There were many other annalists, of whom we know little more than the names, and whose works were used by Livy in compiling his Roman history.

Cato.

Oratory was always cultivated by the Romans as one of the chief avenues to political distinction. Cicero, in his work entitled *Brutus*, has given a long list of distinguished orators whose speeches he had read: but he himself surpassed all his predecessors and contemporaries. In his works the Latin language appears in the highest perfection. Besides his numerous orations he also wrote several treatises on *Rhetoric*, of which the most perfect is a systematic treatise on the art of oratory (*De Oratore*) in three books. His works on

Cicero.

Philosophy were almost the first specimens of this kind of literature ever presented to the Romans in their own language. He does not aim at any original investigation or research. His object was to present in a familiar and attractive form the results at which the Greek philosophers had arrived, not to expound any new theories. His *Epistles,* of which more than eight hundred have come down to us, are among the most valuable remains of antiquity. Cicero, during the most important period of his life, maintained a close correspondence with Atticus and with a wide circle of political friends and connections. These letters supply the most ample materials for a history of the Roman Republic during its last struggles, and afford a clear insight into the personal dispositions and motives of its chief leaders.

Varro.

The most learned Roman under the Republic was M. TERENTIUS VARRO, a contemporary and friend of Cicero. He served as Pompey's lieutenant in Spain in the civil wars, but was pardoned by Caesar after the battle of Pharsalus, and was employed by him in superintending the collection and arrangement of the great library designed for public use. Upon the formation of the second triumvirate, Varro's name appeared upon the list of the proscribed: but he succeeded in making his escape, and, after having remained for some time in concealment, he obtained the protection of Octavian. His death took place 28 B.C., when he was in his 89th year. Not only was Varro the most learned of Roman scholars, but he was likewise the most voluminous of Roman authors. We have his own authority for the assertion that he had composed no less than 490 books, but of these only two have come down to us, and one of them in a mutilated form: 1. *De Re Rustica,* a work on agriculture, in three books, written when the author was eighty years old; 2. *De Lingua Latina,* a grammatical treatise which extended to twenty-five books, but six only have been preserved, and these are in a mutilated condition. The remains of this treatise are particularly valuable. They have preserved many terms and forms which would otherwise have been altogether lost, and much curious information connected with the ancient usages, both civil and religious, of the Romans.

C. JULIUS CAESAR, the great dictator, was also distinguished as an author, and wrote several works, of which his memoirs

(*Commentarii*) alone have come down to us. They relate the history of the first seven years of the Gallic War in seven books, and the history of the Civil War down to the commencement of the Alexandrine in three books. Neither of these works completes the history of the Gallic and Civil Wars. The history of the former was completed in an eighth book, which is usually ascribed to Hirtius. The history of the Alexandrine, African, and Spanish wars was written in three separate books, which are also ascribed to Hirtius, but their authorship is uncertain. The purity of Caesar's Latin and the clearness of his style have deservedly obtained the highest praise.

Caesar.

C. SALLUSTIUS CRISPUS, a contemporary of Caesar, and one of his supporters, was also distinguished as an historian. He was born 86 B.C. at Amiternum, in the country of the Sabines, and died in 34 B.C. After the African War (46 B.C.) he was left by Caesar as governor of Numidia, where he acquired great riches by his oppression of the people. Two of his works have come down to us—the *Catilina*, the history of the suppression of Catiline's conspiracy; and the *Jugurtha*, the history of the war against Jugurtha. Sallust imitated Thucydides, and attained the conciseness, without the obscurity, of his great model.

Sallust.

CORNELIUS NEPOS, the contemporary and friend of Cicero and Atticus, was the author of numerous works, all of which are lost, with the exception of the Biographies of Cato and Atticus, and the Lives of Distinguished Commanders (*Vitae Excellentium Imperatorum*). But even these Lives are possibly an abridgment of the original work of Nepos, made in the fourth century of the Christian era.

Cornelius Nepos.

Of the prose writers of the Augustan age the most distinguished was the historian TITUS LIVIUS, usually called LIVY. He was born at Patavium (*Padua*), 59 B.C. The greater part of his life appears to have been spent in Rome, but he returned to his native town before his death, which happened at the age of seventy-six, in the fourth year of Tiberius, A.D. 17. His literary talents secured the patronage and friendship of Augustus; and his reputation became so widely diffused, that a Spaniard travelled from Cadiz to Rome

Livy.

solely for the purpose of beholding him, and, having gratified his curiosity in this one particular, immediately returned home. Livy's "History of Rome" extended from the foundation of the city to the death of Drusus, 9 B.C., and was comprised in 142 books. Of these thirty-five have descended to us. The whole work has been divided into *decades*, containing ten books each. The First decade (bks. i.-x.) is entire. It embraces the period from the foundation of the city to the year 294 B.C., when the subjugation of the Samnites may be said to have been completed. The Second decade (bks. xi.-xx.) is altogether lost. It included the period from 294 B.C. to 219 B.C., comprising an account, among other matters, of the invasion of Pyrrhus and of the First Punic War. The Third decade (bks. xxi.-xxx.) is entire. It embraces the period from 219 B.C. to 201 B.C., comprehending the whole of the Second Punic War. The Fourth decade (bks. xxxi.-xl.) is entire, and also one-half of the Fifth (bks. xli.-xlv.). These fifteen books continue the history from 201 B.C. to 167 B.C., and develop the progress of the Roman arms in Cisalpine Gaul, in Macedonia, Greece, and Asia, ending with the triumph of Aemilius Paullus. Of the remaining books nothing is extant except inconsiderable fragments. The style of Livy may be pronounced almost faultless. In judging of his merits as an historian, we are bound to ascertain, if possible, the end which he proposed to himself. No one who reads his work with attention can suppose that he ever conceived the project of drawing up a critical history of Rome. His aim was to offer to his countrymen a clear and pleasing narrative, which, while it gratified their vanity, should contain no startling improbabilities or gross amplifications. To effect this purpose he studied with care the writings of some of his more celebrated predecessors in the same field. But in no case did he ever dream of ascending to the fountain-head, and never attempted to test the accuracy of his authorities by examining monuments of remote antiquity.

INDEX.

B.

C.

D.

E.

F.

G.

N.

O.

P.

Q.

R.

S.

T.

U.

V.

X.

Coin of Augustus.

LONDON:
PRINTED BY WILLIAM CLOWES AND SONS, LIMITED,
STAMFORD STREET AND CHARING CROSS.

50, ALBEMARLE STREET, LONDON,
March, 1897.

MR. MURRAY'S LIST OF SCHOOL BOOKS.

MURRAY'S STUDENT'S MANUALS.

A Series of Class-books for advanced Scholars.

FORMING A CHAIN OF HISTORY FROM THE EARLIEST AGES DOWN TO MODERN TIMES.

English History and Literature.

"The great foundation for all useful knowledge we hold, without any doubt, to be the knowledge of the history and literature of our own country. On this ground Mr. Murray is especially strong. We are acquainted with many admirable books on these subjects, issued by various firms of high standing, some of which, such as Mr. Green's and Mr. Bright's, have universally recognized merits; but for the utility and completeness of the course we give the first place to Mr. Murray's series."—*Literary Churchman.*

THE STUDENT'S HUME: A HISTORY OF ENGLAND, FROM THE EARLIEST TIMES TO THE REVOLUTION IN 1688. By DAVID HUME. Incorporating the Researches of recent Historians. **New Edition,** revised, corrected, and continued to the Treaty of Berlin in 1878, by J. S. BREWER, M.A. With Notes, Illustrations, and 7 Coloured Maps and Woodcuts. (830 pp.) Post 8vo. 7*s.* 6*d.*

*** **Also in Three Parts.** 2*s.* 6*d.* each.

I. FROM B.C. 55 TO THE DEATH OF RICHARD III., A.D. 1485.
II. HENRY VII. TO THE REVOLUTION, 1688.
III. THE REVOLUTION TO THE TREATY OF BERLIN, 1878.

*** *Questions on the "Student's Hume."* 12*mo.* 2*s.*

STUDENT'S CONSTITUTIONAL HISTORY OF ENGLAND. FROM THE ACCESSION OF HENRY VII. TO THE DEATH OF GEORGE II. By HENRY HALLAM, LL.D. (680 pp.) Post 8vo. 7*s.* 6*d.*

STUDENT'S MANUAL OF THE ENGLISH LANGUAGE. By GEORGE P. MARSH. (538 pp.) Post 8vo. 7*s.* 6*d.*

STUDENT'S MANUAL OF ENGLISH LITERATURE. By T. B. SHAW, M.A. (510 pp.) Post 8vo. 7*s.* 6*d.*

STUDENT'S SPECIMENS OF ENGLISH LITERATURE. Selected from the BEST WRITERS, and arranged Chronologically. By THOS. B. SHAW, M.A. (560 pp.) Post 8vo. 5*s.*

Scripture and Church History.

STUDENT'S OLD TESTAMENT HISTORY. FROM THE CREATION OF THE WORLD TO THE RETURN OF THE JEWS FROM CAPTIVITY. With an Introduction to the Books of the Old Testament. By PHILIP SMITH, B.A. With 40 Maps and Woodcuts. (630 pp.) Post 8vo. *7s. 6d.*

STUDENT'S NEW TESTAMENT HISTORY. WITH AN INTRODUCTION, CONTAINING THE CONNECTION OF THE OLD AND NEW TESTAMENTS By PHILIP SMITH, B.A. With 30 Maps and Woodcuts. (680 pp.) Post 8vo. *7s. 6d.*

STUDENT'S MANUAL OF ECCLESIASTICAL HISTORY. A History of the Christian Church to the Reformation. By PHILIP SMITH, B.A. 2 vols. Post 8vo. *7s. 6d.* each.

PART I.—A.D. 30—1003. (654 pp.) With Woodcuts.
PART II.—A.D. 1003—1614. (744 pp.) With Woodcuts.

STUDENT'S MANUAL OF ENGLISH CHURCH HISTORY. By G. G. PERRY, M.A., Canon of Lincoln. 3 Vols. *7s. 6d.* each.

1st Period. From the Planting of the Church in Britain to the Accession of Henry VIII. A.D. 596—1509. (576 pp.)

2nd Period. From the ACCESSION OF HENRY VIII. to the Silencing of Convocation in the EIGHTEENTH CENTURY. (A.D. 1509—1717.) (635 pp.)

3rd Period. From the Accession of the House of Hanover to the Present Time. (A.D. 1717—1884.) (578 pp.)

Ancient History.

STUDENT'S ANCIENT HISTORY OF THE EAST. From the Earliest Times to the Conquests of Alexander the Great, including Egypt, Assyria, Babylonia, Media, Persia, Asia Minor, and Phœnicia. By PHILIP SMITH, B.A. With 70 Woodcuts. (608 pp.) Post 8vo. *7s. 6d.*

STUDENT'S HISTORY OF GREECE. FROM THE EARLIEST TIMES TO THE ROMAN CONQUEST. With Chapters on the History of Literature and Art. By SIR WM. SMITH, D.C.L. With Coloured Maps and Woodcuts. (640 pp.) Post 8vo. *7s. 6d.*

*** *Questions on the "Student's Greece."* 12mo. 2s.

STUDENT'S HISTORY OF ROME. FROM THE EARLIEST TIMES TO THE ESTABLISHMENT OF THE EMPIRE. With Chapters on the History of Literature and Art. By DEAN LIDDELL. With Coloured Map and Woodcuts. (686 pp.) Post 8vo. *7s. 6d.*

STUDENT'S HISTORY OF THE ROMAN EMPIRE. FROM THE ESTABLISHMENT OF THE EMPIRE TO THE ACCESSION OF COMMODUS, A.D. 180. With Coloured Maps and Numerous Illustrations. By J. B. BURY, Fellow of Trin. Coll., Dublin. (626 pp.) Post 8vo. *7s. 6d.*

STUDENT'S GIBBON: AN EPITOME OF THE HISTORY OF THE DECLINE AND FALL OF THE ROMAN EMPIRE. By EDWARD GIBBON. Incorporating the Researches of Recent Historians. With 100 Woodcuts. (700 pp.) Post 8vo. *7s. 6d.*

Europe.

STUDENT'S HISTORY OF MODERN EUROPE. FROM THE CAPTURE OF CONSTANTINOPLE BY THE TURKS, 1453, TO THE TREATY OF BERLIN, 1878. By RICHARD LODGE, M.A., Fellow of B.N.C., Oxford. (800 pp.) Post 8vo *7s. 6d.*

"Mr. Lodge has treated this wide subject in a broad and intelligent spirit. While his pages abound in facts, he has not been content to give a mere crowded summary of events: he presents us with many sound and thoughtful remarks on the tendencies of each of his periods. His grasp is firm and he never loses his way amidst a multitude of details . . . above all, we believe that we are justified in saying that it is minutely accurate."—*Journal of Education.*

STUDENT'S HISTORY OF EUROPE DURING THE MIDDLE AGES. By HENRY HALLAM, LL.D. (650 pp.) Post 8vo. *7s. 6d.*

France.

STUDENT'S HISTORY OF FRANCE. FROM THE EARLIEST TIMES TO THE FALL OF THE SECOND EMPIRE. With Notes and Illustrations on the Institutions of the Country. By W. H. JERVIS, M.A. 4 Coloured Maps, and Woodcuts. (760 pp.) *7s. 6d.*

Geography and Geology.

STUDENT'S MANUAL OF ANCIENT GEOGRAPHY. By CANON BEVAN, M.A. 150 Woodcuts. (710 pp.) *7s. 6d.*

STUDENT'S MANUAL OF MODERN GEOGRAPHY. MATHEMATICAL, PHYSICAL, AND DESCRIPTIVE. By CANON BEVAN, M.A. With 120 Woodcuts. (684 pp.) Post 8vo. *7s. 6d.*

STUDENT'S GEOGRAPHY OF BRITISH INDIA, POLITICAL AND PHYSICAL. By GEORGE SMITH, LL.D. With Maps. Post 8vo. *7s. 6d.*

STUDENT'S ELEMENTS OF GEOLOGY. By SIR CHARLES LYELL. A New Edition, thoroughly revised by PROF. J. W. JUDD. With 600 Woodcuts. *9s.*

PHYSICAL GEOGRAPHY. By MARY SOMERVILLE. 7th Edition, corrected and revised. Post 8vo. *9s.*

A DICTIONARY OF PLACE NAMES. Giving their Derivations. By C. BLACKIE. With an Introduction by JOHN STUART BLACKIE. Crown 8vo. *7s.*

Law and Philosophy.

STUDENT'S MANUAL OF MORAL PHILOSOPHY. With Quotations and References. By WILLIAM FLEMING, D.D. (440 pp.) Post 8vo. 7*s.* 6*d.*

STUDENT'S EDITION OF AUSTIN'S JURISPRUDENCE. Compiled from the larger work. By ROBERT CAMPBELL. (544 pp.) Post 8vo. 12*s.*

AN ANALYSIS OF AUSTIN'S JURISPRUDENCE. By GORDON CAMPBELL. (214 pp.) Post 8vo. 6*s.*

Sir Wm. Smith's Smaller Manuals.

These Works have been drawn up for the Lower Forms, at the request of several teachers, who require more elementary books than the STUDENT'S HISTORICAL MANUALS.

SMALLER SCRIPTURE HISTORY OF THE OLD AND THE NEW TESTAMENT. IN THREE DIVISIONS:—I. Old Testament History. II. Connection of Old and New Testaments. III. New Testament History to A.D. 70. Edited by SIR WM. SMITH. With Coloured Maps and 40 Illustrations. (370 pp.) 16mo. 3*s.* 6*d.*

This book is intended to be used with, and not in the place of, the Bible.

"Students well know the value of Dr. Wm. Smith's larger Scripture History. This abridgment omits nothing of importance, and is presented in such a handy form that it cannot fail to become a valuable aid to the less learned Bible Student."—*People's Magazine.*

SMALLER ANCIENT HISTORY OF THE EAST. FROM THE EARLIEST TIMES TO THE CONQUEST OF ALEXANDER THE GREAT. By PHILIP SMITH, B.A. With 70 Woodcuts. (310 pp.) 16mo. 3*s.* 6*d.*

"This book is designed to aid the study of the Scriptures, by placing in their true historical relations those allusions to Egypt, Assyria, Babylonia, Phœnicia, and the Medo-Persian Empire, which form the background of the history of Israel from Abraham to Nehemiah. The present work is an indispensable adjunct of the 'Smaller Scripture History;' and the two have been written expressly to be used together."

SMALLER HISTORY OF GREECE. FROM THE EARLIEST TIMES TO THE ROMAN CONQUEST. By SIR WM. SMITH. With Coloured Maps and 74 Woodcuts. (262 pp.) Crown 8vo. 3*s.* 6*d.*

This history has been drawn up at the request of several teachers, for the use of lower forms' elementary pupils. The table of contents presents a full analysis of the work, and has been so arranged, that the teacher can frame from it QUESTIONS FOR THE EXAMINATION OF HIS CLASS, the answers to which will be found in the corresponding pages of the volume.

SMALLER HISTORY OF ROME. FROM THE EARLIEST TIMES TO THE ESTABLISHMENT OF THE EMPIRE. By SIR WM. SMITH, D.C.L. With Coloured Map and 70 Woodcuts. (324 pp.) 16mo. 3*s.* 6*d.*

The "Smaller History of Rome" has been written and arranged on the same plan, and with the same object, as the "Smaller History of Greece." Like that work it comprises separate chapters on the institutions and literature of the countries with which it deals.

SMALLER CLASSICAL MYTHOLOGY. With Translations from the Ancient Poets, and Questions on the Work. By H. R. LOCKWOOD. With 90 Woodcuts. (300 pp.) 16mo. 3s. 6d.

This work has been prepared by a lady for the use of schools and young persons of both sexes. In common with many other teachers, she has long felt the want of a consecutive account of the heathen deities, which might safely be placed in the hands of the young, and yet contain all that is generally necessary to enable them to understand the classical allusions they may meet with in prose or poetry, and to appreciate the meanings of works of art

A carefully prepared set of QUESTIONS is appended, the answers to which will be found in the corresponding pages of the volume.

SMALLER MANUAL OF ANCIENT GEOGRAPHY. By CANON BEVAN, M.A. (240 pp.) With Woodcuts. 16mo. 3s. 6d.

"This work has been drawn up chiefly for the lower forms in schools, at the request of several teachers who require for their pupils a more elementary work than the 'Student's Manual of Ancient Geography.' The arrangement of the two works is substantially the same. The more important towns alone are mentioned; the historical notices are curtailed; modern names are introduced only in special cases, either for the purpose of identification or where any noticeable change has occurred; and the quotations from classical works are confined for the most part to such expressions as are illustrative of local peculiarities. A very ample Index is supplied, so that the work may supply the place of a dictionary for occasional reference."

SMALLER HISTORY OF ENGLAND. FROM THE EARLIEST TIMES TO THE YEAR 1887. 28th Edition, Revised and Enlarged. By RICHARD LODGE, M.A. With Coloured Maps and 68 Woodcuts. (400 pp.) 16mo. 3s. 6d.

"The most recent authorities have been consulted, and it is confidently believed that the Work will be found to present a careful and trustworthy account of English History for the lower forms in schools, for whose use it is chiefly intended."—*Preface.*

"This little volume is so pregnant with valuable information, that it will enable anyone who reads it attentively to answer such questions as are set forth in the English History Papers in the Indian Civil Service Examinations."—*Reader.*

SMALLER HISTORY OF ENGLISH LITERATURE: Giving a Sketch of the Lives of our Chief Writers. By JAMES ROWLEY. (276 pp.) 16mo. 3s. 6d.

The important position which the study of English literature is now taking in education has led to the publication of this work, and of the accompanying volume of specimens. Both books have been undertaken at the request of many eminent teachers, and no pains have been spared to adapt them to the purpose for which they are designed—as elementary works to be used in schools.

SHORT SPECIMENS OF ENGLISH LITERATURE. Selected from the chief authors and arranged chronologically. By JAMES ROWLEY. With Notes. (368 pp.) 16mo. 3s. 6d.

While the "Smaller History of English Literature" supplies a rapid but trustworthy sketch of the lives of our chief writers, and of the successive influences which imparted to their writings their peculiar character, the present work supplies choice examples of the works themselves, accompanied by all the explanations required for their perfect explanation. The two works are thus especially designed to be used together.

Sir Wm. Smith's Biblical Dictionaries.

DICTIONARY OF THE BIBLE: COMPRISING ITS ANTIQUITIES, BIOGRAPHY, GEOGRAPHY, AND NATURAL HISTORY. By Various Writers. With Illustrations. 3 vols. Enlarged and Revised Edition. Medium 8vo. £4 4*s.*

"The most complete, learned, and trustworthy work of the kind hitherto produced."—*Athenæum.*

CONCISE DICTIONARY OF THE BIBLE. Condensed from the larger Work. For Families and Students. With Maps and 300 Illustrations. (1039 pp.) 8vo. 21*s.*

A Dictionary of the Bible, in some form or another, is indispensable for every family. To students in the Universities, and in the Upper Forms at Schools, to private families, and to that numerous class of persons who desire to arrive at *results* simply, this CONCISE DICTIONARY will, it is believed, supply all that is necessary for the elucidation and explanation of the Bible.

SMALLER DICTIONARY OF THE BIBLE. Abridged from the larger Work. For Schools and Young Persons. With Maps and Illustrations. (620 pp.) Crown 8vo. 7*s.* 6*d.*

"An invaluable service has been rendered to students in the condensation of Dr. Wm. Smith's Bible Dictionary. The work has been done as only a careful and intelligent scholar could do it, which preserves to us the essential scholarship and value of each article."—*British Quarterly Review.*

The two following Works are intended to furnish a complete account of the leading personages, the Institutions, Art, Social Life, Writings, and Controversies of the Christian Church from the time of the Apostles to the Age of Charlemagne. They commence at the period at which the "Dictionary of the Bible" leaves off, and form a continuation of it.

DICTIONARY OF CHRISTIAN ANTIQUITIES. The History, Institutions, and Antiquities of the Christian Church. Edited by SIR WM. SMITH, D.C.L., and ARCHDEACON CHEETHAM, D.D. With Illustrations. 2 vols. Medium 8vo. £3 13*s.* 6*d.*

"The work before us is unusually well done. A more acceptable present for a candidate for holy orders, or a more valuable book for any library, than the 'Dictionary of Christian Antiquities' could not easily be found."—*Saturday Review.*

DICTIONARY OF CHRISTIAN BIOGRAPHY, LITERATURE, SECTS, AND DOCTRINES. Edited by SIR WM. SMITH, D.C.L., and HENRY WACE, D.D. 4 Vols. Medium 8vo. £6 16*s.* 6*d.*

"The value of the work arises, in the first place, from the fact that the contributors to these volumes have diligently eschewed mere compilation. In these volumes we welcome the most important addition that has been made for a century to the historical library of the English theological student."—*Times.*

Sir Wm. Smith's Classical Dictionaries.

AN ENCYCLOPÆDIA OF CLASSICAL ANTIQUITY. By VARIOUS WRITERS. Edited by SIR WM. SMITH, D.C.L. and LL.D.

"It is an honour to this College to have presented to the world so distinguished a scholar as Dr. Wm. Smith, who has, by his valuable manuals of classical antiquity, and classical history and biography, done as much as any man living to promote the accurate knowledge of the Greek and Roman world among the students of this age."—*Mr. Grote at the London University.*

I. DICTIONARY OF GREEK AND ROMAN ANTIQUITIES. Including the Laws, Institutions, Domestic Usages, Painting, Sculpture, Music, the Drama, &c. 3rd Edition, Revised and Enlarged. With 900 Illustrations. 2 Vols. Medium 8vo. £3 3*s.*

II. DICTIONARY OF BIOGRAPHY AND MYTHOLOGY. Containing a History of the Ancient World, Civil, Literary, and Ecclesiastical (3700 pp.) With 560 Illustrations. 3 vols. Medium 8vo. 84*s.*

III. DICTIONARY OF GREEK AND ROMAN GEOGRAPHY. Including the Political History of both Countries and Cities, as well as their Geography. (2500 pp.) With 530 Illustrations. 2 vols. Medium 8vo. 56*s.*

FOR SCHOOLS AND COLLEGES.

CLASSICAL DICTIONARY OF BIOGRAPHY, MYTHOLOGY, AND GEOGRAPHY. For the Higher Forms in Schools. Condensed from the larger Dictionaries. New and Revised Edition, by G. E. MARINDIN. With over 800 Woodcuts 8vo. 18*s.*

SMALLER CLASSICAL DICTIONARY. For Junior Classes. Abridged from the above Work. With 200 Woodcuts. Crown 8vo. 7*s.* 6*d.*

SMALLER DICTIONARY OF ANTIQUITIES. For Junior Classes. Abridged from the larger Work. With 200 Woodcuts. Crown 8vo. 7*s.* 6*d.*

Sir Wm. Smith's Ancient Atlas.

AN ATLAS OF ANCIENT GEOGRAPHY, BIBLICAL AND CLASSICAL. Intended to illustrate the "Dictionary of the Bible," and the "Classical Dictionaries." Compiled under the superintendence of SIR WM. SMITH, D.C.L., and SIR GEORGE GROVE, LL.D. With Descriptive Text, Indices, &c. With 43 Maps. Folio, half-bound. Price Six Guineas.

"The students of Dr. Smith's admirable Dictionaries must have felt themselves in want of an Atlas constructed on the same scale of precise and minute information with the article they were reading. This want has at length been supplied by the superb work before us. The indices are full, the engraving is exquisite, and the delineation of the natural features very minute and beautiful. It may safely be pronounced—and higher praise can scarcely be bestowed—to be a worthy companion of the volumes which it is intended to illustrate."—*Guardian.*

Sir Wm. Smith's Latin Dictionaries.

"I consider Dr. Wm. Smith's Dictionaries to have conferred a great and lasting service on the cause of classical learning in this country."—Dean LIDDELL.

"I have found Dr. Wm. Smith's Latin Dictionary a great convenience to me. I think that he has been very judicious in what he has omitted, as well as what he has inserted."—Dr. SCOTT.

A COMPLETE LATIN-ENGLISH DICTIONARY. BASED ON THE WORKS OF FORCELLINI AND FREUND. With Tables of the Roman Calendar, Measures, Weights, Money, and a DICTIONARY OF PROPER NAMES. By SIR WM. SMITH, D.C.L. and LL.D. (1200 pp.) Medium 8vo. 21st Edition. 16*s*.

This work aims at performing the same service for the Latin language as Liddell and Scott's Lexicon has done for the Greek. Great attention has been paid to Etymology, in which department especially this work is admitted to maintain a superiority over all existing Latin Dictionaries.

A SMALLER LATIN-ENGLISH DICTIONARY. WITH A SEPARATE DICTIONARY OF PROPER NAMES, TABLES OF ROMAN MONEYS, &c. 33rd Edition. Thoroughly revised and in great part re-written. Edited by SIR WM. SMITH and T. D. HALL, M.A. The Etymological portion by JOHN K. INGRAM, LL.D. Square 12mo. 7*s*. 6*d*.

This edition of Dr. Smith's 'Smaller Latin-English Dictionary' is to a great extent a new and original Work. Every article has been carefully revised.

A COPIOUS AND CRITICAL ENGLISH-LATIN DICTIONARY. Compiled from Original Sources. By SIR WM. SMITH, D.C.L. and T. D. HALL, M.A. (970 pp.) Medium 8vo. 5th Edition. 16*s*.

It has been the object of the Authors of this Work to produce a more complete and more perfect ENGLISH-LATIN DICTIONARY than yet exists, and every article has been the result of original and independent research.

Each meaning is illustrated by examples from the classical writers; and those phrases are as a general rule given in both English and Latin.

A SMALLER ENGLISH-LATIN DICTIONARY. Abridged from the above Work, by SIR WM. SMITH and T. D. HALL, M.A., for the use of Junior Classes. 16th Edition. (730 pp.) Square 12mo. 7*s*. 6*d*.

"An English-Latin Dictionary worthy of the scholarship of our age and country. It will take absolutely the first rank, and be the standard English-Latin Dictionary as long as either tongue endures. Even a general examination of the pages will serve to reveal the minute pains taken to ensure its fulness and philological value, and the 'work is to a large extent a dictionary of the English language, as well as an English-Latin Dictionary.'"—*English Churchman.*

A NEW GRADUS AD PARNASSUM.

AN ENGLISH-LATIN GRADUS, OR VERSE DICTIONARY, on a new plan, with carefully selected Epithets and Synonyms, intended to Simplify the Composition of Latin Verses. By A. C. AINGER, M.A., Trinity Coll., Cambridge, and H. G. WINTLE, M.A., Christ Church, Oxford. (450 pp.) Crown 8vo. 9*s*.

Sir Wm. Smith's Educational Series.

Latin Course.

THE YOUNG BEGINNER'S COURSE.

2s. each.

I. **FIRST LATIN BOOK.**—Grammar, Easy Questions, Exercises, and Vocabularies.

II. **SECOND LATIN BOOK.**—An easy Latin Reading Book with Analysis of Sentences.

III. **THIRD LATIN BOOK.**—Exercises on the Syntax, with Vocabularies.

IV. **FOURTH LATIN BOOK.**—A Latin Vocabulary for Beginners, arranged according to Subjects and Etymologies.

PRINCIPIA LATINA, Part I. FIRST LATIN COURSE. Grammar, Delectus, Exercises, and Vocabularies. (218 pp.) 12mo. 3*s.* 6*d.*

APPENDIX TO PRINCIPIA LATINA, Part I. Containing Additional Exercises, with Examination Papers. (125 pp.) 12mo. 2*s.* 6*d.*

PRINCIPIA LATINA, Part II. READING BOOK. An Introduction to Ancient Mythology, Geography, Roman Antiquities, and History. With Notes and a Dictionary. (268 pp.) 12mo. 3*s.* 6*d.*

PRINCIPIA LATINA, Part III. POETRY. 1. Easy Hexameters and Pentameters. 2. Eclogæ Ovidianæ. 3. Prosody and Metre. 4. First Latin Verse Book. (160 pp.) 12mo. 3*s.* 6*d.*

PRINCIPIA LATINA, Part IV. PROSE COMPOSITION. Rules of Syntax, with Examples, Explanations of Synonyms, and Exercises on the Syntax. (194 pp.) 12mo. 3*s.* 6*d.*

PRINCIPIA LATINA, Part V. SHORT TALES AND ANECDOTES FROM ANCIENT HISTORY, FOR TRANSLATION INTO LATIN PROSE. With an English-Latin Vocabulary. By SIR WM. SMITH, LL.D. 10th Edition. Revised and considerably Enlarged. By T. D. HALL, M.A. (182 pp.) 3*s.* 6*d.*

THE STUDENT'S LATIN GRAMMAR. FOR THE USE OF COLLEGES AND THE HIGHER FORMS IN SCHOOLS. By SIR WM. SMITH, LL.D. and T. D. HALL. *Thirteenth Edition, thoroughly revised and partly re-written.* (450 pp.) Post 8vo. 6*s.*

SMALLER LATIN GRAMMAR. FOR THE MIDDLE AND LOWER FORMS. *New and thoroughly revised Edition.* (260 pp.) 12mo. 3*s.* 6*d.*

TRANSLATION AT SIGHT; OR, AIDS TO FACILITY IN THE TRANSLATION OF LATIN. Passages of Graduated Difficulty, carefully Selected from Latin Authors, with Explanations, Notes, &c. *An entirely New and Original Work.* By Professor T. D. HALL, M.A. Crown 8vo. 2*s.*

A CHILD'S FIRST LATIN BOOK. COMPRISING NOUNS, PRONOUNS, AND ADJECTIVES, WITH THE VERBS. With ample and varied Practice of the easiest kind. Both old and new order of Cases given. By T. D. HALL, M.A. (124 pp.) New and Enlarged Edition, including the Passive Verb. 16mo. 2*s.*

*** *Keys may be had by* AUTHENTICATED TEACHERS *on application.*

Sir Wm. Smith's Greek Course.

INITIA GRÆCA, Part I. A FIRST GREEK COURSE, containing Grammar, Delectus, Exercise Book, and Vocabularies. (284 pp.) 12mo. 3s. 6d.

*** *The present Edition has been very thoroughly revised, and many additions and improvements have been introduced.*

The great object of this work, as of the "Principia Latina," is to make the study of the language as easy and simple as possible, by giving the grammatical forms only as they are wanted, and by enabling the pupil to translate from Greek into English and from English into Greek as soon as he has learnt the Greek characters and the First Declension. For the convenience of teachers the cases of the nouns, &c., are given according to the ordinary grammars as well as according to the arrangement of the Public Schools Latin Primer.

APPENDIX TO INITIA GRÆCA, Part I. Containing Additional Exercises, with Examination Papers and Easy Reading Lessons with the Sentences Analysed, serving as an Introduction to INITIA GRÆCA, Part II. (110 pp.) 12mo. 2s. 6d.

INITIA GRÆCA, Part II. A READING BOOK. Containing short Tales, Anecdotes, Fables, Mythology, and Grecian History. With a Lexicon. (220 pp.) 12mo. 3s. 6d.

INITIA GRÆCA, Part III. PROSE COMPOSITION. Containing the Rules of Syntax, with Copious Examples and Exercises. (202 pp.) 12mo. 3s. 6d.

THE STUDENT'S GREEK GRAMMAR. FOR THE HIGHER FORMS. By PROFESSOR CURTIUS. Edited by SIR WM. SMITH, D.C.L. (386 pp.) Post 8vo. 6s.

The Greek Grammar of Dr. Curtius is acknowledged by the most competent scholars to be the best representative of the present advanced state of Greek scholarship. It is, indeed, almost the only Grammar which exhibits the inflexions of the language in a really scientific form; while its extensive use in schools, and the high commendations it has received from practical teachers, are a sufficient proof of its excellence as a school-book.

A SMALLER GREEK GRAMMAR. FOR THE MIDDLE AND LOWER FORMS. Abridged from the above Work. (220 pp.) 12mo. 3s. 6d.

THE GREEK ACCIDENCE. Extracted from the above Work. (125 pp.) 12mo. 2s. 6d.

HALL'S INTRODUCTION TO THE GREEK TESTAMENT. A work designed for students possessing no previous knowledge of Greek. (210 pp.) Crown 8vo. 3s. 6d.

LEATHES' HEBREW GRAMMAR. With the Hebrew Text of Genesis i.—vi., and Psalms i.—vi. Grammatical Analysis and Vocabulary. (252 pp.) Post 8vo. 7s. 6d.

*** *Keys may be had by* AUTHENTICATED TEACHERS *on application.*

Sir Wm. Smith's French Course.

FRENCH PRINCIPIA, Part I. A FIRST FRENCH COURSE, containing Grammar, Delectus and Exercises, with Vocabularies and Materials for French Conversation. (202 pp.) 12mo. 3*s.* 6*d.*

This work has been compiled at the repeated request of numerous teachers who, finding the "Principia Latina" and "Initia Græca" *the easiest books for learning Latin and Greek,* are anxious to obtain equally elementary French books on the same plan. There is an obvious gain in studying a new language on the plan with which the learner is already familiar. The main object is to enable a beginner to acquire an accurate knowledge of the chief grammatical forms, to learn their usage by constructing simple sentences as soon as he commences the study of the language, and to accumulate gradually a stock of words useful in conversation as well as in reading.

APPENDIX TO FRENCH PRINCIPIA, Part I. Containing Additional Exercises and Examination Papers. (110 pp.) 12mo. 2*s.* 6*d.*

FRENCH PRINCIPIA, Part II. A READING BOOK. Containing Fables, Stories, and Anecdotes, Natural History, and Scenes from the History of France. With Grammatical Questions, Notes, and copious Etymological Dictionary. (376 pp.) 12mo. 4*s.* 6*d.*

FRENCH PRINCIPIA, Part III. PROSE COMPOSITION. Containing a Systematic Course of Exercises on the Syntax, with the Principal Rules of Syntax. 12mo. 4*s.* 6*d.*

THE STUDENT'S FRENCH GRAMMAR: PRACTICAL AND HISTORICAL. FOR THE HIGHER FORMS. By C. HERON-WALL, with INTRODUCTION by M. LITTRÉ. (490 pp.) Post 8vo. 6*s.*

This Grammar is the work of a practical teacher of twenty years' experience in teaching English boys. It has been his special aim to produce a book which would work well in schools where Latin and Greek form the principal subjects of study.

"This book as a whole is quite a monument of French Grammar, and cannot fail to become a standard work in high-class teaching."—*School Board Chronicle.*

"It would be difficult to point more clearly to the value of Mr. Wall's work, which is intended for the use of Colleges and Upper Forms in schools, than by quoting what M. Littré says of it in an introductory letter:—'I have carefully tested the principal parts of your work, and have been completely satisfied with the accuracy and correctness which I found there.'"—*Saturday Review.*

A SMALLER FRENCH GRAMMAR. FOR THE MIDDLE AND LOWER FORMS. Abridged from the above Work. (230 pp.) 12mo. 3*s.* 6*d.*

*** *Keys may be had by* AUTHENTICATED TEACHERS *on application.*

Sir Wm. Smith's German Course.

GERMAN PRINCIPIA, Part I. A FIRST GERMAN COURSE. Containing Grammar, Delectus, Exercises, Vocabularies and materials for German Conversation. (244 pp.) 12mo. 3s. 6d.

*** *The present edition has undergone a very careful revision, and various improvements and additions have been introduced.*

This work is on the same plan as the "French Principia," and therefore requires no further description, except in one point. Differing from the ordinary grammars, all German words are printed in Roman, and not in the old German characters. The Roman letters are used by many modern German writers, and also in Grimm's great Dictionary and Grammar; and it is believed that this alteration will facilitate, more than at first might be supposed, the acquisition of the language. But at the same time, as many German books continue to be printed in the German characters, the exercises are printed in both German and Roman letters.

GERMAN PRINCIPIA, Part II. A READING BOOK. Containing Fables, Stories, and Anecdotes, Natural History, and Scenes from the History of Germany. With Grammatical Questions, Notes, and Dictionary. (272 pp.) 12mo. 3s. 6d.

PRACTICAL GERMAN GRAMMAR. With a Sketch of the Historical Development of the Language and its Principal Dialects. (240 pp.) Post 8vo. 3s. 6d.

*** *Keys may be had by* AUTHENTICATED TEACHERS *on application.*

Sir Wm. Smith's Italian Course.

ITALIAN PRINCIPIA, Part I. A FIRST ITALIAN COURSE. Containing a Grammar, Delectus, Exercise Book, with Vocabularies, &c. By SIGNOR RICCI, Professor of Italian at the City of London School. (288 pp.) 12mo. 3s. 6d.

ITALIAN PRINCIPIA, Part II. A FIRST ITALIAN READING-BOOK, containing Fables, Anecdotes, History, and Passages from the best Italian Authors, with Questions, Notes, and an Etymological Dictionary. By SIGNOR RICCI. 12mo. 3s. 6d.

*** *Keys may be had by* AUTHENTICATED TEACHERS *on application.*

English Course.

A READABLE ENGLISH DICTIONARY. Etymologically arranged. By DAVID MILNE, M.A. Crown 8vo. 7s. 6d.

"An excellent book. . . . We gladly allow that its contents justify the title. . . . It is sound matter very skilfully arranged."—*Pall Mall Gazette.*

"Mr. Milne has, we think, in his new Readable English Dictionary, hit the right nail on the head. . . . We have no hesitation in pronouncing his Dictionary to be one of the most entertaining and instructive and readable books of the season."—*Bookseller.*

English Course—continued.

PRIMARY ENGLISH GRAMMAR for Elementary Schools. With 134 Exercises and carefully graduated parsing lessons. By T. D. HALL, M.A. (120 pp.) 16mo. 1*s.*

This Work aims at the clearest and simplest statement possible of the first principles of English Grammar for the use of children from about eight to twelve years of age.

"We doubt whether any grammar of equal size could give an introduction to the English language more clear, concise, and full than this."—*Watchman.*

SCHOOL MANUAL OF ENGLISH GRAMMAR. With 194 Exercises. By SIR WM. SMITH, D.C.L., and T. D. HALL, M.A. With Appendices. Eighth Edition, carefully revised. (270 pp.) Post 8vo. 3*s.* 6*d.*

This Work has been prepared with a special view to the requirements of Schools in which English, *as a living language*, is systematically taught, and differs from most modern grammars in its thoroughly practical character. A distinguishing feature of the book is the constant appeal for every usage to the authority of Standard English Authors.

"An admirable English Grammar. We cannot give it higher praise than to say that as a school grammar it is the best in this country."—*English Churchman.*

⁂ Keys may be had by AUTHENTICATED TEACHERS *on application.*

MANUAL OF ENGLISH COMPOSITION. With Copious Illustrations and Practical Exercises. Suited equally for Schools and for Private Students of English. By T. D. HALL, M.A. Fourth Edition. (210 pp.) 12mo. 3*s.* 6*d.*

"Certainly the most sensible and practical book upon English composition that we have lately seen. The great variety of subjects which it suggests as themes for exercising the imagination as well as the literary powers of young students will be found a great assistance to teachers, who must often be sorely puzzled to hit upon subjects sufficiently diversified without being ridiculously beyond the scope of youthful experience."—*Saturday Review.*

PRIMARY HISTORY OF BRITAIN for Elementary Schools. Edited by SIR WM. SMITH, D.C.L. and LL.D. With a Map. (430 pp.) 12mo. 2*s.* 6*d.*

A New and thoroughly revised Edition, continued down to 1880.

Eton College Books.

THE ETON LATIN GRAMMAR. An entirely New Work. For use in the Higher Forms. By F. H. RAWLINS, M.A., and W. R. INGE, M.A., Fellows of King's Coll., Cambridge, and Assistant-Masters at Eton Coll. (396 pp.) Crown 8vo. 6*s.*

THE ETON ELEMENTARY LATIN GRAMMAR. For Use in the Lower Forms. Compiled with the sanction of the Headmaster. By C. A. AINGER, M.A., Trinity College, Cambridge, and H. G. WINTLE, M.A., Christ Church, Oxford, Assistant Masters at Eton College. (327 pp.) Crown 8vo. 3*s.* 6*d.*

THE ETON PREPARATORY GRAMMAR. Abridged from the above Work. (108 pp.) Post 8vo. 2*s.*

***THE ETON FIRST LATIN EXERCISE BOOK.** Adapted to the Eton Latin Grammar. (152 pp.) Crown 8vo. 2*s.* 6*d.*

THE ETON FOURTH FORM OVID. Being Easy Passages selected from the ELEGIAC POEMS of OVID and TIBULLUS. With Explanatory Notes. By H. G. WINTLE. (155 pp.) 2*s.* 6*d.*

THE ETON HORACE. THE ODES, EPODES, AND CARMEN SÆCULARE. With Notes. By F. W. CORNISH, M.A., Assistant-Master at Eton College. With Maps. (380 pp.) Crown 8vo. 6*s.*

THE ETON MATHEMATICAL SERIES.

I. *ETON EXERCISES IN ALGEBRA. By E. P. ROUSE and A. COCKSHOTT. Crown 8vo. 3*s.*

II. *ETON EXERCISES IN ARITHMETIC. By REV. T. DALTON, M.A., Assistant Master at Eton College. Crown 8vo. 3*s.*

Keys may be purchased by AUTHENTICATED TEACHERS *on written application to the Publisher.*

Natural Philosophy and Science.

WORKS BY SAMUEL NEWTH, M.A., D.D.

Specially adapted to the Regulations of the Examinations of the University of London.

FIRST BOOK OF NATURAL PHILOSOPHY, an Introduction to the Study of Statics, Dynamics, Hydrostatics, Light, Heat, and Sound, with Examples. (200 pp.) 3*s.* 6*d.*

ELEMENTS OF MECHANICS, INCLUDING HYDROSTATICS. With numerous Examples. (362 pp.) 8*s.* 6*d.*

MATHEMATICAL EXAMPLES. A Graduated Series of Elementary Examples in Arithmetic, Algebra, Logarithms, Trigonometry, and Mechanics. (378 pp.) 8*s.* 6*d.*

University Extension Manuals.

Edited by PROFESSOR KNIGHT, of St. Andrew's University.

The following are now ready :—

AN INTRODUCTION TO MODERN GEOLOGY. By Dr. R. D. ROBERTS. Illustrations and Maps. 5*s.*

THE REALM OF NATURE: A Manual of Physiography. By DR. HUGH ROBERT MILL. 19 Coloured Maps and 68 Illustrations. 5*s.*

THE STUDY OF ANIMAL LIFE. By J. ARTHUR THOMSON. With many Illustrations. 5*s.*

THE ELEMENTS OF ETHICS. By J. H. MUIRHEAD. 3*s.*

ENGLISH COLONIZATION AND EMPIRE. By A. CALDECOTT. Coloured Maps and Diagrams. 3*s.* 6*d.*

THE FINE ARTS. By Prof. BALDWIN BROWN. Illustrations. 3*s.* 6*d.*

THE USE AND ABUSE OF MONEY. By Professor CUNNINGHAM, D.D. 3*s.*

THE PHILOSOPHY OF THE BEAUTIFUL. By Professor KNIGHT. Parts I. and II. 3*s.* 6*d.* each part.

FRENCH LITERATURE. By H. G. KEENE. 3*s.*

THE RISE OF THE BRITISH DOMINION IN INDIA. By SIR ALFRED LYALL. With Maps. 4*s.* 6*d.*

THE PHYSIOLOGY OF THE SENSES. By Professor McKENDRICK and Dr. SNODGRASS. With Illustrations. 4*s.* 6*d.*

CHAPTERS IN MODERN BOTANY. By Professor PATRICK GEDDES. With Illustrations. 3*s.* 6*d.*

THE FRENCH REVOLUTION. By C. E. MALLET, 3*s.* 6*d.*

ENGLISH LITERATURE. By W. RENTON. 3*s.* 6*d.*

LOGIC, INDUCTIVE AND DEDUCTIVE. By WILLIAM MINTO, late Professor of Logic, University of Aberdeen. With Diagrams. 4*s.* 6*d.*

GREECE IN THE AGE OF PERICLES. By A. J. GRANT, King's College, Cambridge, Professor of History, Yorkshire College, Leeds. With Illustrations. 3*s.* 6*d.*

THE JACOBEAN POETS. By EDMUND GOSSE. 3*s.* 6*d.*

THE ENGLISH NOVEL. By Professor RALEIGH, University College, Liverpool. 3*s.* 6*d.*

HISTORY OF RELIGION. By ALLAN MENZIES, D.D. 5*s.*

LATIN LITERATURE. By J. W. MACKAIL, Balliol College, Oxford. 3*s.* 6*d.*

SHAKSPERE AND HIS PREDECESSORS IN THE ENGLISH DRAMA. By F. S. BOAS, Balliol College, Oxford. 6*s.*

ELEMENTS OF PSYCHOLOGY. By GEORGE CROOM ROBERTSON, late Grote Professor, University College, London. Edited by Mrs. C. A. F. RHYS DAVIDS, M.A. 3*s.* 6*d.*

ELEMENTS OF PHILOSOPHY. By GEORGE CROOM ROBERTSON, late Grote Professor, University College, London. Edited by Mrs. C. A. F. RHYS DAVIDS, M.A. 3*s.* 6*d.*

Mrs. Markham's Histories.

"Mrs. Markham's Histories are constructed on a plan which is novel and we think well chosen, and we are glad to find that they are deservedly popular, for they cannot be too strongly recommended."—JOURNAL OF EDUCATION.

HISTORY OF ENGLAND, FROM THE FIRST INVASION BY THE ROMANS TO 1880. *New and revised edition.* With Conversations at the end of each Chapter. 100 Woodcuts. (528 pp.) 3*s.* 6*d.*

HISTORY OF FRANCE, FROM THE CONQUEST OF GAUL BY JULIUS CÆSAR TO 1878. *New and revised edition.* Conversations at the end of each Chapter. 70 Woodcuts. (550 pp.) 3*s.* 6*d.*

HISTORY OF GERMANY, FROM ITS INVASION BY MARIUS TO 1880. *New and revised edition.* 50 Woodcuts. (460 pp.) 3*s.* 6*d.*

LITTLE ARTHUR'S HISTORY OF ENGLAND. By LADY CALLCOTT. *New and revised edition.* Continued down to 1878. 500*th thousand.* With 36 Woodcuts. 16mo. 1*s.* 6*d.*

"I never met with a history so well adapted to the capacities of children or their entertainment, so philosophical, and written with such simplicity." —Mrs. MARCETT.

LITTLE ARTHUR'S HISTORY OF FRANCE. FROM THE EARLIEST TIMES TO THE FALL OF THE SECOND EMPIRE. With Map and Illustrations. 16mo. 2*s.* 6*d.*

"The jaded schoolboy, surfeited with tales and the 'over-pressure' arising from long attention to lives and adventures, will, towards the latter part of his holiday, turn with some relief to this book, and begin feasting afresh. Those who know what 'Little Arthur's England' did to popularise the subject among little folks, will know what to expect in this 'France.' The book is capitally illustrated, and very wisely the compiler does not reject the exciting and legendary parts of the subject."—*Schoolmaster.*

ÆSOP'S FABLES. A NEW VERSION. Chiefly from the Original Sources. By REV. THOMAS JAMES. With 100 Woodcuts. Illustrations by JOHN TENNIEL. (168 pp.) Post 8vo. 2*s.* 6*d.*

"Of ÆSOP'S FABLES there ought to be in every school many copies, full of pictures."—*Fraser's Magazine.*

THE BIBLE IN THE HOLY LAND. Extracted from Dean Stanley's work on Sinai and Palestine. With Woodcuts. (210 pp.) Crown 8vo. 3*s.* 6*d.*

SERMONS FOR CHILDREN PREACHED IN WESTMINSTER ABBEY. By DEAN STANLEY. Post 8vo. 3*s.* 6*d.*

JOHN MURRAY, ALBEMARLE STREET.

Bradbury, Agnew & Co. Ld.] [Printers, London and Tonbridge.